Planning, Implementing, and Maintaining a Microsoft® Windows® Server 2003 Active Directory Infrastructure

Project Lab Manual

Exam 70-294

Planning, Implementing, and Maintaining a Microsoft® Windows® Server 2003 Active Directory Infrastructure

Project Lab Manual
Exam 70-294

First Edition

Kenneth C. Laudon, Series Designer
L. Ward Ulmer, MCSE, MCT
Robin L. Pickering

The Azimuth Interactive MCSE/MCSA Team

Carol G. Traver, Series Editor
Kenneth Rosenblatt
Russell Polo
David Langley
Stacey McBrine, MCSE, MCSA
Richard Watson, MCSE
Brien Posey, MCSE
Tim Oliwiak, MCSE, MCT
David Lundell, MCSE, MCT
L. Ward Ulmer, MCSE, MCT
Wale Soyinka, MCP
Simon Sykes-Wright, MCSE
David W. Tschanz, MCSE
Mark Maxwell

PEARSON
Prentice Hall

Upper Saddle River, New Jersey, 07458

Senior Vice President/Publisher: Natalie Anderson
Acquisitions Editor: Steven Elliot
Senior Marketing Manager: Steven Rutberg
Assistant Editor: Laura Burgess
Manager, Print Production: Christy Mahon
Production Editor & Buyer: Wanda Rockwell
Composition: Azimuth Interactive, Inc.
Quality Assurance: Digital Content Factory, Ltd.
Cover Printer: Phoenix Color
Printer/Binder: Technical Communication Services

PEARSON
Prentice
Hall

10 9 8 7 6 5 4 3
ISBN 0-13-189314-9

Brief Contents

Contents

***To our families,
for their love, patience,
and inspiration.***

Preface

The purpose of this Project Lab Manual is to provide you, the student, with another opportunity to review Windows Server 2003 concepts and skills, and to apply them to situations that you are likely to encounter on the job. The Prentice Hall Certification Series textbooks contain a great deal of conceptual and hands-on material. The Prentice Hall Certification Series Project Lab Manuals are designed to give you an opportunity to put those concepts and skills to work in a variety of different real-world on-the-job situations, and to understand the textbook contents in greater depth.

The Project Lab Manuals are organized in the same two-page highly illustrated format with conceptual material and instructions on the left-hand page, and screenshots and conceptual diagrams on the right-hand page. The Lessons in the Project Lab Manuals follow the Lessons in the textbook. Each Project Lab Manual Lesson is composed of a number of projects that reinforce the concepts and skills taught in the accompanying textbooks.

Project Lab Manual Lesson Contents

The Project Lab Manual Lessons have a number of elements designed to speed your learning and help you understand key concepts and skills.

Introductory Page: Each Lesson begins with an introductory page that reviews the key concepts and skills that you will be asked to apply in the lesson.

Scenario: Each Lesson has a brief scenario that describes the setting in which the projects take place. These scenarios provide you with a sense of how the concepts and skills that you have learned in the book are used in realistic business settings.

Project/Objective Table: Each Lesson includes a table that lists the Lesson projects and the corresponding exam objective supported. Where the project relates to a basic understanding of the subject matter, this is referred to as "Basic knowledge." You will always know how a project relates to MCSE/MCSA exam requirements.

General Requirements: At the beginning of each Lesson, there is a description of the hardware and software that you will need to complete the projects in the Lesson.

Project's Exam Objective: For each project there is a description of the specific MCSA/MCSE exam objective supported by the project.

Overview: Each project presents a specific assignment that builds on the Lesson's main scenario.

Learning Objective: Each project includes a specific learning objective that describes what you will be able to do after completing the project.

Specific Requirements: A list of specific requirements for each project is provided.

Estimated Completion Time: For each project, there is an estimated time for completion based on the experience of MCSE/MCSA professionals and instructors in colleges and training institutes. You should use these estimates only as a guide because your actual completion times will depend on your prior experience with Windows Server 2003.

Project Steps: Each project includes a set of step-by-step instructions for completing the project. These instructions are similar to those in the main textbook, but often differ because new options and pathways may be explored in the Project Lab Manuals.

Tips: Throughout the Project Lab Manuals you will find Tips and Cautions that offer you suggestions or comments about completing the project and working with Windows Server 2003.

Graphics and Illustrations: As you can expect from the Prentice Hall Certification Series, there are many screenshots and conceptual graphics provided that show you how the software should look at various points in the project. These are intended to familiarize you with the Windows Server 2003 environment and assure you that you are on the right track.

Quality Assurance

We have made every effort to ensure that the Project Lab Manuals are written to the same quality standards as the main textbook and the Interactive Solution CD-ROM. The Project Lab Manuals are written by MCSE and MCSA professionals with many years of real-world experience. The initial instructions and scenarios are then reviewed by independent technical editors who test each project, and each step. These results are then verified by the MCSE/MCSA team at Azimuth and the Series Designer and Editor. The end result is a product that students and instructors can understand and trust.

Notice

The projects in the Project Lab Manuals have been built using the most recent release of Windows Server 2003, Windows 2000 Server, and Windows XP Professional software. Your school or other institution may be using an earlier release of the software, or its environment may differ in some respects from the environment in which the projects were built. At times, these variations in environment and service packs can cause variations in the progression of steps and screenshots so that a screenshot in the book does not precisely match the screen you may be looking at. If this should occur, please report this to the authors at the Web site for this book.

LESSON 1

Introducing Active Directory Services in Windows Server 2003

The directory service for Microsoft Windows Server 2003 is called Active Directory. A directory service is a database that stores information about users and resources on a network. It also provides ways to access and distribute that information. Active Directory is used by administrators to efficiently design a network structure and to manage network resources.

In order to administer an Active Directory infrastructure effectively, you must be familiar with how objects—such as users, groups, organizational units (OUs), sites, and domains—are used in Active Directory. These objects, along with their attributes, are stored in the searchable Active Directory database.

An important distinction in Active Directory is the division between the logical structure and the physical structure. Although the logical structure and the physical structure are independent of one another, proper integration of the two structures is critical to ensure a smoothly operating network. The logical structure is concerned with how the organization is administered, while the physical structure deals with the physical location of objects in the network.

This lesson contains projects that will enable you to practice creating an Active Directory domain structure, expanding both the logical and physical structures, and handling multiple account policies within a single organization.

Scenario

You are the Senior Network Administrator for APB Industries, a record company based in Toronto, Canada. The company is growing quickly, and you are responsible for designing a suitable network infrastructure that will ease administration, as well as allow for future expansion. You have decided that Windows Server 2003 with Active Directory implemented is the most flexible solution. Currently, APB Industries is based out of a single location, with the following departments:

Human Resources

20 employees, 4 printers, 1 network administrator

Accounting

25 employees, 6 printers, 1 network administrator

Sales

60 employees, 12 printers, 2 network administrators

Each department has its own Network Administration team that operates independently, but they still must fall under the control of you and your team. Additionally, as the Senior Network Administrator, management wants you to have control over account policy (password strength, expiration, etc.) for the entire organization.

Lesson 1 Introducing Active Directory Services in Windows Server 2003

Project	Exam 70-294 Objective
1.1 Planning an Active Directory Domain Structure	Basic knowledge
1.2 Expanding the Logical Active Directory Structure	Basic knowledge
1.3 Expanding the Physical Active Directory Structure	Basic knowledge
1.4 Dealing with Separate Account Policies	Basic knowledge

General Requirements

There are no special requirements for this lesson. However, you may find it helpful to refer to Lesson 1 in your Prentice Hall Certification Series Exam 70-294 textbook for further information about the topics covered by the projects in this lesson.

project 1.1

Planning an Active Directory Domain Structure

exam objective

Basic knowledge

overview

Based on the information given to you in the scenario, create a domain plan that includes the top-level domain apbindustries.com, child domains (if applicable), organizational units (if applicable), and a group structure plan.

learning objective

After completing this project, you will know how to create a basic domain plan.

specific requirements

None

estimated completion time

15 minutes

project steps

1. Create a diagram that outlines your network hierarchy. Ensure that you include all child domains and/or organizational units that you plan on creating.
2. Create a group structure that reflects the departmental organization of APB Industries.

Figure 1-1 A typical network hierarchy

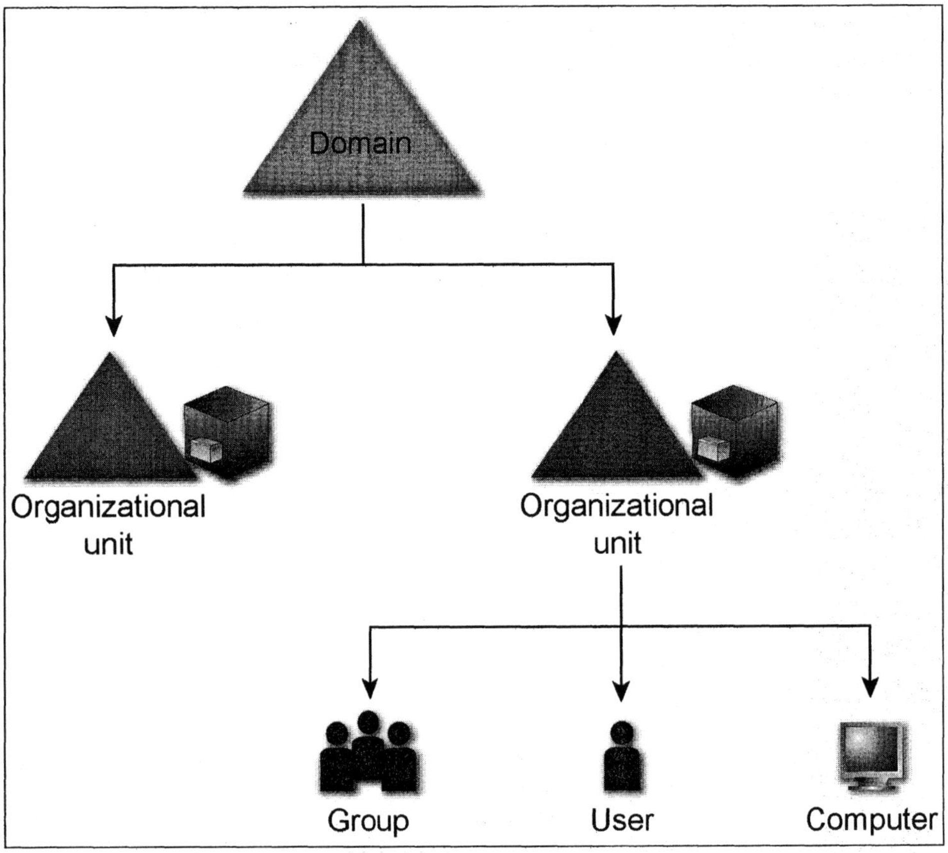

Figure 1-2 Examples of naming conventions

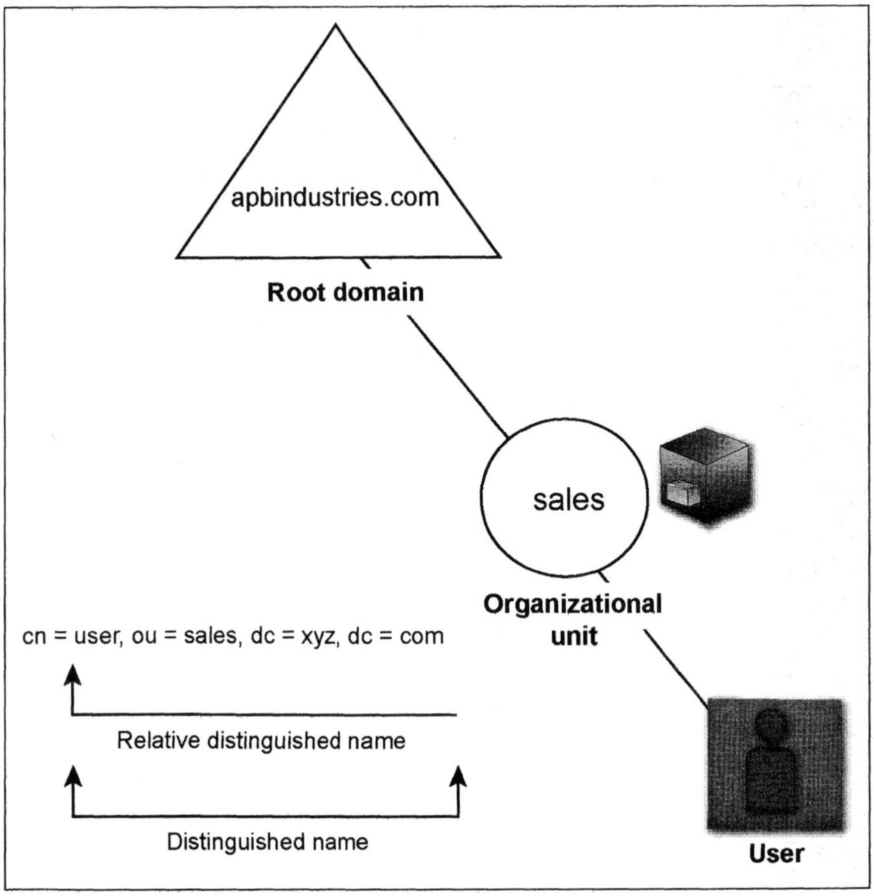

project 1.2

Expanding the Logical Active Directory Structure

exam objective

Basic knowledge

overview

APB Industries has decided to modify the logical structure of its Active Directory so that all Network Administrators are grouped together into one container.

learning objective

After completing this project, you will know how to expand the logical Active Directory structure.

specific requirements

None

estimated completion time

10 minutes

project steps

1. Modify your existing domain structure diagram so that there is a separate Active Directory container (child domain or organizational unit) for Network Administrators. Keep in mind that there are two levels of Network Administrators: top-level Network Administrators and departmental Network Administrators.

tip

It is best to restrict the number of domains in your organization to the absolute minimum necessary. Use OUs instead of additional domains wherever possible.

Figure 1-3 Domain models

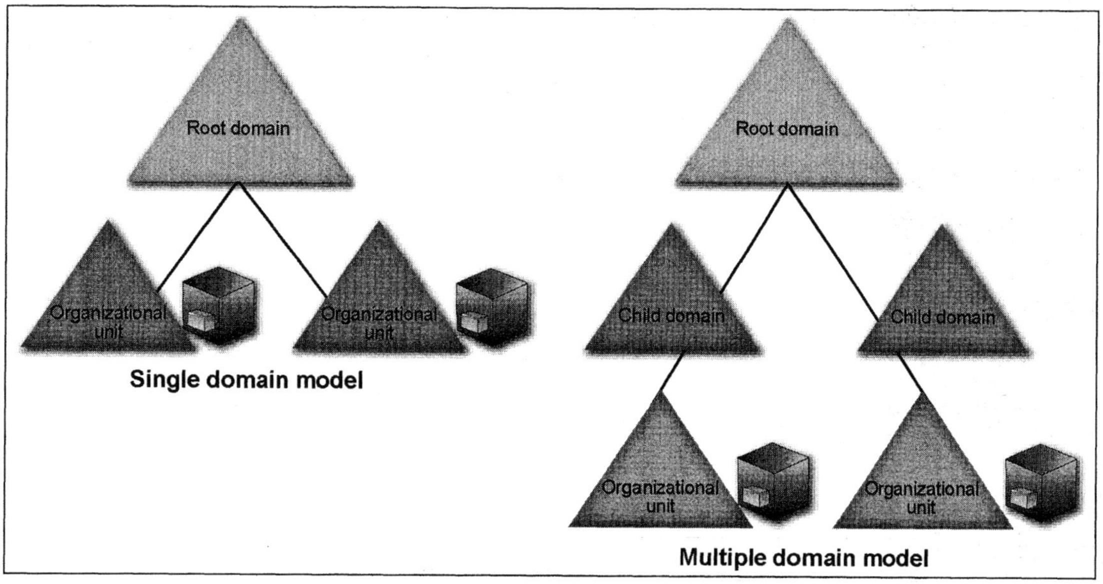

project 1.3

Expanding the Physical Active Directory Structure

exam objective

Basic knowledge

overview

APB Industries is expanding its operations. The company will open a new office overseas in Oslo, Norway. There will be only five employees at this location initially, and they all will be part of the Sales department. Since the office is so small, there will be no in-house network administrator. The one server at this location will act as a domain controller. Since overseas-dedicated data connections are expensive, bandwidth between the two locations is limited to 56 Kbps. Keep that in mind as you modify the physical structure of Active Directory.

learning objective

After completing this project, you will know how to expand the physical Active Directory structure.

specific requirements

None

estimated completion time

10 minutes

project steps

1. Modify your existing domain structure diagram to reflect the new location in Oslo, Norway.

tip

Site objects allow you to control Active Directory replication traffic across low bandwidth connections.

Figure 1-4 Site structure

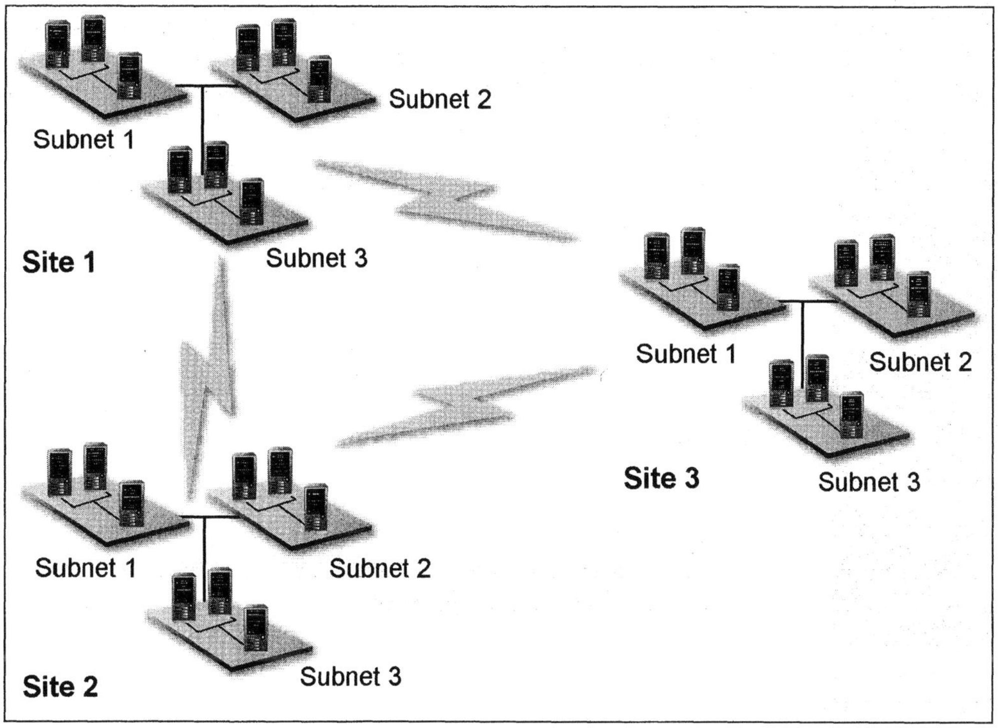

project 1.4

Dealing with Separate Account Policies

exam objective

Basic knowledge

overview

APB Industries now needs a Research and Development department, which will operate out of its Toronto location. Due to the sensitive nature of the data that the Research and Development department will produce, it will require a separate account policy. This will allow the R&D administrators to set a minimum password length of 8 characters and a maximum password age of 14 days, which is much stricter than for the rest of the organization.

learning objective

After completing this project, you will know how to handle multiple account policies within a single organization.

specific requirements

None

estimated completion time

10 minutes

project steps

tip

The account policies section of a Group Policy Object only can be applied at the domain level.

1. Modify your existing domain structure diagram to reflect the addition of the Research and Development department. Keep in mind the need for a more secure password policy.

Figure 1-5 Account policies only can be applied at the domain level

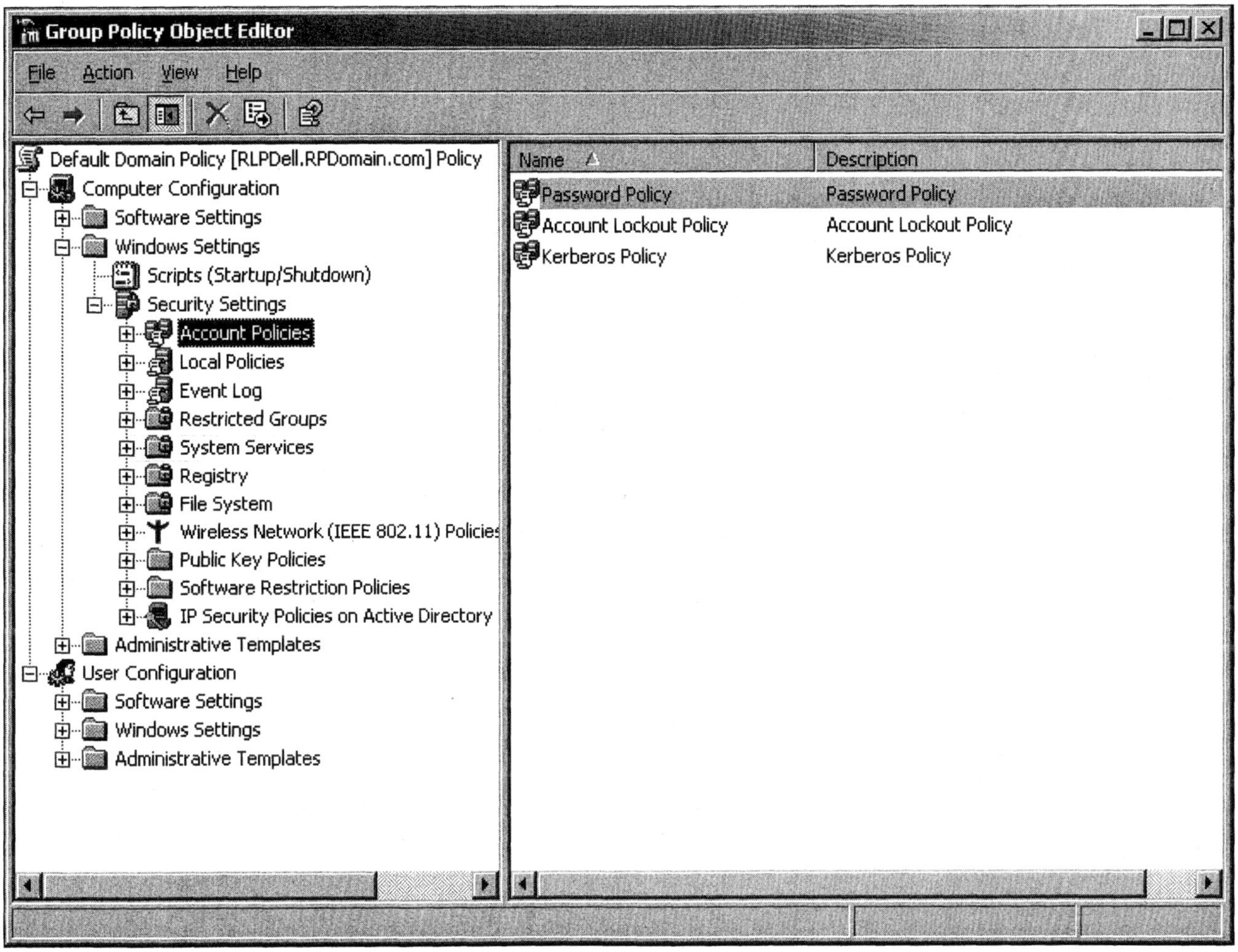

LESSON 2

Implementing Active Directory

Active Directory is not installed as part of the Windows Server 2003 default installation. Therefore, to take advantage of Active Directory's features, you must install Active Directory on at least one Windows Server 2003 computer in your organization.

During the installation of Active Directory, a Windows Server 2003 computer is promoted to a domain controller. During installation, you can create a new child domain, a new domain in an existing forest of domains, or a new domain in a new forest of domains. In order to verify proper installation, you must ensure that all Active Directory components, such as the database, the shared system volume, and DNS are present.

In an Active Directory forest, certain domain controllers act as operations masters. Operations masters are assigned control over specific tasks that cannot be performed under the multi-master model of Active Directory. These operations masters are also referred to as FSMOs, or Flexible Single Masters of Operation. It is critical to know which roles are forest-wide (Schema Master and Domain Naming Master) and which roles are domain-wide (RID Master, Infrastructure Master, and PDC Emulator). Occasionally, you may want to change the default operations master role assignments. Active Directory enables you to seize the operations master role, or transfer it, to other domain controllers in the domain or forest.

An OU is a container that can store users, groups, computers, printers, shared folders, and other OUs. A proper OU structure makes administration of the domain much easier, while also allowing for delegation of control over specific areas of an organization.

Scenario

APB Industries is ready to deploy their planned Active Directory infrastructure. As the Senior network administrator, you are responsible for installing and verifying Active Directory. You will also need to transfer an operations master role from one domain controller to another. Lastly, you will create an OU structure to simplify your administration, and to enable you to delegate control.

Lesson 2 Implementing Active Directory

Project	Exam 70-294 Objective
2.1 Installing Active Directory	Implement an Active Directory directory service forest and domain structure. Create the forest root domain. Install and configure an Active Directory domain controller.
2.2 Verifying Active Directory Installation	Manage an Active Directory forest and domain structure.
2.3 Installing a Child Domain in Active Directory	Create a child domain. Install forests, trees, and domains.
2.4 Managing Domain and Forest Functional Levels	Set an Active Directory forest and domain functional level based on requirements. Manage an Active Directory forest and domain structure.
2.5 Viewing and Transferring Operations Master Roles	Plan flexible operations master role placement. Plan for business continuity of operations master roles. Identify operations master role dependencies.
2.6 Implementing an Organizational Unit Structure within a Domain	Plan an OU structure. Analyze the administrative requirements for an OU. Implement an OU structure. Create an OU. Move objects within an OU hierarchy.

General Requirements

To complete the projects in this lesson, you will need to have administrative rights on a Windows Server 2003 computer on a network. At least one of this computer's hard disk partitions must be configured to use the NTFS file system. You will also need the Windows Server 2003 installation CD. For Project 3 and Project 4, you will need an additional Windows Server 2003 computer that can act as domain controller for a child domain of the domain you will create in Project 1. You may also find it helpful to refer to Lesson 2 in your Prentice Hall Certification Series Exam 70-294 textbook for further information about the topics covered by the projects in this lesson.

project 2.1

Installing Active Directory

exam objective

Implement an Active Directory directory service forest and domain structure. Create the forest root domain. Install and configure an Active Directory domain controller.

overview

In this project, you will be installing the first Active Directory domain controller in your organization. Not only will you be creating a new domain tree, you will also be creating a new forest.

learning objective

After completing this project, you will know how to install Active Directory.

specific requirements

Administrative rights on a computer running Windows Server 2003. At least one of the computer's hard disk partitions must be formatted with the NTFS file system. You will also need the Windows Server 2003 installation CD.

estimated completion time

30 minutes

project steps

1. Log on to a computer running Windows Server 2003 with an account that has administrative rights. Throughout this text, this computer will be known as SERVERA.
2. Click **Start**, point to **Control Panel**, point to **Network Connections**, and then click **Local Area Connection** to open the **Local Area Connection** dialog box.
3. Click **Properties** to open the **Local Area Connection Properties** dialog box. Select **Internet Protocol (TCP/IP)** and click **Properties (Figure 2-1)**.
4. In the **Internet Protocol (TCP/IP) Properties** dialog box, select the **Use the following IP address** option button and type the IP address **192.168.1.235** in the **IP address** text box. Type **255.255.255.0** in the **Subnet mask** text box and **192.168.1.254** in the **Default gateway** text box. Click **OK** and close all open dialog boxes and windows.
5. Click **Start**, click **Run** and in the **Open** text box, type **dcpromo** and click **OK** to open the **Active Directory Installation Wizard**.
6. Click **Next** in each of the next four screens to accept the default configuration information. These defaults are the most common settings.
7. When the **New Domain Name** screen appears, enter **apbindustries.com** in the **Full DNS name for the new domain** text box **(Figure 2-2)** and click **Next**.
8. Accept the default NetBIOS name by clicking **Next**.
9. The Database and Log folders screen opens with the default location ***%Systemroot%*\SYSVOL** entered in the **Folder location** text box. Click **Next** to accept the default database folder and Active Directory log locations.
10. The **Shared System Volume** screen opens. Select **Next** to accept the default SYSVOL folder location.
11. At this point, the **DNS Registration Diagnostics** screen may appear if the Wizard could not determine the name and address of the DNS server with which this domain controller will be registered. Select the **Install and configure the DNS server on this computer, and set this computer to use this DNS server as its preferred DNS server** option button, if it is not already selected, and click **Next**.

tip

In a Microsoft environment, passwords and pre-shared keys are the ONLY items that are case-sensitive. Users names are not case-sensitive.

Figure 2-1 Local Area Connection Properties dialog box

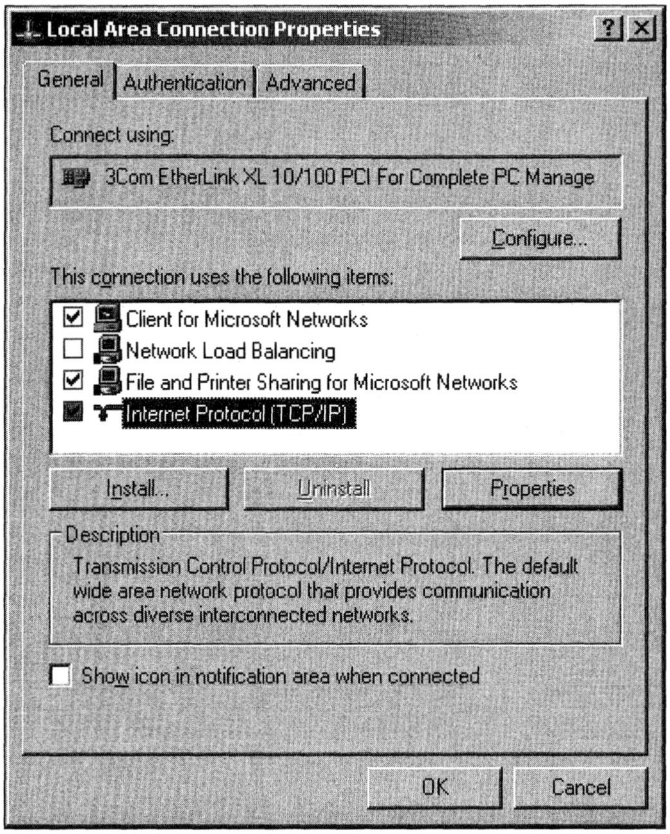

Figure 2-2 Specifying a DNS name for the new domain

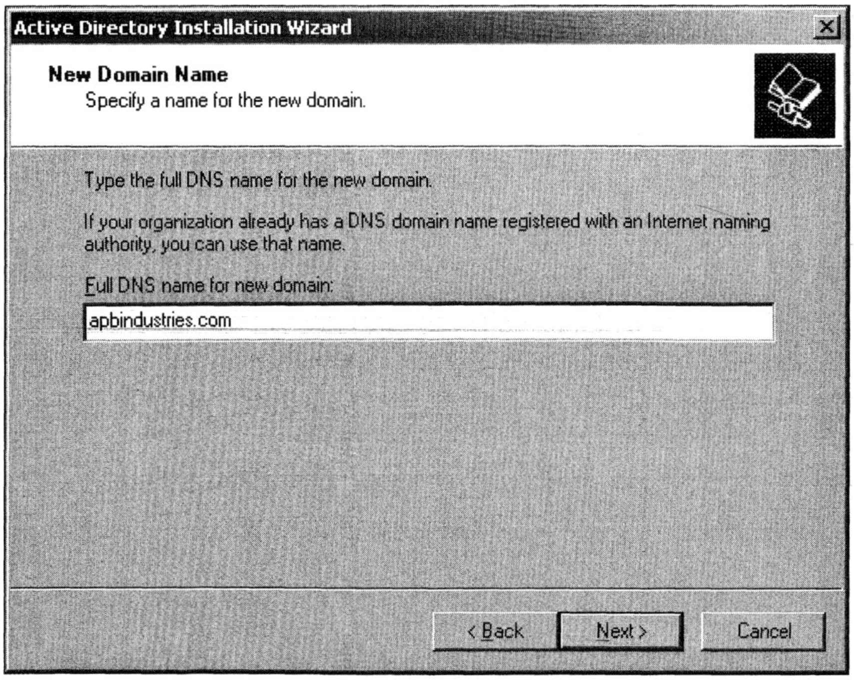

project 2.1

Installing Active Directory *(cont'd)*

exam objective

Implement an Active Directory directory service forest and domain structure. Create the forest root domain. Install and configure an Active Directory domain controller.

project steps

12. The **Permissions** screen opens (**Figure 2-3**). Accept the default permissions for user and group objects by clicking **Next**.
13. The **Directory Services Restore Mode Administrator Password** screen opens (**Figure 2-4**). In the **Restore Mode Password** text box, enter and confirm the password, **ADRestore**, remembering that it is case-sensitive. Note that this is not the administrator password but is used only in directory services restore operations. Click **Next**.
14. Review the **Summary** screen and click **Next** to accept it.
15. The **Active Directory Installation Wizard** will begin installing Active Directory. The **Configuring Active Directory** progress indicator displays as Active Directory is being installed. This process may take several minutes, depending on system performance.
16. When the process is complete, click **Finish**.
17. A message box asking for your confirmation to restart the computer will open. Click **Restart Now** to restart your server and to complete the installation. When the server reboots, it will be a domain controller in the **apbindustries.com** domain.

Figure 2-3 The Permissions screen

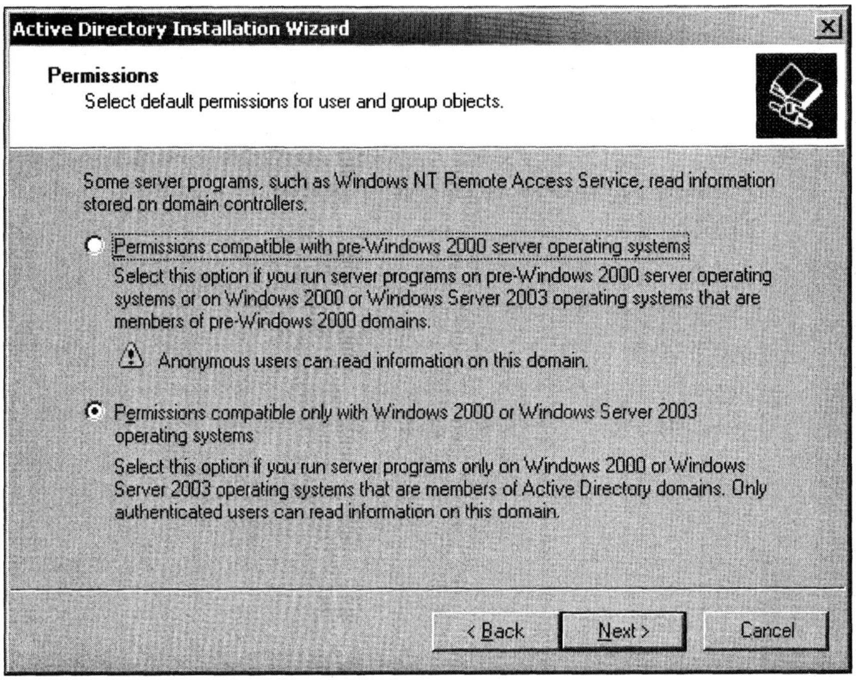

Figure 2-4 The Directory Services Restore Mode Administrator Password screen

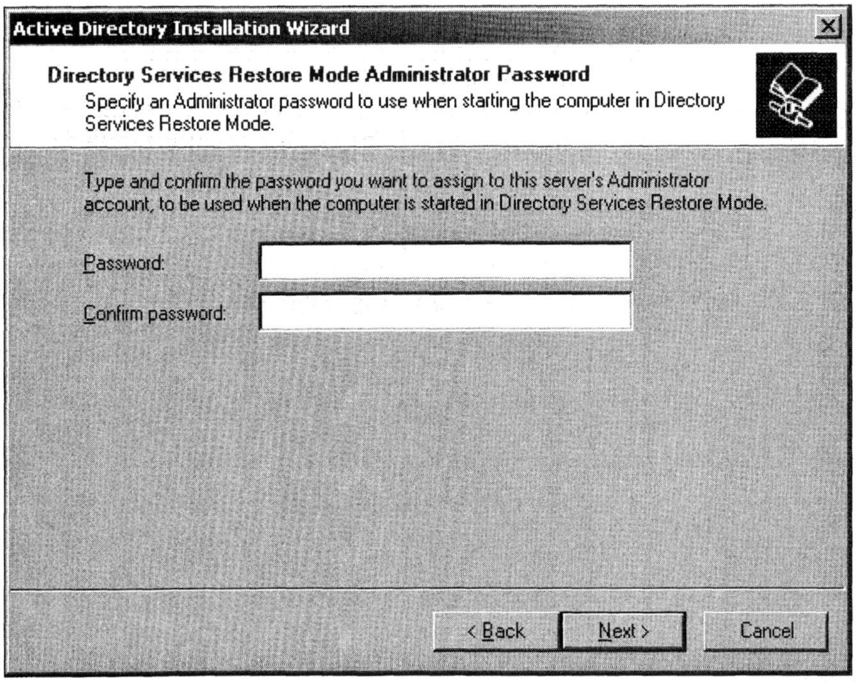

project 2.2

Verifying Active Directory Installation

exam objective

Manage an Active Directory forest and domain structure.

overview

You have finished the Active Directory installation process. To confirm a successful installation, you will now verify that all the Active Directory components are present, including the default containers, the default Domain Controllers OU, the default site, the global catalog server, the Active Directory database, and the shared system volume. You must also verify that the computer role is properly registered and that the Service Resource Records exist in the DNS database.

learning objective

After completing this project, you will know how to verify the installation of Active Directory.

specific requirements

Successful completion of Project 2.1 and administrative rights on SERVERA, the Windows Server 2003 computer that has been configured as the domain controller for the apbindustries.com domain.

estimated completion time

20 minutes

project steps

1. Using an account that has administrative rights, log on to **SERVERA**, the Windows Server 2003 domain controller for the apbindustries.com domain.
2. Click **Start**, point to **Administrative Tools**, and click **DNS** to open the DNS console.
3. Double-click **Forward Lookup Zones** in the tree and then verify that **_msdcs.apbindustries.com** and **apbindustries.com** appear in the details pane **(Figure 2-5)**.
4. Double-click **apbindustries.com** and verify that **SOA**, **NS** and two **A** records have been created. Then close the console window.
5. Open **Windows Explorer**. Expand drive **C:**, expand the ***%Systemroot%*** folder. This folder usually will be **C:\Windows**, but it may be **WINNT** if the computer was upgraded from Windows 2000 Server. Verify the existence of the **SYSVOL** directory and the **NTDS** directory in the tree.
6. Close **Windows Explorer**.
7. Click **Start**, point to **Administrative Tools**, and verify that **Active Directory Domains and Trusts**, **Active Directory Sites and Services**, and **Active Directory Users and Computers** have been added to the Administrative Tools menu **(Figure 2-6)**. Click **Active Directory Users and Computers**.
8. Expand **apbindustries.com** and double-click **Domain Controllers**. Verify that **SERVERA** is in the details pane **(Figure 2-7)**.
9. Double-click **Builtin** in the console tree and verify the existence of sixteen objects **(Figure 2-8)**. These are the groups installed by default in Active Directory.
10. Close all windows.

Figure 2-5 Forward Lookup Zone Verification

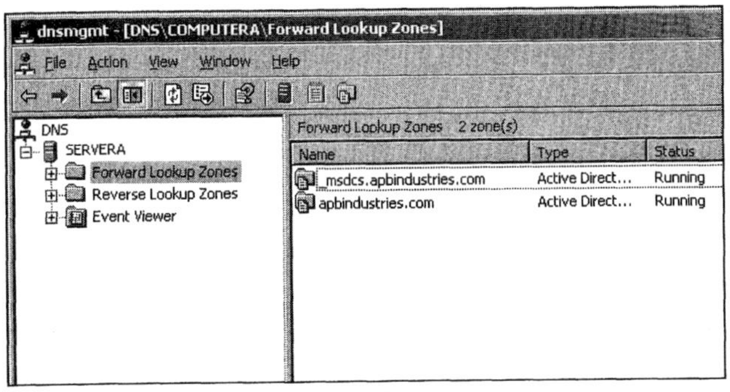

Figure 2-6 Active Directory tools

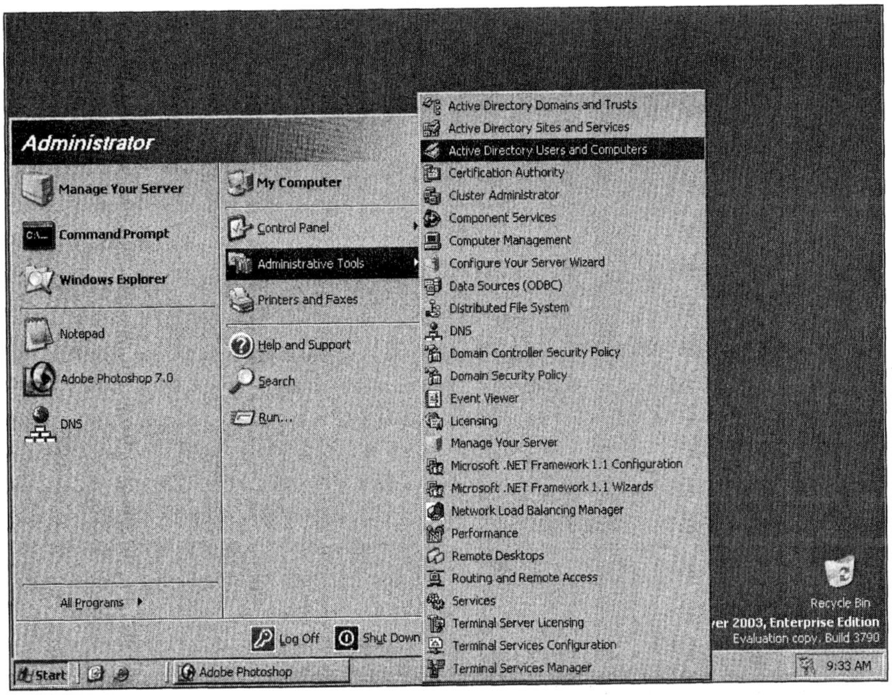

Figure 2-7 SERVERA in the details pane

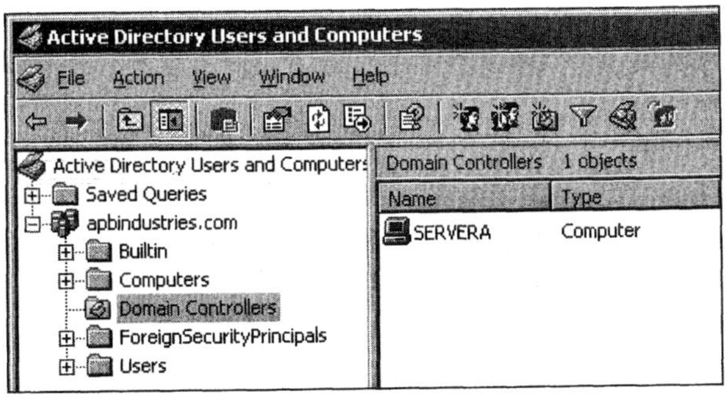

Figure 2-8 Active Directory Builtin Groups

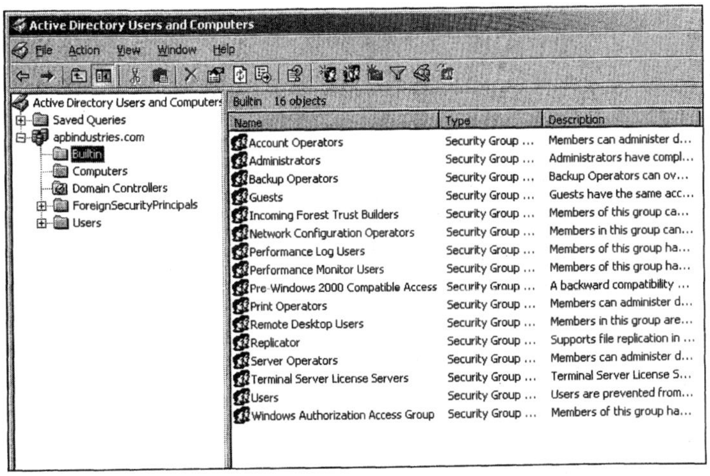

project 2.3

Installing a Child Domain in Active Directory

exam objective

Create a child domain. Install forests, trees, and domains.

overview

Now that you have verified the installation of the first Active Directory domain, you will add a child domain for the Research and Development department of APB Industries. This child domain will be called rnd.apbindustries.com.

learning objective

After completing this project, you will know how to add a child domain to an existing Active Directory domain.

specific requirements

Successful completion of Project 2.1, a second Windows Server 2003 computer that you can promote to a domain controller, and the Windows Server 2003 installation CD.

estimated completion time

50 minutes

project steps

1. Log on to a computer running Windows Server 2003, using an account with administrative rights.
2. Click **Start**, point to **Control Panel**, point to **Network Connections**, and click **Local Area Connection** to open the **Local Area Connection Status** dialog box **(Figure 2-9)**.
3. Click the **Properties** button. In the **Local Area Connection Properties** dialog box, select **Internet Protocol (TCP/IP)** and click **Properties**.
4. In the **Internet Protocol (TCP/IP) Properties** dialog box, select the **Use the following IP address** option button and type the IP address **192.168.1.234** in the **IP address** text box.
5. Type **255.255.255.0** in the **Subnet mask** text box. Type **192.168.1.254** in the **Default gateway** text box.
6. The **Use the following DNS server addresses** option button was automatically selected when you selected the **Use the following IP address** option in Step 4. Type **192.168.1.235** in the **Preferred DNS Server** text box **(Figure 2-10)**.
7. Click **OK** and close all other open dialog boxes and windows.
8. Click **Start**, click **Run**, and in the **Open** text box, type **dcpromo** and click **OK** to open the **Active Directory Installation Wizard**.
9. Click **Next** in each of the next three screens to accept the default configuration information.

Figure 2-9 The Local Area Connection Status dialog box

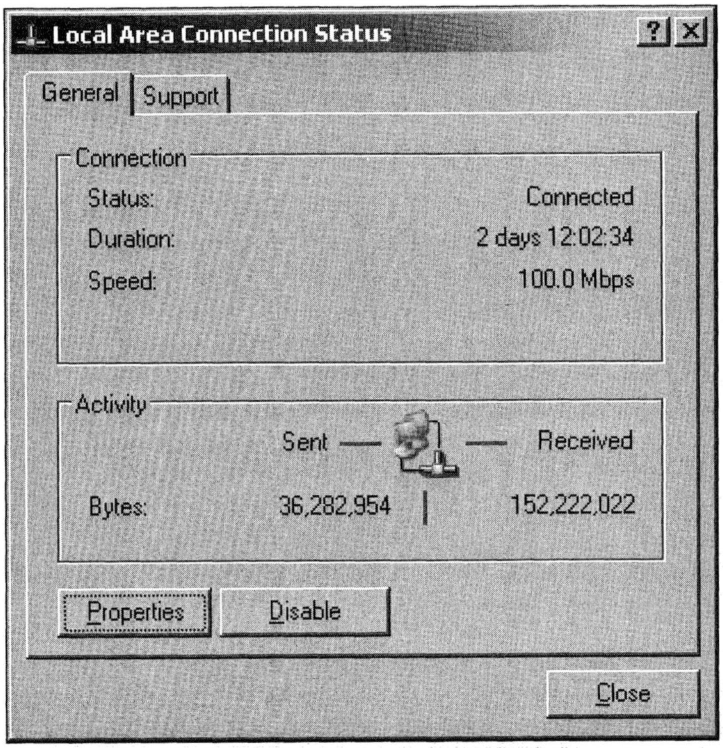

Figure 2-10 IP Address, Subnet Mask, and Default Gateway for SERVERB

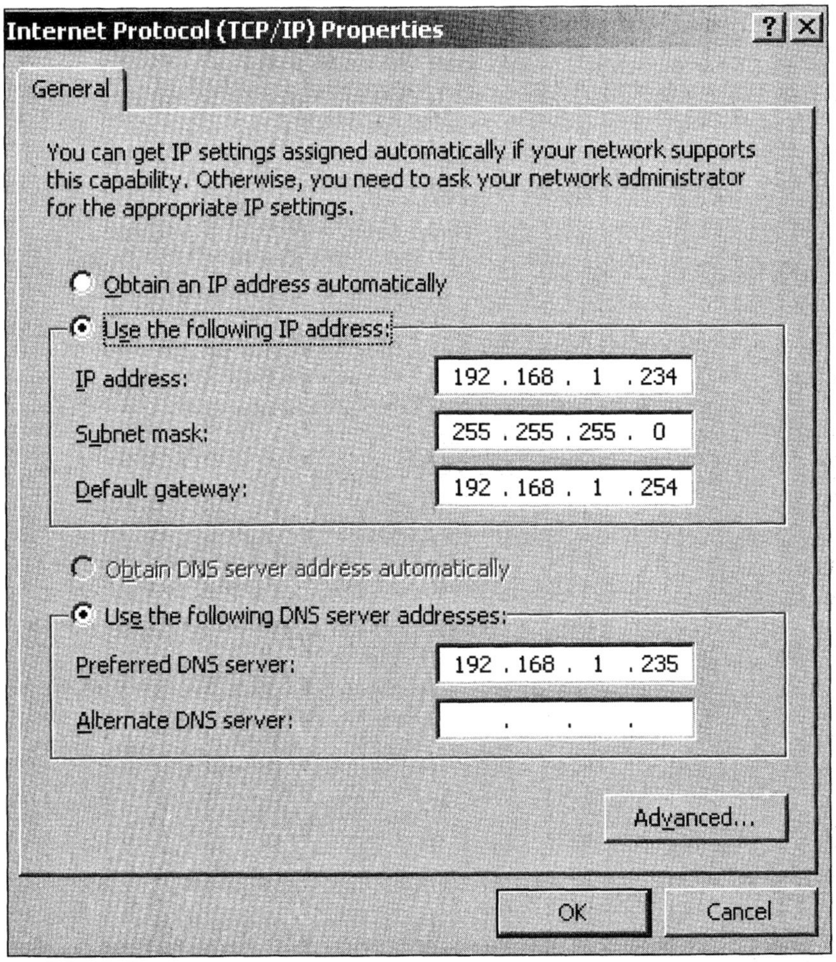

project 2.3

Installing a Child Domain in Active Directory *(cont'd)*

exam objective

Create a child domain. Install forests, trees, and domains.

project steps

caution

You should use a simple password, like the one in Step 8, only for practice purposes. In actual work situations, create more difficult passwords that mix letters with numbers, and that do not resemble the word "password."

10. When the **Create a New Domain** screen appears, select the **Child domain in an existing domain tree** option button **(Figure 2-11)**. Click **Next**.
11. In the **Network Credentials** screen, enter the administrative account's user name and password, and the domain **apbindustries** in the appropriate text boxes. Click **Next**.
12. The **Child Domain Installation** screen opens. Select the **Browse** button to the right of the **Parent domain** text box. Select **apbindustries.com** and click **OK**. In the **Child domain** text box, type **rnd (Figure 2-12)**. Click **Next**.
13. Accept the default NetBIOS name by clicking **Next**.
14. Click **Next** to accept the default database folder and Active Directory log locations.
15. Click **Next** to accept the default SYSVOL folder location.
16. The **DNS Registration Diagnostics** screen opens. DNS support for the domain controller should be verified. The primary DNS server tested should be **servera.apbindustries.com (192.168.1.235)**. Click **Next**.
17. Click **Next** to accept the default permissions.
18. The **Directory Services Restore Mode Administrator Password** screen opens. In the **Restore Mode Password** text box, enter and confirm the password, **ADRestore**, remembering that it is case sensitive. Note that this is not the administrator password but is used only in directory services restore operations. Click **Next**.
19. Click **Next** to accept the **Summary** screen.
20. The **Active Directory Installation Wizard** will configure Active Directory. This may take a few minutes based on system performance.
21. Click **Finish** to close the Wizard. Click **Restart Now**.
22. Log on as an **Administrator**. If the **Manage Your Server** window opens, select the **Don't display this page at logon** check box. Close the window.

Figure 2-11 Creating a child domain in an existing domain tree

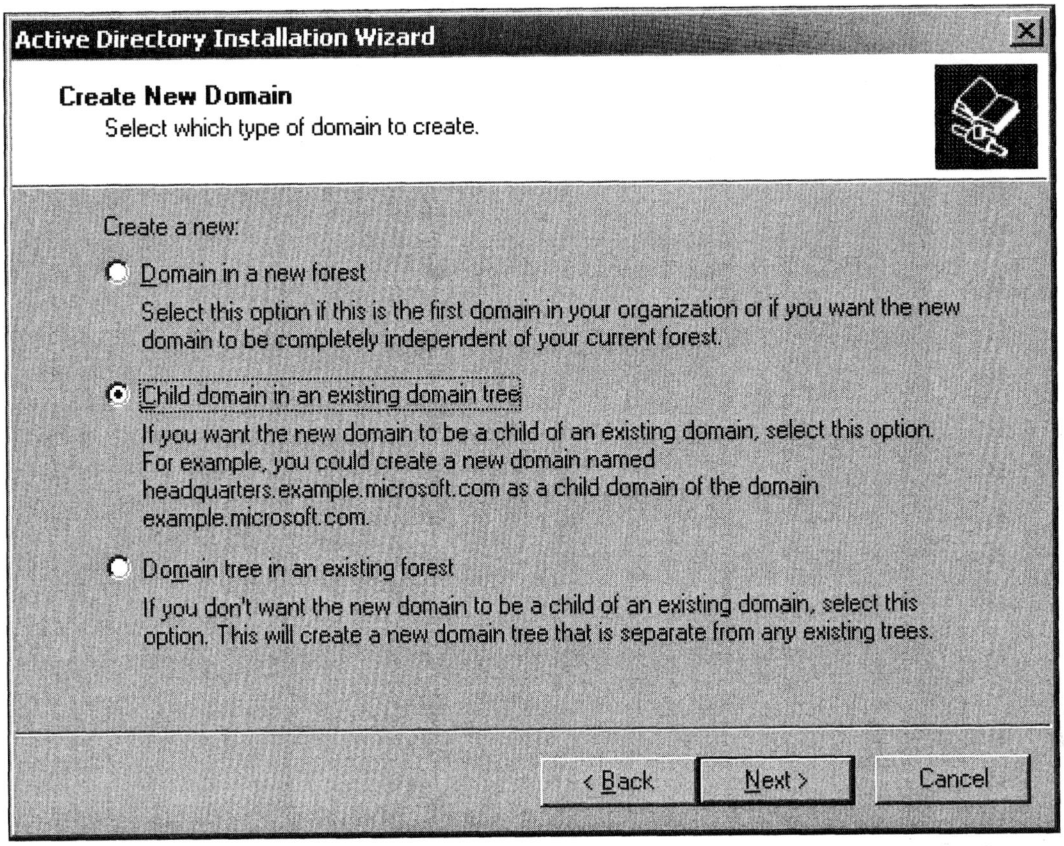

Figure 2-12 The Child Domain Installation screen

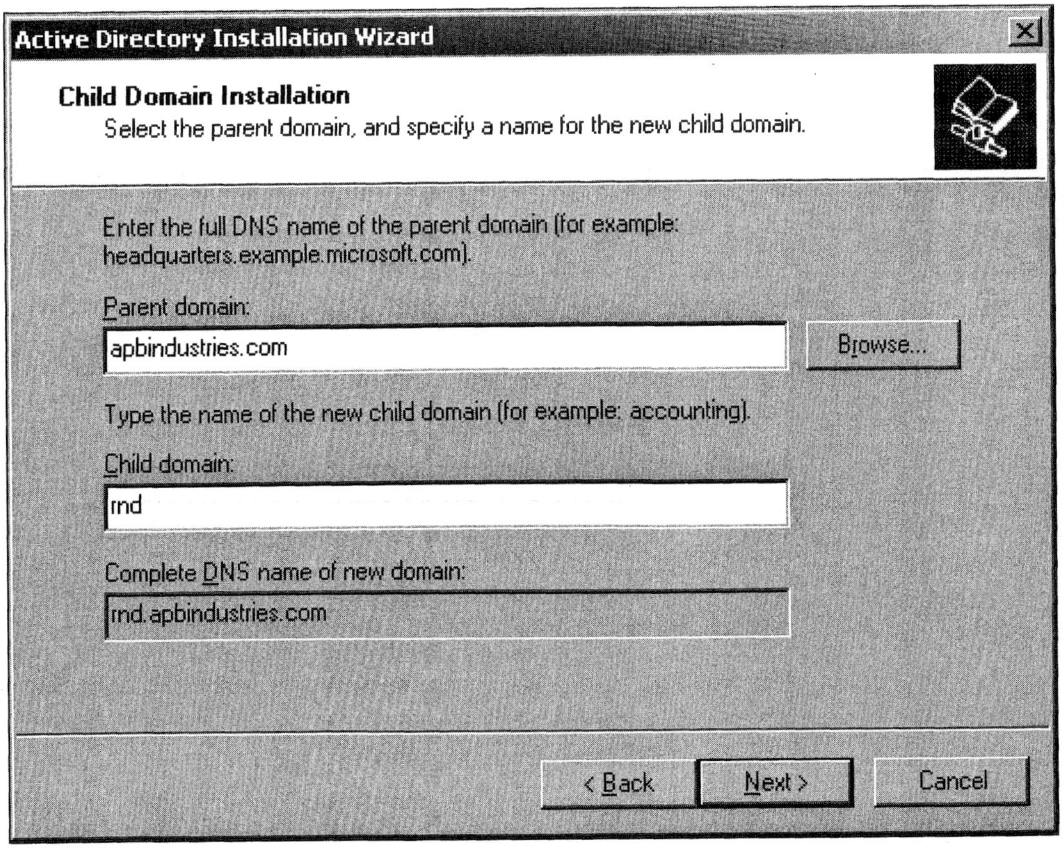

project 2.4

Managing Domain and Forest Functional Levels

exam objective

Set an Active Directory forest and domain functional level based on requirements. Manage an Active Directory forest and domain structure.

overview

Active Directory provides four domain and forest functional levels, or modes: Windows 2000 mixed mode, Windows 2000 native mode, Windows Server 2003 interim mode, and Windows Server 2003 mode. When you create a domain, by default, the domain is configured to run in Windows 2000 mixed mode. This mode allows the coexistence of Windows NT, Windows 2000, and Windows Server 2003 domains. If your domain consists of only Windows 2000 domain controllers, you can use Windows 2000 native mode. This mode supports Windows 2000 and Windows Server 2003 domains. If your domain has only Windows NT 4.0 servers, and you upgrade a server to Windows Server 2003, you can use Windows Server 2003 interim mode. This level is used when there are no Windows 2000 servers and you upgrade a Windows NT PDC (primary domain controller) to Windows Server 2003. APB Industries, however, has only Windows Server 2003 domain controllers. This means that you can switch the domain to Windows Server 2003 mode, which supports the full Windows Server 2003 Active Directory implementation. Note however that the decision to raise the domain or forest functional levels to Windows Server 2003 mode is final. Be certain that you do not need to add Windows 2000 domain controllers anywhere in the forest before performing this procedure. Once the Active Directory forest is upgraded to Windows Server 2003, you cannot add Windows 2000 Active Directory sub-domains.

learning objective

After completing this project, you will know how to raise the functional level of domains and forests.

specific requirements

Administrative rights on SERVERA, the Windows Server 2003 that is acting as a domain controller for apbindustries.com.

estimated completion time

5 minutes

project steps

1. Log on to **SERVERA** with an account that has administrative rights.
2. Click **Start**, point to **Administrative Tools**, and click **Active Directory Domains and Trusts** to open the **Active Directory Domains and Trusts** console.
3. Expand **apbindustries.com** and right-click **rnd.apbindustries.com**.
4. Select **Raise Domain Functional Level (Figure 2-13)**.
5. The **Raise Domain Functional Level** dialog box opens. In the **Select an available domain functional level** list box **(Figure 2-14)**, select **Windows Server 2003**.
6. Click the **Raise** button.
7. The **Raise Domain Functional Level** warning dialog box opens to remind you that this change will affect the entire domain and that the process cannot be reversed. Click **OK**.
8. The **Raise Domain Functional Level** information dialog box opens to confirm that the functional level was successfully raised. Click **OK** again.
9. Right-click **apbindustries.com**. Select **Raise Domain Functional Level**. In the **Select an available domain functional level** list box, select **Windows Server 2003**. Click **Raise**. Click **OK**. Click **OK** again.
10. Close all open dialog boxes and windows.

Figure 2-13 Raise Domain Functional Level command

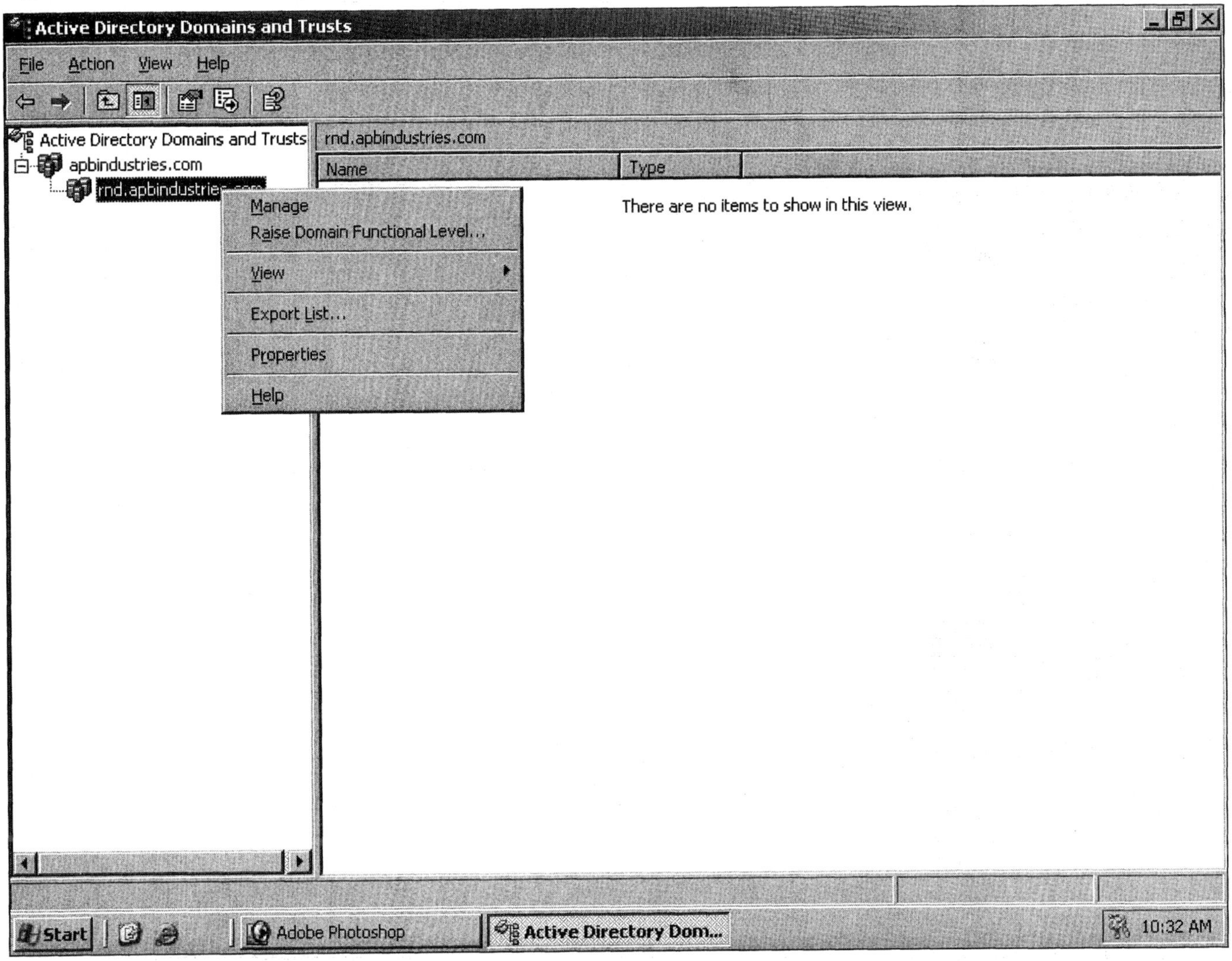

Figure 2-14 Specifying Windows Server 2003 Domain Functional Level

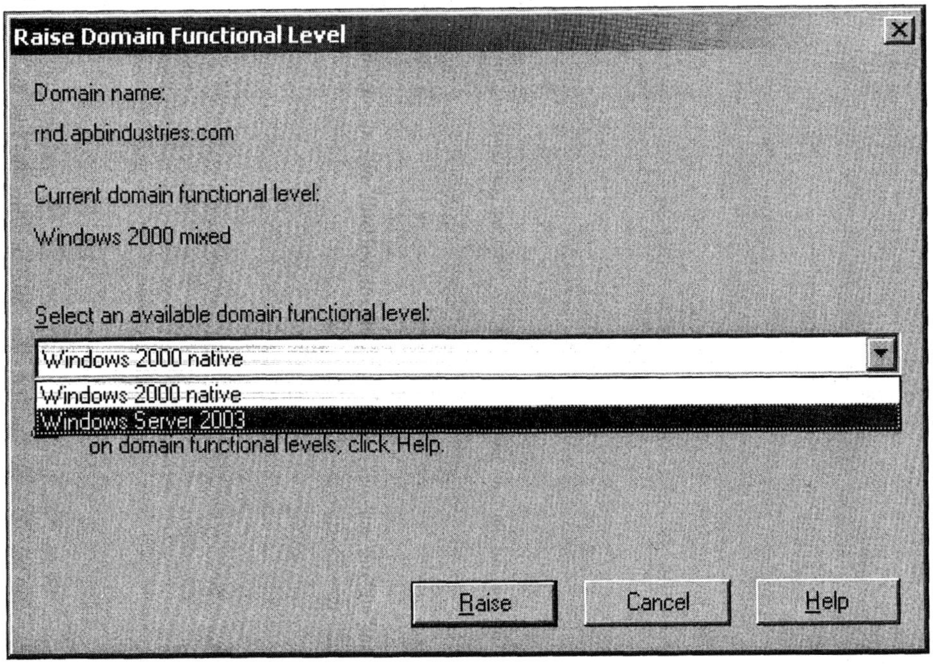

project 2.5

Viewing and Transferring Operations Master Roles

exam objective

Plan flexible operations master role placement. Plan for business continuity of operations master roles. Identify operations master role dependencies.

overview

You will now view the forest-wide and domain-wide operations master roles. The domain controller for the apbindustries.com domain holds both of the forest-wide operations masters, so you will transfer one of those operations master roles to the domain controller of the rnd.apbindustries.com.

learning objective

After completing this project, you will know how to view and transfer operations master roles.

specific requirements

Administrative rights on SERVERA, the Windows Server 2003 computer that is acting as a domain controller for apbindustries.com, as well as the successful completion of Project 2.3.

estimated completion time

10 minutes

project steps

1. Log on to **SERVERA** with an account that has administrative rights.
2. Open the **Active Directory Domains and Trusts** console.
3. Right-click **Active Directory Domains and Trusts** and select **Connect to Domain Controller** to open the **Connect to Domain Controller** dialog box.
4. Select the **Browse** button to the right of the **Domain** text box to open the **Browse for Domain** dialog box.
5. Expand **apbindustries.com** and select **rnd.apbindustries.com**. Click **OK**.
6. Click **OK** to close to close the Connect to Domain Controller dialog box.
7. Right-click **Active Directory Domains and Trusts** and select **Operations Master (Figure 2-15)** to open the **Change Operations Master** dialog box. View the current location for the **Domain naming operations master** (It is located on SERVERA.).
8. Select the **Change** button **(Figure 2-16)**.
9. An **Active Directory Domains and Trusts** warning dialog box opens to confirm that you want to transfer the operations master role. Click **Yes**.
10. An **Active Directory Domains and Trusts** information dialog box opens to confirm that the operations master was successfully transferred. Click **OK**. Notice that **serverb.rnd.apbindustries.com** is now the **Domain Naming Master (Figure 2-17)**.
11. Close all open dialog boxes and windows.
12. Click **Start**, point to **Administrative Tools**, and click **Active Directory Users and Computers** to open the **Active Directory Users and Computers** console.
13. Right-click **apbindustries.com** and select **Operations Master** to open the **Operations Masters** dialog box **(Figure 2-18)**.
14. View the location of the **RID**, **PDC**, and **Infrastructure** by clicking the respective tabs.

Figure 2-15 Operations Master command

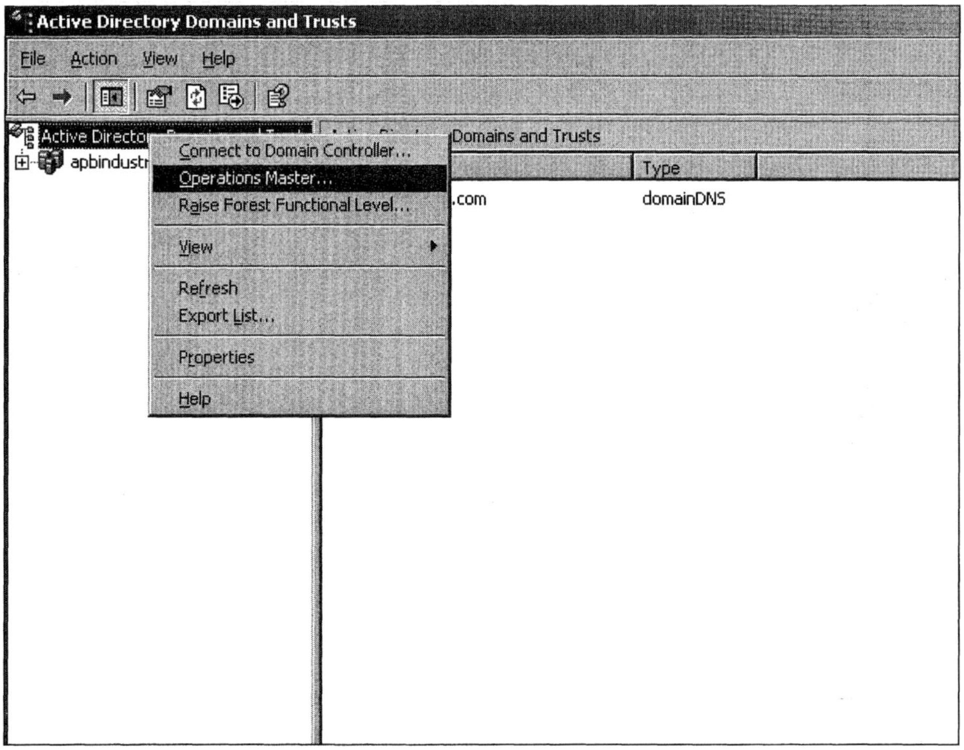

Figure 2-16 Changing the Operations Master

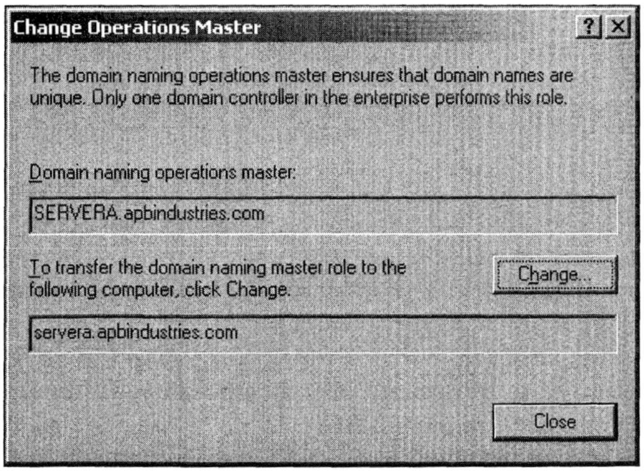

Figure 2-17 Newly Appointed Operations Master

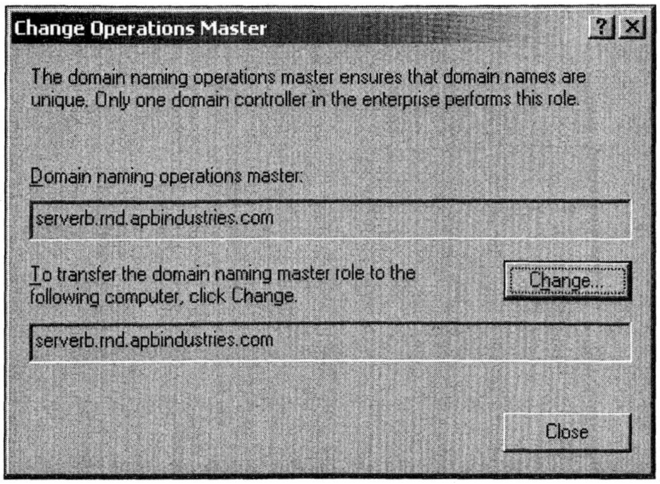

Figure 2-18 RID Pools displaying SERVERA

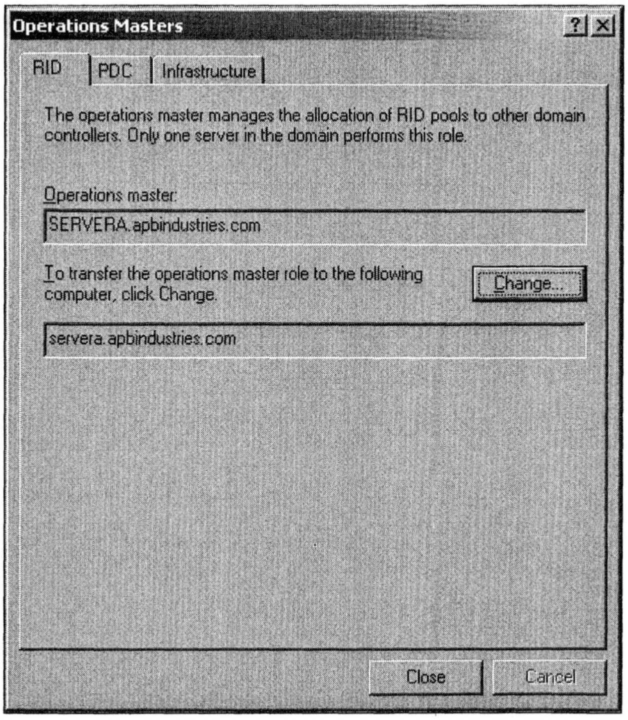

project 2.6

Implementing an Organizational Unit Structure within a Domain

exam objective

Plan an OU structure. Implement an OU structure. Analyze the administrative requirements for an OU. Create an OU. Move objects within an OU hierarchy.

overview

Now that you have completed the installation of your planned Active Directory infrastructure, you will create an OU structure that supports the organizational model outlined in Project 1.

learning objective

After completing this project, you will know how to implement an OU structure.

specific requirements

Administrative rights on SERVERA, the Windows Server 2003 computer that acts as a domain controller for apbindustries.com.

estimated completion time

5 minutes

project steps

1. Log on to **SERVERA** with an account that has administrative rights.
2. Open the **Active Directory Users and Computers** console.
3. Right-click **apbindustries.com**, point to **New**, and click **Organizational Unit (Figure 2-19)**.
4. The **New Object – Organizational Unit** dialog box opens. In the **Name** text box, type **HR**.
   Click **OK** to create the OU. Repeat the process for Accounting and Sales, naming them **Acct** and **Sales**, respectively.
6. Right-click **Active Directory Users and Computers** and select **Connect to Domain** to open the **Connect to Domain** dialog box.
7. Click the **Browse** button to open the **Browse for Domain** dialog box.
8. Expand **apbindustries.com**. Select **rnd.apbindustries.com**. Click **OK** to close the Browse for Domain dialog box.
9. Click **OK** to close the Connect to Domain dialog box.
10. Right-click **rnd.apbindustries.com**, point to **New**, and click **Organizational Unit**. In the **Name** text box, type **rnd.apbindustries.com**. Click **OK**.
11. Close the Active Directory and Computers console.

Figure 2-19 Creating a new Organizational Unit

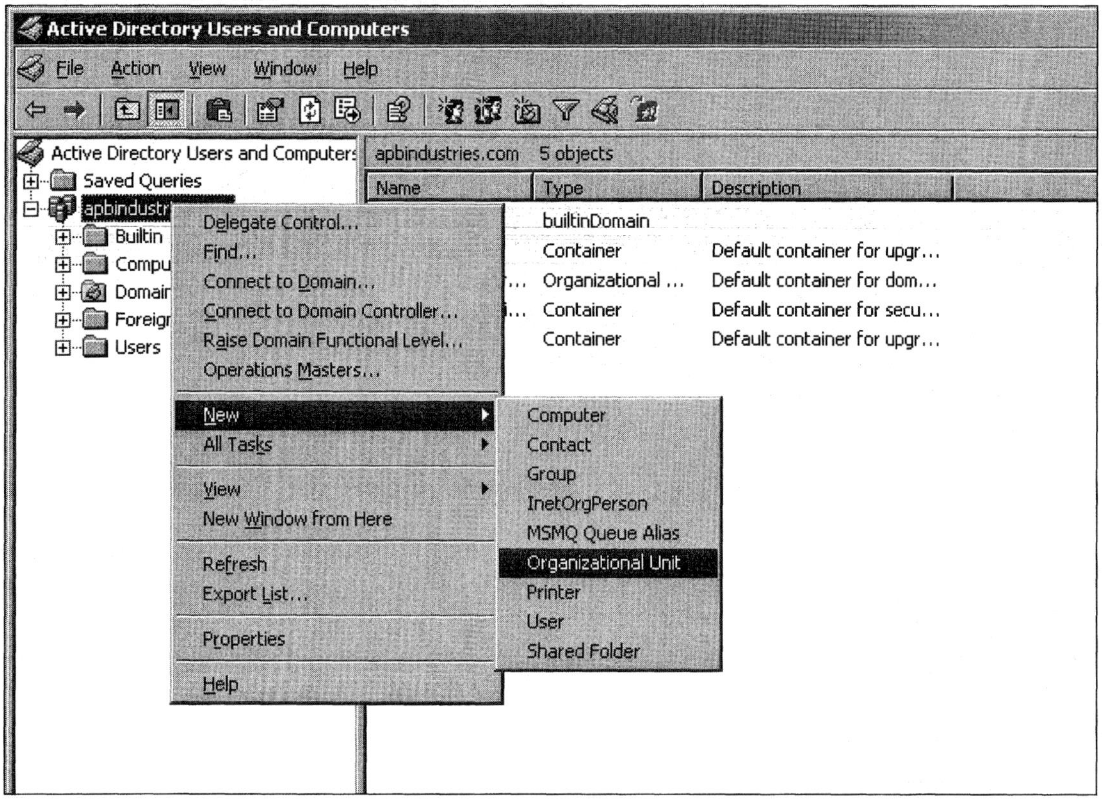

Figure 2-20 The New Object – Organizational Unit dialog box

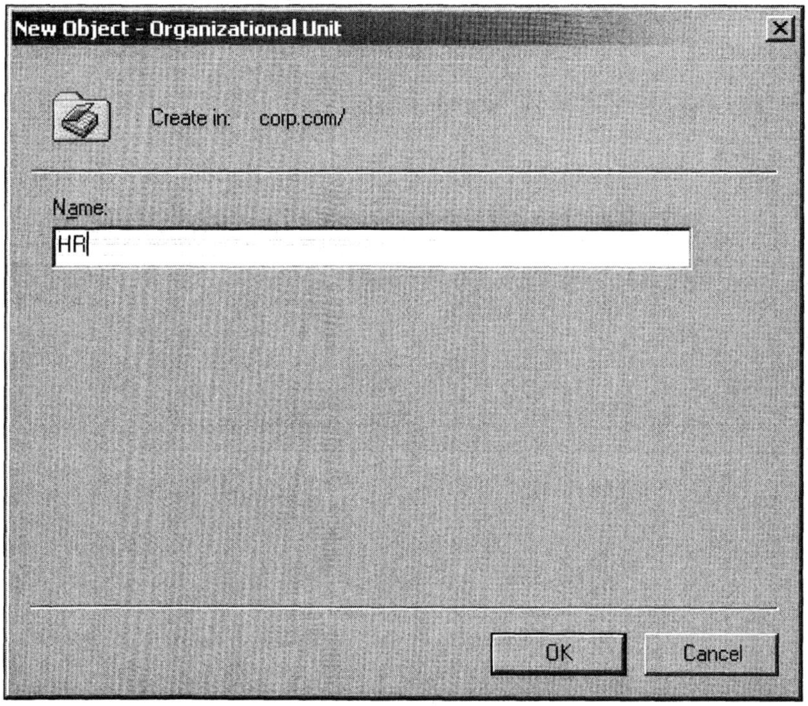

LESSON 3

Configuring Site Settings and Inter-Site Replication

Active Directory sites make it possible to have a global network consisting of a single domain. This is the major factor in creating significant scalability. A properly designed site layout tells Active Directory how your network is physically built. Site links tell Active Directory which sites are linked to one another and the cost (relative speed and reliability) of the physical link. Active Directory uses site information to determine how inter-site Active Directory database replication should occur, which domain controllers should respond to user requests, which global catalog servers to contact, and which resources are closest to the end user for site-aware applications (such as Distributed File System).

Scenario

The Toronto, Canada office of APB Industries is expanding and has purchased a new office across town where the Sales department will eventually be moved. There will be a dedicated 128 Kbps connection between the two sites. To simplify administration, the Sales department will remain in the same domain, apbindustries.com. When the Sales department is moved, they will also take with them a new domain controller that will reside at the new location. To limit the effect that Active Directory replication traffic has on other types of more business-critical traffic (such as file and database access), sites will be implemented. This will allow the Network Administration team to control when and how often Active Directory replication occurs.

Lesson 3 Configuring Site Settings and Inter-Site Replication

Project	Exam 70-294 Objective
3.1 Creating Sites to Develop a Directory Structure	Basic knowledge
3.2 Configuring a Subnet	Basic knowledge
3.3 Creating Site Links	Implement an Active Directory site topology. Configure site links.
3.4 Creating Site Link Bridges	Implement an Active Directory site topology. Configure site links.
3.5 Selecting a Bridgehead Server Basic knowledge for Inter-Site Replication	Basic knowledge
3.6 Checking Replication Topology	Monitor Active Directory replication failures. Monitor Active Directory replication.
3.7 Designating a Global Catalog Server	Plan a strategy for placing global catalog servers. Evaluate network traffic considerations when placing global catalog servers. Evaluate the need to enable universal group caching.

General Requirements

To complete the projects in this lesson, you will need administrative rights on two Windows Server 2003 computers: SERVERA, the domain controller for the apbindustries.com domain, and SERVERB, the domain controller for the rnd.apbindustries.com domain. You will also need the Windows Server 2003 installation CD-ROM. You may also find it helpful to refer to Lesson 3 in your Prentice Hall Certification Series Exam 70-294 textbook for further information about the topics covered by projects in this lesson.

project 3.1

Creating Sites to Develop a Directory Structure

exam objective

Basic knowledge

overview

In this project, you will be creating an Active Directory site for the new location that APB Industries will be acquiring, in addition to the existing APB Industries site in Oslo, Norway.

learning objective

After completing this project, you will know how to create a site in Active Directory.

specific requirements

Administrative rights on SERVERA, the Windows Server 2003 computer that is acting as a domain controller for apbindustries.com.

estimated completion time

10 minutes

project steps

1. Log on to **SERVERA** using an account that has administrative rights.
2. Click **Start**, point to **Administrative Tools**, and then click **Active Directory Sites and Services**. The **Active Directory Sites and Services** console opens.
3. Expand **Sites**. Right-click **Sites** and click **New Site**. The **New Object – Site** dialog box opens.
4. Type **TorontoSalesSite1** in the **Name** text box.
5. Click **DEFAULTIPSITELINK** and then click **OK (Figure 3-1)**.
6. This opens an **Active Directory** message box that lists the tasks you need to perform in order to complete the configuration of the newly created site. Click **OK**.
7. Repeat steps 3 and 4 to create another site called **OsloSalesSite1**. This is the site for the Oslo, Norway location.
8. Right-click **Default-First-Site-Name** and select **Rename**. Name it **TorontoMainSite**.
9. The new sites, **TorontoMainSite**, **TorontoSalesSite1**, and **OsloSalesSite1** now appear in the tree below **Sites (Figure 3-2)**.

tip

When Active Directory is installed, DEFAULTIPSITELINK is automatically created as the default site link.

Figure 3-1 Specifying DEFAULTIPSITELINK

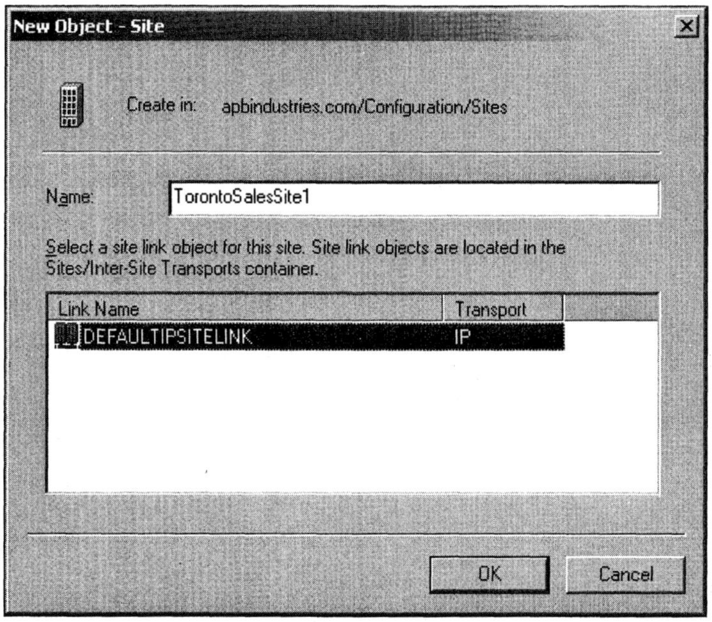

Figure 3-2 New sites in the Active Directory Sites and Services console

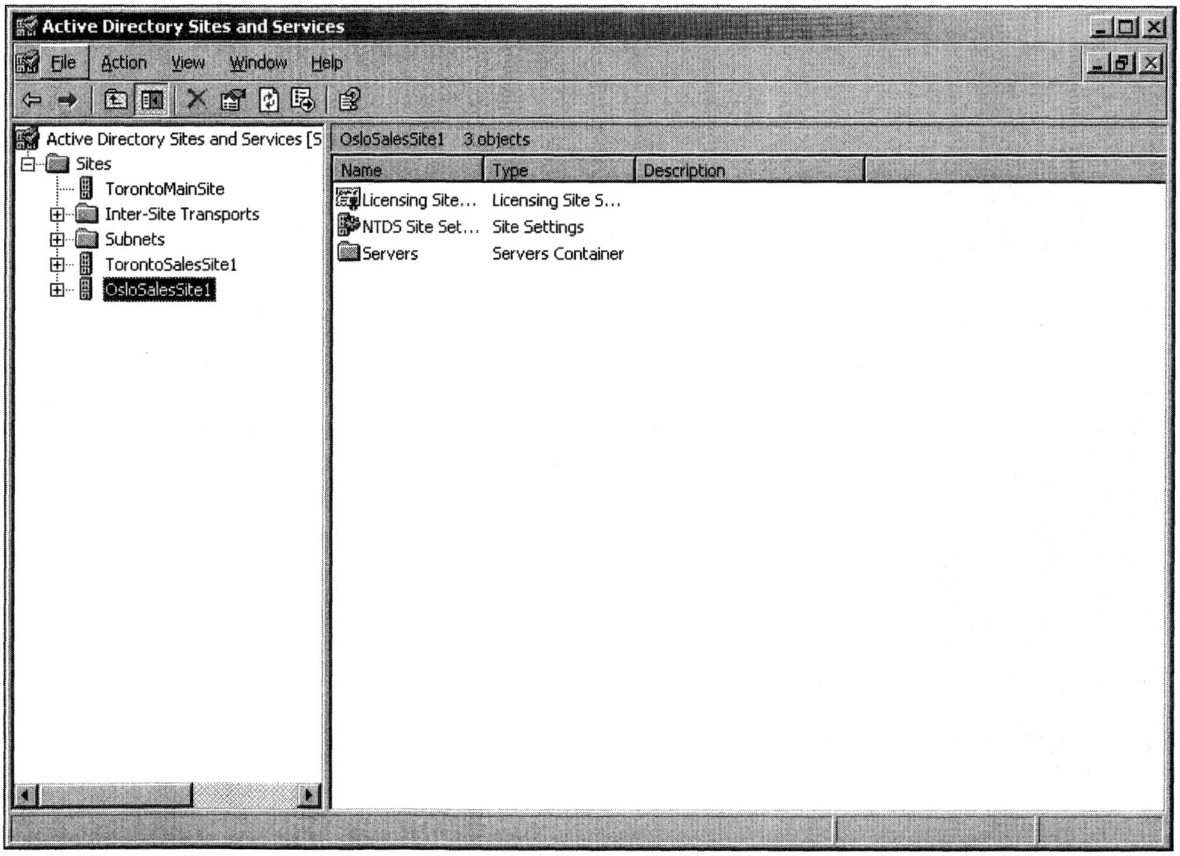

project 3.2

Configuring a Subnet

exam objective

Basic knowledge

overview

In order to function properly, at least one subnet must be assigned to each site. You will create a subnet object each for the existing main Toronto location, the new Toronto location, and the existing Oslo, Norway location.

learning objective

After completing this project, you will know how to create subnets.

specific requirements

Administrative rights on SERVERA, the Windows Server 2003 computer that is acting as a domain controller for apbindustries.com.

estimated completion time

10 minutes

project steps

1. In the **Active Directory Sites and Services** console, right-click the **Subnets** folder under the **Sites** container. Click **New Subnet**. The **New Object—Subnet** dialog box opens.
2. In the **Address** text box, type **192.168.1.0**.
3. In the **Mask** text box, type **255.255.255.0**. This will create a subnet with the **Name 192.168.1.0/24**. This will be the IP subnet of the existing Toronto location.
4. In the **Select a site object for this subnet** box, select **TorontoMainSite**. Click **OK (Figure 3-3)**.
5. Right-click **Subnets** under the **Sites** container. Click **New Subnet**. The **New Object – Subnet** dialog box appears.
6. In the **Address** text box, type **192.168.2.0**.
7. In the **Mask** text box, type **255.255.255.0**. This will create a subnet with the **Name 192.168.2.0/24**. This will be the IP subnet that the existing Oslo, Norway location will be using.
8. In the **Select a site object for this subnet** box, select **OsloSalesSite1**. Click **OK**.
9. Right-click **Subnets** under the **Sites** container. Click **New Subnet**. The **New Object – Subnet** dialog box opens.
10. In the **Address** text box, type **192.168.3.0**.
11. In the **Mask** text box, type **255.255.255.0**. This will create a subnet with the **Name 192.168.3.0/24**. This will be the IP subnet that the new Toronto location will be using.
12. In the **Select a site object for this subnet** box, select **TorontoSalesSite1**. Click **OK**.
13. Expand the **Subnets** folder in order to see the three subnets that you just created **(Figure 3-4)**.

tip

Membership in a site is defined by the IP subnet that a computer belongs to. Each site can be made up of one or more IP subnets. The IP subnets that will belong to a specific site are defined using the subnets node in the AD Sites and Services console.

Figure 3-3 Assigning a subnet to the Default-First-Site-Name site

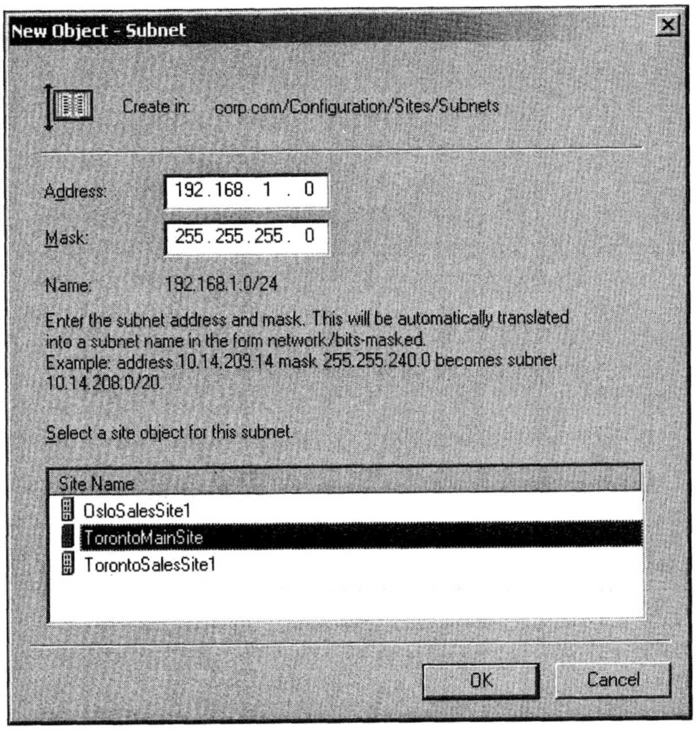

Figure 3-4 New subnets in the Active Directory Sites and Services console

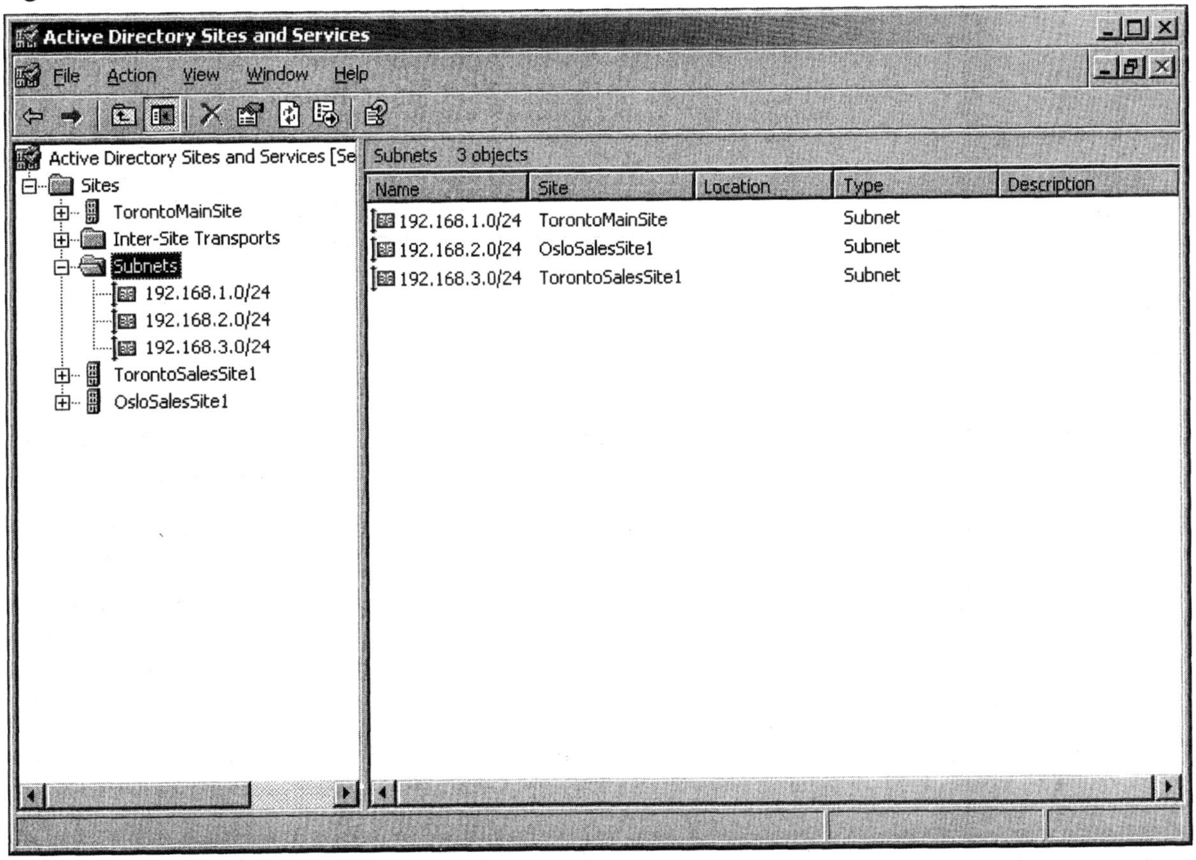

project 3.3 Creating Site Links

exam objective

Implement an Active Directory site topology. Configure site links.

overview

Site links are connections between sites that allow Active Directory inter-site replication to occur. Inter-site replication will not happen unless there is a correctly configured site link between the two sites in question. The most common protocol to use for inter-site replication is Remote Procedure Call (RPC) over IP, although the SMTP protocol can be used in some situations. Once a site link is created, you can modify such attributes as site link cost, replication frequency, and replication schedule.

learning objective

After completing this project, you will know how to create site links and configure attributes such as site link cost, replication frequency, and replication schedule.

specific requirements

Administrative rights on SERVERA, the Windows Server 2003 computer that is acting as a domain controller for apbindustries.com.

estimated completion time

20 minutes

project steps

1. In the **Active Directory Sites and Services** console, expand the **Inter-Site Transports** folder.
2. Right-click **IP** and click **New Site Link**. The **New Object – Site Link** dialog box opens.
3. In the **Name** text box, type **TorontoMain-OsloSales.**
4. In the **Sites not in this site link** selection box, select **TorontoMainSite**. Click **Add**.
5. In the **Sites not in this site link** selection box, select **OsloSalesSite1**. Click **Add**. Click **OK (Figure 3-5)**.
6. Right-click **IP** and click **New Site Link**. The **New Object – Site Link** dialog box opens.
7. In the **Name** text box, type **TorontoMain-TorontoSales**.
8. In the **Sites not in this site link** selection box, select **TorontoMainSite**. Click **Add**.
9. In the **Sites not in this site link** selection box, select **TorontoSalesSite1**. Click **Add.** Click **OK.**
10. In the **Inter-Site Transport** folder, click **IP**. In the details pane, right-click **DEFAULTIPSITELINK** and select **Delete**. A warning dialog box prompts you to confirm that you are sure you want to delete this object. Click **Yes**.
11. The two new site links that you just created remain in the console **(Figure 3-6)**.
12. Right-click the **TorontoMain-OsloSales** site link and click **Properties**. Click **Change Schedule**.
13. The **Schedule for TorontoMain-OsloSales** dialog box opens. On the right side, click the **Replication Not Available** option button.
14. Click and drag from **Monday** at **12 pm** to **Friday** at **12 am**. On the right side, click the **Replication Available** option button **(Figure 3-7)**. Click **OK**. This will allow replication between the hours of 12 Noon and 12 Midnight, Monday through Friday, Eastern Standard Time across this site link.
15. Click **OK** to close the TorontoMain-OsloSales Properties dialog box.
16. Right-click the **TorontoMain-TorontoSales** site link and click **Properties**. In the **Replicate every** spin box, type **20**. Click **OK (Figure 3-8)**. This allows replication to occur every 20 minutes, 24 hours a day across this site link.
17. Click **OK** to close the TorontoMain-TorontoSales Properties dialog box.

tip

Since in our example there are no redundant links between sites, it is not useful to modify the site link cost.

caution

Remember that there is a six-hour time zone difference between Toronto and Oslo. This difference can significantly affect system performance, scheduled maintenance, and related factors.

Figure 3-5 Creating a new site link

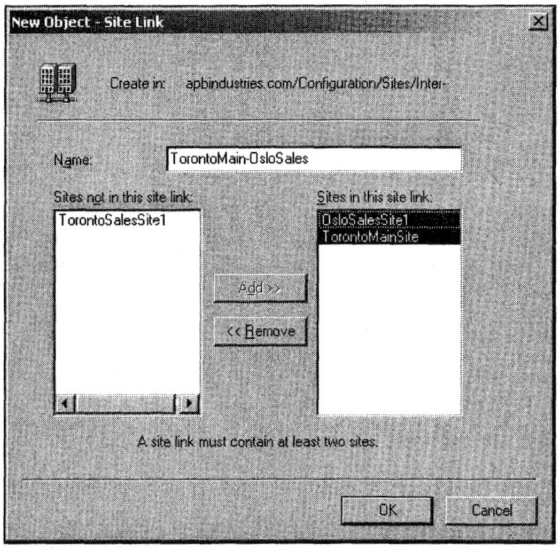

Figure 3-6 Newly created site links viewed in the Active Directory Sites and Services console

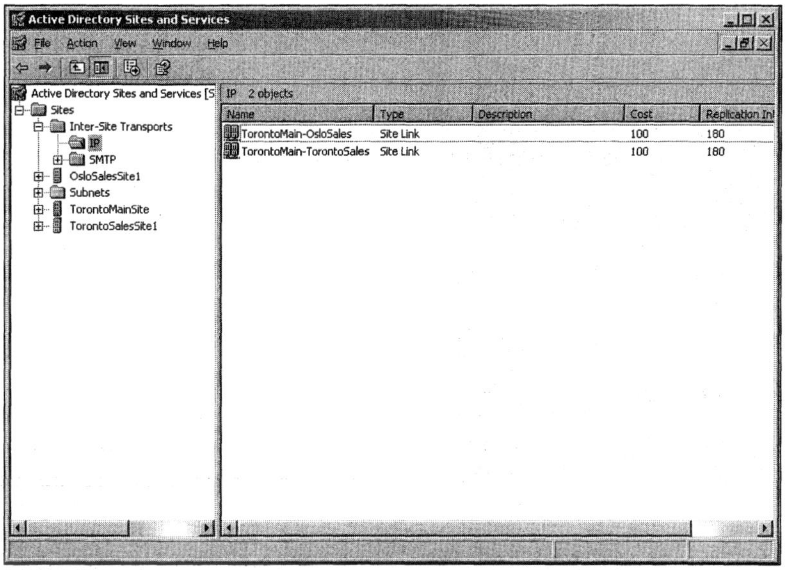

Figure 3-7 Modifying the replication schedule for a site link

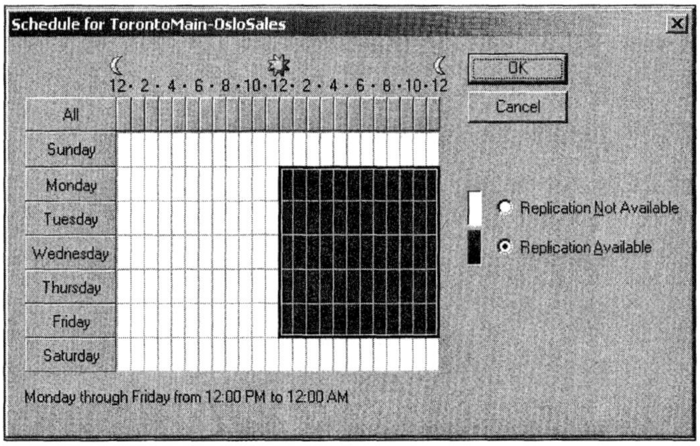

Figure 3-8 Modifying the replication frequency for a site link

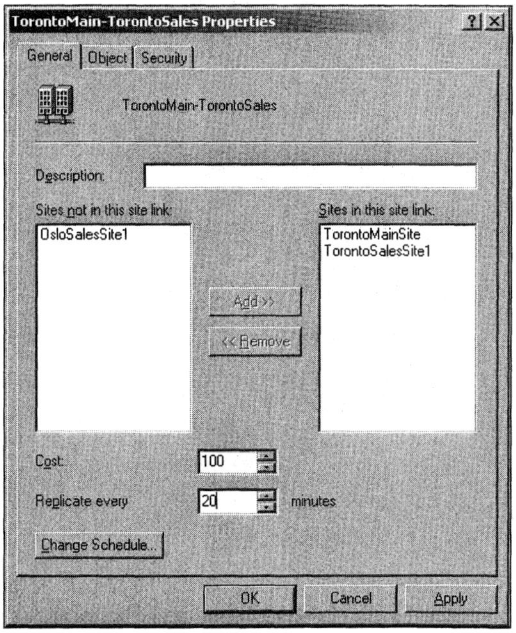

project 3.4 Creating Site Link Bridges

exam objective

Implement an Active Directory site topology. Configure site links.

overview

A site link bridge is an Active Directory object that links two or more indirectly connected sites for replication. By default, all site links that use the same transport (IP or SMTP) are automatically bridged. It is possible, however, if your situation requires it, to disable automatic site link bridging and to manually create site link bridges.

learning objective

After completing this project, you will know how to disable automatic site link bridging and manually create a site link bridge.

specific requirements

Administrative rights on SERVERA, the Windows Server 2003 computer that is acting as a domain controller for apbindustries.com, and the successful completion of Project 3.3.

estimated completion time

5 minutes

project steps

1. In the **Active Directory Sites and Services** console, right-click **IP** under **Inter-Site Transports**. Click **Properties** to open the **IP Properties** dialog box.
2. Remove the check mark from the **Bridge all site links** check box **(Figure 3-9)**. Click **OK**. This disables automatic site link bridging.
3. Right-click **IP** under **Inter-Site Transports**. Click **New Site Link Bridge**. The **New Object – Site Link Bridge** dialog opens.
4. In the **Name** text box, type **OsloSales-TorontoSales-Bridge (Figure 3-10)**. Since there are only two site links (and since a site link bridge requires at least two site links), the **Site links in this site link bridge** list box is populated automatically. Click **OK**.
5. Double-click **OsloSales-TorontoSales-Bridge** in the details pane to open the **OsloSales-TorontoSales-Bridge Properties** dialog box. This is the site link bridge that you just created **(Figure 3-11)**. Click **OK** to close the Properties dialog box.
6. The newly created site link bridge is stored in the **IP** folder **(Figure 3-12)**.

caution

If you do not disable automatic site link bridging before manually creating a site link bridge, you will be creating a redundant connection.

Figure 3-9 Disabling automatic site link bridging

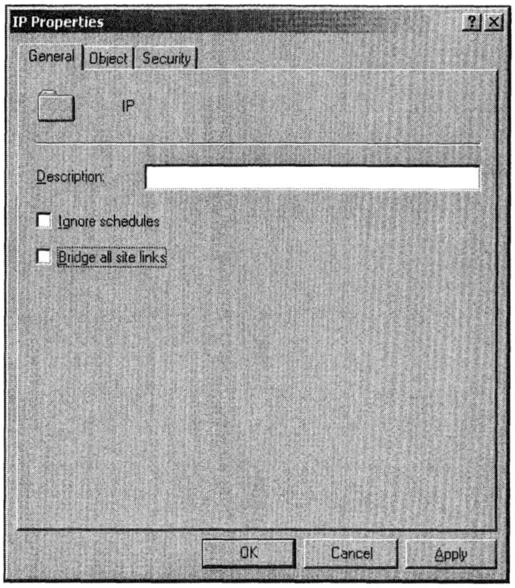

Figure 3-10 Site Link Bridge for OsloSales-TorontoSales

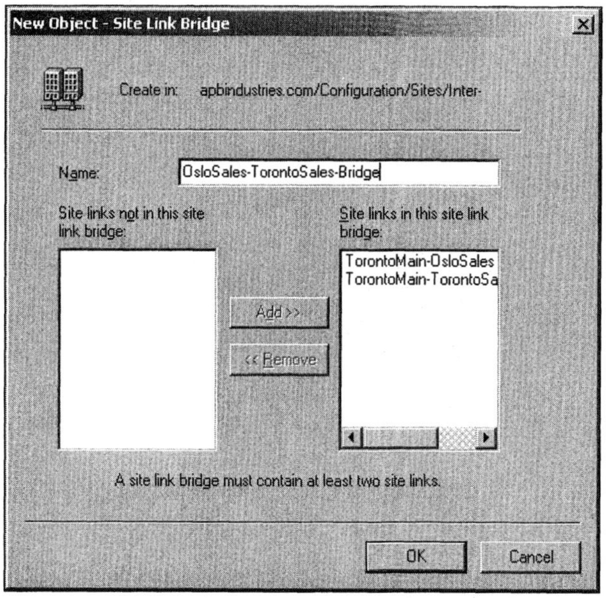

Figure 3-11 Creating a new site link bridge

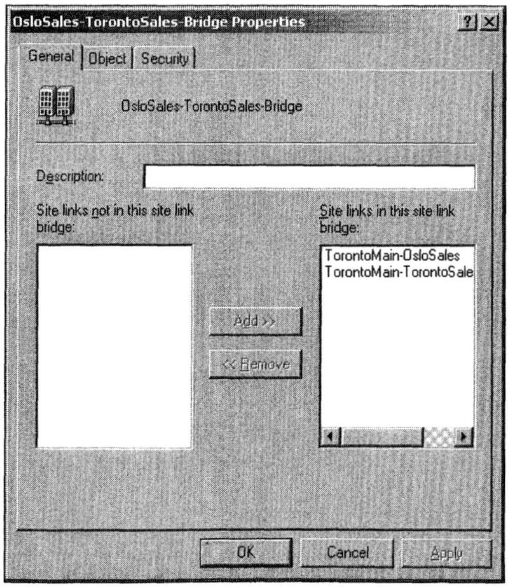

Figure 3-12 New site link bridge in the IP folder

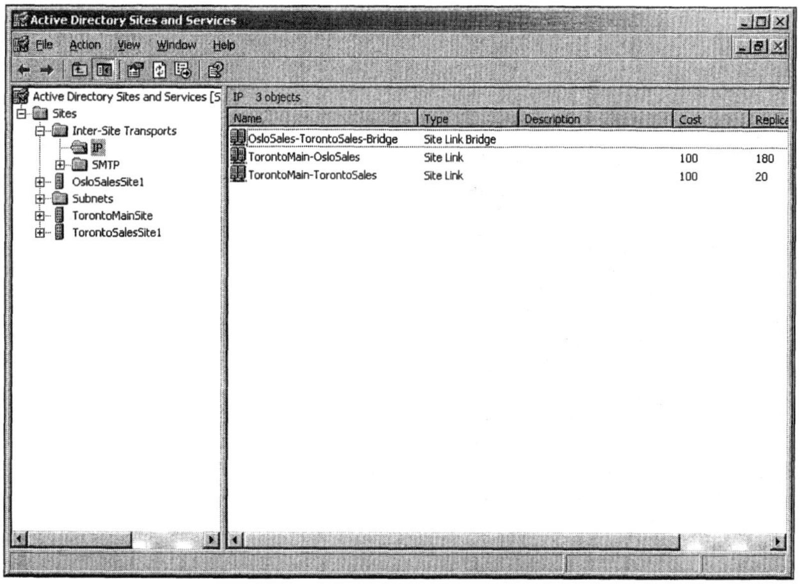

project 3.5

Selecting a Bridgehead Server for Inter-Site Replication

exam objective

Basic knowledge

overview

The Knowledge Consistency Checker (KCC) on one domain controller in each site is responsible for assigning a bridgehead server for the site in which it is a member. To limit replication traffic between sites, bridgehead servers are the only domain controllers that participate in inter-site replication. As with other KCC tasks, usually it is best to allow the KCC to assign bridgehead servers. However, you sometimes may have to assign specific servers as bridgehead servers. You can manually assign one or more preferred bridgehead servers per site.

learning objective

After completing this project, you will know how to assign a domain controller for apbindustries.com.

specific requirements

Administrative rights on SERVERA, the Windows Server 2003 computer that is acting as a domain controller for apbindustries.com.

estimated completion time

5 minutes

project steps

1. In the **Active Directory Sites and Services** console, expand **TorontoMainSite**. Expand the **Servers** folder.
2. Right-click **SERVERA** and click **Properties** to open the **SERVERA Properties** dialog box.
3. In the **Transports available for inter-site data transfer** list box, select **IP** and click **Add** (**Figure 3-13**). Click **OK**. SERVERA is now assigned as a preferred bridgehead server for the TorontoMain site.
4. Close the **Active Directory Sites and Services** console.

Figure 3-13 Specifying Transports available for SERVERA

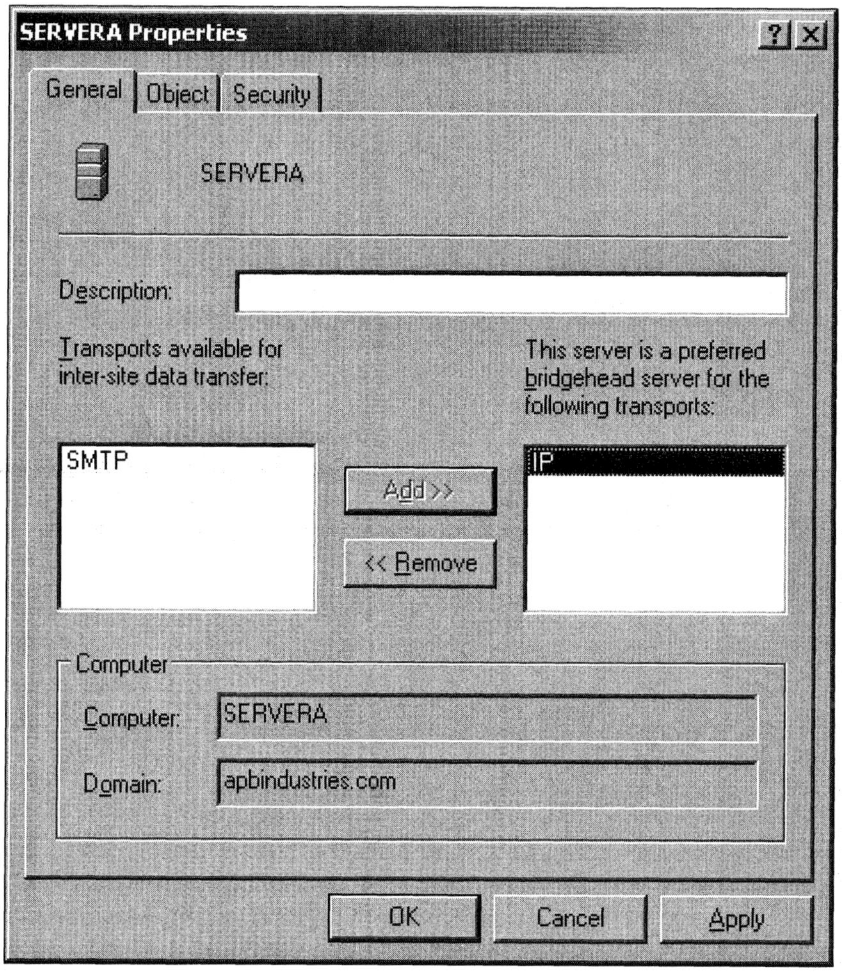

project 3.6

Checking Replication Topology

exam objective

Monitor Active Directory replication failures. Monitor Active Directory replication.

overview

The Knowledge Consistency Checker (KCC) periodically monitors the Active Directory replication topology and makes any necessary changes. However, if necessary, you can speed up the process of topology regeneration by forcing the KCC to reexamine the replication topology. You can do this in either the Active Directory Sites and Services console or the Active Directory Replication Monitor (part of the Windows Server 2003 Support Tools package, available in the Support\Tools folder on the Windows Server 2003 installation CD). The Active Directory Replication Monitor is a useful tool for examining replication issues because you can obtain a lot of replication-related information from this tool.

learning objective

After completing this project, you will know how to use the Active Directory Replication Monitor to trigger the KCC to check the replication topology, as well as obtain a graphical view of replication connections between domain controllers in your enterprise.

specific requirements

Administrative rights on SERVERA, the Windows Server 2003 computer that is acting as a domain controller for apbindustries.com and SERVERB, the Windows Server 2003 computer that is acting as a domain controller for rnd.apbindustries.com. Additionally, the Windows Server 2003 installation CD-ROM is required to install the Windows Support Tools.

estimated completion time

20 minutes

project steps

1. Log on to **SERVERA** and insert the **Windows Server 2003 installation CD-ROM** into the CD-ROM drive.
2. Open **Windows Explorer**.
3. Right-click the CD-ROM drive and click **Explore**.
4. Expand the **Support** folder. Expand the **Tools** folder. Double-click **supporttools.msi**. This will start the **Windows Support Tools Setup Wizard**. Follow the installation process, selecting the defaults to complete the installation. Once the installation is complete, close Windows Explorer.
5. Click **Start** and then click **Run** to open the **Run** dialog box. In the **Open** text box, type **replmon**. Click **OK**.
6. Right-click **Monitored Servers** and click **Add Monitored Server**. The **Add Monitored Server Wizard** starts.
7. Accept the default setting, **Add the server explicitly by name** and click **Next**.
8. In the **Enter the name of the server to monitor explicitly** text box, type **SERVERB**. Click **Finish**. SERVERB is now in the list of Monitored Servers **(Figure 3-14)**.
9. Right-click **SERVERB** and click **Check Replication Topology (Figure 3-15)**. An **Active Directory Replication Monitor** dialog box informs you that the KCC has been triggered. Click **OK**. The KCC will now examine the current connection objects and will recalculate the topology based on server availability.
10. Right-click **SERVERB** and click **Show Replication Topologies**. The **View Replication Topology** window opens. Open the **View** menu and select **Connections Objects Only**. Two objects, **SERVERA** and **SERVERB**, should appear.
11. Right-click **SERVERA** and select **Show Intra-Site Connections**. Do the same for **SERVERB**. You should now see a graphical representation of the replication topology between SERVERA and SERVERB **(Figure 3-16)**.
12. Close the **View Replication Topology** window. Close the **Active Directory Replication Monitor**.

tip

The KCC uses the Inter-site Topology Generator (ISTG) to create connection objects between domain controllers in different sites, and it runs all by itself.

Figure 3-14 The Active Directory Replication Monitor

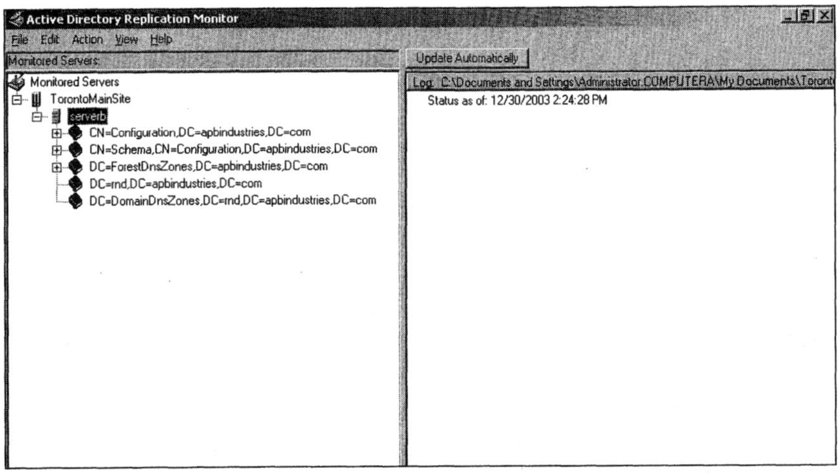

Figure 3-15 Triggering the KCC to check the replication topology

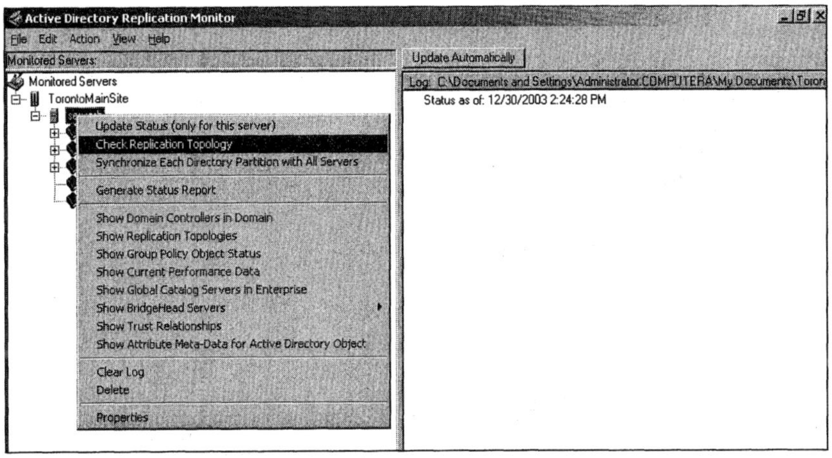

Figure 3-16 Viewing a graphical representation of connection objects between domain controllers

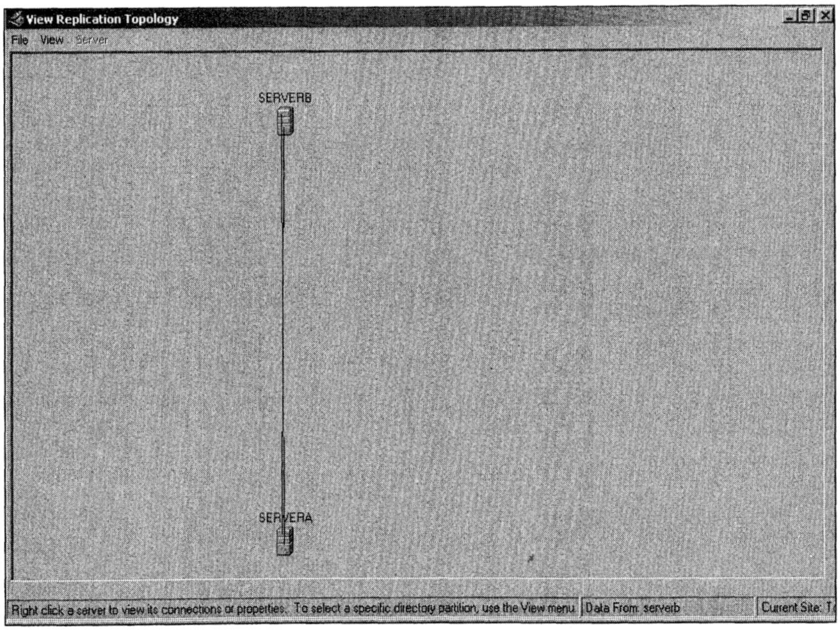

project 3.7

Designating a Global Catalog Server

exam objective

Plan a strategy for placing global catalog servers. Evaluate network traffic considerations when placing global catalog servers. Evaluate the need to enable universal group caching.

overview

A global catalog is a database that stores a full, writable copy of the directory data for its own domain and a partial, read-only copy of the directory databases for every other domain in the forest. The global catalog is stored on domain controllers that are designated as global catalog servers. By default, the first domain controller in a forest is the only automatically assigned global catalog server. However, it is possible to manually assign as many domain controllers as you wish as global catalog servers. Caution is needed though, because even though more global catalog servers can save time and bandwidth in answering queries, each additional global catalog server increases the amount of replication overhead.

learning objective

After completing this project, you will know how to designate a domain controller as a global catalog server.

specific requirements

Administrative rights on SERVERA, the Windows Server 2003 computer that is acting as a domain controller for apbindustries.com.

estimated completion time

5 minutes

project steps

1. In the **Active Directory Sites and Services** console, expand **TorontoMainSite** if necessary.
2. Expand the **Servers** folder.
3. Expand the **SERVERB** node.
4. Right-click **NTDS Settings** and click **Properties** to open the **NTDS Settings Properties** dialog box.
5. Select the **Global Catalog** check box to designate this domain controller as a global catalog server **(Figure 3-17)**. Click **OK**.
6. Close the **Active Directory Sites and Services** console.

Figure 3-17 Designating a global catalog server

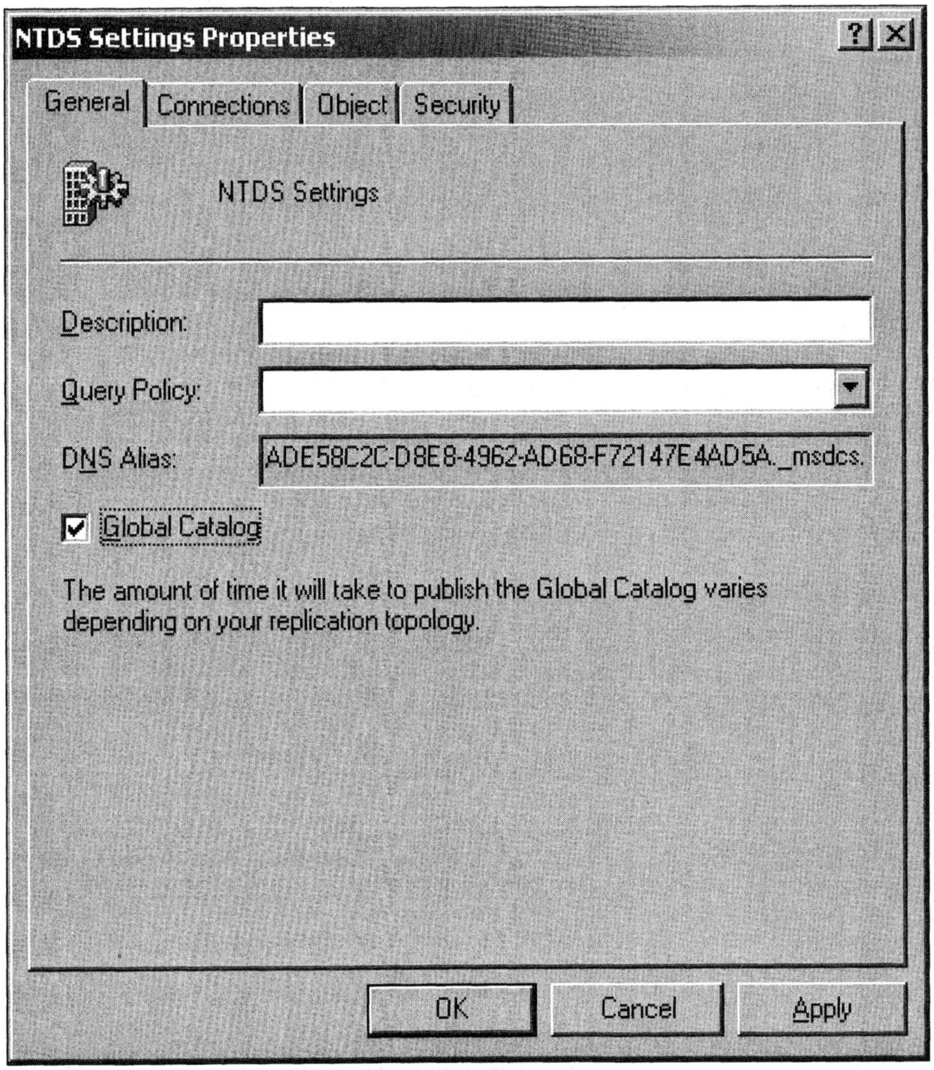

LESSON

4 Integrating the Domain Name System with Active Directory

In a TCP/IP network, every host (computer or other network connected device) has a unique IP address, such as 192.168.10.5, to allow it to communicate on the network. Due to their numerical format, IP addresses can be difficult to remember. The Domain Name System (DNS) is a method used to resolve easy-to-remember host names to IP addresses.

In Windows Server 2003, DNS is the native method for resolving host names to IP addresses (Windows Server 2003 also supports NetBIOS name resolution for backwards compatibility). A properly configured DNS infrastructure is important in a Windows Server 2003 network, particularly if Active Directory is installed. Note that although the Active Directory namespace and the DNS namespace map directly to each other, they are two totally separate namespaces. It is important to understand this critical difference in order to avoid confusion.

Windows Server 2003's implementation of DNS includes some key enhancements, some of which originated with other companies, that greatly reduce the administrative overhead required to maintain a DNS structure. These enhancements include the following:

- *Dynamic DNS (DDNS) Support:* This feature allows the automatic registration of DNS records by compliant hosts or DHCP servers.
- *Secure dynamic DNS updates:* This ensures that a DNS record is updated by only the host that originally registered that record.
- *Active Directory-integrated zones:* This is a type of zone that eliminates standard text-based zone files and the entire zone-transfer process by integrating all of the DNS records for a particular zone into Active Directory. The benefits of this type of zone include a reduction in zone transfer traffic, automatic replication, increased replication security, and multi-master replication.
- *Incremental zone transfers (IXFR):* This support allows DNS servers to transfer only changes that have been made to a zone rather than transferring the entire zone whenever a change has been made to the zone.
- *Service Location record support:* This allows Service Location (SRV) DNS records to be registered in the DNS database. SRV records are used to register the location of particular services such as LDAP, Kerberos, and global catalogs.

Scenario

APB Industries is planning to acquire some new Sales software in the near future. However, before a decision can be made, the software must be tested to ensure that it can integrate into APB Industries' current network configuration. This software relies very heavily on DNS, particularly dynamic DNS support. In this lesson, you will be installing and configuring a test DNS infrastructure to determine whether it can support the software you are evaluating.

Lesson 4 Integrating the Domain Name System with Active Directory

Project	Exam 70-294 Objective
4.1 Installing the DNS Service	Basic knowledge
4.2 Creating Lookup Zones	Basic knowledge
4.3 Delegating Zones	Basic knowledge
4.4 Configuring Dynamic DNS	Basic knowledge
4.5 Implementing Zone Replication and Zone Transfer	Basic knowledge
4.6 Setting Debugging Options for DNS Servers	Basic knowledge

General Requirements

To complete the projects in this lesson, you must have administrative rights on two Windows Server 2003 computers: the domain controller for the apbindustries.com domain (SERVERA), which has DNS installed, and the domain controller for the rnd.apbindustries.com domain (SERVERB), which does not have DNS installed. You will also need the Windows Server 2003 installation CD-ROM. You may also find it helpful to refer to Lesson 4 in your Prentice Hall Certification Series Exam 70-294 textbook for further information about the topics covered by the projects in this lesson.

project 4.1

Installing the DNS Service

exam objective

Basic knowledge

overview

In this project, you install the DNS service on a Windows Server 2003 computer.

learning objective

After completing this project, you will know how to install DNS in a Windows Server 2003 environment.

specific requirements

Administrative rights on a computer running Windows Server 2003. The computer does not have to be a domain controller. If you have been following the projects in order, you should perform this exercise on SERVERB.

estimated completion time

10 minutes

project steps

1. Log on to **SERVERB** with an account that has administrative rights.
2. Click **Start**, point to **Control Panel**, and click **Add or Remove Programs**.
3. In the **Add or Remove Programs** window, click the **Add/Remove Windows Components** button to start the **Windows Components Wizard**.
4. Click the **Networking Services** option *(not the check box)* displayed in the list **(Figure 4-1)**.
5. Click **Details** to open the **Networking Services** dialog box.
6. Click the check box to the left of the **Domain Name System (DNS)** option displayed in the list **(Figure 4-2)**.
7. Click **OK** to close the **Networking Services** dialog box.
8. Click **Next** in the **Windows Components Wizard** to begin the installation of DNS. You may be prompted to insert the Windows Server 2003 installation CD. If you are, click **Exit** to leave the Welcome screen.
9. When the Wizard is complete, click **Finish**.
10. Close the **Add/Remove Programs** window.
11. To verify that DNS has been installed, click **Start** and point to **Administrative Tools**. You should see DNS listed on the **Administrative Tools** menu **(Figure 4-3)**.

caution

DNS servers must have statically assigned IP addresses. Therefore, ensure that you have a static IP address on the server on which you plan to install DNS.

Figure 4-1 Selecting Networking Services

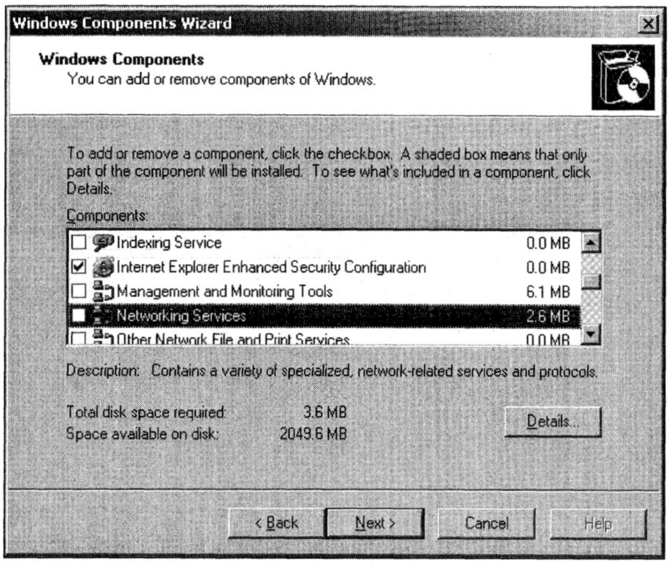

Figure 4-2 Adding DNS Service

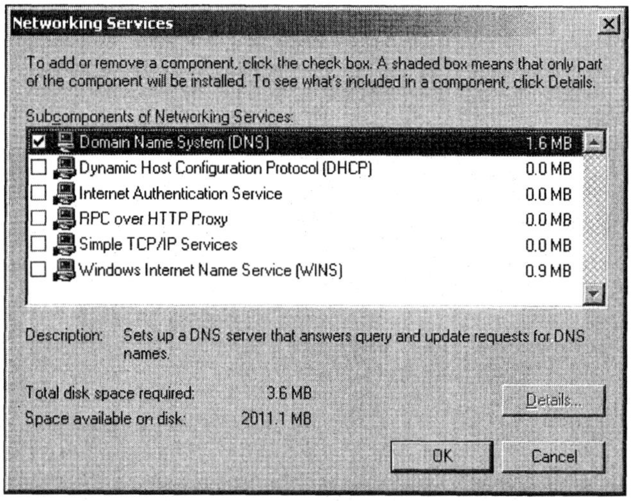

Figure 4-3 Verifying the installation of DNS

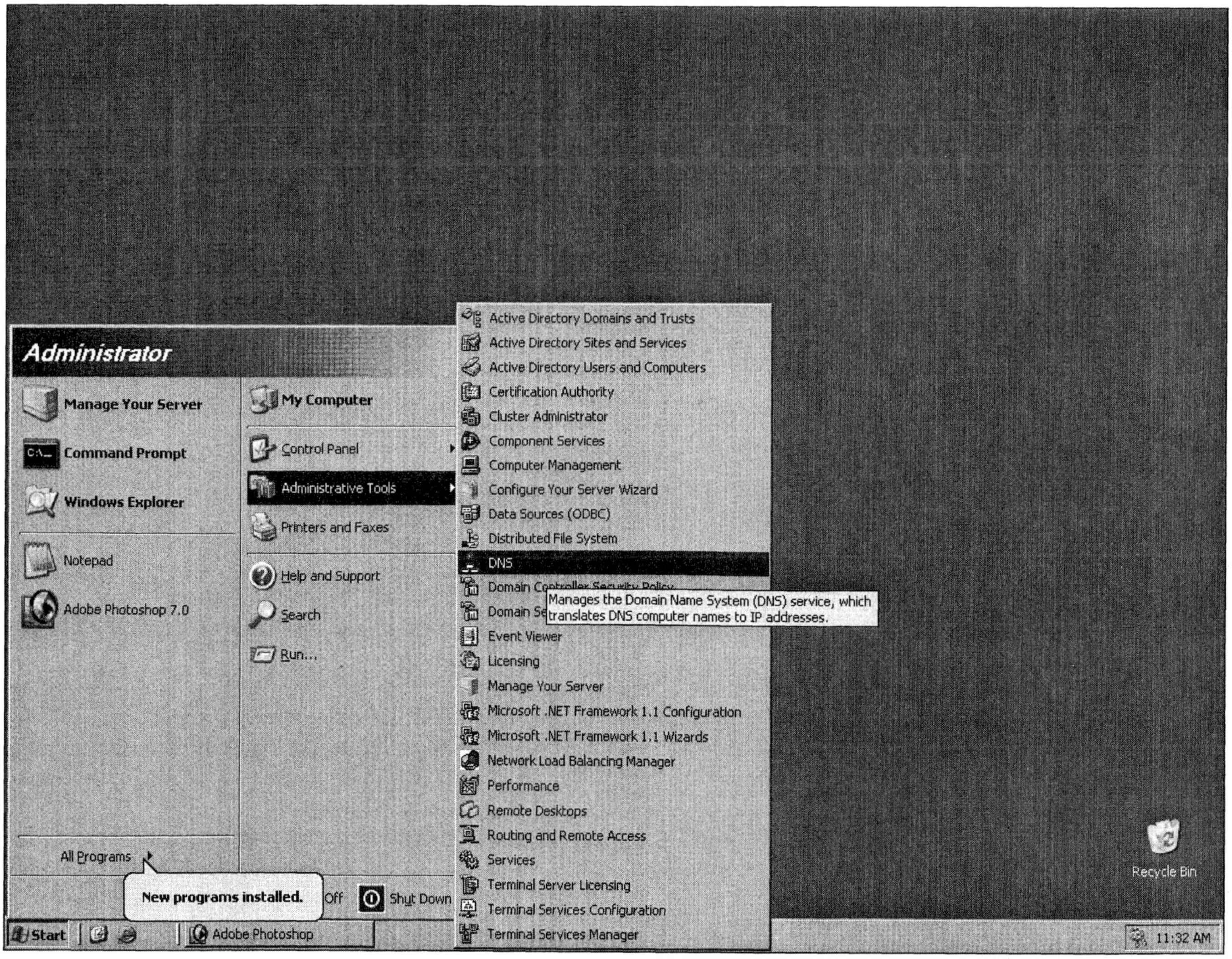

project 4.2

Creating Lookup Zones

exam objective

Basic knowledge

overview

Now that you have installed DNS onto a second server in your network environment, you will create a test lookup zone. Since the apbindustries.com lookup zone hosted on SERVERA is an Active Directory-integrated zone, you will be creating a primary zone in this exercise.

learning objective

After completing this project, you will know how to manually create a primary zone, create a DNS record, and use Nslookup to test the presence of newly created DNS records.

specific requirements

Successful completion of Project 4.1 and administrative rights on a Windows Server 2003 computer with DNS installed (SERVERB).

estimated completion time

20 minutes

project steps

1. Log on to **SERVERB** with an account that has administrative rights.
2. Click **Start**, point to **Administrative Tools**, and click **DNS**.
3. Double-click **SERVERB** in the tree and click **Forward Lookup Zones**. Notice that there are no zones currently configured on this DNS server.
4. Right-click **Forward Lookup Zones**. Click **New Zone** to open the **New Zone Wizard**.
5. Click **Next**. The **Zone Type** screen opens. Make sure that **Primary zone** is selected. Clear the **Store the zone in Active Directory** check box **(Figure 4-4)**. Click **Next**.
6. The **Zone Name** screen opens. In the **Zone name** text box, enter **apbtest.com**. Click **Next**.
7. The **Zone File** screen opens. In the **Create a new file with this file name** text box, accept the default, **apbtest.com.dns**. Click **Next**. The **Dynamic Update** screen opens. Click **Next** to accept the default.
8. The **Completing the New Zone Wizard** screen opens. Click **Finish**.
9. Double-click **Forward Lookup Zones**. A new zone, **apbtest.com**, is listed.
10. Double-click **apbtest.com**. Right-click **apbtest.com**. Click **New Host (Figure 4-5)** to open the **New Host** dialog box. In the **Name** text box, type **www**. In the **IP address** text box, type the IP address **192.168.1.230**. Note that the IP address does not have to be a currently used IP address. Click **Add Host**, click **OK**, and then click **Done**. Notice the new **Host** record present in the **apbtest.com** zone.
11. Close the **DNS** console.
12. Click **Start**, click **Run**, and then type **cmd** in the **Open** text box. Click **OK** to to open a command prompt window.
13. Change the current working directory to ***%Systemroot%*\System32\DNS** by typing **cd %systemroot%\system32\dns** and then pressing **[Enter]**.
14. Type **dir** and press **[Enter]**. There should be a file listed with the name **apbtest.com.dns.** This is the zone database file that stores all the information for the zone.
15. Type **nslookup** and press **[Enter]**. Type **server 192.168.1.234** (the IPaddress of the DNS server hosting the apbtest.com zone) and press **[Enter]**. This will set the default name server to the DNS server hosting the **apbtest.com** zone.
16. Type **www.apbtest.com** and press **[Enter]**. You should get a response indicating that the record **www.apbtest.com** points to the IP address entered when you created the **www** record.
17. Type **exit** to close Nslookup. Type **exit** again to close the command prompt.

tip

NSLOOKUP simply tests for the presence of a DNS record within the DNS database, not the presence of an actual host on the network.

tip

If you receive an error message "Can't find server name for address" when you run NSLOOKUP, make sure that the reverse lookup zone for SERVERA (the primary DNS server) is properly configured and that a pointer (PTR) record has been created for SERVERA.

Figure 4-4 New Zone Wizard

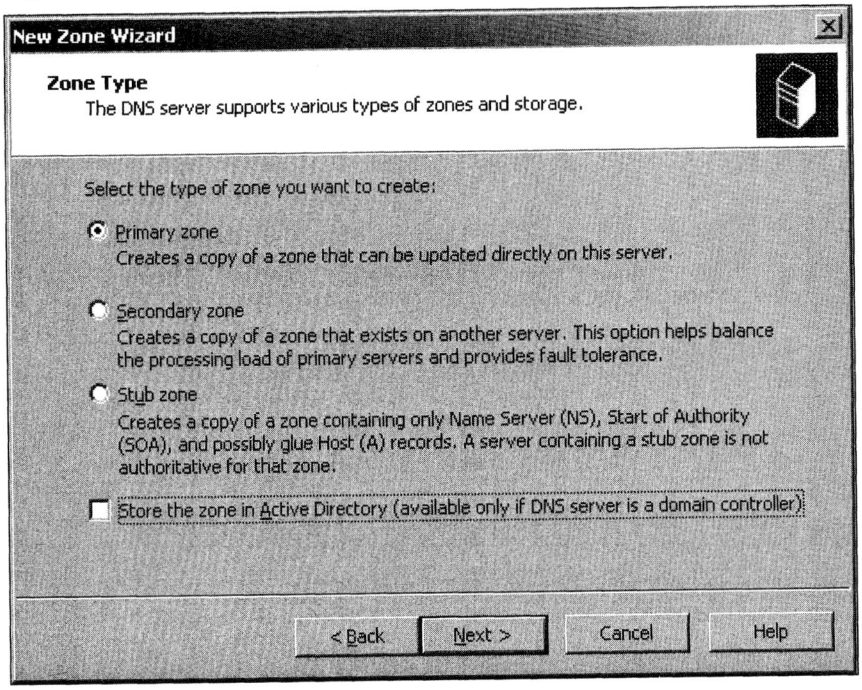

Figure 4-5 Creating a new Host (A) record

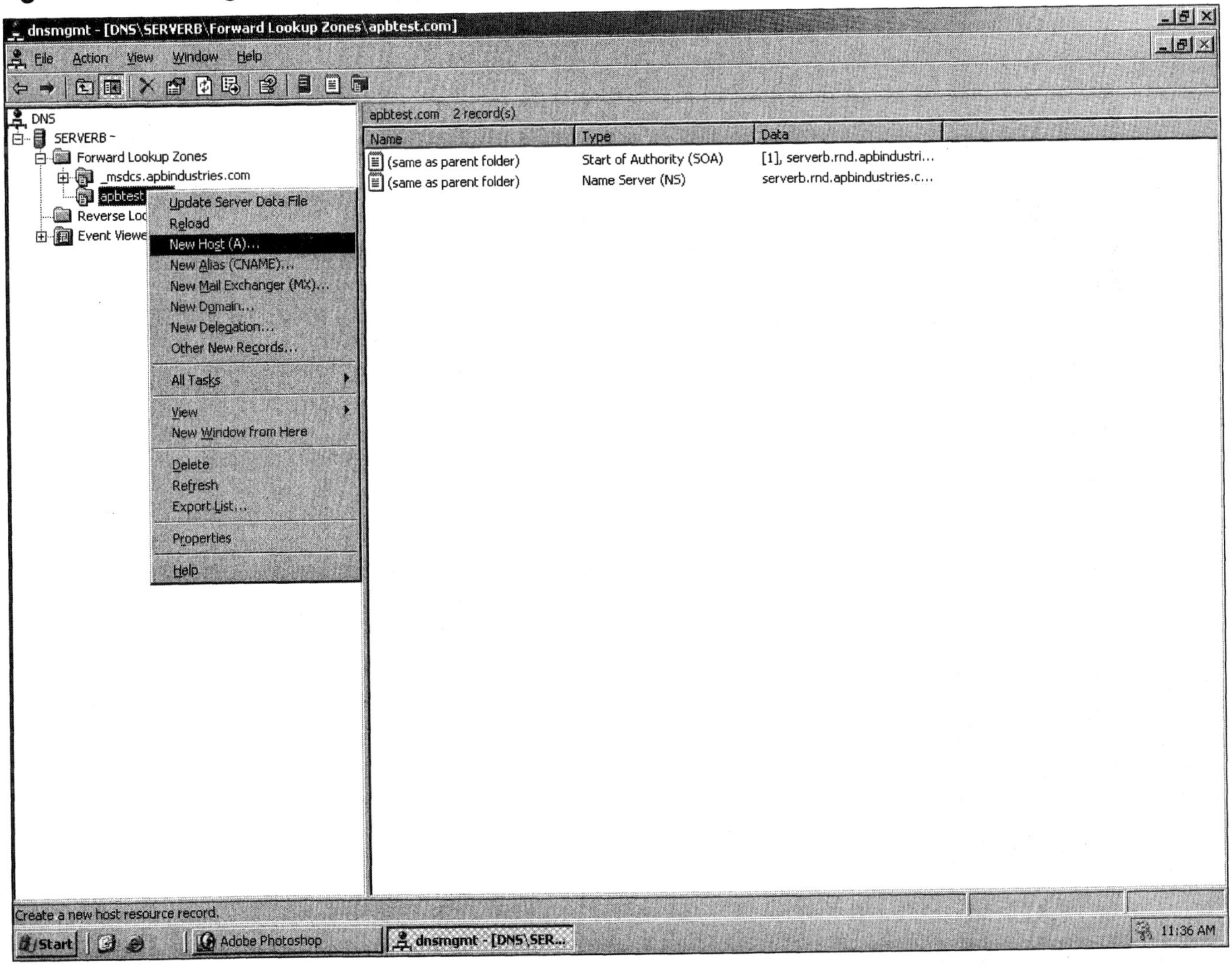

project 4.3 Delegating Zones

exam objective

Basic knowledge

overview

In order to DNS simplify administration, you can create subdomains within the DNS hierarchy. Subdomains can be located in the same zone as the parent domain. Alternatively, subdomains can be located in a separate zone, hosted on the same DNS server, or on a different DNS server from the parent domain. This project will help you to better understand the concept of delegating DNS zones.

learning objective

After completing this project, you will know how to delegate a zone using the New Delegation Wizard, as well as how to create a new zone on a DNS server that has been delegated authority for a zone.

specific requirements

Administrative rights on the computer you used for Project 4.2 (SERVERB) and successful completion of Project 4.2.

estimated completion time

15 minutes

project steps

tip

You could successfully create the sales subdomain on SERVERA without first delegating authority for that zone. However, unless a DNS client is configured to point to SERVERA, name resolution will not succeed because SERVERA will not be authoritative within the DNS hierarchy.

1. Log on to **SERVERB** with an account that has administrative rights.
2. Click **Start**, point to **Administrative Tools**, and click **DNS** to open the **DNS Management** console.
3. Double-click **Forward Lookup Zones** to expand the tree. Click **apbtest.com**. Right-click **apbtest.com** and select **New Delegation** to start the **New Delegation Wizard**.
4. The **Welcome to the New Delegation Wizard** screen opens. Click **Next**.
5. The **Delegated Domain Name** screen opens. In the **Delegated domain** text box, type **sales**. The **Fully qualified domain name** text box will automatically be populated with **sales.apbtest.com**. This is the DNS subdomain that will be delegated to a different zone. Click **Next**.
6. The **Name Servers** screen opens. Click **Add** to open the **New Resource Record** dialog box.
7. In the **Server fully qualified name (FQDN)** text box, type **servera.apbindustries.com** and click **Resolve**. The IP address of **SERVERA** should automatically be added to the **IP address** list. Click **OK**.
8. Click **Next** on the **Name Servers** screen. Click **Finish** to complete the New Delegation Wizard.
9. Notice the **sales** delegation record located within the **apbtest.com** domain **(Figure 4-6)**. It has a **Name Server** record that points to **servera.apbindustries.com**. This means that the DNS server service on SERVERA has been delegated authority for the **sales.apbtest.com** DNS zone.
10. Log on to **SERVERA** with an account that has administrative rights and open the DNS Management console.
11. Expand **SERVERA** and then expand **Forward Lookup Zones**.
12. Right-click **Forward Lookup Zones** and click **New Zone** to start the **New Zone Wizard**. Click **Next**.
13. The **Zone Type** screen opens. Ensure that **Primary zone** is selected and clear the **Store the zone in Active Directory** check box. Click **Next**.
14. The **Zone Name** screen opens. In the **Zone name** text box, type **sales.apbtest.com** **(Figure 4-7)**. Click **Next**.
15. The **Zone File** screen opens. Click **Next**. Click **Next** again to accept the default. Click **Finish**.
16. You have now successfully created the DNS subdomain **sales.apbtest.com** on the server that has been delegated authority for that zone.

Figure 4-6 Viewing a delegation record in the DNS console

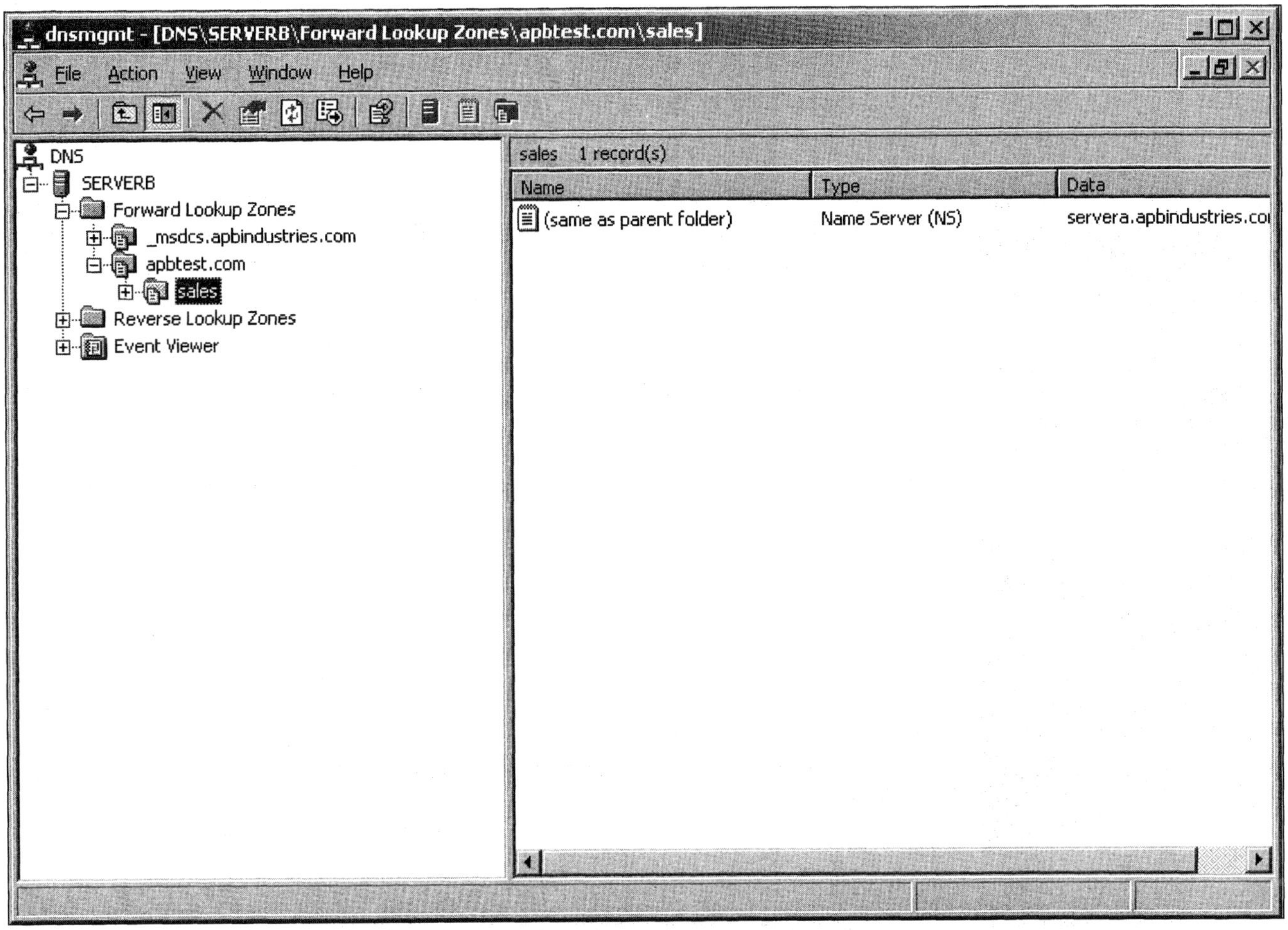

Figure 4-7 Specifying sales.apbtest.com as the zone name

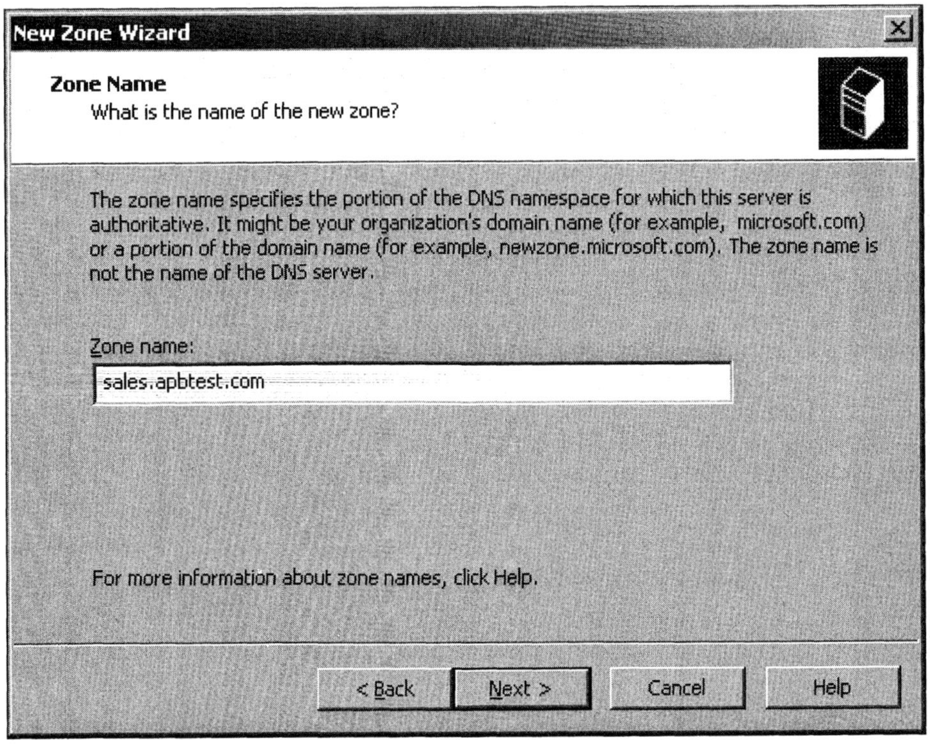

project 4.4 Configuring Dynamic DNS

exam objective

Basic knowledge

overview

In order for a DNS zone to accept dynamic updates from DDNS-enabled clients and/or a DDNS-enabled DHCP server, you must first configure the zone to allow dynamic updates. Once a zone is configured to allow dynamic updates, it is important to configure scavenging to ensure that old records are cleared out of the zone.

learning objective

After completing this project, you will know how to configure a Primary DNS zone to accept dynamic updates. You will also know how to configure scavenging options.

specific requirements

Administrative rights on the domain controller for the apbindustries.com domain (SERVERA) and successful completion of Project 4.3.

estimated completion time

10 minutes

project steps

1. Log on to **SERVERA** with an account that has administrative rights.
2. Click **Start**, point to **Administrative Tools**, and click **DNS** to open the **DNS Management** console
3. Expand **Forward Lookup Zones** and then expand **sales.apbtest.com**. Right-click **sales.apbtest.com** and click **Properties**.
4. In the **Dynamic updates** list box, click **Nonsecure and secure (Figure 4-8)**.
5. Click the **Aging** button to open the **Zone Aging/Scavenging Properties** dialog box.
6. Select the **Scavenge stale resource records** check box. In the **No-refresh interval** text box, type **5**.
7. In the **Refresh interval** text box, type **10**. Records will not be scavenged until both the no-refresh and refresh intervals expire, which in this case is 15 days **(Figure 4-9)**.
8. Click **OK**.
9. Since dynamic updates are not supported by all DNS servers, you will receive a message warning you that, once aging is enabled, the zone file format will change. As a result, the zone file may not be loaded on non-Windows 2000 or later DNS servers. Click **Yes.**
10. Click **OK**.
11. Expand apbindustries.com. Right-click **apbindustries.com** and click **Properties** to open the **apbindustries Properties** dialog box.
12. In the **Dynamic updates** list box, notice the third option, **secure only**, that was not available on the other zone **(Figure 4-10)**. This option is available because this zone is an Active Directory-integrated zone. Click **Cancel**.
13. Close the DNS Management console.

Figure 4-8 Configuring a zone for DDNS

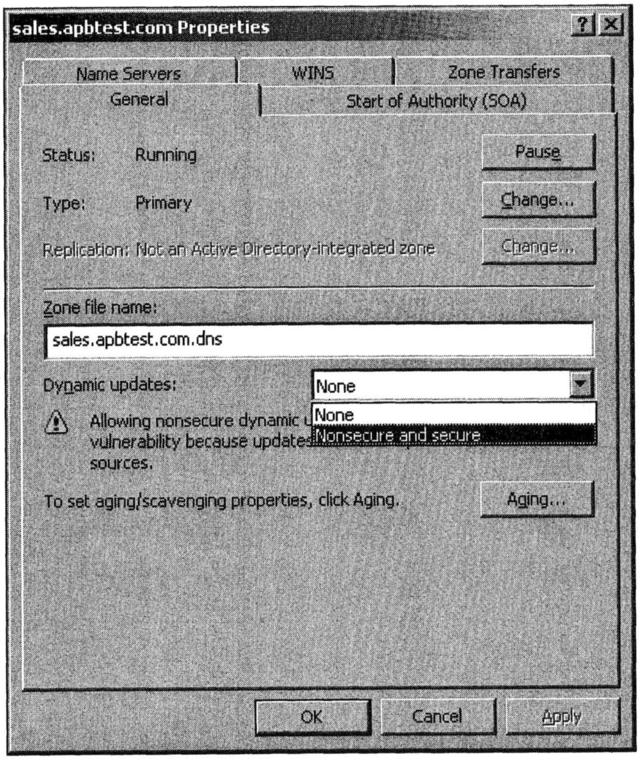

Figure 4-9 Setting Aging/Scavenging properties for a zone

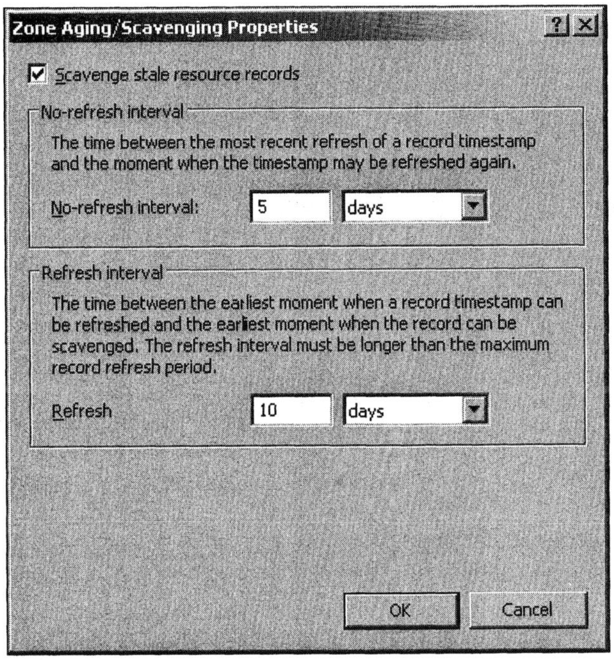

Figure 4-10 DDNS settings for an Active Directory-integrated zone

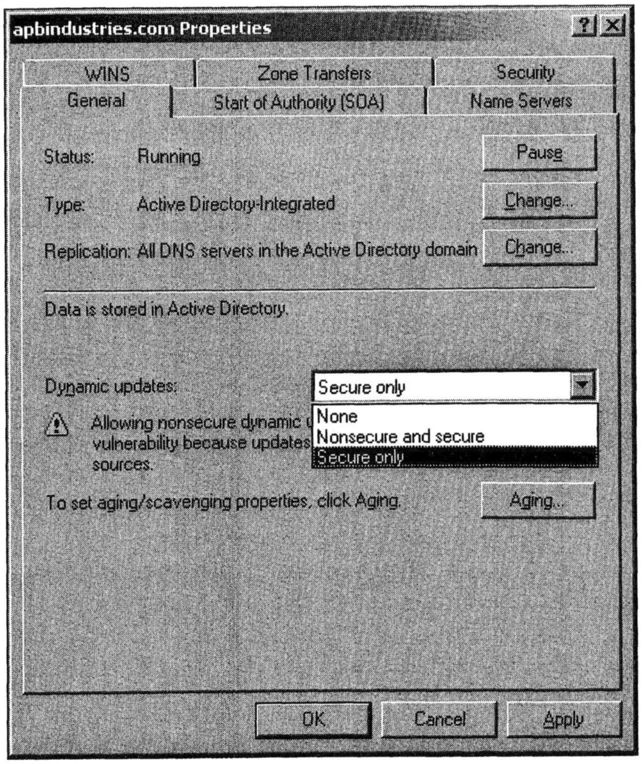

project 4.5 Implementing Zone Replication and Zone Transfer

exam objective

Basic knowledge

overview

DNS replication facilitates redundancy and load balancing. Replication of an Active Directory-integrated zone is automatic between all domain controllers based on the Active Directory replication model. However, you must manually configure the replication and transfer parameters for DNS zones.

learning objective

After completing this project, you will know how to create a secondary DNS zone and configure it to replicate from the DNS server that holds the primary copy of the zone.

specific requirements

Administrative rights on the domain controller for the apbindustries.com domain (SERVERA) and successful completion of Project 4.4.

estimated completion time

10 minutes

project steps

1. Log on to **SERVERA** with an account that has administrative rights.
2. Click **Start**, point to **Administrative Tools**, and click **DNS**.
3. Expand **Forward Lookup Zones**. Right-click **Forward Lookup Zones** and select **New Zone** to start the **New Zone Wizard**. Click **Next**.
4. The **Zone Type** screen opens. Click the **Secondary zone** option button **(Figure 4-11)**. Click **Next**.
5. The **Zone Name** screen opens. In the **Zone name** text box, type **apbtest.com**. Click **Next**.
6. The **Master DNS Servers** screen opens (**Figure 4-12**). In the **IP address** text box, enter the IP address of **SERVERB (192.168.1.234)**. Click **Add**.
7. Click **Next** to open the **Completing the New Zone Wizard** screen. Click **Finish**.
8. Click **apbtest.com**, which is located under sales.apbtest.com in the SERVERA node. Notice the error message **Zone not loaded by DNS Server (Figure 4-13).** This message appears because SERVERA has not been given the right to act as a secondary DNS server for the **apbtest.com** zone.
9. If SERVERB is not listed in the **DNS** console, right-click **DNS** and click **Connect To DNS Server** to open the **Connect to DNS Server** dialog box.
10. Select the **The following computer** option button and type **SERVERB** in the text box. Click **OK** to add SERVERB to the console.
11. Expand **SERVERB**. Expand **Forward Lookup Zones**. Expand **apbtest.com**.
12. Right-click **apbtest.com** and select **Properties** to open the **apbtest.com Properties** dialog box.
13. Click the **Name Servers** tab. Click **Add** to open the **New Resource Record** dialog box. Enter the FQDN for **SERVERA** in the **Server fully qualified domain name (FQDN)** text box **(Figure 4-14)**.
14. Click **Resolve**. Click **OK** to close the New Resource Record dialog box. Ensure that **SERVERA** is listed in the **Server Fully Qualified Domain Name (FQDN)** list.
15. Click the **Zone Transfers** tab. Make sure the **Only to servers listed on the Name Servers** tab is selected. Click **OK** to close the apbtest.com Properties dialog box.
16. Right-click the **apbtest.com** secondary zone located on SERVERA and select **Transfer from master**. The zone should successfully replicate, and you should see an exact replica of the **apbtest.com** zone on SERVERA.
17. Close the **DNS** console.

tip

Windows Server 2003 DNS servers support incremental zone transfers (IXFR), which reduce network traffic by only replicating changes that have been made to the zone database file. This contrasts a full zone transfer (AXFR), which replicates the entire zone database file every time zone transfer occurs.

Figure 4-11 Creating a replica DNS zone

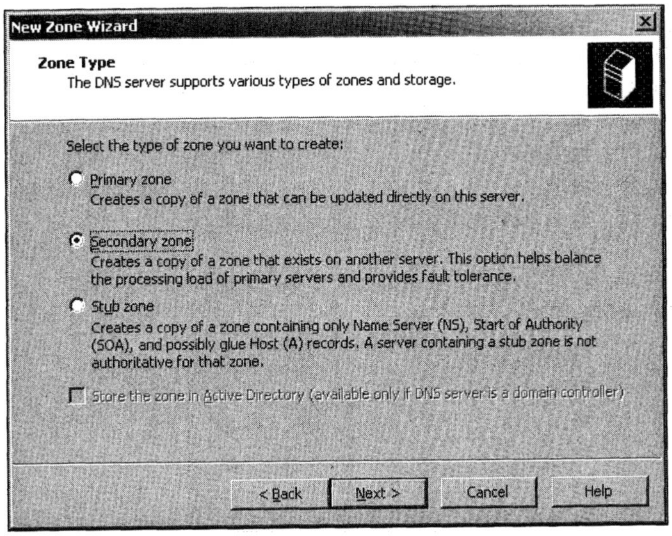

Figure 4-12 Specifying a DNS server that hosts the master DNS zone

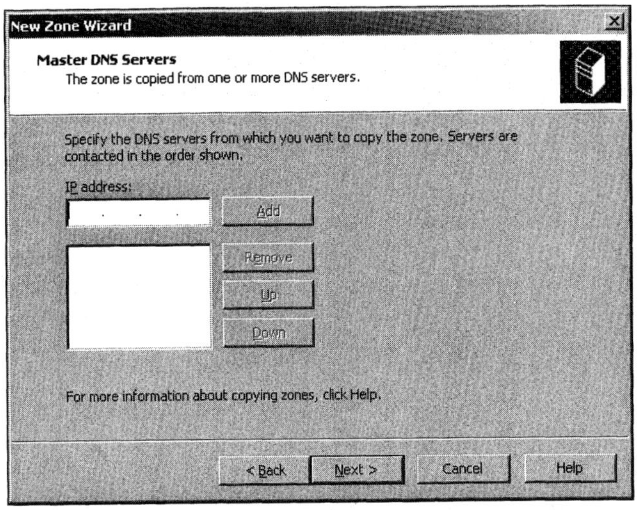

Figure 4-13 Zone transfer error message

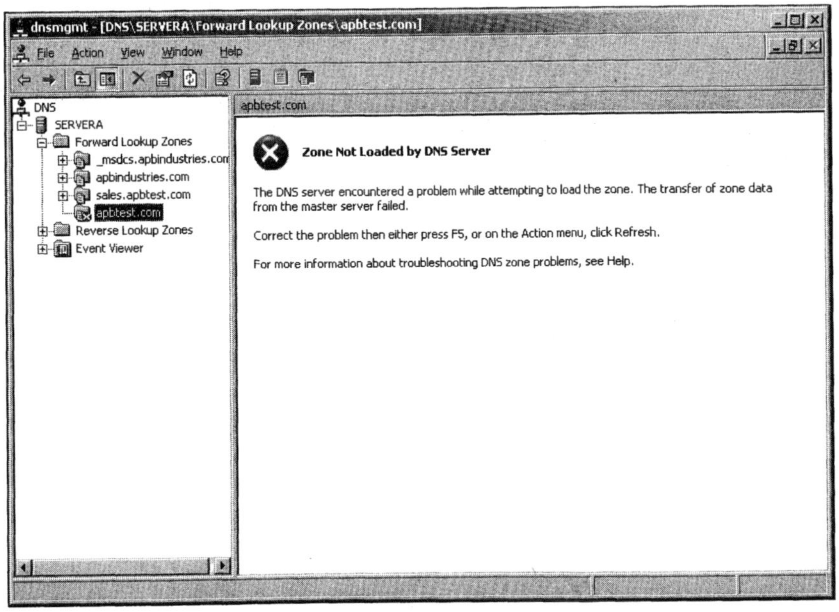

Figure 4-14 Specifying a new name server for a zone

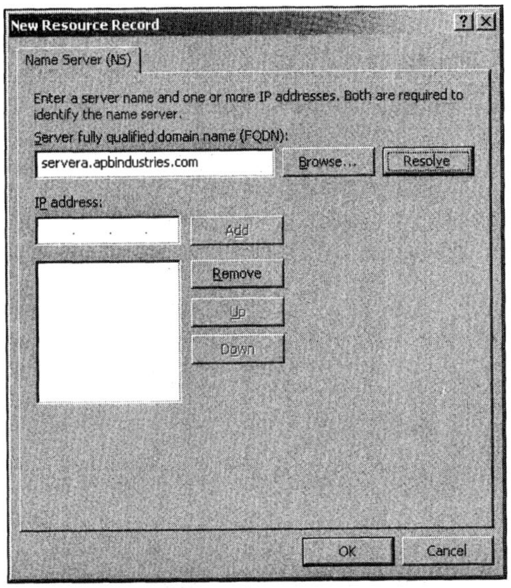

project 4.6

Setting Debugging Options for DNS Servers

exam objective

Basic knowledge

overview

The DNS server log located in Event Viewer contains basic events logged by the DNS Server service. However, occasionally you may require advanced debugging information. In these cases, you can set advanced debug options to create a temporary trace log to use for troubleshooting.

learning objective

After completing this project, you will know how to view the DNS server log using the Event Viewer and how to set debug logging options for the DNS server service.

specific requirements

Administrative rights on a Windows Server 2003 computer with the DNS Server service installed (SERVERA).

estimated completion time

10 minutes

project steps

1. Log on to **SERVERA** with a user account that has administrative rights.
2. Click **Start**, point to **Administrative Tools**, and click **Event Viewer**. Click **DNS Server**. In the right pane, you will see all of the events that have been logged by the DNS Server service **(Figure 3-16)**.
3. Close the **Event Viewer** console.
4. Click **Start**, point to **Administrative Tools**, and click **DNS**.
5. Right-click **SERVERA** and click **Properties**. Click the **Debug Logging** tab.
6. Put a check in the **Log Packets for debugging** check box to enable debugging.
7. In the **Log file** section, type **c:\windows\system32\dns\servera.txt** in the **File path and name** text box **(Figure 4-17)**. Click OK.
8. Wait several minutes before viewing the log file **servera.txt**, located in the ***%Systemroot%*\System32\DNS** folder.

tip

If the computer that you are working on (SERVERA) has been upgraded from Windows 2000 Server, the *%Systemroot%* folder may be C:\WINNT.

Figure 4-15 Event Viewer showing the DNS server

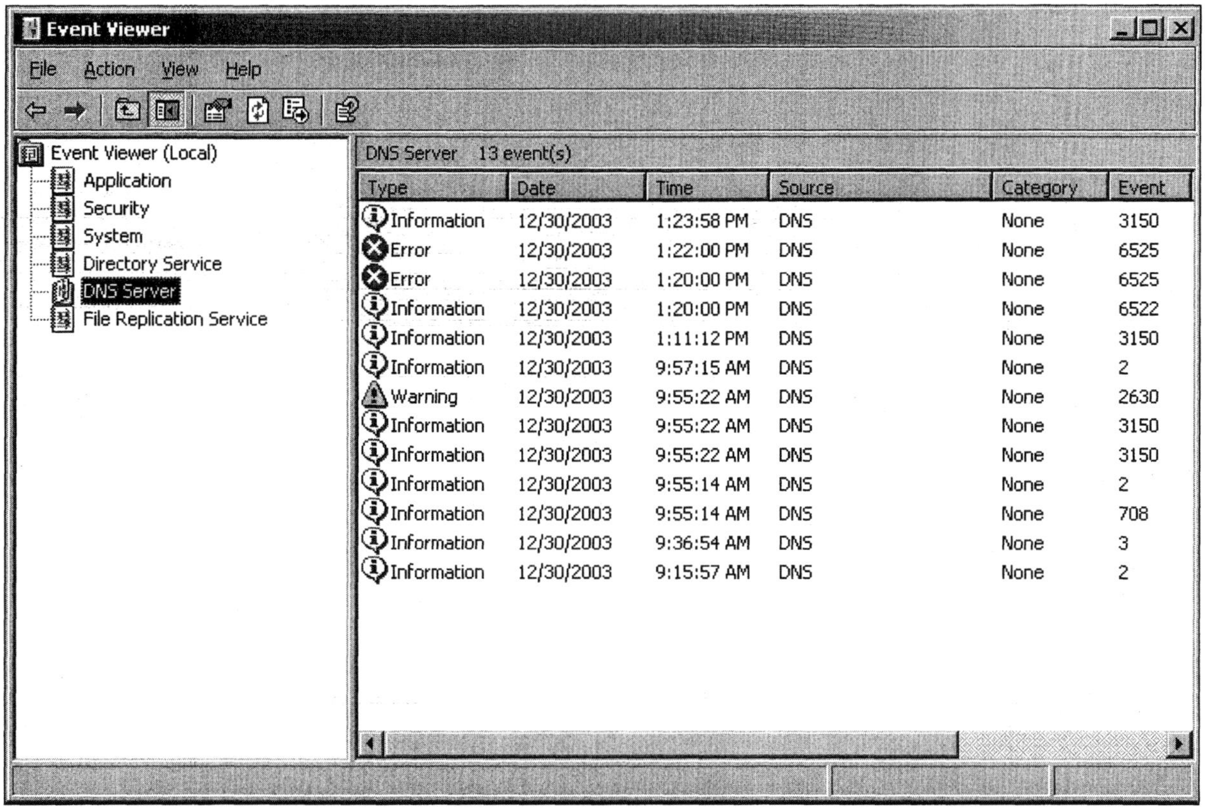

Figure 4-16 Specifying file path and name for servera.txt

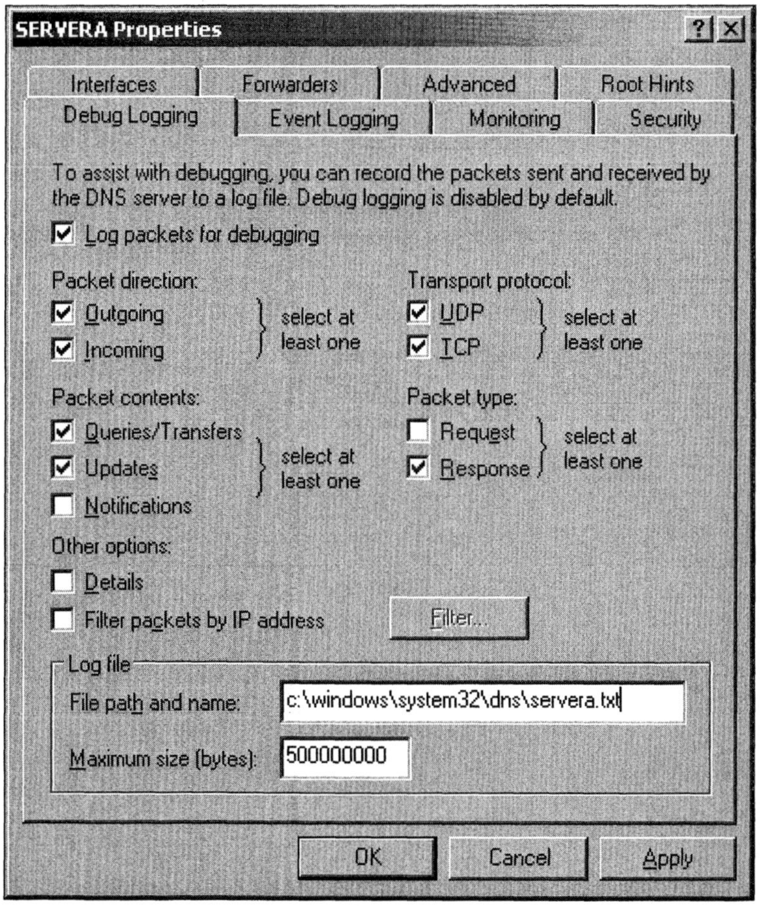

LESSON

5 Administering User Accounts

Active Directory stores user information such as the first name, last name, logon name, and password as user account attributes. A user account is a security principal that identifies a user and is used to either grant or deny access to network resources. In an Active Directory environment, there are two types of user accounts: domain user accounts and built-in user accounts. Domain user accounts are used to grant or deny access to resources on a network. Built-in user accounts are created automatically during installation. Examples of built-in user accounts are Administrator and Guest. Although you can rename them, you cannot delete the Administrator or Guest built-in accounts. In fact, for security reasons, it is recommended that the Administrator account be renamed. Local user accounts are available on Windows Server 2003 computers that are not domain controllers. Local user accounts can only be used to grant or deny access to local resources.

Whenever a user logs on, a user profile is accessed, which contains user-defined desktop settings, network connections, printers, etc. There are three types of user profiles: local user profiles, roaming user profiles, and mandatory profiles. A local user profile is stored on the computer that the user is actually using. A roaming user profile is stored on a network share and is accessible from any Windows computer in the enterprise. A mandatory user profile is similar to a roaming user profile, except that it is read-only, meaning that only people who have been assigned permission can make permanent changes to the profile. One of the responsibilities of an administrator is to manage and maintain user accounts. This includes such tasks as modifying user account attributes, resetting passwords, disabling user accounts, and renaming user accounts.

Scenario

As the Network Administrator for APB Industries, you are responsible for the creation and maintenance of all user accounts in Active Directory. In this lesson, you will be creating user accounts for a group of new employees. Some of these users will be using local user profiles, while others will need roaming user profiles. A couple of temporary contract employees will require a mandatory profile. All users will have their home directory configured to point to a network share, located on a server.

Lesson 5 Administering User Accounts

Project	Exam 70-294 Objective
5.1 Creating Domain User Accounts	Basic knowledge
5.2 Setting User Account Properties	Create and manage objects manually or by using scripting.
5.3 Introducing User Profiles	Basic knowledge
5.4 Creating a Roaming User Profile	Basic knowledge
5.5 Creating a Mandatory User Profile	Basic knowledge
5.6 Creating a Home Folder on a Server	Basic knowledge
5.7 Maintaining User Accounts	Create and manage objects manually or by using scripting.

General Requirements

To complete the projects in this lesson, you will need administrative rights on two Windows Server 2003 computers: SERVERA, the Windows Server 2003 computer acting as a domain controller for the apbindustries.com domain, and SERVERB, the Window Server 2003 computer that is acting as a domain controller for the rnd.apbindustries.com domain. You also will need to know how to use Windows Explorer to navigate through the file system and create folders, as well as the ability to create a network share. You may also find it helpful to refer to Lesson 5 in your Prentice Hall Certification Series Exam 70-294 textbook for further information about the topics covered by the projects in this lesson.

project 5.1 Creating Domain User Accounts

exam objective

Basic knowledge

overview

Due to expansion, APB Industries is hiring some new employees. It is your responsibility to create the new user accounts for these new employees. Following the steps below, create a user account for each of the following employees. All of these users will be created in the apbindustries.com domain. The user logon name format will be the first initial of the first name, and then the full last name.

Employee user logon names are as follows:

- Steven Groth (SGroth)
- Peter Murphy (PMurphy)
- Daniel Ash (DAsh)
- David Jay (DJay)
- Kevin Haskins (KHaskins)
- Ronan Harris (RHarris)
- Mark Jackson (MJackson)

learning objective

After completing this project, you will know how to create user accounts in an Active Directory environment.

specific requirements

Administrative rights on SERVERA, the Windows Server 2003 computer that is acting as a domain controller for apbindustries.com.

estimated completion time

15 minutes

project steps

1. Log on to **SERVERA** with an account that has administrative rights.
2. Click **Start**, point to **Programs**, point to **Administrative Tools**, and click **Active Directory Users and Computers** to open the **Active Directory Users and Computers** console.
3. Expand **apbindustries.com**. Right-click **Users**, point to **New**, and click **User** to open the **New Object – User** dialog box.
4. In the **First name** text box, type **Steven**. In the **Last name** text box, type **Groth**. In the **User logon name** text box, type **SGroth (Figure 5-1)**. Click **Next**.
5. Type a password in the **Password** and **Confirm password** text boxes.
6. Clear the **User must change password at next logon** check box. Select the **User cannot change password** check box (**Figure 5-2**). Click **Next**.
7. Review the settings and click **Finish**.
8. Repeat steps 4 through 5 to create user accounts for the six remaining employees.
9. The newly created users will now appear in the **Users** container **(Figure 5-3)**.

tip

You should use the administrator account ONLY for administrative purposes. For day to day tasks, create and use a standard user account. This adds to the overall security plan.

Figure 5-1 Creating a domain user account

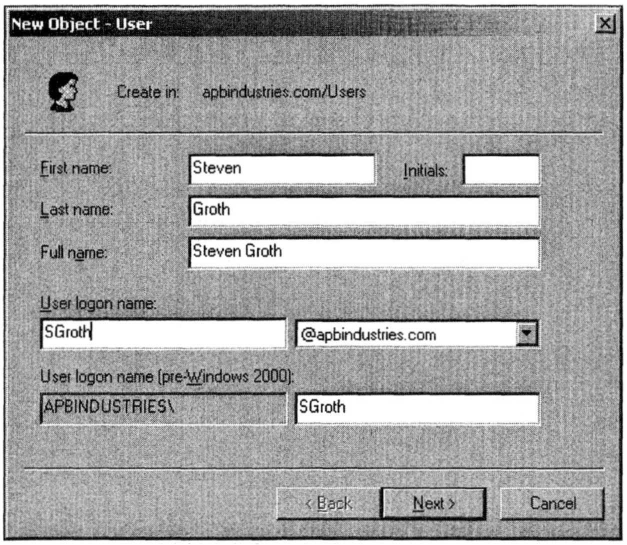

Figure 5-2 Specifying a password for a new domain user account

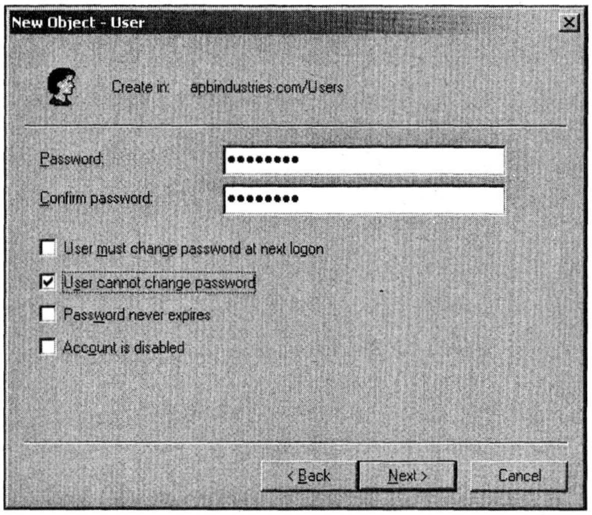

Figure 5-3 The new users in the Active Directory Users and Computers console

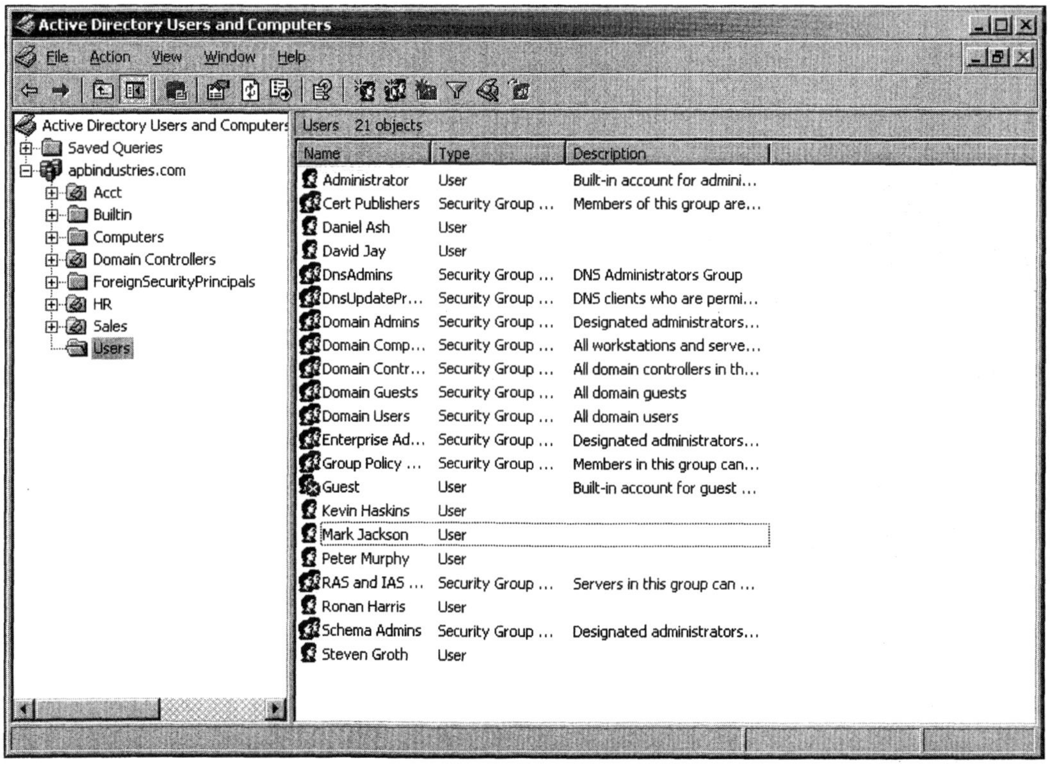

project 5.2

Setting User Account Properties

exam objective

Create and manage objects manually or by using scripting.

overview

One of the users created in Project 5.1 has special needs. You must modify the domain user account settings for this user to reflect his requirements. Steven Groth is a temporary contractor. For security reasons, management wants his user account to expire when it is no longer needed. Management also does not want him to be able to access Terminal Services.

learning objective

After completing this project, you will know how to examine and modify domain user account properties.

specific requirements

Administrative rights on SERVERA, the Windows Server 2003 computer that is acting as a domain controller for apbindustries.com, and successful completion of Project 5.1

estimated completion time

5 minutes

project steps

1. In the **Active Directory Users and Computers** console, click **Users**. Right-click **Steven Groth** and click **Properties**.
2. On the **General** tab, type **Temporary Contractor** in the **Description** text box.
3. Click the **Account** tab. At the bottom of the tab, in the **Account expires** area, click the **End of** option button. The default expiration date is one month from the current date **(Figure 5-4)**. Leave the default.
4. Click the **Terminal Services Profile** tab. Remove the check mark from the **Allow logon to terminal server** check box **(Figure 5-5)**.
5. Click **OK** to close the **Properties** dialog box and to apply the changes.

Figure 5-4 Setting a user account expiration date

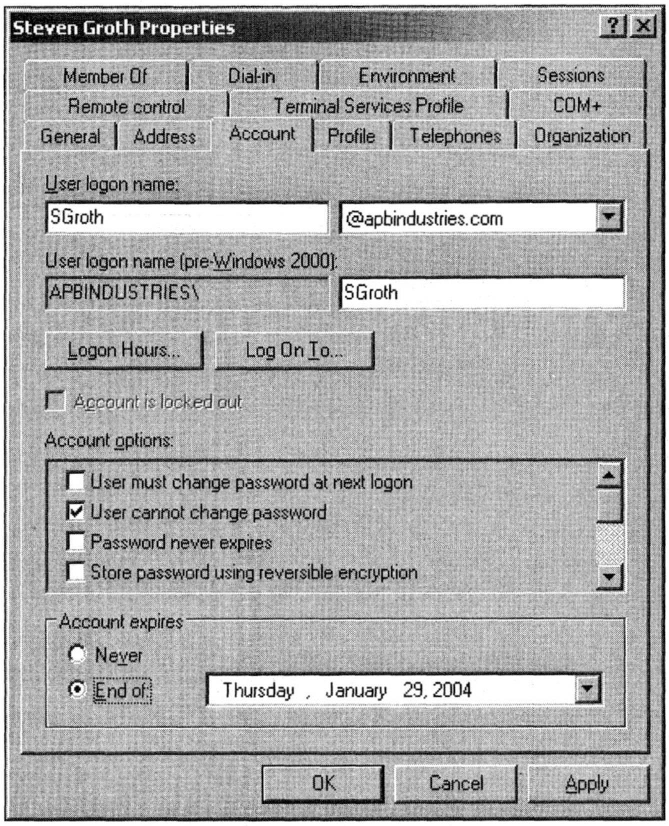

Figure 5-5 Restricting a user account from logging on to a terminal server

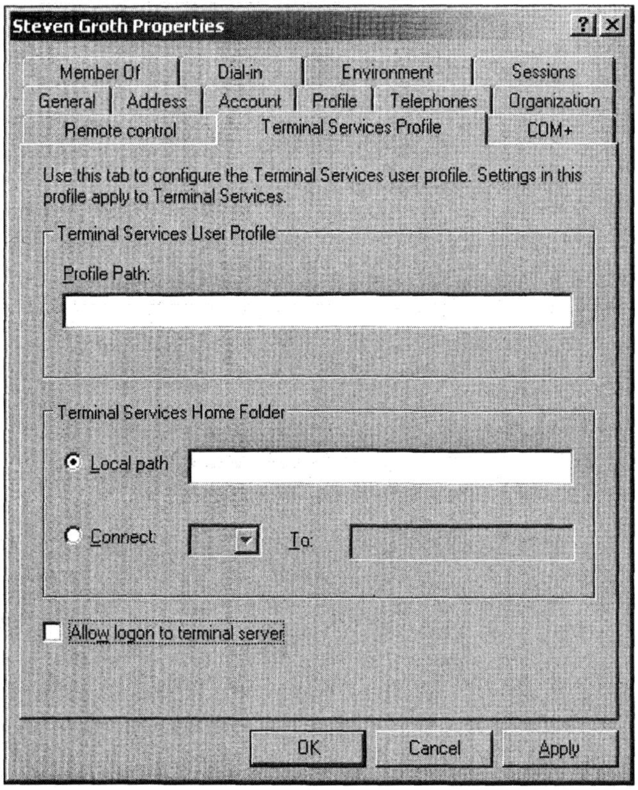

project 5.3

Introducing User Profiles

exam objective

Basic knowledge

overview

To simplify administration, you will modify the Default User profile so that whenever a new user logs on to that computer, that user's profile will automatically have a desktop shortcut to the WordPad application. This will prevent you from having to manually add this shortcut to each new user's profile. Additionally, you will modify the All Users profile to place a text document on the desktop. This will place the text document on the desktop for every user profile on that computer, even those that have already been created.

learning objective

After completing this project, you will know how to make changes to the Default User and All Users profiles.

specific requirements

Administrative rights on SERVERA, the Windows Server 2003 computer that is acting as a domain controller for apbindustries.com, and successful completion of Project 5.1.

estimated completion time

15 minutes

project steps

1. In the **Active Directory Users and Computers** console, right-click the **Peter Murphy** user account and click **Properties**. Click the **Member Of** tab. Click the **Add** button to open the **Select Groups** dialog box.
2. Click the **Advanced** button to expand the dialog box. Click the **Find Now** button. Select **Print Operators** in the **Search results** pane and click **OK** to add the **Printer Operators** group to the **Enter the object names to select** box.
3. Click **OK** to close the Select Groups dialog box. This action also adds Peter Murphy to the Print Operators group so that he can log on to the domain controller. Close the Peter Murphy Properties dialog box and the **Active Directory Users and Computers** console.
4. Click **Start**. Click **Run**. In the **Open** text box, type **explorer**. Click **OK** to open **Windows Explorer**. Open the **Tools** menu and click **Folder Options** to open the **Folder Options** dialog box.
5. Click the **View** tab. Remove the check mark from the **Hide protected operating system files (Recommended)** check box. A warning message box will appear. Click **Yes.**
6. Click **OK** to close the Folder Options dialog box.
7. Expand **My Computer** and then expand **C:** (if Windows Server 2003 was installed on a drive other than **C:**, expand the appropriate drive). Expand **Documents and Settings**.
8. Expand the **Default User** folder. Click the **Desktop** folder. In the right pane, right-click an empty space, point to **New**, and click **Shortcut** to start the **Create Shortcut Wizard**.
9. In the **Type the location of the item** text box, enter or browse to the pathway and filename **c:\Program Files\Windows NT\Accessories\wordpad.exe**. (Click **OK** to close the Browse for Folder dialog box, if needed.) Click **Next** to open the **Select a Title for the Program** screen. Click **Finish** to accept the default name, **wordpad.exe**, in the **Type a name for this shortcut** text box. Close **Windows Explorer** and log off.
10. Log on with the user account **PMurphy**, using the password that you set for this account in Project 5.1. Notice that there is a **wordpad** icon on the desktop. This is because the first time the PMurphy user account was used, a user profile was created based on the Default User template. Log off.
11. Log on as a user with administrative rights. Open **Windows Explorer** and then expand the **C:** drive (if Windows Server 2003 was installed on a drive other than C:, expand the appropriate drive). Navigate to **Documents and Settings\All Users\Desktop**.
12. Right-click inside the **Desktop** folder, point to **New**, and click **Text Document**. Name the file **allusers.txt**. A new icon, **allusers.txt**, immediately appears on the desktop. Log off.
13. Log on with the user account **PMurphy**. A new icon, **allusers**, now appears on the desktop of this user profile **(Figure 5-6)**. Log off.

tip

When logging on as Peter Murphy, the allusers.txt file appears simply as allusers. This is because the Peter Murphy user profile has not been configured to show file extensions of known file types.

Figure 5-6 Wordpad.exe and allusers.txt shortcuts on desktop

project 5.4 Creating a Roaming User Profile

exam objective

Basic knowledge

overview

Whenever a user logs on to a computer for the first time, a local user profile is created for that user account. If that same user logs on to a different computer, a new local user profile will be created. This can be confusing for users. To avoid this confusion, roaming user profiles can be implemented. When a roaming user profile is used, the user profile is stored on a network share, and is accessible to that user from any Windows computer in the enterprise.

learning objective

After completing this project, you will know how to copy user profiles. You will also know how to create roaming user profiles.

specific requirements

Administrative rights on SERVERA, the Windows Server 2003 computer that is acting as a domain controller for apbindustries.com, and on SERVERB, the Windows Server 2003 computer that is acting as a domain controller for rnd.apbindustries.com. Additionally, successful completion of Projects 5.1 and 5.3 is required.

estimated completion time

15 minutes

project steps

1. Log on to **SERVERB** with a user account that has administrative rights.
2. Create the folder **C:\RoamingProfiles**, share it as **Roaming**, and assign the **Full Control** share permission to the **Authenticated Users** group. Remove the **Everyone** group for security purposes.
3. Log on to **SERVERA** using an account with administrative rights and open the **Active Directory Users and Computers** console.
4. Select the **Users** folder. Right-click **Mark Jackson** and click **Properties** to open the **Properties** dialog box for the user.
5. Open the **Member Of** tab. Click the **Add** button to open the **Select Groups** dialog box.
6. Click the **Advanced** button to expand the dialog box.
7. Click the **Find Now** button. Select the **Print Operators** group in the **Search** results list.
8. Click **OK** to add the **Print Operators** group to the **Enter the object names to** select box.
9. Click **OK** to close the Select Groups dialog box and make Mark a member of Print Operators group so that he can log on to the domain controller.
10. Click **OK** to close the Properties dialog box.
11. Log off and log back on as **MJackson** using the password that you set for this account in Project 5.1. A local user profile is automatically created.
12. Right-click the **Desktop** and click **Properties** to open the **Display Properties** dialog box.
13. Open the **Desktop** tab and select **Stonehenge** as the background.
14. Click **OK** to close the Display Properties dialog box. If you get a warning message, click **Yes**. Log off.
15. Log on to **SERVERA** with a user account that has administrative rights.
16. Click **Start**, point to **Control Panel** and click **System** to open the **System Properties** dialog box.
17. Open the **Advanced** tab (**Figure 5-7**). In the **User profiles** section, click the **Settings** button to open the **User Profiles** dialog box (**Figure 5-8**).
18. Select the **APBINDUSTRIES\MJackson** profile and click the **Copy To** button to open the **Copy To** dialog box.
19. In the **Copy profile to** text box, enter **\\serverb\roaming\sgroth**.
20. In the **Permitted to use** box, click the **Change** button to open the **Select User or Group** dialog box.
21. Click **Advanced** to expand the dialog box.
22. Click **Find Now**. Select **Steven Groth** in the **Search results** pane (**Figure 5-9**).

tip

If possible, it is best to locate roaming user profiles on a member server rather than a domain controller.

caution

Application shortcuts can be included in a roaming user profile. However, the shortcut will not work unless the application is installed on the computer on which the roaming user is logging on.

Figure 5-7 Accessing the Advanced tab through System Properties

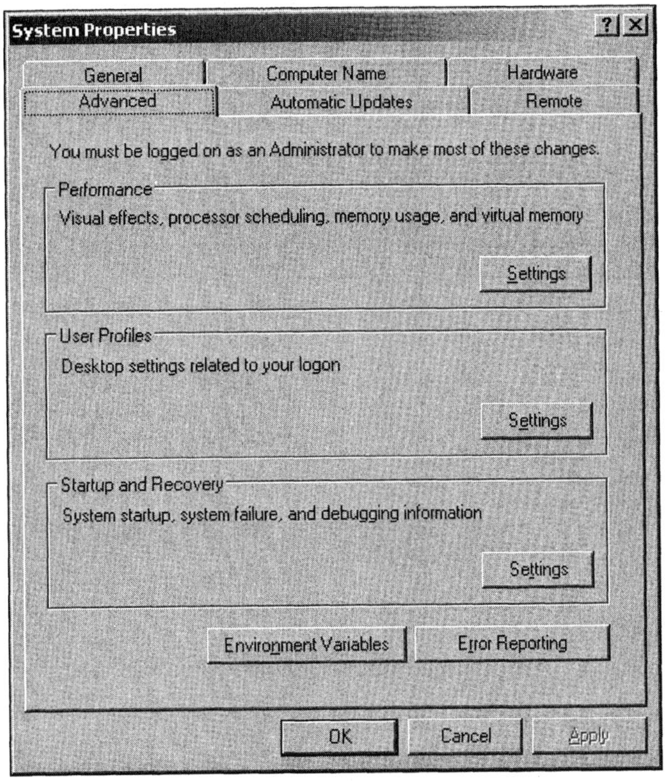

Figure 5-8 The User Profiles dialog box

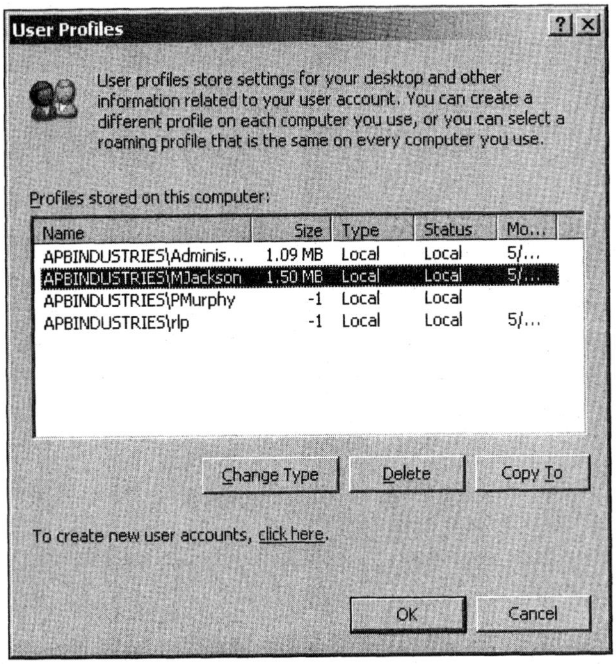

Figure 5-9 Making a copy of a user profile on a shared folder

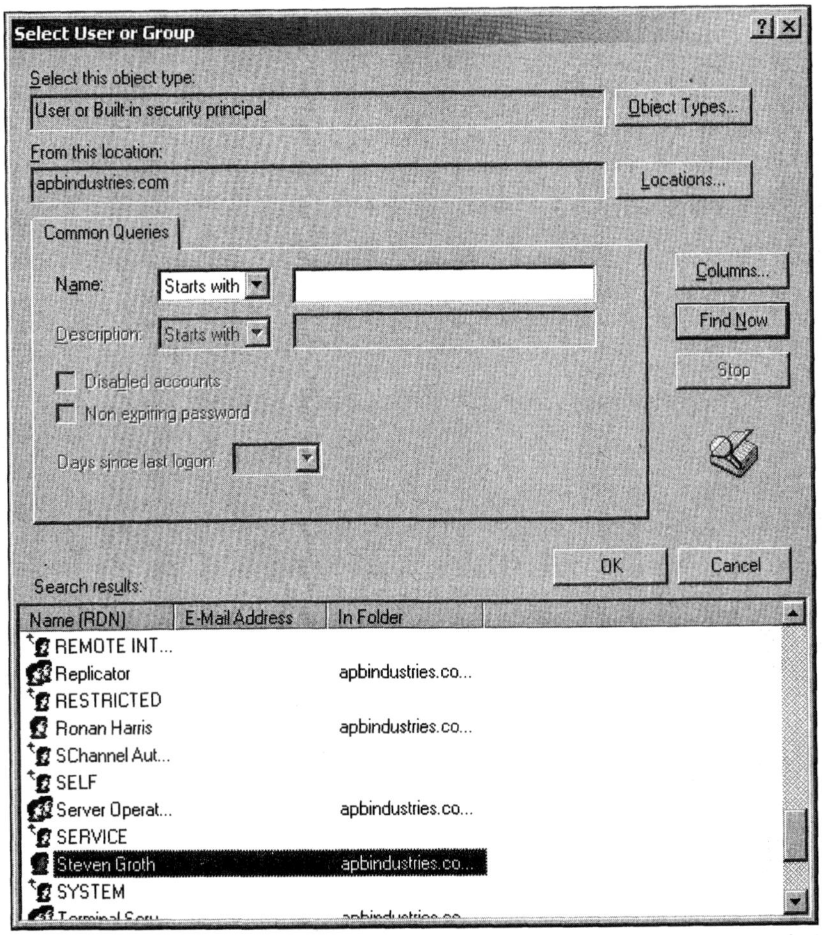

project 5.4

Creating a Roaming User Profile (cont'd)

exam objective

Basic knowledge

project steps

23. Click OK to enter the user account in the **Enter the object name to** select box.
24. Click **OK** to close the Select User or Group dialog box. APBINDUSTRIES\SGroth is permitted to use the copy of the MJackson profile (**Figure 5-10**).
25. Click **OK** to close the Copy To dialog box.
26. Click **OK** to close the User Profiles dialog box.
27. Click **OK** to close the System Properties dialog box.
28. Open the **Active Directory Users and Computers** console.
29. Click the **Users** container. Right-click **Steven Groth** and click **Properties**. Click the **Profile** tab.
30. In the **Profile path** text box, type **\\serverb\roaming\sgroth (Figure 5-11**).
31. Open the **Member Of** tab. Click the **Add** button to open the **Select Groups** dialog box.
32. Click the **Advanced** button to expand the dialog box.
33. Click **Find Now**.
34. Select the **Print Operators** group in the **Search results** list.
35. Click **OK** to add the Print Operators group to the **Enter the object names to select** box.
36. Click **OK** to close the Select Groups dialog box. This will allow this user account to log on to the SERVERA domain controller to test the roaming profile.
37. Click **OK** to close the Steven Groth Properties dialog box.
38. Close the Active Directory Users and Computers console.
39. Log off.
40. Log on to either **SERVERA** or any other Windows Server 2003 or Windows 2000 or XP Professional computer that is part of the apbindustries.com domain with the user account SGroth, using the password that you set for this account in Project 5.1. The profile that was copied from MJackson's profile should appear.
41. Log off.

Figure 5-10 The Copy To dialog box

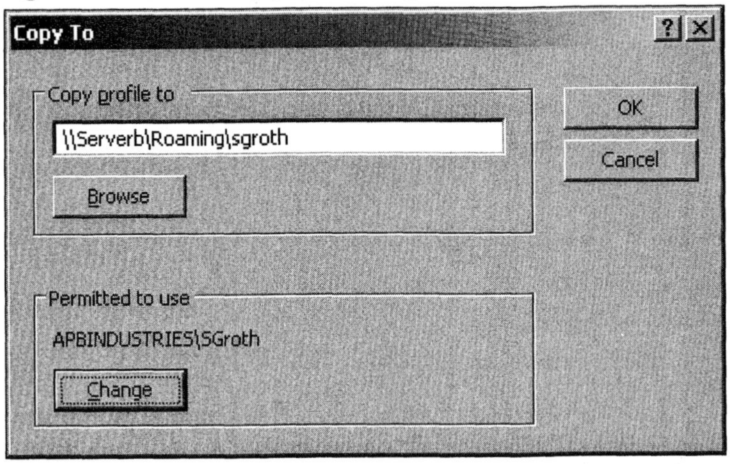

Figure 5-11 Specifying the network path to the roaming user profile

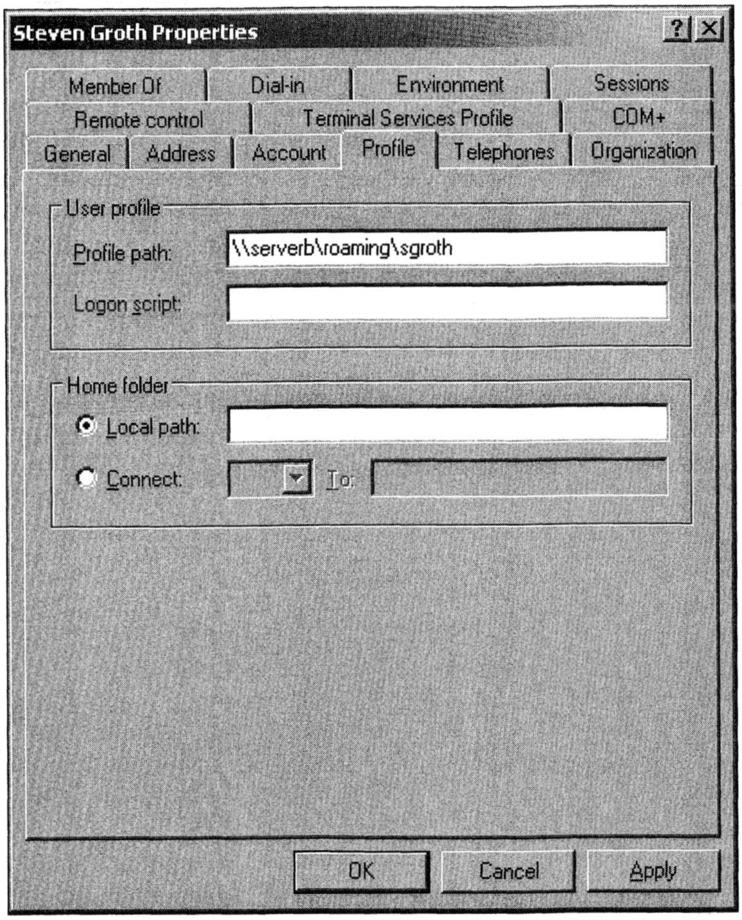

project 5.5 Creating a Mandatory User Profile

exam objective

Basic knowledge

overview

To simplify administration, it may be desirable to prevent users from making changes to their profiles. This can be accomplished by implementing a mandatory user profile. A mandatory user profile is a roaming user profile that is read-only. Changes can be made to the profile during a user's session, but those changes are lost once the user logs off.

learning objective

After completing this project, you will know how to change a roaming user profile into a mandatory user profile.

specific requirements

Access to SERVERA, and administrative rights on SERVERB, the Windows Server 2003 computer that is acting as a domain controller for rnd.apbindustries.com. Additionally, successful completion of Projects 5.1, 5.3, and 5.4 is required.

estimated completion time

10 minutes

project steps

1. Log on to **SERVERB** with a user account that has administrative rights.
2. Open **Windows Explorer**.
3. Navigate to **C:\RoamingProfiles\sgroth**.
4. Select the hidden file **Ntuser.dat** and press **[F2]**. Change the name of the file to **Ntuser.man (Figure 5-12)**. Close Windows Explorer.
5. Log on to **SERVERA** with the **SGroth** user account, using the password that you set for this account in Project 5.1.
6. Delete the **wordpad.exe** icon from the desktop. Log off.
7. Log back on using the **SGroth** user account. Notice that the icon you deleted is on the Desktop. The icon has not been deleted because only administrators are permitted to make changes to mandatory user profiles. Log off.

tip

Only roaming user profiles can be made mandatory. Local user profiles cannot be designated as mandatory.

Figure 5-12 Creating a mandatory user profile

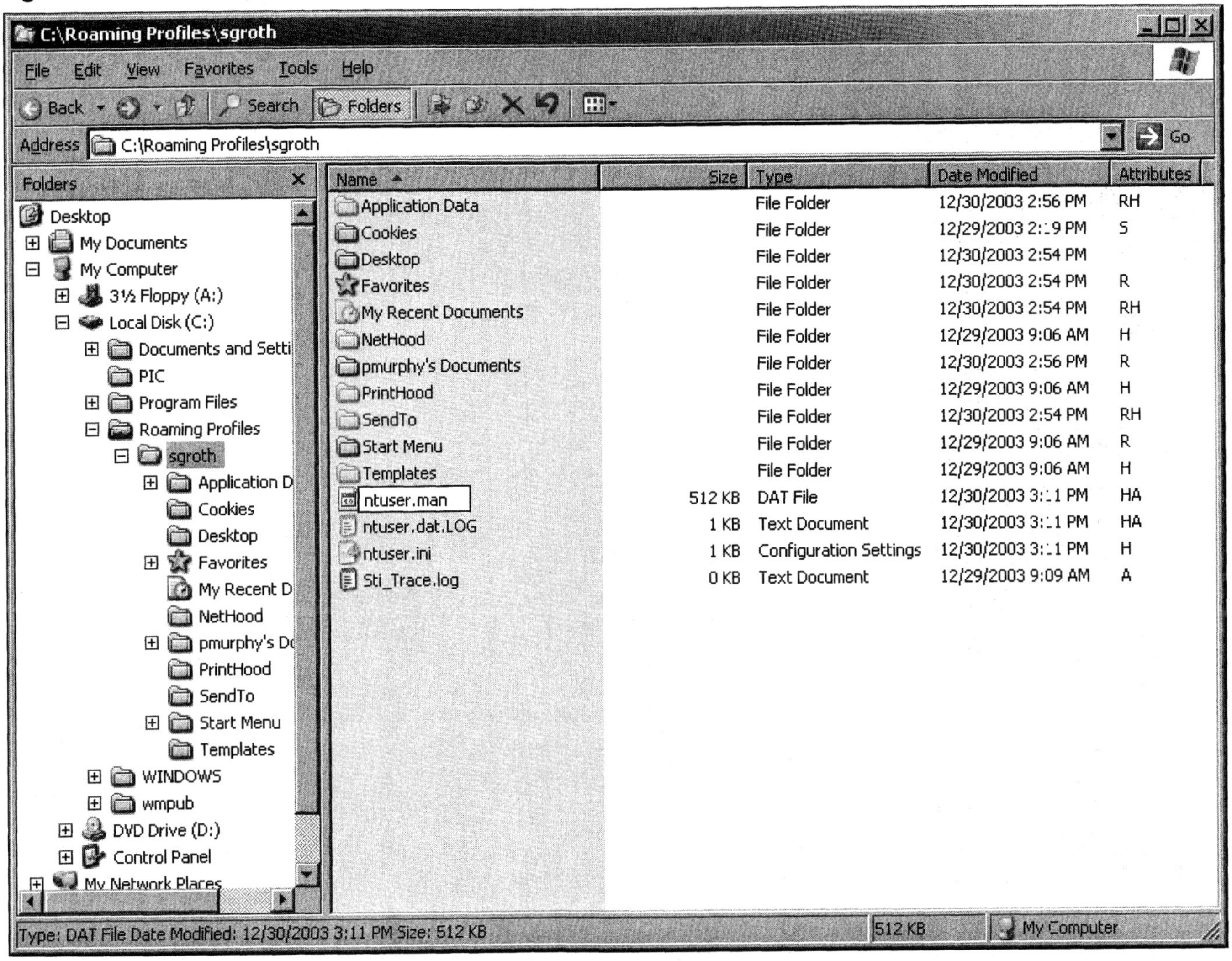

project 5.6 Creating a Home Folder on a Server

exam objective

Basic knowledge

overview

The default location for users to store their data is the My Documents folder, which is part of each user's profile. However, this folder is located on the local computer, which can prevent a user from accessing documents when not at their specific computer. An alternative is to create a home folder on a server. This will allow documents to be accessed in a uniform fashion no matter which computer the user logs on to.

learning objective

After completing this project, you will know how to create a home folder for a user located on a network share.

specific requirements

Administrative rights on SERVERA, the Windows Server 2003 computer that is acting as a domain controller for apbindustries.com, and successful completion of Project 5.1.

estimated completion time

10 minutes

project steps

1. Log on to **SERVERB** with a user account that has administrative rights.
2. Create the folder **C:\HomeFolders**, share it as **Home**, and grant the Full Control share permission to the **Domain Users** group.
3. Log on to **SERVERA** with a user account that has administrative rights.
4. Open the **Active Directory Users and Computers** console. Click the **Users** container. Right-click **Peter Murphy** and click **Properties**. Click the **Profile** tab.
5. In the **Home folder** box, choose the **Connect** option. In the drop-down list, select any unused drive letter to specify the drive for the existing network share. In the **To** text box, type **\\serverb\home*%username%*** (**Figure 5-13**). Click **OK**. Close the **Active Directory Users and Computers** console.
6. Navigate to the **Home Folders** folder on **SERVERB** to confirm that the **PMurphy** folder has been automatically created.
7. Right-click the **PMurphy** folder and select **Properties**. Click the **Security** tab. Notice that the permissions have been automatically set to only allow Administrators and the home folder owner access to the folder (**Figure 5-14**). Click **OK**.
8. Log on to SERVERA as **PMurphy** using the password that you set for this account in Project 5.1.
9. Open **Window Explorer**. Select **My Computer**. You will notice that the drive you selected in Step 4 has been automatically mapped to the specified network share (**Figure 5-15**).
10. Log off.

tip

Since the My Documents folder is part of a user's profile, using it can hinder network performance if roaming user profiles are implemented. Using a home folder on a server instead can prevent large amounts of user data from being sent across the network during logon and logoff.

Figure 5-13 Specifying a home folder for a user

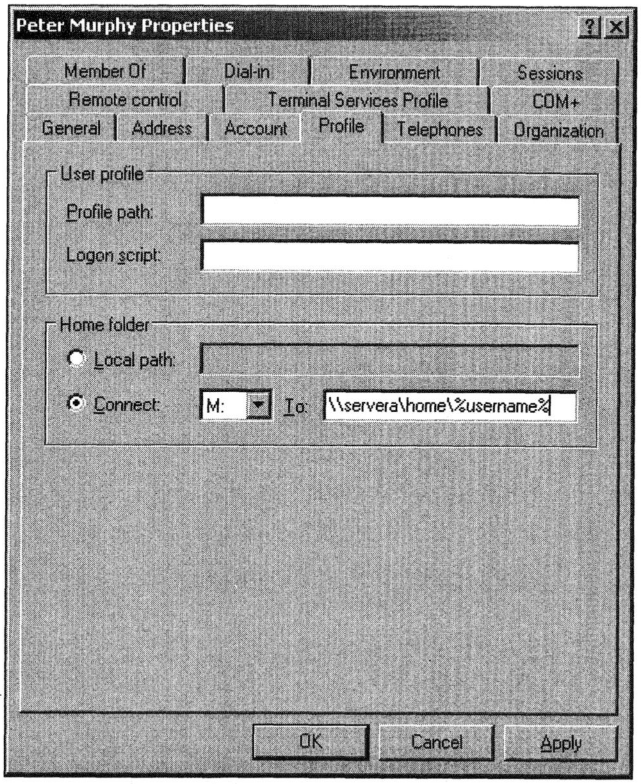

Figure 5-14 Viewing the security settings for a user's home folder

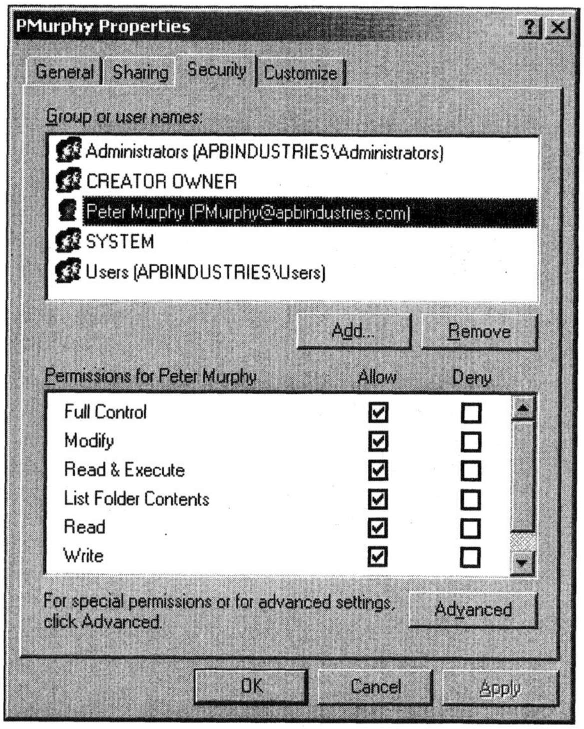

Figure 5-15 Viewing the automatically generated home folder drive mapping

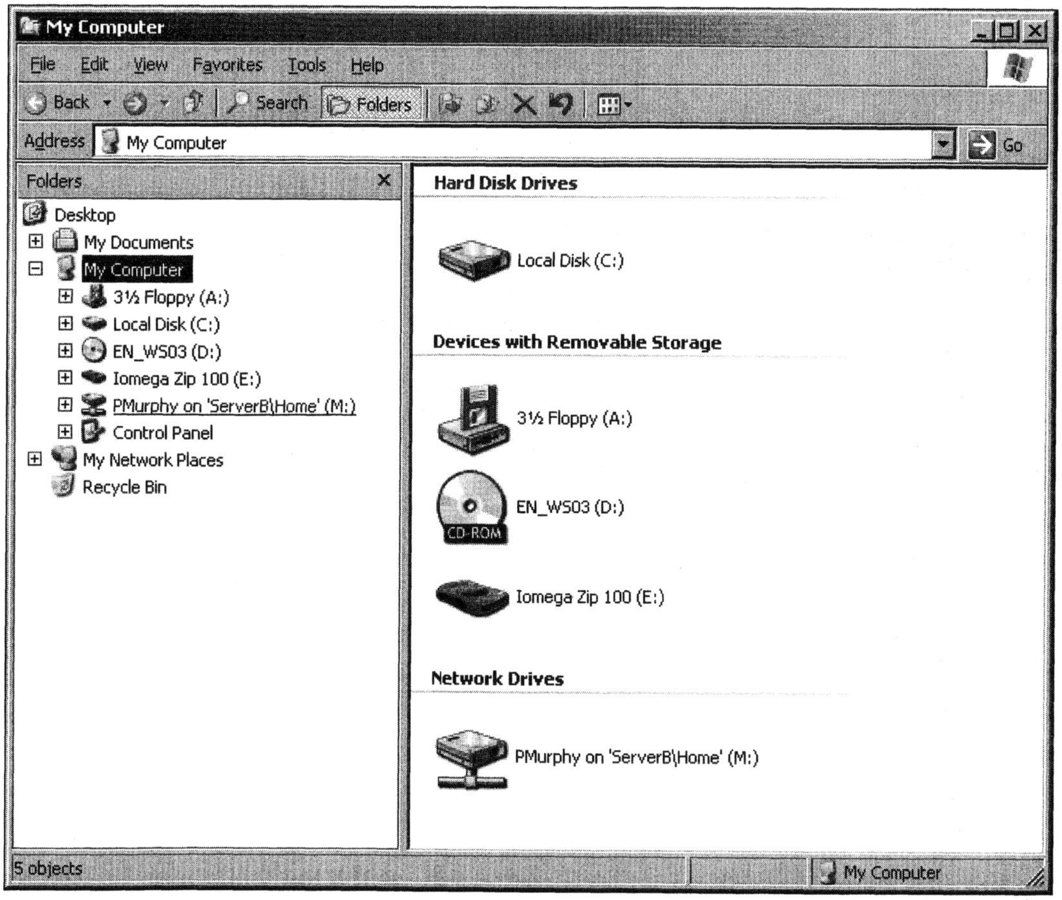

project 5.7

Maintaining User Accounts

exam objective

Create and manage objects manually or by using scripting.

overview

Managing a network includes maintaining user accounts. This can include renaming user accounts, resetting passwords, disabling and enabling user accounts, and deleting user accounts.

learning objective

After completing this project, you will know how to maintain user accounts by resetting passwords, renaming user accounts, and deleting user accounts.

specific requirements

Administrative rights on SERVERA, the Windows Server 2003 computer that is acting as a domain controller for apbindustries.com.

estimated completion time

10 minutes

project steps

1. Log on to **SERVERA** with a user account that has administrative rights.
2. Open the **Active Directory Users and Computers** console. Right-click the **Users** container, point to **New**, and click **User**.
3. Create a user named **Markus Reinhardt** with a user logon name of **MReinhardt** and the password, **password**. Clear the **User must change password at next logon** check box. Put a check in the box for **User cannot change password**. Click **Next**. Click **Finish**.
4. Right-click **Markus Reinhardt** and click **Reset Password**.
5. Type **wolfsheim** in both the **New password** and **Confirm password** text boxes (**Figure 5-16**). Click **OK**. A message appears indicating that the password was successfully changed. Click **OK.**
6. Right-click **Markus Reinhardt** and then click **Disable account**. A message appears informing you that the object has been disabled. Click **OK**. Notice that the user account now has a red X, showing that it is disabled **(Figure 5-17)**.
7. Right-click **Markus Reinhardt** and click **Rename**. Rename the user account as **Andy Kreuger**. Press **Enter**. The **Rename User** dialog box opens. Modify the information to reflect the new user account name **(Figure 5-18)**. Click **OK**.
8. Right-click **Andy Kreuger** and click **Delete**. A message box opens, asking you to confirm the deletion **(Figure 5-19)**. Click **Yes**.
9. Close the **Active Directory Users and Computers** console.

tip

A red X on a user account indicates that the user account is either disabled or has been locked out.

caution

Once a user account is deleted, all security related information is also deleted. Even if a new user account is created with the exact same name, it will not have the same security relationships as the original account.

Figure 5-16 Resetting a user's password

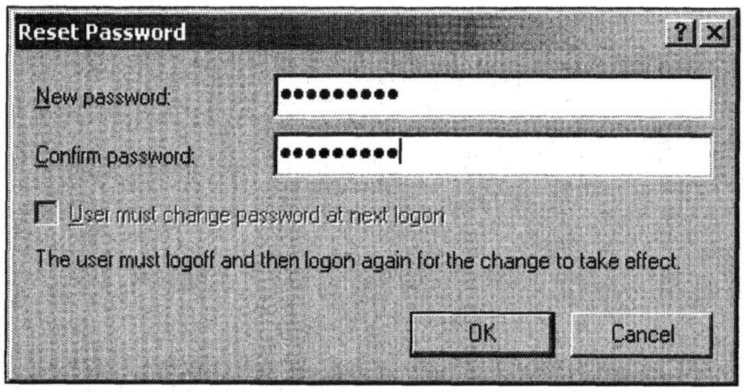

Figure 5-17 Viewing a disabled user account in the Active Directory Users and Computers console

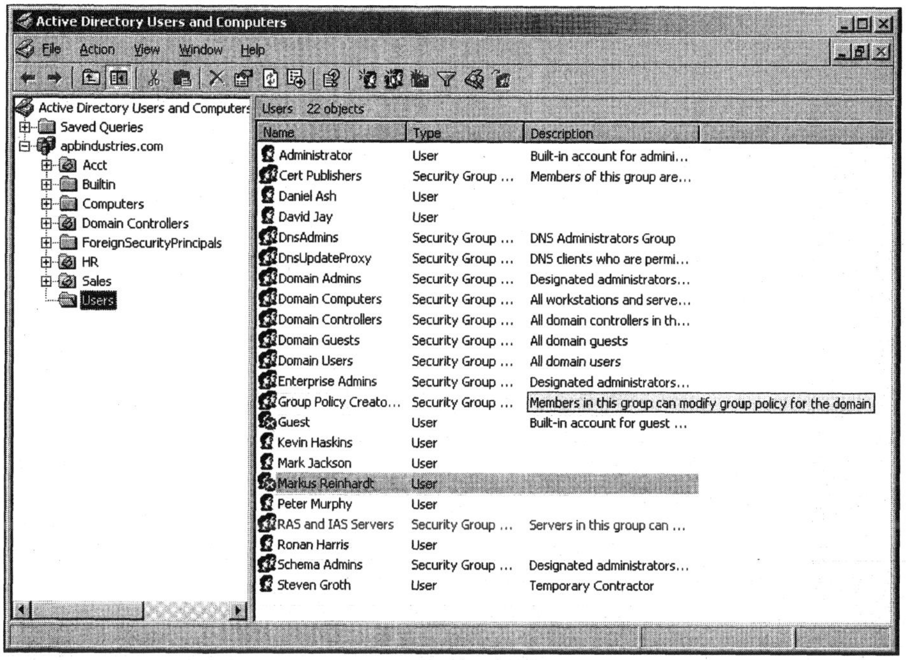

Figure 5-18 Renaming a user account

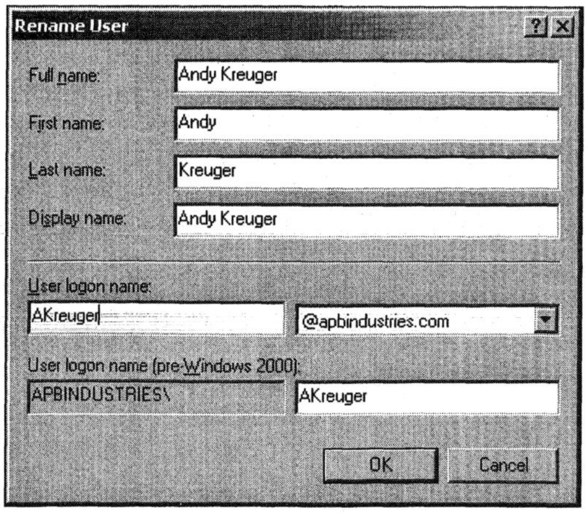

Figure 5-19 Confirming the deletion of a user object

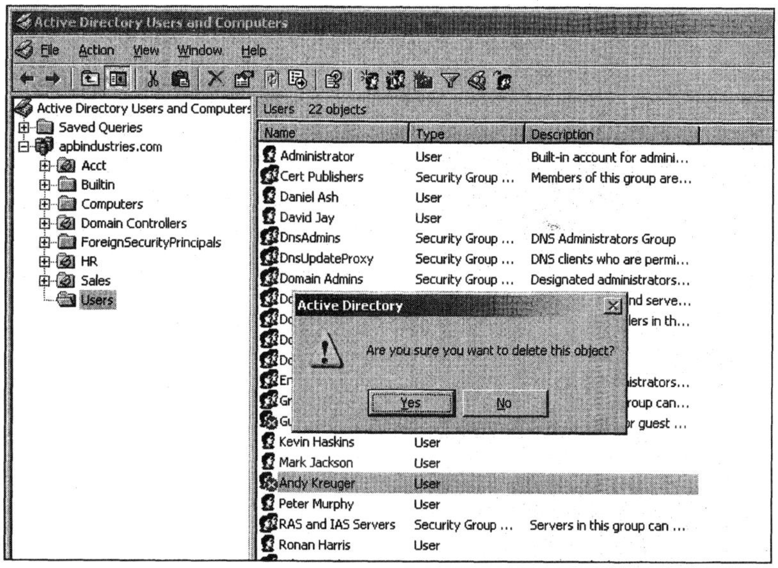

LESSON

6 Implementing Groups in Active Directory

Active Directory simplifies network management by allowing administrators to organize users into groups. Using security groups allows administrators to assign access permissions to a number of users at one time. It also allows administrators to delegate administrative privileges and rights to many users at once. In Active Directory, multiple users can be part of a single group. Conversely, one user can be a member of multiple groups. Crcating groups ensures that the administrator does not need to assign similar permissions to individual users separately.

There are two types of groups: distribution and security. Distribution groups are used only for the distribution of messages by applications such as Microsoft Exchange Server. They cannot be used to assign permissions to users. Security groups are used to define the rights and permissions users will have to access resources on a computer or a network. In order to use security groups effectively administrators must devise group strategies that address the group scopes to be used and the nesting strategy in order to assign the appropriate level of access.

There are three group scopes: domain local, global, and universal. Domain local groups are used to assign permissions for resources in the domain in which the group is created. Global groups are used to assign permissions for resources in any domain. When all domain controllers in a domain have been upgraded to Windows 2000 and Windows Server 2003, and Active Directory has been transferred to Windows 2000 native mode or Windows Server 2003 mode, you can also create universal groups, which can have members from many different domains and permissions assigned for resources in any domain.

The most commonly used nesting strategy is known as "the Microsoft rule" and it is the preferred strategy for building and using groups. First, you create one global group for each position or job function since all users with a particular job function will generally be granted the same access permissions. Then, each time you create a share, you typically create four separate domain local groups for different levels of access to the share. Finally, you make the global group, or groups, members of the appropriate domain local group. Even if you have only a single domain, this global-domain local group nesting strategy is an effective method for assigning permissions to network resources.

Scenario

Groups have not been implemented in the APB Industries environment yet. To prevent a future administrative headache, groups will now be created and group membership will be assigned. File shares will also be created, and the appropriate groups will be given the appropriate permissions to the shares.

Lesson 6 Implementing Groups in Active Directory	
Project	**Exam 70-294 Objective**
6.1 Creating Groups	Basic knowledge
6.2 Setting Group Properties	Basic knowledge
6.3 Modifying Group Properties	Basic knowledge

General Requirements

To complete the projects in this lesson, you will need administrative rights on SERVERA, the Windows Server 2003 computer that is acting as a domain controller for the apbindustries.com domain, as well as the successful completion of the projects in Lesson 5. You will also need to know how to use Windows Explorer to navigate through the file system, how to create folders, and how to create a network share. You may also find it helpful to refer to Lesson 6 in your Prentice Hall Certification Series Exam 70-294 textbook for further information about the topics covered by the projects in this lesson.

project 6.1

Creating Groups

exam objective

Basic knowledge

overview

Currently, permissions and rights are being assigned on a user-by-user basis. This can become a headache as the number of employees grows. To avoid this problem, three global groups will be created: Sales, Human Resources, and Information Technology.

learning objective

After completing this project, you will know how to create groups.

specific requirements

Administrative rights on SERVERA, the Windows Server 2003 computer that is acting as a domain controller for apbindustries.com.

estimated completion time

5 minutes

project steps

1. Log on to SERVERA with a user account that has administrative rights.
2. Open the **Active Directory Users and Computers** console. Right-click **Users**, point to **New**, and click **Group**. The **New Object-Group** dialog box opens.
3. In the **Group name** text box, type **Sales-G**. The **G** (for **Global**) after the name of the group will make it easier to visually determine the group scope.
4. Ensure that the **Global** option is selected in the **Group scope** box, and the **Security** option is selected in the **Group type** box **(Figure 6-1)**. Click **OK**.
5. Repeat steps 2 and 3 for the remaining two groups, **HR-G** and **IT-G**. The three newly created groups now appear in the **Active Directory Users and Computers** console **(Figure 6-2)**.

Figure 6-1 Creating a group

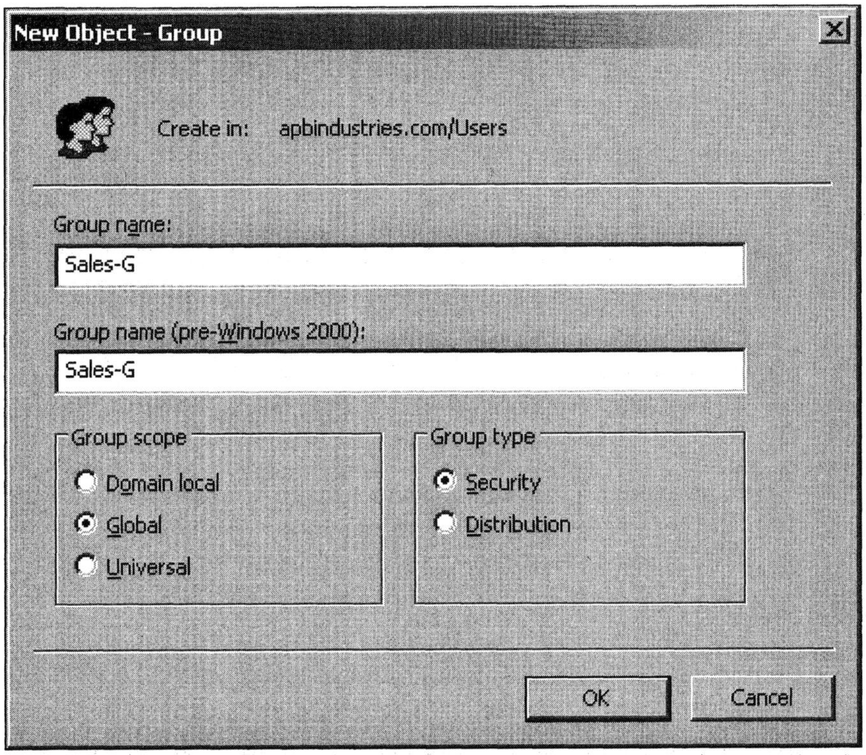

Figure 6-2 Viewing the new groups in the Active Directory Users and Computers console

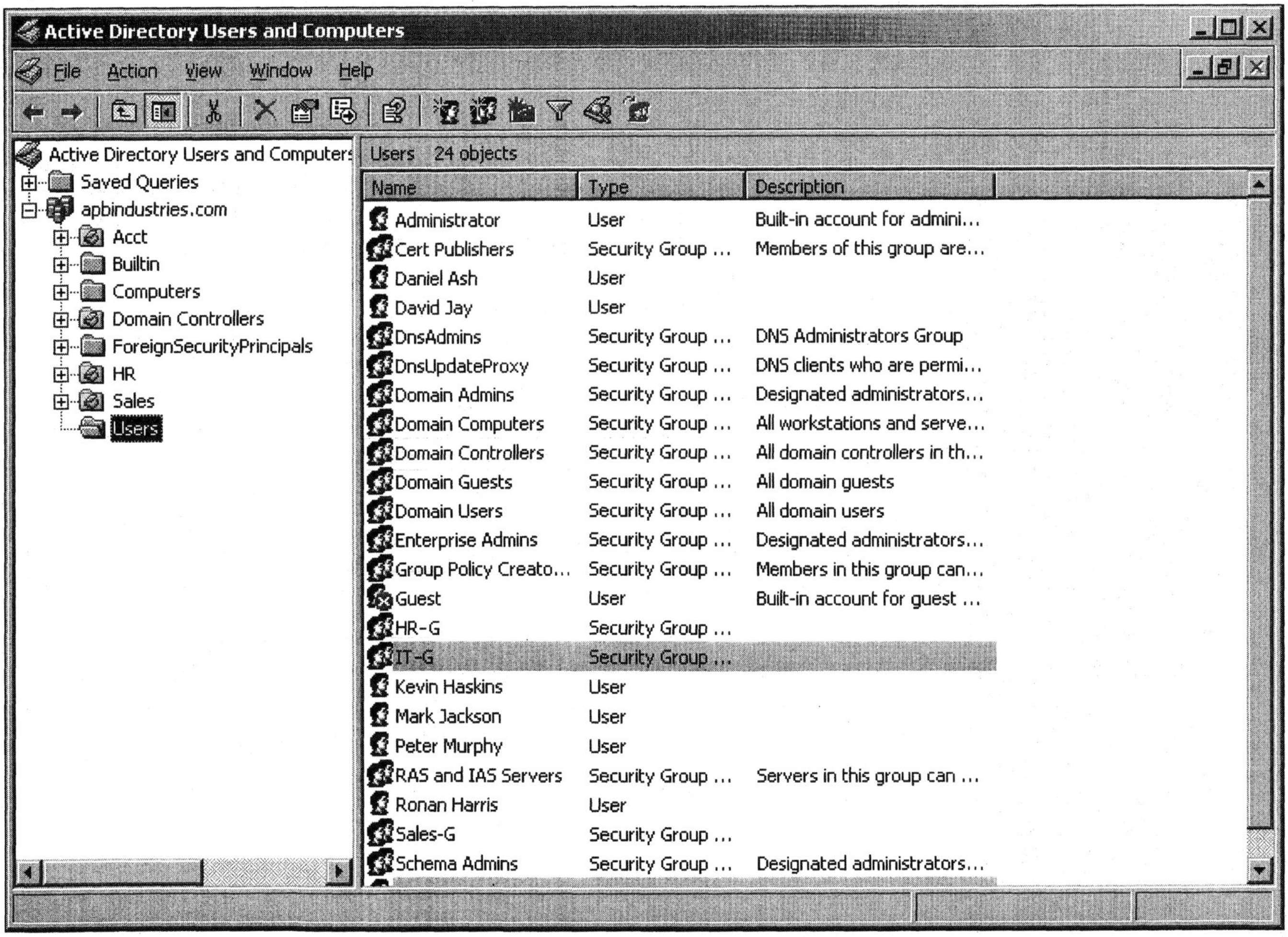

project 6.2 Setting Group Properties

exam objective

Basic knowledge

overview

Now that the appropriate groups have been created, the group properties need to be modified.

learning objective

After completing this project, you will know how to set group properties.

specific requirements

Administrative rights on SERVERA, the Windows Server 2003 computer that is acting as a domain controller for apbindustries.com, and successful completion of Project 6.1.

estimated completion time

10 minutes

project steps

1. In the **Active Directory Users and Computers** console, click the **Users** folder. Right-click the **Sales-G** security group and select **Properties** to open the Properties dialog box for the group.
2. Open the **Members** tab. Click the **Add** button to open the **Select Users, Contacts, Computers, or Groups** dialog box.
3. Click the **Advanced** button to expand the dialog box. Click **Find Now**. Select **Steven Groth** in the **Search results** pane. Click **OK** to enter **Steven Groth** in the **Enter the object names to select** box.
4. Click **Advanced**. Click **Find Now**. Select **Peter Murphy** in the **Search results** pane. Click **OK** to enter **Peter Murphy** in the **Enter the object names to select** box.
5. Click **OK** to close the Select Users, Contacts, Computers, or Groups dialog box.
6. The two users you just added are listed in the **Members** list in the Sales-G Properties dialog box **(Figure 6-3)**.
7. Click **OK** to close the Sales-G Properties dialog box.
8. Repeat steps 1 through 5 to add **Daniel Ash**, **David Jay**, and **Kevin Haskins** to the **HR-G** group.
9. In the Active Directory Users and Computers console, select the **Users** folder.
10. Right-click the user account for **Ronan Harris** and select **Add to a group** to open the **Select Group** dialog box. Click **Advanced.** Click **Find Now**. Select **IT-G** in the **Search results** pane.
11. Click **OK** to add the IT-G group to the **Enter the objects names to select** box.
12. Click **OK** to close the Select Group dialog box. A message box informs you that the Add to Group operation was successfully completed **(Figure 6-4)**. Click **OK** to close the message box.
13. Right-click **Ronan Harris** and select **Properties** to open the **Properties** dialog box for the user account. Open the **Member Of** tab. **IT-G** has been added to the list of groups in which **Ronan Harris** is a member. Click **OK** to close the Properties dialog box.
14. Repeat Steps 10 through 12 to add **Mark Jackson** to the **IT-G** group.

Figure 6-3 Viewing current members of the group

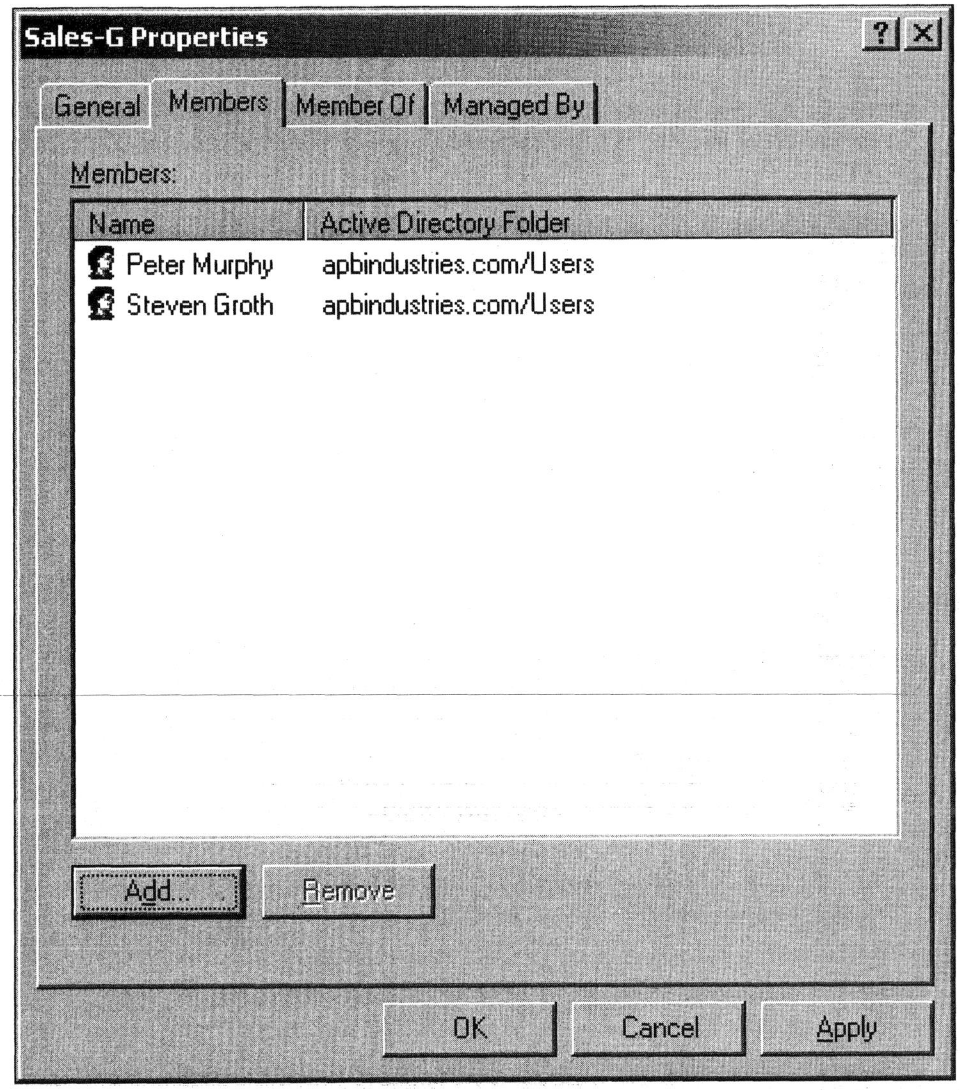

Figure 6-4 Viewing the groups that a user is currently a member of

project 6.3

Modifying Group Properties

exam objective

Basic knowledge

overview

Group properties can be modified in a number of ways and for a number of different reasons. For instance, you can change the scope of a group if necessary.

learning objective

After completing this project, you will know how to modify group properties, specifically, the group scope.

specific requirements

Administrative rights on SERVERA, the Window Server 2003 computer that is acting as a domain controller for apbindustries.com, and successful completion of Project 6.1.

estimated completion time

5 minutes

project steps

1. In the **Users** folder in the **Active Directory Users and Computers** console, right-click the **IT-G** group and click **Properties** to open the **Properties** dialog box for the group.
2. In the **Group scope** section on the **General** tab, notice that the group scope can be changed. Select the **Universal** option button **(Figure 6-5)**. Click **OK**.
3. Click the **IT-G** group in the **Users** folder. Press **[F2]**. Rename the group **IT-U**. Press **Enter** to open the **Rename Group** dialog box.
4. In the **Group name (pre-Windows 2000)** text box, change the group name to **IT-U** **(Figure 6-6)**. Click **OK**.
5. Close the **Active Directory Users and Computers** console.

tip

Group scopes and types can be changed only when Windows Server 2003 Active Directory operates in Windows 2000 native mode or in Windows Server 2003 mode. If your domain is in Windows 2000 mixed mode, you must first raise the functional level of the domain to Windows 2000 native mode or to Windows Server 2003 mode before you can change the group scope or type. Remember that this process is irreversible.

tip

In Step 3, changing the **G** to a **U** will make it easier to visually identify the group as Universal.

Figure 6-5 Changing the scope of a group

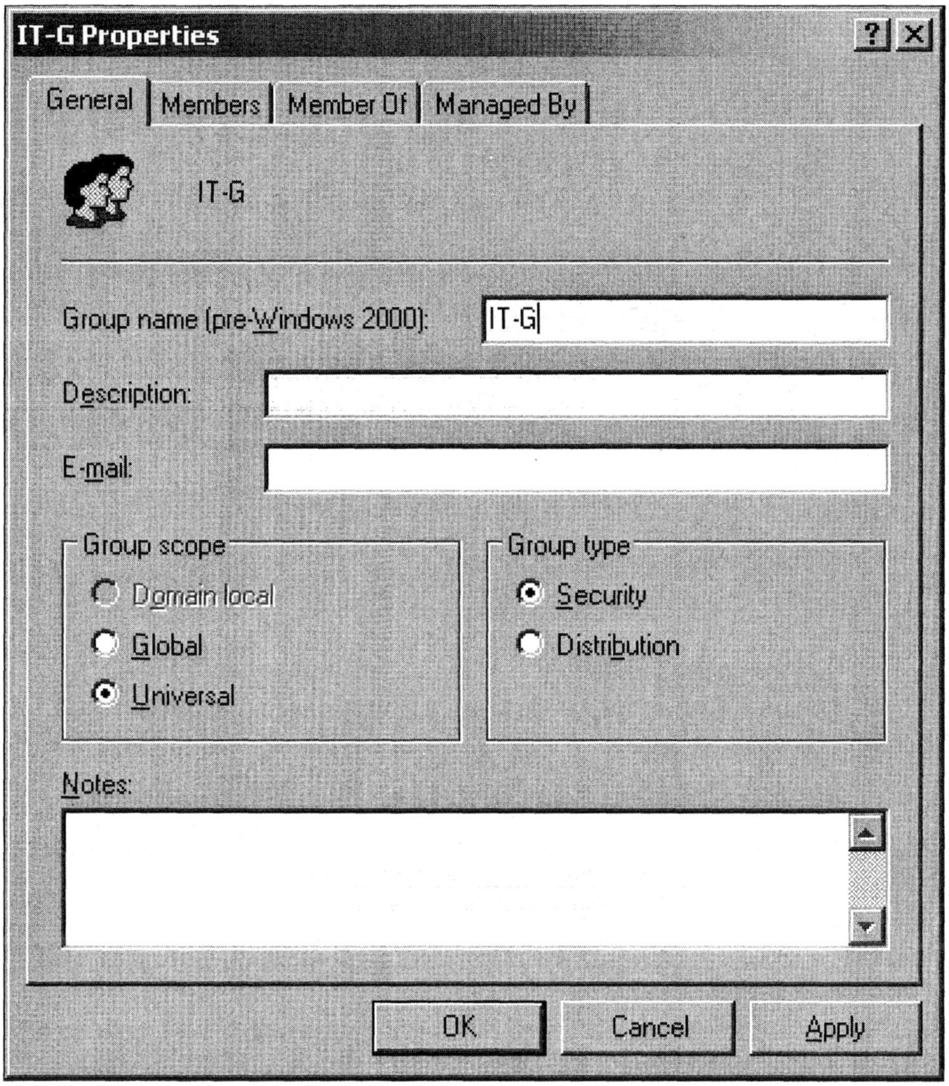

Figure 6-6 Renaming a group

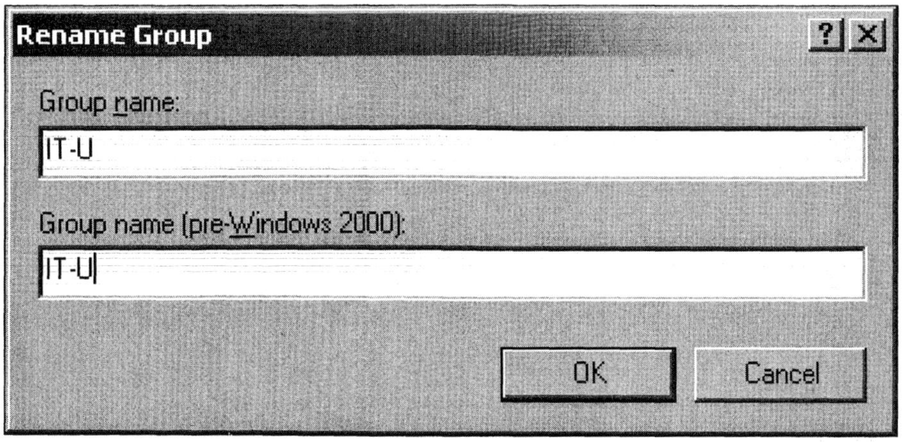

LESSON 7

Performing Active Directory Administrative Tasks

As a network grows, it typically becomes more and more difficult to locate objects. Active Directory uses the Lightweight Directory Access Protocol (LDAP) to perform object searches within the domain or throughout the forest. Occasionally, as the administrator, you may be required to control which users (or groups) are permitted access to certain objects. This can be accomplished by setting security permissions for Active Directory objects.

Especially in a large network, it can be difficult for users to find the resources (such as network shares or network printers) that they need. Active Directory allows you to create objects that represent resources in the Active Directory database. This makes it much easier for users to locate resources simply by doing a search of Active Directory. Another issue on large networks is the administrative load for performing routine tasks, such as creating new user accounts or changing a forgotten password. Active Directory allows administrators to delegate full or partial control over an area of Active Directory (typically an organizational unit) to specific users or groups. Using the Delegation of Control Wizard, the administrator can off-load routine tasks to a trusted individual, thereby freeing up time for more critical issues.

Scenario

As an administrator for the APB Industries network, it is your responsibility to perform certain basic administrative tasks. This includes searching for objects (users, printer, file shares, etc.) in Active Directory, setting access permissions for objects, advertising resources in Active Directory, moving objects, and delegating control over objects. This lesson will explore those tasks.

Lesson 7 Performing Active Directory Administrative Tasks

Project	Exam 70-294 Objective
7.1 Searching for Active Directory Objects on a Network	Basic knowledge
7.2 Publishing Resources in Active Directory	Basic knowledge
7.3 Setting Standard Active Directory Object Permissions	Implement an OU structure. Delegate permissions for an OU to a user or to a security group. Plan an administrative delegation strategy.
7.4 Moving Active Directory Objects Within a Domain	Implement an OU structure. Move objects within an OU hierarchy.
7.5 Delegating Active Directory Permissions	Implement an OU structure. Delegate permissions for an OU to a user or security group. Plan an administration delegation strategy. Plan an OU structure based on delegation requirements.

General Requirements

To complete the projects in this lesson, you will need administrative rights on SERVERA, the Windows Server 2003 computer that is acting as a domain controller for the apbindustries.com domain, as well as the successful completion of the projects in Lessons 5 and 6. You may also find it helpful to refer to Lesson 7 in your Prentice Hall Certification Series Exam 70-294 textbook for further information about the topics covered by the projects in this lesson.

project 7.1

Searching for Active Directory Objects on a Network

exam objective

Basic knowledge

overview

Especially in a larger network environment, it can be difficult to locate an object such as a user account or computer. Active Directory uses the Lightweight Directory Access Protocol (LDAP) to perform searches on the Active Directory database to find objects.

learning objective

After completing this project, you will know how to search for objects in Active Directory.

specific requirements

Administrative rights on SERVERA, the Windows Server 2003 computer that is acting as a domain controller for apbindustries.com.

estimated completion time

10 minutes

project steps

1. Log on to **SERVERA** with an account that has administrative rights.
2. Open the **Active Directory Users and Computers** console.
3. Right-click **apbindustries.com** and select **Find**. The **Find Users, Contacts, and Groups** dialog box opens.
4. In the **Name** text box, type **peter**. Click **Find Now**. After searching, one object should be returned, a user named **Peter Murphy (Figure 7-1)**.
5. In the **Find** list box, select **Computers**. Click **OK** to clear the current search results.
6. In the **In** list box, select **rnd** to choose the child domain **rnd.apbindustries.com**.
7. In the **Computer name** text box, type **SERVERB**.
8. In the **Role** list box, select **Workstations and Servers**. Click **Find Now**. Notice that no results are returned **(Figure 7-2)**.
9. In the **Role** list box, select **Domain Controller** and click **Find Now**. Notice that the **SERVERB** object appears in the **Search results** pane **(Figure 7-3)**.
10. Close the **Find Computers** dialog box.

Figure 7-1 Search attributes for a user in the local domain

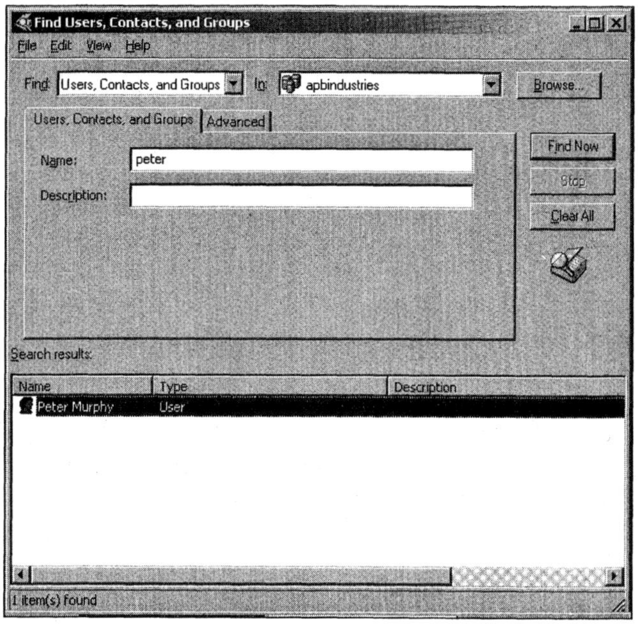

Figure 7-2 Search attributes for a computer in a child domain

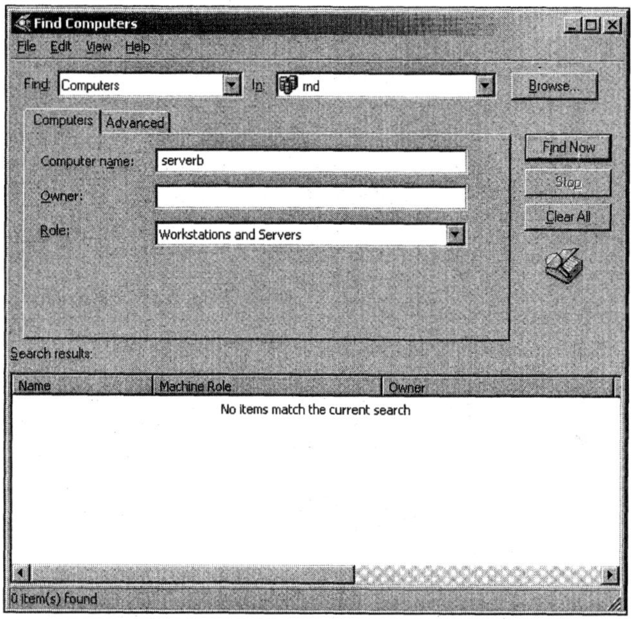

Figure 7-3 Search attributes for a computer in a child domain

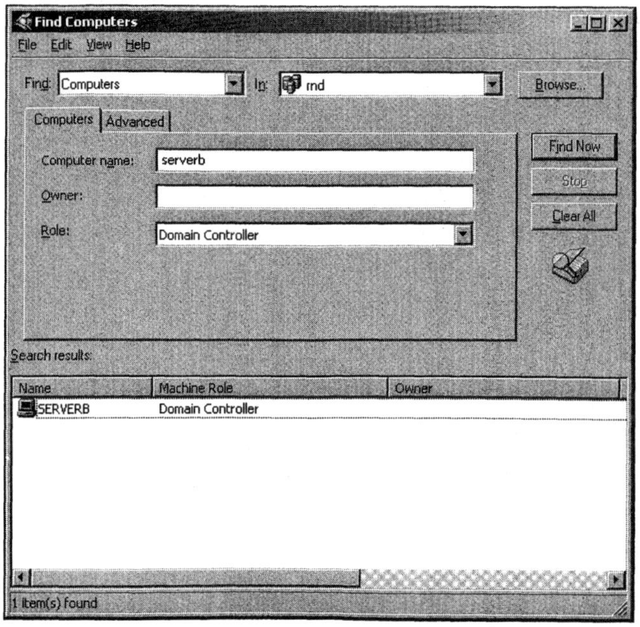

project 7.2

Publishing Resources in Active Directory

exam objective

Basic knowledge

overview

The new president of APB Industries, Robert Smith, needs a shared folder on the network that only he will be permitted to access. Additionally, he wants it published in Active Directory, so that it is easy for him to find when he is traveling between offices.

learning objective

After completing this project, you will know how to publish resources in Active Directory.

specific requirements

Administrative rights on SERVERA, the Windows Server 2003 computer that is acting as a domain controller for apbindustries.com and successful completion of Lesson 5.

estimated completion time

15 minutes

project steps

1. In the **Active Directory Users and Computers** console, create a new user in the **Users** container named **Robert Smith**, with the user logon name **RSmith** and the password, **password**.
2. In **Windows Explorer**, create a folder on the **C:** drive called **President** and share it as **private**.
3. In the **Active Directory Users and Computers** console, right-click the **HR OU**, point to **New**, and click **Shared Folder** to open the **New Object—Shared Folder** dialog box.
4. In the **Name** text box, type **PresidentPrivate**. In the **Network path** text box, type **\\SERVERA\PRIVATE (Figure 7-4)**. Click **OK** to publish the **\\SERVERA\PRIVATE** share in Active Directory so that it can be searched for there.
5. In the **Active Directory Users and Computers** console, open the **View** menu and select **Advanced Features**.
6. In the **HR OU**, right-click the **PresidentPrivate** object and click **Properties**. Click the **Security** tab. Remove the **Authenticated Users** access control entry from the access control list.
7. Click **Add**. Click **Advanced**. Click **Find Now**. Double-click **Robert Smith** to add the user account to the **Enter the object names to select** box. Click **OK** to close the Select Users, Computers, or Groups dialog box.
8. Select **Robert Smith** in the access control list. Click the **Allow** check box for the **Full Control** permission to give Robert Smith full control over the published folder **(Figure 7-5)**.
9. Click **OK** to close the PresidentPrivate Properties dialog box.
10. Close the Active Directory Users and Computers console.

Figure 7-4 Publishing a shared folder in Active Directory

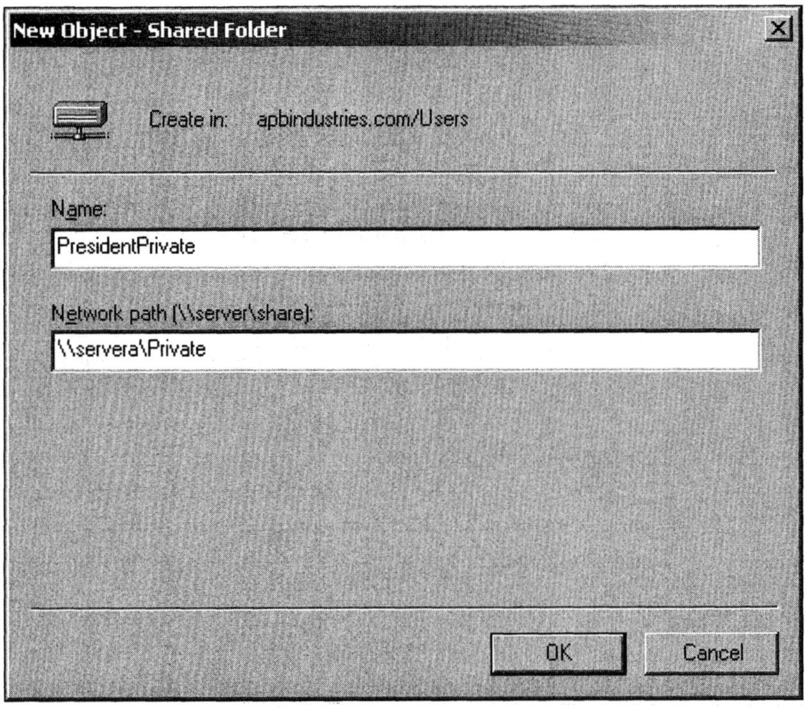

Figure 7-5 Assigning full control permissions over an Active Directory object to a user

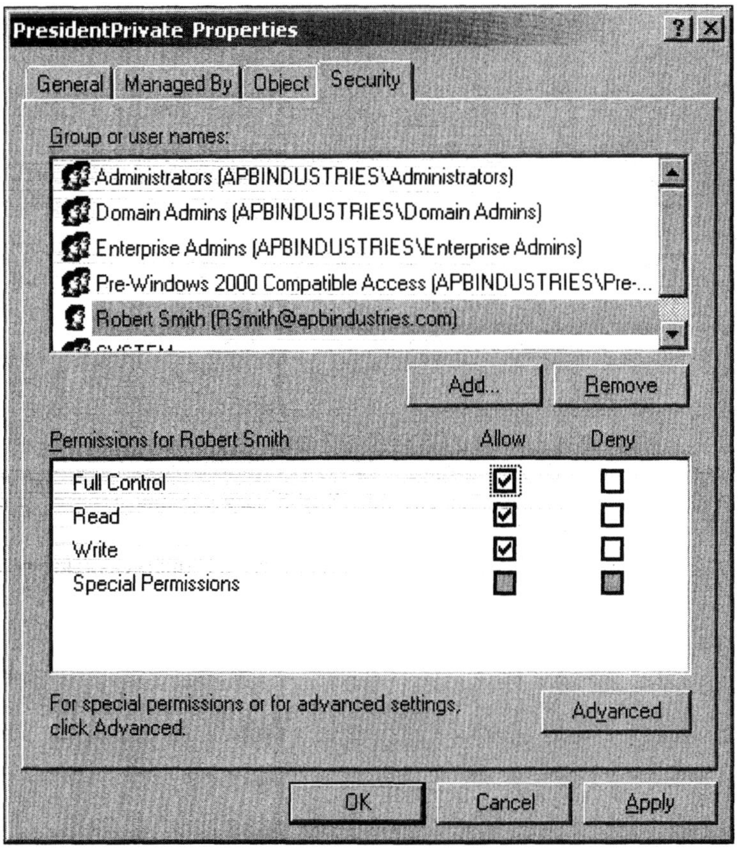

project 7.2

Publishing Resources in Active Directory *(cont'd)*

exam objective

Basic knowledge

project steps

11. Click **Start**, point to **Administrative Tools**, and click **Group Policy Management** to open the **Group Policy Management** console.
12. Expand the **apbindustries.com** node. Expand the **Domain Controllers** OU.
13. Right-click **Default Domain Controllers Policy** and click **Edit** to open the **Group Policy Object Editor** for the policy.
14. Expand the **Computer Configuration** node, if necessary. Expand **Windows Settings**, **Security Settings**, and **Local Policies**.
15. Select **User Rights Assignment** to display the User Rights assignment policies in the details pane.
16. Double-click **Allow logon locally** to open the **Allow logon locally Properties** dialog box.
17. Click the **Add User or Group** button to open the **Add User or Group** dialog box.
18. Type **RSmith** in the **User and group names** text box. Click **OK** to close the Add User or Group dialog box. Click **OK** to close the Allow logon locally Properties dialog box.
19. Close the Group Policy Object Editor and the GPMC. Log off.
20. Log on as **PMurphy**, using the password you set for this account in Project 5.1.
21. Click **Start** and then click **Run**. In the **Open** text box, type **mmc** and press **[Enter]** to open an mmc console.
22. Open the **File** menu and click **Add/Remove Snap-in** to open the **Add/Remove Snap-in** dialog box.
23. Click the **Add** button to open the **Add Standalone Snap-in** dialog box. Select **Active Directory Users and Computers**. Click **Add**. Click **Close**. Click **OK** to close the Add/Remove Snap-in dialog box.
24. Expand **Active Directory Users and Computers**. Expand **apbindustries.com**. Select the **HR** OU.
25. Double-click **PresidentPrivate**. The Active Directory object cannot be displayed because the PMurphy user account does not have access to the published folder **(Figure 7-6)**.
26. Click **OK** to close the PresidentPrivate Properties dialog box. Close the mmc console. Do not save the console settings when prompted. Log off.
27. Log on as **RSmith**. Click **Start** and then click **Run**. In the **Open** text box, type **mmc** and press **[Enter]**.
28. Open the **File** menu and click **Add/Remove Snap-in**. Click **Add** to open the **Add Standalone Snap-in** dialog box.
29. Select **Active Directory Users and Computers**. Click **Add**. Click **Close**.
30. Click **OK** to close the Add/Remove Snap-in dialog box.
31. Expand **Active Directory Users and Computers**. Expand **apbindustries.com**. Select the **HR** OU. Double-click **PresidentPrivate**. This time you can view the **Properties** dialog box because the RSmith user account has full control access to the published folder **(Figure 7-7)**.
32. Click OK to close the PresidentPrivate Properties dialog box. Close the mmc console. Do not save the console settings when prompted. Log off.

tip

The permissions that were set in step 7 only apply to the object in Active Directory that represents the file share. If a user knows the exact UNC path to the share, they can access files located in that share. In order to prevent this from happening, share-level and/or file-level NTFS permissions must be implemented.

Figure 7-6 Search results from a user that does not have access permissions to the object being searched for

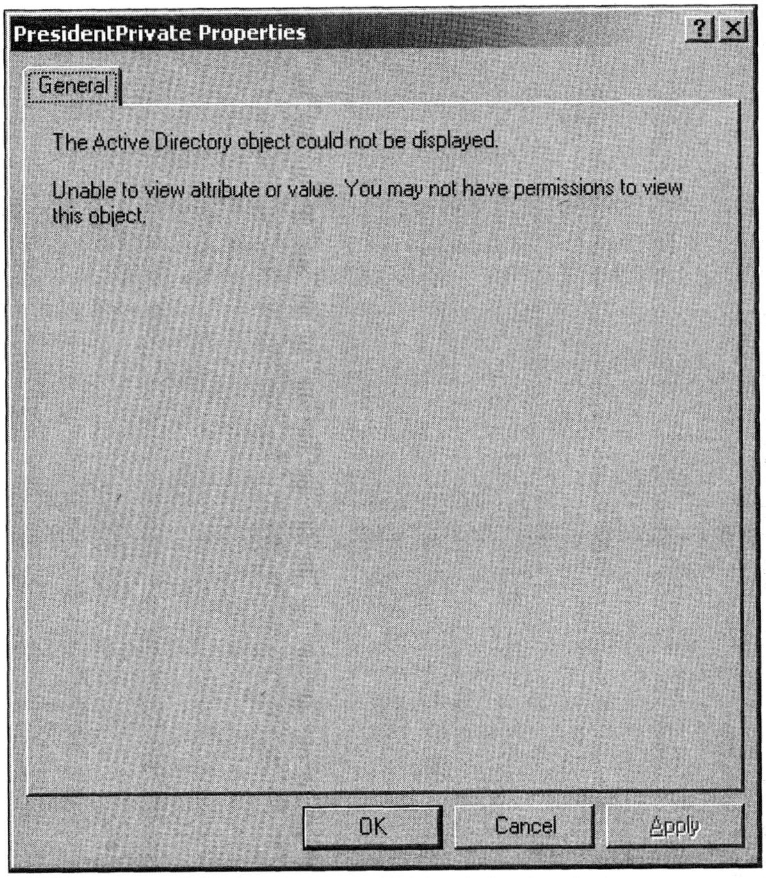

Figure 7-7 Search results from a user that has access permissions to the object being searched for

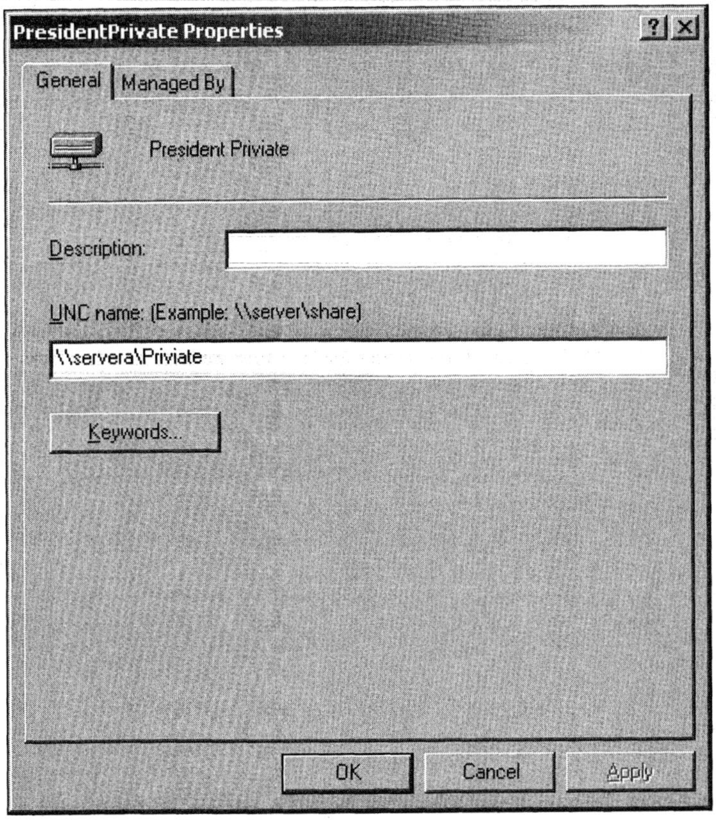

project 7.3

Setting Standard Active Directory Object Permissions

exam objective

Implement an OU structure. Delegate permissions for an OU to a user or to a security group. Plan an administrative delegation strategy.

overview

Every Active Directory object has a security descriptor associated with it that contains an access control entry for every user or group that has been allowed or denied a certain type of access to that object. A user's effective permissions are a combination of permissions assigned to that user and to any groups in which the user is a member. However, deny permissions take precedence over all other permissions assigned.

learning objective

After completing this project, you will know how to set standard permissions for Active Directory objects.

specific requirements

Administrative rights on SERVERA, the Windows Server 2003 computer that is acting as a domain controller for apbindustries.com and successful completion of Lesson 5.

estimated completion time

15 minutes

project steps

1. Log on to **SERVERA** with a user account that has administrative rights. Open the **Active Directory Users and Computers** console. In the **Users** container, right-click **Robert Smith** and click **Properties**. Open the **Security** tab. Click **Add**. Click **Advanced**. Click **Find Now**.
2. Double-click **IT-U** in the **Search results** list and click **OK** to close the Select Users, Computers, or Groups dialog box. In the **Permissions for IT-U** box, scroll down and select the **Allow** check box for the **Reset Password** permission **(Figure 7-8)**. Click **OK** so any member of the IT-U group can reset the password for the Robert Smith user object. Close the Active Directory Users and Computers console. Log off.
3. Log on as **PMurphy** using the password that you set for this account in Project 5.1.
4. Click **Start**; click **Run**. In the **Open** text box, type **mmc.** Press **[Enter]**. Open the **File** menu and click **Add/Remove Snap-in**. Click **Add**.
5. In the Add Standalone Snap-in dialog box, select **Active Directory Users and Computers**. Click **Add**. Click **Close**. Click **OK** to close the dialog box. Expand **Active Directory Users and Computers**. Expand **apbindustries.com**. Select **Users**.
6. Right-click **Robert Smith** and select **Reset Password** to open the **Reset Password** dialog box. In the **New password** and **Confirm password** text boxes, type **Rachel1293**. Click **OK**.
7. An **Active Directory** dialog box informs you that the password change cannot be completed because access is denied **(Figure 7-9)**. This is because PMurphy does not have permission to reset the password for Robert Smith.
8. Click **OK**. Close the mmc console. Do not save the changes when prompted. Log off.
9. Log on as **MJackson** using the password that you set for this account in Project 5.1.
10. Click **Start** and then click **Run**. In the **Open** text box, type **mmc** and press **[Enter]**. Open the **File** menu and click **Add/Remove Snap-in**. Click **Add** to open the **Add Standalone Snap-in** dialog box.
11. Select **Active Directory Users and Computers**. Click **Add**. Click **Close**. Click **OK** to close the Add/Remove Snap-in dialog box. Expand **Active Directory Users and Computers**. Expand **apbindustries.com**. Select **Users**.
12. Right-click **Robert Smith** and select **Reset Password** to open the **Reset Password** dialog box. In the **New password** and **Confirm password** text boxes, type **Rachel1293**. Click **OK**.
13. An **Active Directory** dialog box informs you that the password has been successfully changed **(Figure 7-10)**. This is because MJackson has permission, as a member of the IT-U group, to reset the password for the Robert Smith user object. Click **OK**. Log off. Do not save the console settings when prompted.

tip

To view the **Security** tab of the **Properties** dialog box for an object, you must ensure that the **Advanced Features** option is enabled in the **View** menu in the **Active Directory Users and Computers** console.

Figure 7-8 Setting permissions for an Active Directory user object

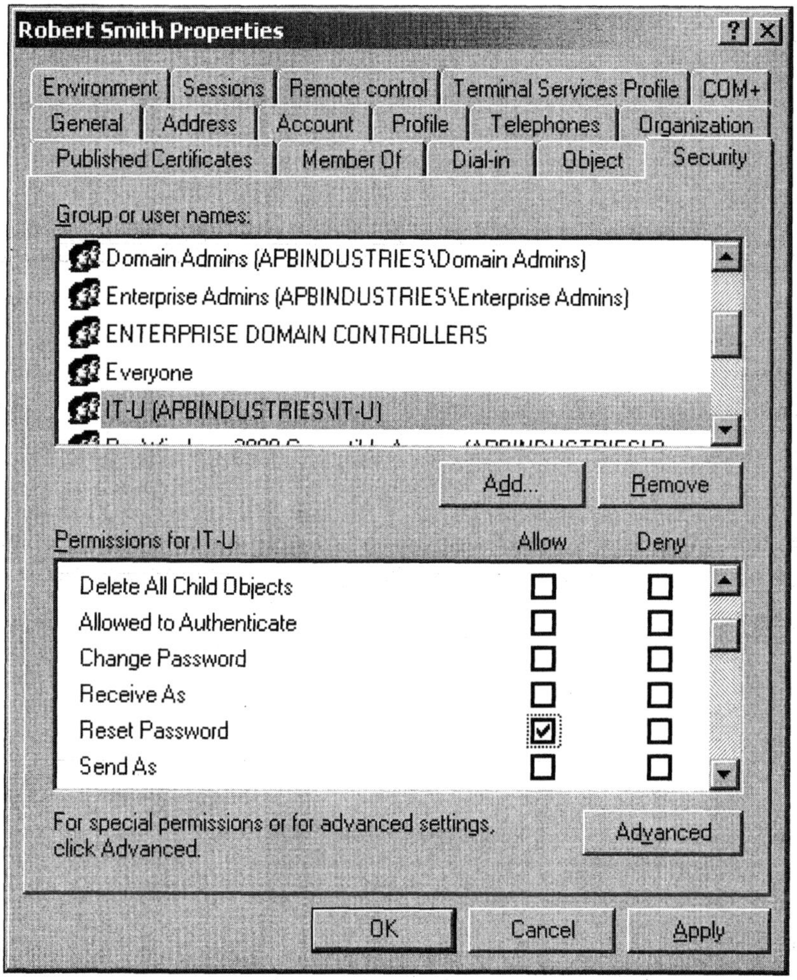

Figure 7-9 Error message informing you that the user's password cannot be changed

Figure 7-10 Message confirming that the users password has been successfully changed

project 7.4

Moving Active Directory Objects Within a Domain

exam objective

Implement an OU structure. Move objects within an OU hierarchy.

overview

Occasionally, organizational or other changes within your company may require you to move Active Directory objects to different containers. When an object is moved, permissions that have been inherited from its parent container are lost, and are replaced with the permissions from the new parent container. However, permissions that were explicitly assigned to that object are retained.

learning objective

After completing this project, you will know how to move objects within Active Directory.

specific requirements

Administrative rights on SERVERA, the Windows Server 2003 computer that is acting as a domain controller for apbindustries.com, and successful completion of Project 2.6 and the projects in Lessons 5 and 6.

estimated completion time

10 minutes

project steps

1. Log on to **SERVERA** with a user account that has administrative rights. Open the **Active Directory Users and Computers** console.
2. Right-click **apbindustries.com**, point to **New**, and click **Organizational Unit** to open the **New Object – Organizational Unit** dialog box.
3. In the **Name** text box, type **IT** (**Figure 7-11**). Click **OK**.
4. Create another OU in apbindustries.com named **Exec**.
5. In the **Users** container, right-click **Daniel Ash**, and click **Move** to open the **Move** dialog box. Select the **Sales** OU (**Figure 7-12**).
6. Click **OK** to close the Move dialog box.
7. Repeat the procedure to move **David Jay** and **Kevin Haskins** to the **Sales** organizational unit that you created in Project 2.6.
8. Move **Steven Groth** and **Peter Murphy** to the **HR** organizational unit that you created in Project 2.6.
9. Click and drag **Ronan Harris** and **Mark Jackson** to the **IT** organizational unit.
10. Click and drag **Robert Smith** to the **Exec** organizational unit.
11. Select the **HR** OU in the console tree. Move the **PresidentPrivate** shared folder to the **Exec** OU.
12. Move the **Sales-G**, **HR-G**, and **IT-U** groups to their corresponding organizational units.
13. Select the **Exec** organizational unit in the console tree to view the two newly moved objects (**Figure 7-13**).

Figure 7-11 Creating a new organizational unit

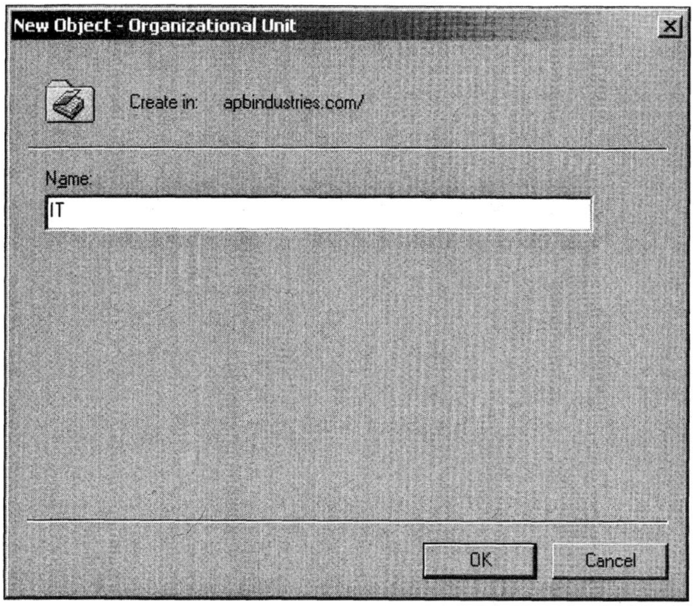

Figure 7-12 Selecting a new location for an object

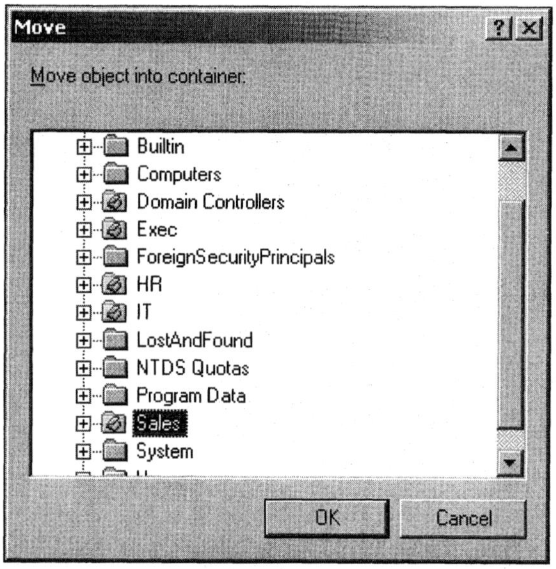

Figure 7-13 Viewing the newly moved objects

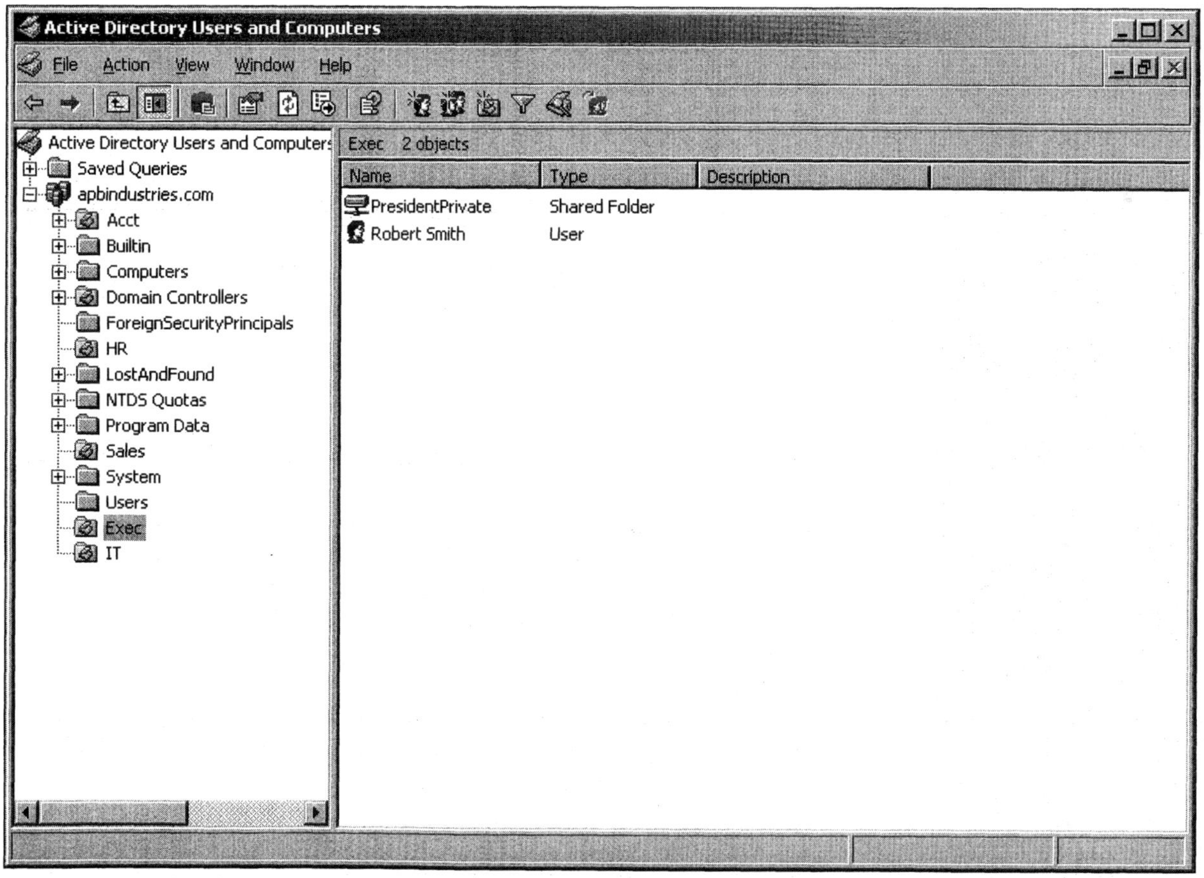

project 7.5

Delegating Active Directory Permissions

exam objective

Implement an OU structure. Delegate permissions for an OU to a user or security group. Plan an administration delegation strategy. Plan an OU structure based on delegation requirements.

overview

Active Directory allows administrators to delegate certain administrative tasks to other individuals. This lets administrators off-load routine or time-consuming tasks, such as resetting passwords, to free up their time for other critical administrative tasks. The Active Directory Users and Computers console includes a Delegation of Control Wizard to assist in assigning certain tasks to non-administrators.

learning objective

After completing this project, you will know how to delegate administrative control for objects in Active Directory.

specific requirements

Administrative rights on SERVERA, the Windows Server 2003 computer that is acting as a domain controller for apbindustries.com.

estimated completion time

10 minutes

project steps

1. Right-click the **HR** organizational unit and click **Delegate Control** to start the **Delegation of Control Wizard**.
2. Click **Next** to open the **Users or Groups** screen. Click **Add** to open the **Select Users, Computers, or Groups** dialog box.
3. Click **Advanced**. Click **Find Now**. Double-click **Peter Murphy** in the **Search results** list. Click **OK** to close the Select Users, Computers, or Groups dialog box and to add Peter Murphy to the **Selected users and groups** box.
4. Click **Next** to open the **Tasks to Delegate** screen. In the **Delegate the following common tasks** box, select the **Create, delete, and manage user accounts** and **Reset user passwords and force password change at next logon** check boxes **(Figure 7-14)**.
5. Click **Next** to open the **Completing the Delegation of Control Wizard** screen. Click **Finish**.
6. Close the Active Directory Users and Computers console. Log off.
7. Log on as **PMurphy** using the password that you set for this account in Project 5.1.
8. Click **Start** and then click **Run**. In the **Open** text box, type **mmc** and press **[Enter]**.
9. Open the **File** menu and click **Add/Remove Snap-in**. Click **Add** to open the **Add Standalone Snap-in** dialog box.
10. Select **Active Directory Users and Computers**. Click **Add**. Click **Close**.
11. Click **OK** to close the **Add/Remove Snap-in** dialog box.
12. Open the **File** menu and click **Save As** to open the **Save As** dialog box. In the **File name** list box, type **AD Users and Computers**. In the **Save in** list box, select **Desktop** **(Figure 7-15)**.
13. Click **Save** to save the mmc console.
14. Expand **Active Directory Users and Computers**. Expand **apbindustries.com**. Right-click the **HR** OU and point to **New**. Notice that there are only two options: **Printer** and **User**. The **Printer** option is there because Peter Murphy is a member of the Print Operators group. The **User** option is there because of the permissions granted in step 3.
15. Right-click the **Sales** organizational unit and point to **New**. Notice that there is only one option, **Printer (Figure 7-16)**. The User option is not present because control was not delegated to **Peter Murphy** for the **Sales** OU.
16. Close the AD Users and Computers console. Save the changes when prompted. Log off.

Figure 7-14 Selecting the tasks to be delegated

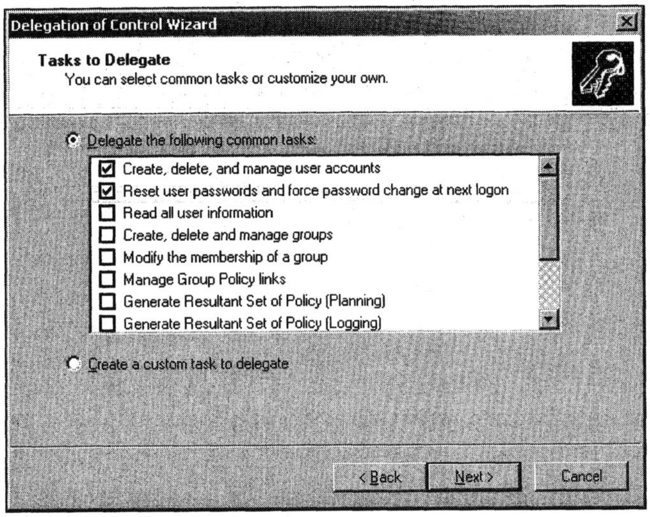

Figure 7-15 Saving an mmc console

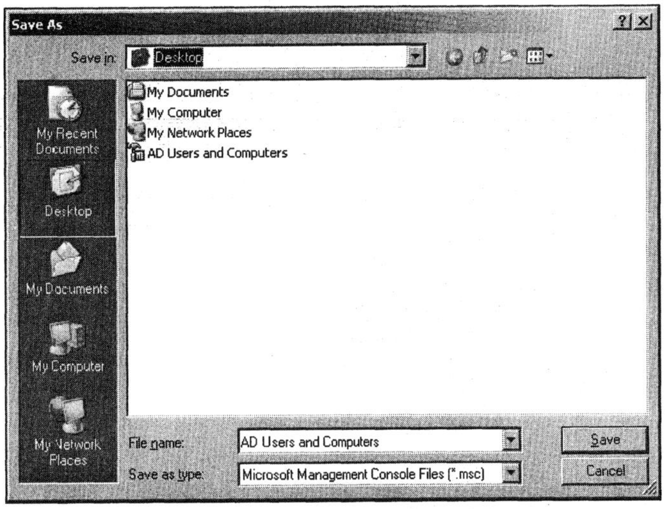

Figure 7-16 Comparing an organizational unit that has not had control delegated over it to the current user

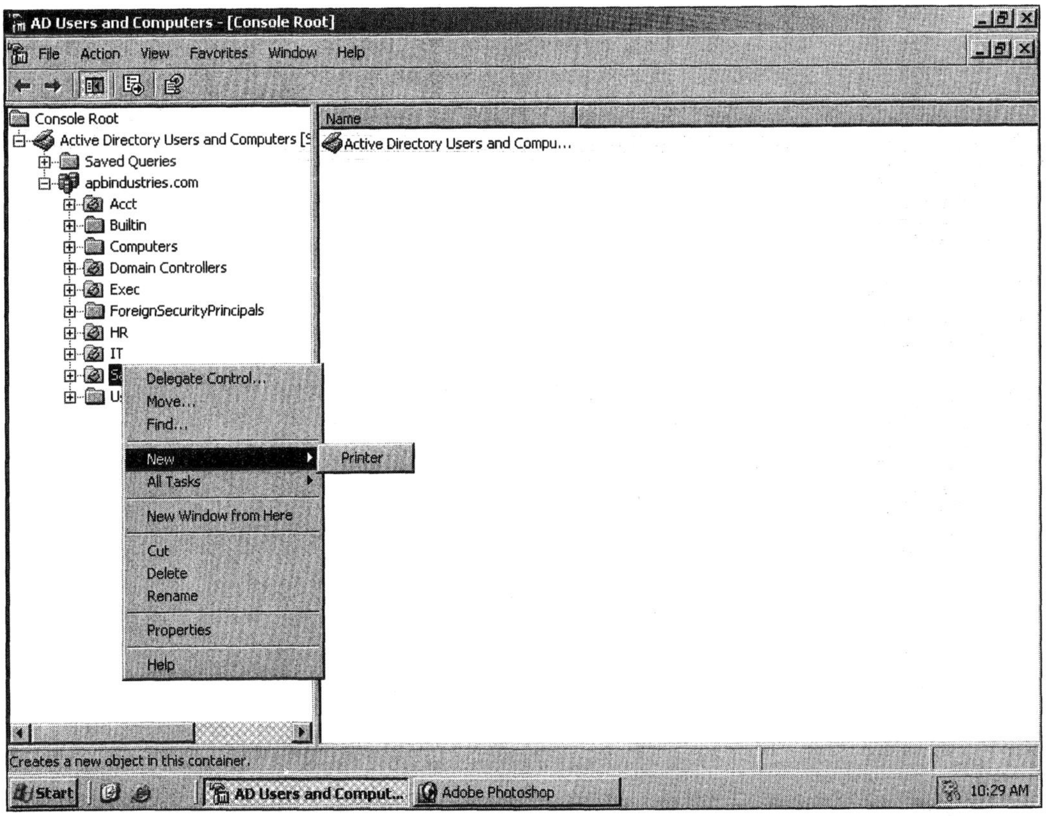

LESSON 8

Backing Up and Restoring Active Directory

Active Directory is the backbone of a Windows Server 2003-based network. It is a service that helps in locating and accessing network objects. Active Directory relies on a series of database and log files in order to function properly. If, for some reason, these files become corrupt, Active Directory will not function. Catastrophic hardware failure can also cause Active Directory failure. In this case, a recent backup of the Active Directory database is required in order to restore Active Directory to its previously functioning state.

Windows Server 2003 includes a backup tool that provides a user friendly way to back up Active Directory. A critical feature of this backup utility is that it allows for the regular scheduling of backup tasks, which enables the administrative team to set the schedule and not have to worry about manually performing a backup on a daily basis. If an Active Directory backup is performed daily, this ensures that a recent backup is available in the event of a serious failure.

The Active Directory database can be restored in two ways: non-authoritative and authoritative. A non-authoritative restore is a simple restore of Active Directory that will restore the entire database. An authoritative restore is used to overwrite a change that has been made to an object or to restore a deleted object.

Scenario

In order to make recovery possible, it is critical to have a regular backup schedule. Additionally, it is very important to test the restore process to ensure that all the correct steps are taken in order get Active Directory up and functioning as quickly as possible. This lesson deals with backing up Active Directory and testing the restore procedure.

Lesson 8 Backing Up and Restoring Active Directory	
Project	**Exam 70-294 Objective**
8.1 Using the Backup Tool to Back Up Active Directory	Troubleshoot Active Directory. Diagnose and resolve issues related to the Active Directory database.
8.2 Scheduling Active Directory Backups	Troubleshoot Active Directory. Diagnose and resolve issues related to the Active Directory database.
8.3 Executing a Non-authoritative Restore	Restore Active Directory directory services. Perform a non-authoritative restore of Active Directory. Recover from a system failure.
8.4 Executing an Authoritative Restore	Restore Active Directory directory services. Perform an authoritative restore of Active Directory.

General Requirements

To complete the projects in this lesson, you will need administrative rights on SERVERA, the Windows Server 2003 computer that is acting as a domain controller for the apbindustries.com domain, as well as administrative rights on SERVERB, the Windows Server 2003 computer that is acting as a domain controller for the rnd.apbindustries.com domain. You also will need to create a folder on SERVERB named AD_backup and share it as AD_backup. You may also find it helpful to refer to Lesson 8 in your Prentice Hall Certification Series Exam 70-294 textbook for further information about the topics covered by the projects in this lesson.

project 8.1

Using the Backup Tool to Back Up Active Directory

exam objective

Troubleshoot Active Directory. Diagnose and resolve issues related to the Active Directory database.

overview

In order to back up the Active Directory database using the Windows Server 2003 Backup tool, you must be a member of the Administrators or Backup Operators group. To back up Active Directory, you must back up the System State of a domain controller. In addition to the Active Directory database and the SYSVOL folder, the System State includes the Registry, COM+ Class Registration database, and Boot files.

learning objective

After completing this project, you will know how to manually backup the Active Directory database.

specific requirements

Administrative rights on SERVERA, the Windows Server 2003 computer that is acting as a domain controller for apbindustries.com and SERVERB, the Windows Server 2003 computer that is acting as a domain controller for the rnd.apbindustries.com domain.

estimated completion time

15 minutes

project steps

tip

You cannot backup individual components of the System State. You must back up the entire System State.

1. Log on to **SERVERB** with a user account that has administrative rights.
2. Open **Windows Explorer**. Select **Local Disk (C:)**. Open the **File** menu, point to **New**, and click **Folder**. Type **AD_Backup**. Press **Enter**.
3. Right-click **AD_Backup** and select **Sharing and Security** to open the **AD_Backup Properties** dialog box.
4. Click **Share this folder**. Click the **Permissions** button to open the **Permissions for AD_Backup** dialog box. Assign the **Full Control** share permission to the **Everyone** group.
5. Click **OK** to close the Permissions for AD_Backup dialog box. Click **OK** to close the AD_Backup Properties dialog box. Close Windows Explorer.
6. Log on to **SERVERA** with a user account that has administrative rights.
7. Click **Start** and then click **Run**. In the **Open** text box, type **cmd**. Click **OK**. Type **net use m: \\SERVERB\AD_Backup**. Press **[Enter]**. A message indicating that the command has completed successfully should appear. **\\SERVERB\AD_Backup** is now mapped to the **M:** drive. Close the command prompt.
8. Click **Start**, point to **All Programs**, point to **Accessories**, point to **System Tools**, and click **Backup** to open the **Backup or Restore Wizard**.
9. Click **Next** to open the **Backup or Restore** screen. Make sure that the **Back up files and settings** option is selected. Click **Next** to open the **What to Back Up** screen. Select **Let me choose what to back up**. Click **Next** to open the **Items to Back Up** screen. Expand **My Computer**. Put a check in the **System State** check box.
10. Click **Next** to open the **Backup Type, Destination, and Name** screen. Click **Browse** to open the **Save As** dialog box. In the **Save in** list box, select **AD_Backup on 'Serverb' (M:)**. In the **File name** list box, accept the default, **Backup.bkf (Figure 8-1)**. Click **Save**.
11. The backup destination is entered in the **Choose a place to save your backup** list box and the backup name is entered in the **Type a name for this backup text box (Figure 8-2)**.
12. Click **Next** to open the **Completing the Backup or Restore** screen. Click **Finish**.
13. The **Backup Progress** dialog box opens, summarizing details about the backup job **(Figure 8-3)**. After the backup is complete, click **Close**. You have successfully backed up the System State of SERVERA, including the Active Directory database.

Figure 8-1 Manually backing up the System State

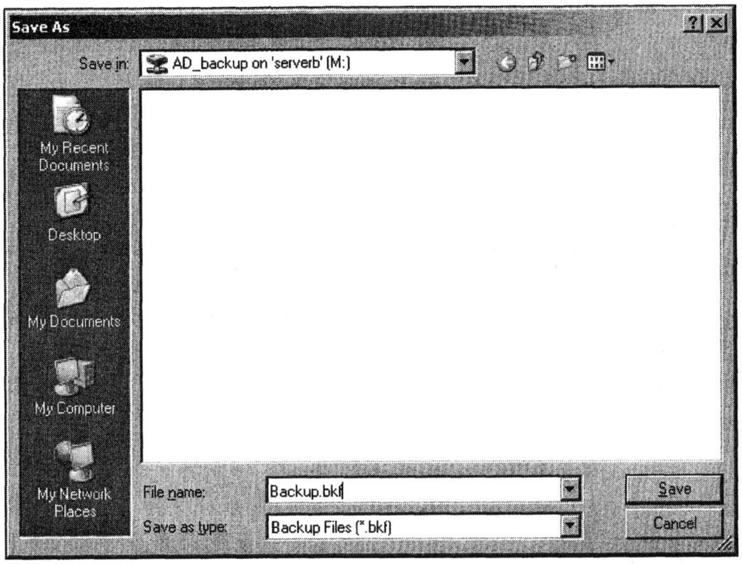

Figure 8-2 Selecting a description for the backup job

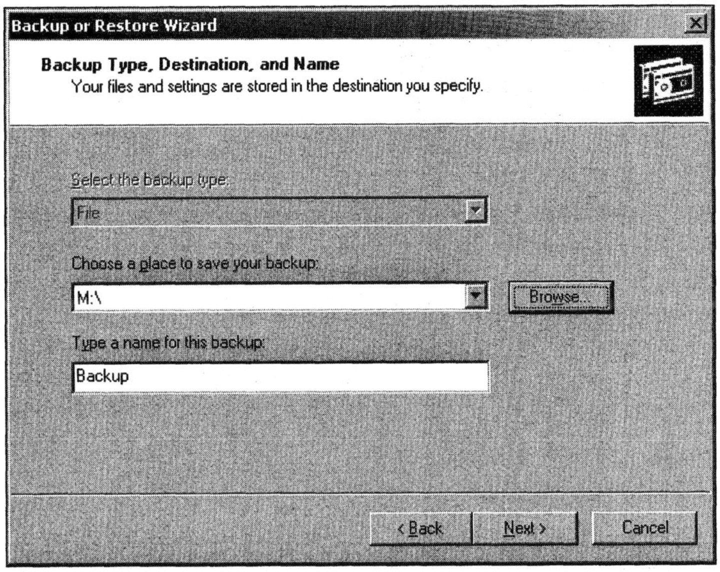

Figure 8-3 Backup Progress dialog box

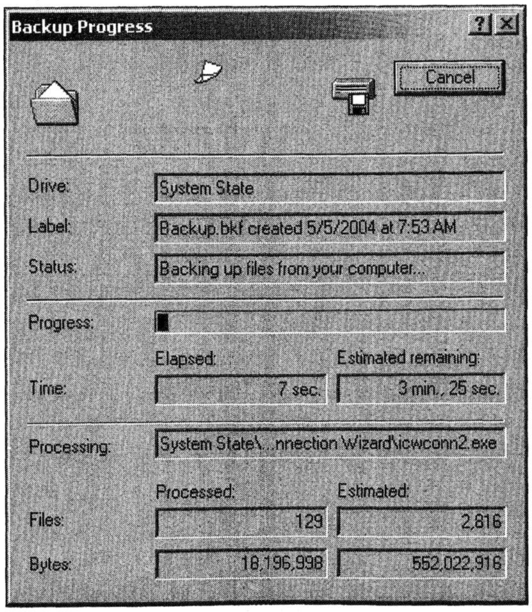

project 8.2

Scheduling Active Directory Backups

exam objective

Troubleshoot Active Directory. Diagnose and resolve issues related to the Active Directory database.

overview

Manually backing up data on a regular basis can be tedious. It is also very easy to forget to perform a regular backup. Fortunately, the Backup tool that is included with Windows Server 2003 allows an administrator to schedule backups to be run at specific times. This allows the administrator to set the backup and not have to worry about manually starting each one.

learning objective

After completing this project, you will know how to schedule a backup job.

specific requirements

Administrative rights on SERVERA, the Windows Server 2003 computer that is acting as a domain controller for apbindustries.com.

estimated completion time

10 minutes

project steps

1. Click **Start**, point to **All Programs**, point to **Accessories**, point to **System Tools**, and click **Backup** to open the **Backup or Restore Wizard**.
2. Click **Next** to open the **Backup or Restore** screen. Make sure that the **Backup files and settings** option is selected.
3. Click **Next** to open the **What to Back Up** screen. Select **Let me choose what to back up**.
4. Click **Next** to open the **Items to Back Up** screen. Expand **My Computer**. Put a check in the **System State** check box.
5. Click **Next** to open the **Backup Type, Destination, and Name** screen. Click **Browse** to open the **Save As** dialog box. In the **Save in** list box, select **AD_Backup on 'Serverb' (M:)**. Click **Save**.
6. Click **Next** to open the **Completing the Backup or Restore Wizard** screen.
7. Click the **Advanced** button to open the **Type of Backup** screen. In the **Select the type of backup** list box, select **Daily**.
8. Click **Next** to open the **How to Back Up** screen. Select the **Verify data after backup** check box to make sure that data is checked for consistency after the backup operation.
9. Click **Next** to open the **Backup Options** screen. Select the **Append this backup to the existing backups** option button, if necessary.
10. Click **Next** to open the **When to Back Up** screen. Select the **Later** option button. In the **Job name** text box, type **Daily System State**.
11. Click the **Set Schedule** button to open the **Schedule Job** dialog box. In the **Schedule Task** spin box, select **Daily**. In the **Start time** spin box, enter **12:01 AM (Figure 8-6)**. Click **OK** to close the Schedule Job dialog box.
12. The **Set Account Information** dialog box opens. Enter and confirm the password for the **Administrator** account. Click **OK**.
13. Click **Next** to open the **Completing the Backup or Restore Wizard** screen. If the **Set Account Information** dialog box reopens, enter and confirm the password again. Click **OK**.
14. Click **Finish**. A backup of the System State has now been scheduled to run every day at 12:01 AM.

tip

ALWAYS remember your backups. Even if a schedule is set, you must monitor backup logs and perform test restores to ensure that your backups are functioning correctly.

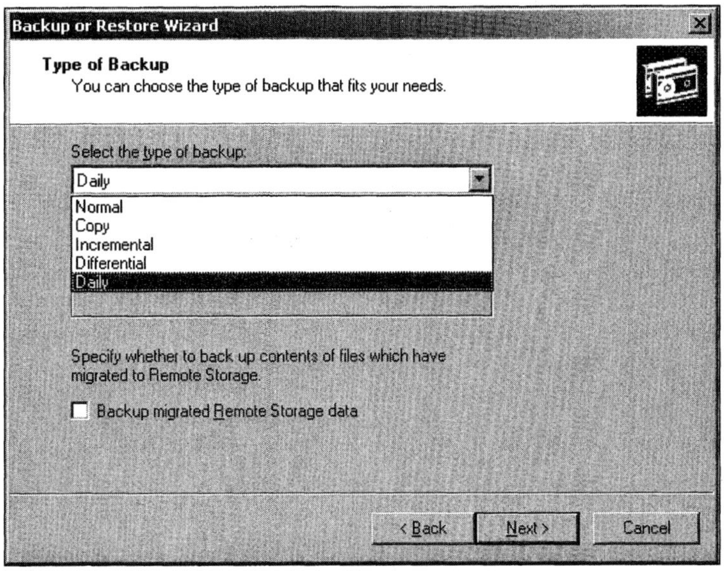

Figure 8-4 Choosing to backup the System State data

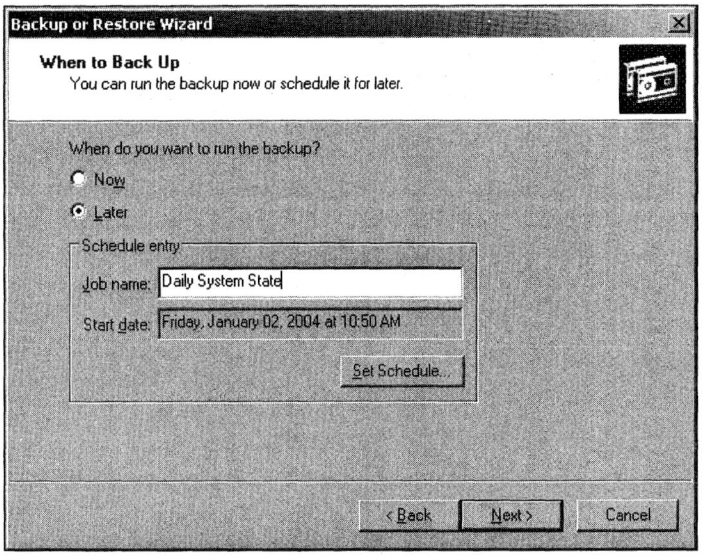

Figure 8-5 Selecting when and how often the backup job will execute

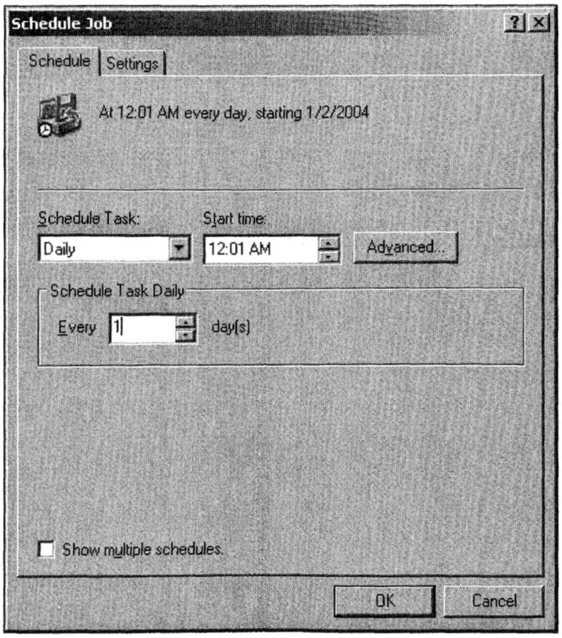

Figure 8-6 Viewing the scheduled jobs on the calendar

project 8.3

Executing a Non-authoritative Restore

exam objective

Restore Active Directory directory services. Perform a non-authoritative restore of Active Directory. Recover from a system failure.

overview

A non-authoritative restore is a full Active Directory database restore. This type of restore would be used to recover from a failure of a domain controller that was the only domain controller in the domain.

learning objective

After completing this project, you will know how to perform a non-authoritative restore.

specific requirements

Administrative rights on SERVERA, the Windows Server 2003 computer that is acting as a domain controller for apbindustries.com.

estimated completion time

20 minutes

project steps

1. Open the **Active Directory Users and Computers** console and delete the **Peter Murphy** user account. Close the console.
2. Restart **SERVERA**.
3. As soon as the computer reboots, or when the boot menu appears, press **[F8]** to open the **Windows Advanced Options** menu.
4. Select **Directory Services Restore Mode (Windows domain controllers only)**. Press **[Enter]**. You choose this option to ensure that Active Directory is not connected to the network.
5. If necessary, select the operating system (there should be only one: **Windows Server 2003, Enterprise or Standard**). The startup procedure continues.
6. Log on using the **Administrator** account and the **Directory Services Restore Mode (DSRM) Administrator** password that you set for **SERVERA** in Project 2.1 (**ADRestore**).
7. A Desktop message box informs you that Windows is running in **Safe Mode.** Click **OK** to close the message box and continue the startup process.
8. The desktop appears with the words *Safe Mode* in all four corners.
9. Click **Start**, point to **All Programs**, point to **Accessories**, point to **System Tools**, and click **Backup** to open the **Backup or Restore Wizard**.
10. Click **Next** to open the **Backup or Restore** screen. Select **Restore files and settings**.
11. Click **Next** to open the **What to Restore** screen. Expand **File**. Expand the **Backup.bkf** option that corresponds to the most recent backup of the System State. Put a check mark beside **System State (Figure 8-7)**.
12. Click **Next** to open the **Completing the Backup or Restore Wizard** screen.
13. Click **Finish** to start the restoration process. A **Warning** dialog box opens to remind you that the current System State will be overwritten unless you are restoring to an alternate location **(Figure 8-8)**.
14. Click **OK** to close the dialog box and begin the restore. The **Restore Progress** dialog box opens.
15. If the **Check Backup File Location** dialog box opens, click **OK** to verify the source of the backup file.
16. When the restore is complete, click **Close**. A **Backup Utility** warning dialog box opens to inform you that some of the files restored require you to restart the computer **(Figure 8-9)**.
17. Click **Yes** to restart the computer. You have just performed a non-authoritative restore.

tip

Non-authoritative restores depend on at least one other domain controller being available in your domain so that the restored Active Directory data can be updated. After you perform a non-authoritative restore, the Active Directory replication system will update the restored data with more recent versions of Active Directory objects (those with higher update sequence numbers).

Figure 8-7 Selecting Directory Services Restore Mode on the boot menu

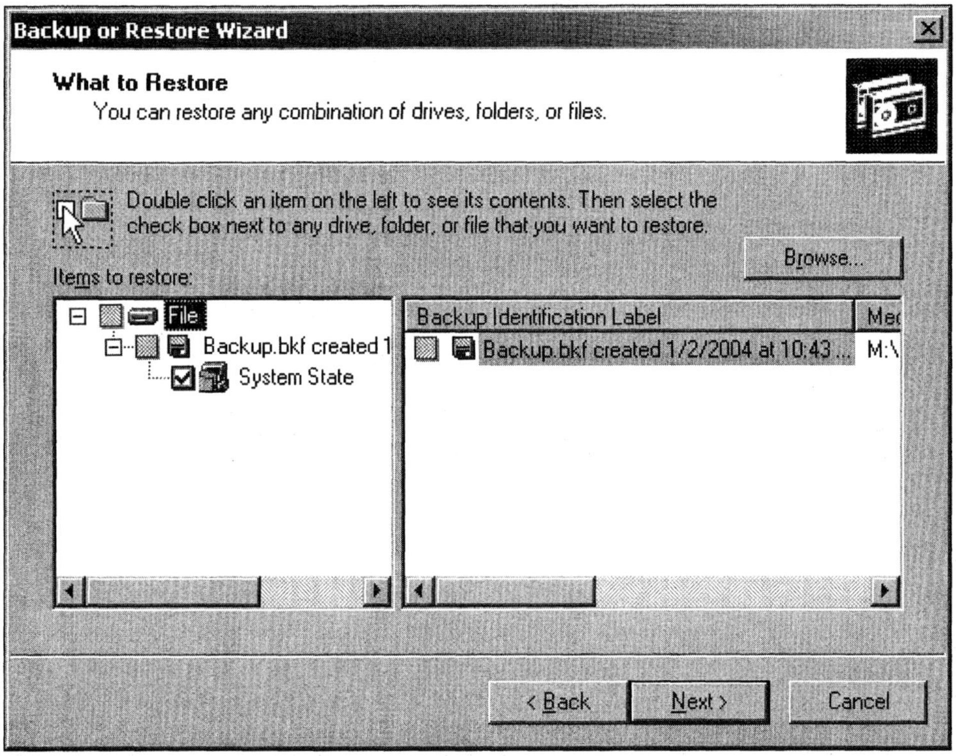

Figure 8-8 The Warning dialog box

Figure 8-9 The Backup Utility warning dialog box

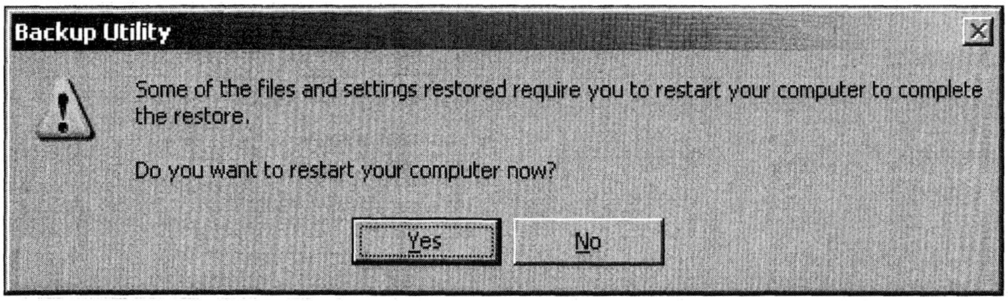

project 8.4 Executing an Authoritative Restore

exam objective

Restore Active Directory directory services. Perform an authoritative restore of Active Directory.

overview

An authoritative restore is used to recover specific Active Directory objects, for example, when a user account has been accidentally deleted. If there is more than one domain controller in the domain, all domain controllers will be aware of the deletion of that user account. A non-authoritative restore is performed on one domain controller to bring that user account back. However, once that domain controller is rebooted, it will initiate replication with its replication partners. Since the deleted version of the user account in question is newer than the recently restored version, the user account in question will be re-deleted. An authoritative restore is used to flag specific objects as 'authoritative' and, as such, they will not be re-deleted upon replication.

learning objective

After completing this project, you will know how to perform an authoritative restore.

specific requirements

Administrative rights on SERVERA, the Windows Server 2003 that is acting as a domain controller for apbindustries.com.

estimated completion time

25 minutes

project steps

1. Restart **SERVERA**.
2. Perform a non-authoritative restore, following the steps in Project 8.3. However, when the restore is complete, do NOT restart the computer.
3. Click **Start** and then click **Run**. In the **Open** text box, type **cmd** and click **OK** to open a command prompt window.
4. Type **ntdsutil** and press **[Enter]** to open the ntdsutil prompt.
5. Type **authoritative restore** to open the authoritative restore prompt.
6. To restore the deleted object Peter Murphy, type **restore subtree "cn=Peter Murphy,ou=HR,dc=apbindustries,dc=com" (Figure 8-10)**.
7. Press **[Enter]**. The **Authoritative Restore Confirmation** dialog box prompts you to confirm that you want to perform the authoritative restore **(Figure 8-11)**. Click **Yes**.
8. If the syntax is correct, a message indicates that one record has been successfully updated **(Figure 8-12).**
9. Type **quit** to exit the authoritative restore prompt.
10. Type **quit** to exit ntdsutil.
11. Type **exit** to close the command prompt.
12. Restart the computer.
13. Open the **Active Directory Users and Computers** console and verify the existence of the Peter Murphy user account.

tip

If there are any spaces in the object name or OU name, you must enclose the full path in quotation marks (" ").

Figure 8-10 Specifying the object to perform an authoritative restore on in Ntdsutil

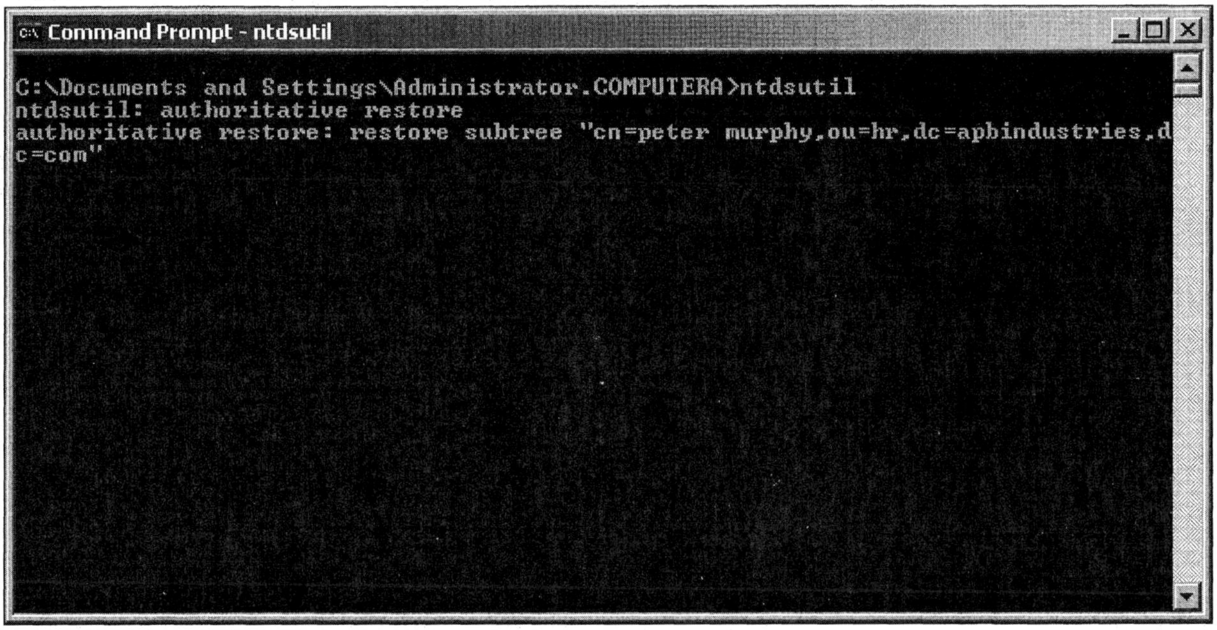

Figure 8-11 The Authoritative Restore Confirmation dialog box

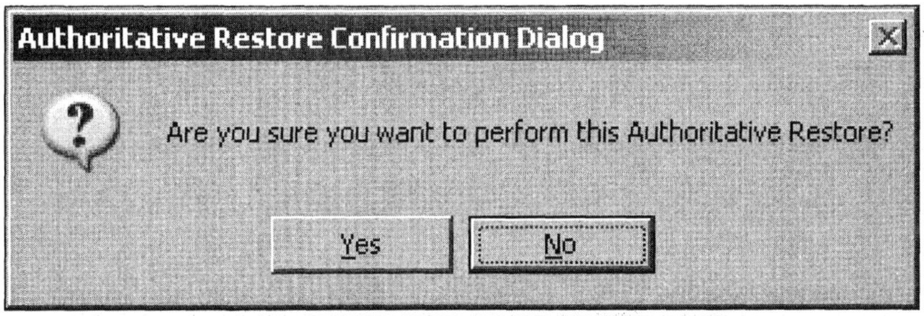

Figure 8-12 Ntdsutil's successful completion of an authoritative restore

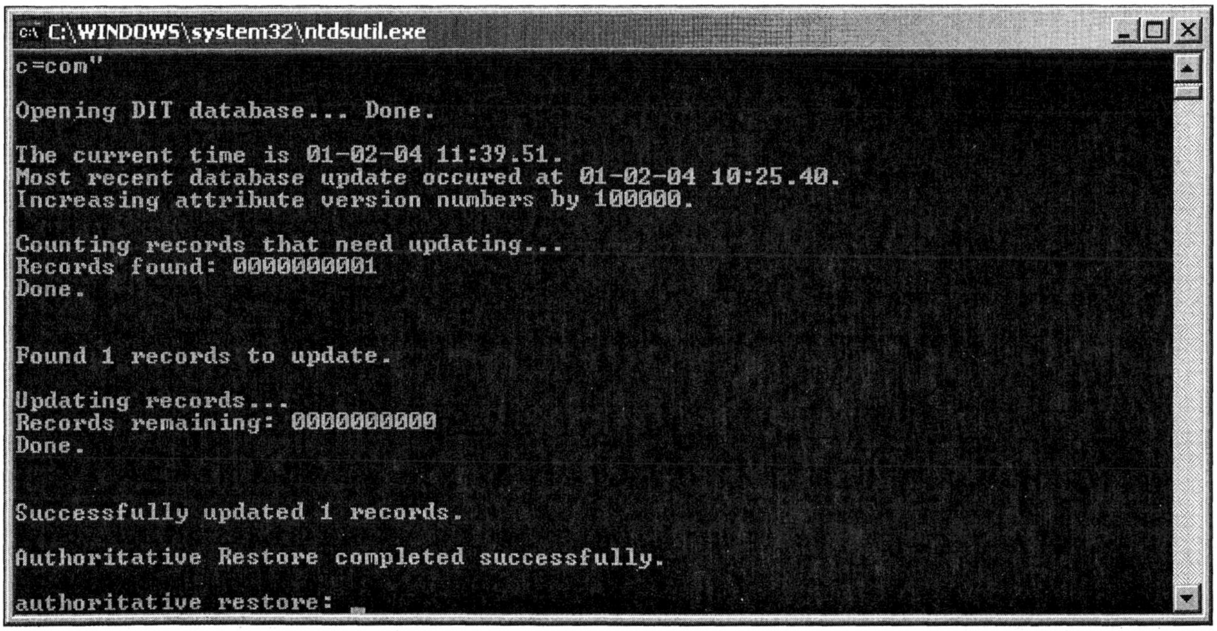

LESSON 9

Implementing Group Policy

Managing the user environment is a very important task for an Active Directory administrator. Active Directory includes a feature called Group Policy, which allows administrators to automatically deploy user and computer settings, in turn, easing the burden of controlling the computing environment. Group Policy is implemented using one or more Group Policy Objects (GPOs). A GPO is an Active Directory object that contains a collection of Group Policy settings.

GPOs can be applied to various Active Directory containers, such as sites, domains, and organizational units (OUs). GPOs can exist in any or all of these containers. As a result, there is a potential for conflicting settings. To deal with this, there is a specific order in which GPOs are processed. The order in which GPOs are processed is as follows: Local, Site, Domain, and OUs (LSDOU).

As with other Active Directory objects, you can delegate administrative control for individual GPOs in order to disperse the administrative burden.

The Group Policy Management Console (GPMC) is a comprehensive new tool in Windows Server 2003 that combines the functionality of Active Directory Users and Computers, Active Directory Sites and Services, the ACL Editor, the Delegation Wizard, and the Resultant Set of Policy tool. It can be used to control Group Policy administration in Windows 2000 and Windows Server 2003 domains.

Scenario

A powerful aspect of Active Directory is Group Policy. In order to fully take advantage of Group Policy, it is critical that you have a good knowledge of the different components of a Group Policy Object, as well as the different settings of a Group Policy Object. This lesson introduces you to the basics of a Group Policy Object.

Lesson 9 Implementing Group Policy

Project	Exam 70-294 Objective
9.1 Introducing Group Policy	Basic knowledge
9.2 Creating a Group Policy Object	Basic knowledge
9.3 Delegating Control for a Group Policy Object	Basic knowledge
9.4 Configuring Policy Settings for a GPO	Basic knowledge

General Requirements

To complete the projects in this lesson, you will need administrative rights on SERVERA, the Windows Server 2003 computer that is acting as a domain controller for the apbindustries.com domain. You may also find it helpful to refer to Lesson 9 in your Prentice Hall Certification Series Exam 70-294 textbook for further information about the topics covered by the projects in this lesson.

project 9.1

Introducing Group Policy

exam objective

Basic knowledge

overview

A Group Policy Object (GPO) consists of two components. One part is a Group Policy Container (GPC). A GPC is an Active Directory component that contains GPO attributes, extensions, and version information. Each GPO has a corresponding GPC that is accessible through the System\Policies folder in the Active Directory Users and Computers console. The name of the GPC corresponds to the Globally Unique Identifier (GUID) of the GPO. The second part of a GPO is the Group Policy Template (GPT). A GPT is a collection of folders stored in *%Systemroot%*\SYSVOL\sysvol*domain_name*\Policies on each Windows 2003 domain controller. Like the GPC, the GPT folder is also named after the GUID of the GPO with which it is associated.

learning objective

After completing this project, you will be familiar with the location of the Group Policy Container and Group Policy Template portions of a Group Policy Object. You will also know where to find the GUID for a GPO so that you can determine the GPO with which the GPC and the GPT are associated.

specific requirements

Administrative rights on SERVERA, the Windows Server 2003 computer that is acting as a domain controller for apbindustries.com.

estimated completion time

5 minutes

project steps

1. Log on to **SERVERA** with a user account that has administrative rights.
2. Open the **Active Directory Users and Computers** console. Open the **View** menu and make sure that there is a check mark by **Advanced Features**.
3. Expand **apbindustries.com**. Expand **System**. Select **Policies**. In the details pane, you will see a corresponding GroupPolicyContainer for each GPO in the domain **(Figure 9-1)**.
4. Close the Active Directory Users and Computers console.
5. Open **Windows Explorer**. Then navigate to ***%Systemroot%*\SYSVOL\sysvol \apbindustries.com\Policies**. Here you will see a corresponding folder (**Group Policy Template**) for each GPO in the domain **(Figure 9-2)**.
6. Close Windows Explorer.
7. Open the **Group Policy Management** console.
8. Expand the **Forest** node, if necessary. Expand the **Domains** node, if necessary.
9. Expand **apbindustries.com**. Select **Default Domain Policy**. If the **Group Policy Management Console** dialog box opens, select the **Do not show this message again** check box and click **OK** to confirm that you understand that if you make changes to the properties for the GPO link, they will affect all linked GPO's.
10. Open the **Details** tab. The **Unique ID** field displays the GUID for the GPO.
11. Expand the **Domain Controllers** node. Select the **Default Domain Controllers Policy**.
12. Open the **Details** tab. The **Unique ID** field displays the GUID for the GPO.
13. Close the GPMC.

tip

%Systemroot% is an environment variable that points to the folder in which Windows Server 2003 was installed. Typically, the value of *%Systemroot%* is **C:\Windows** or **C:\WINNT**.

Figure 9-1 Group Policy Containers in Active Directory Users and Computers

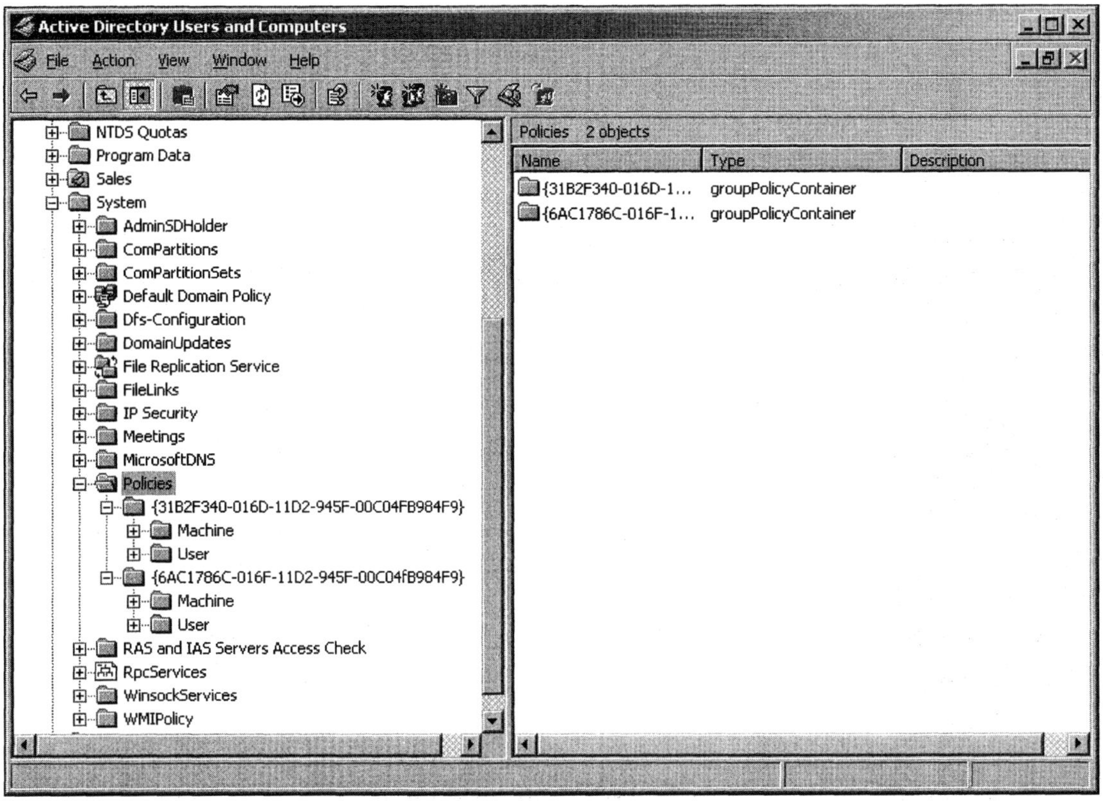

Figure 9-2 Group Policy Templates in Windows Explorer

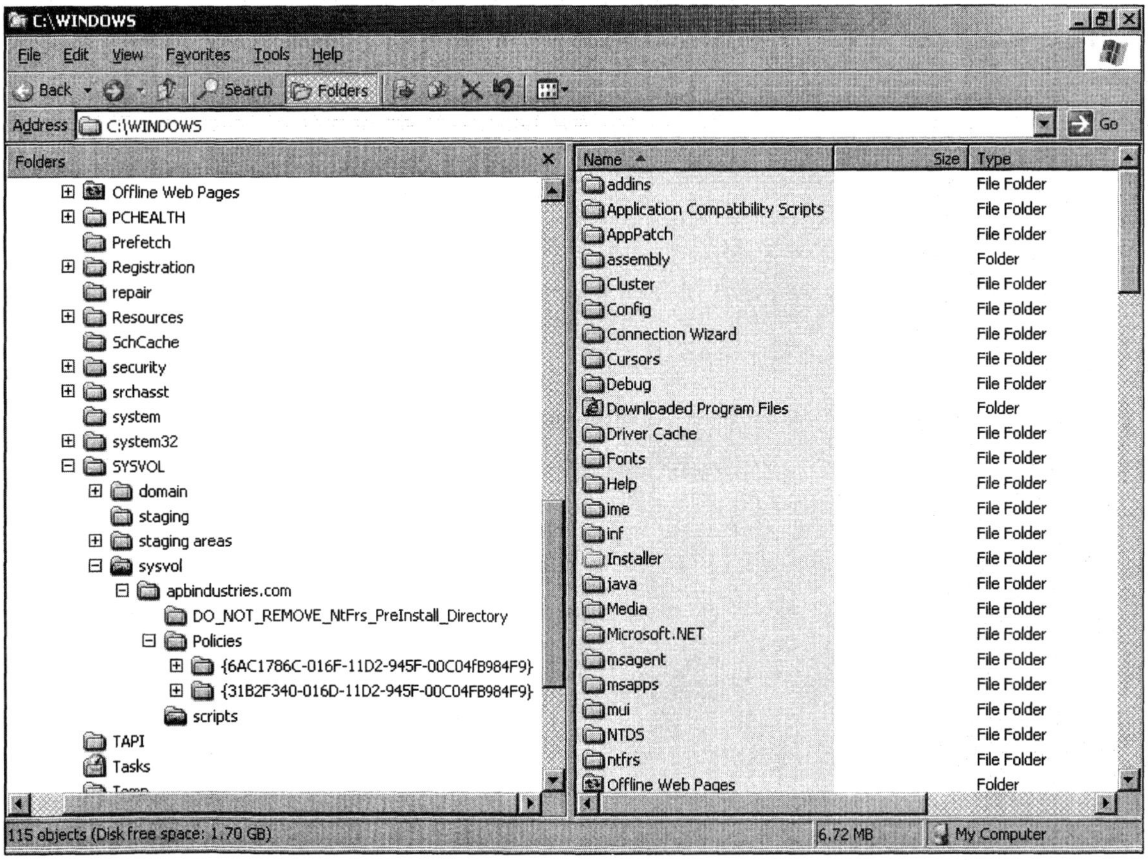

project 9.2 Creating a Group Policy Object

exam objective

Basic knowledge

overview

When Active Directory is installed, two GPOs (Default Domain Policy and Default Domain Controllers Policy) are automatically created and linked. However, there will be situations when the default GPOs do not serve the needs of the network. In these cases, additional GPOs can be created at the site, domain, or OU level.

learning objective

After completing this project, you will know how to create a Group Policy Object.

specific requirements

Administrative rights on SERVERA, the Windows Server 2003 computer that is acting as a domain controller for apbindustries.com.

estimated completion time

10 minutes

project steps

1. Log on to **SERVERA** with a user account that has administrative rights.
2. Open the **Group Policy Management** console.
3. Right-click the **HR** OU and click **Create and Link a GPO Here** to open the **New GPO** dialog box.
4. In the **Name** text box, type **Password Policy**. Press **[Enter] (Figure 9-3)**.
5. Expand the **HR** node.
6. Right-click **Password Policy** and click **Enforced (Figure 9-4)**. This will prevent other Group Policy Objects from overriding the settings in this Group Policy Object.
7. Select **Password Policy**. On the **Scope** tab, in the **Links** section, select **Entire forest** in the **Display links in this location** list box **(Figure 9-5)**. The sites, domains, and OUs that are linked to the Password Policy GPO are displayed in the box.
8. Close the Group Policy Management console.

Figure 9-3 Creating a new GPO

Figure 9-4 Selecting the No Override Link Option

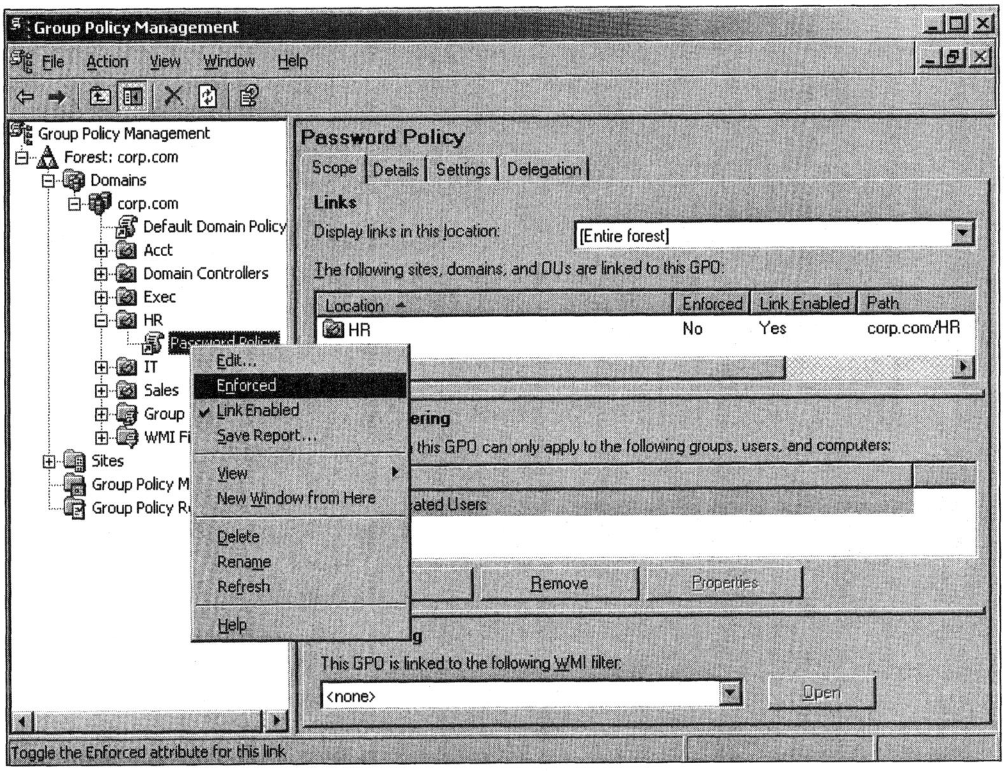

Figure 9-5 Determining how many containers a GPO is linked to

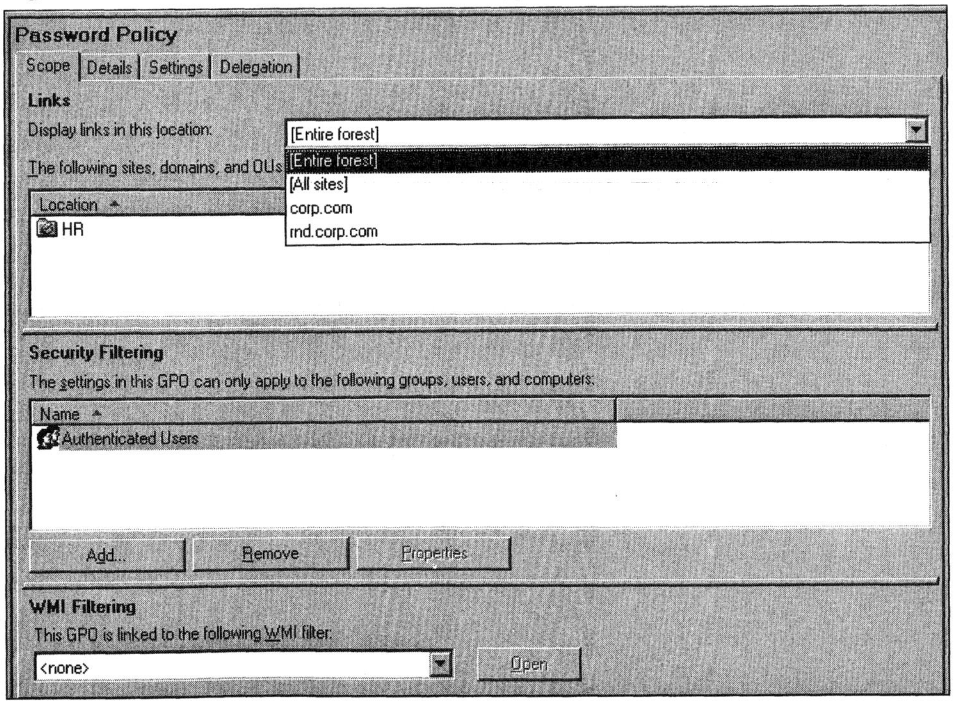

project 9.3

Delegating Control for a Group Policy Object

exam objective

Basic knowledge

overview

When a GPO is created, it may be necessary to delegate control to another administrator. This relieves the administrative burden that would fall on a single individual. To delegate administrative control over a GPO, the Read and Write permissions must be set to Allow for the user(s) or group(s) that are to have control over the GPO.

learning objective

After completing this project, you will know how to delegate control of a Group Policy Object.

specific requirements

Administrative rights on SERVERA, the Windows Server 2003 computer that is acting as a domain controller for apbindustries.com.

estimated completion time

5 minutes

project steps

1. Open the **Group Policy Management** console.
2. Expand the **HR** OU, if necessary.
3. Select the **Password Policy GPO**.
4. Click the **Delegation** tab.
5. Click the **Add** button to open the **Select User, Computer, or Group** dialog box.
6. Click the **Advanced** button to expand the dialog box.
7. Click **Find Now**.
8. Double-click **Steven Groth** in the **Search results** list to add his name to the **Enter the object names to** select box. **(Figure 9-6)**. Click **OK**.
9. The **Add Group or User** dialog box opens. **APBINDUSTRIES\SGroth** has been entered in the **Group or user name** label.
10. In the **Permissions** list box, select **Edit settings, delete, modify security**.
11. Click **OK** to close the Add Group or User dialog box.
12. **Steven Groth** is added to the list on the **Delegation** tab **(Figure 9-7)**.
13. Close the GPMC.

tip

To delegate permissions for a GPO, you must have the **Edit settings, delete, and modify security** permission for the GPO.

tip

You must assign the Edit settings, delete, and modify security permission to at least one user or group for each GPO. If only one user or group has this permission level, then you cannot remove this user or group.

Figure 9-6 Selecting a user to assign control over the GPO to

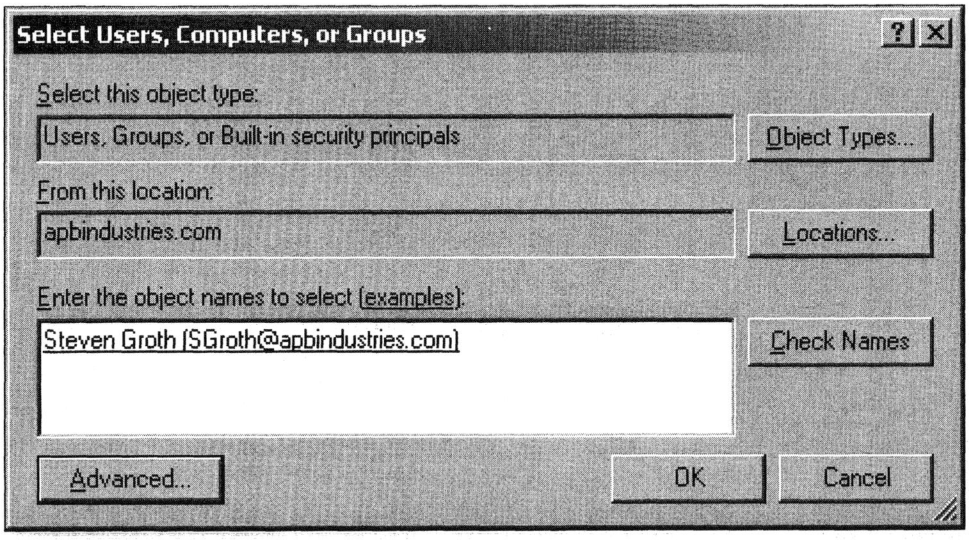

Figure 9-7 Settings permissions

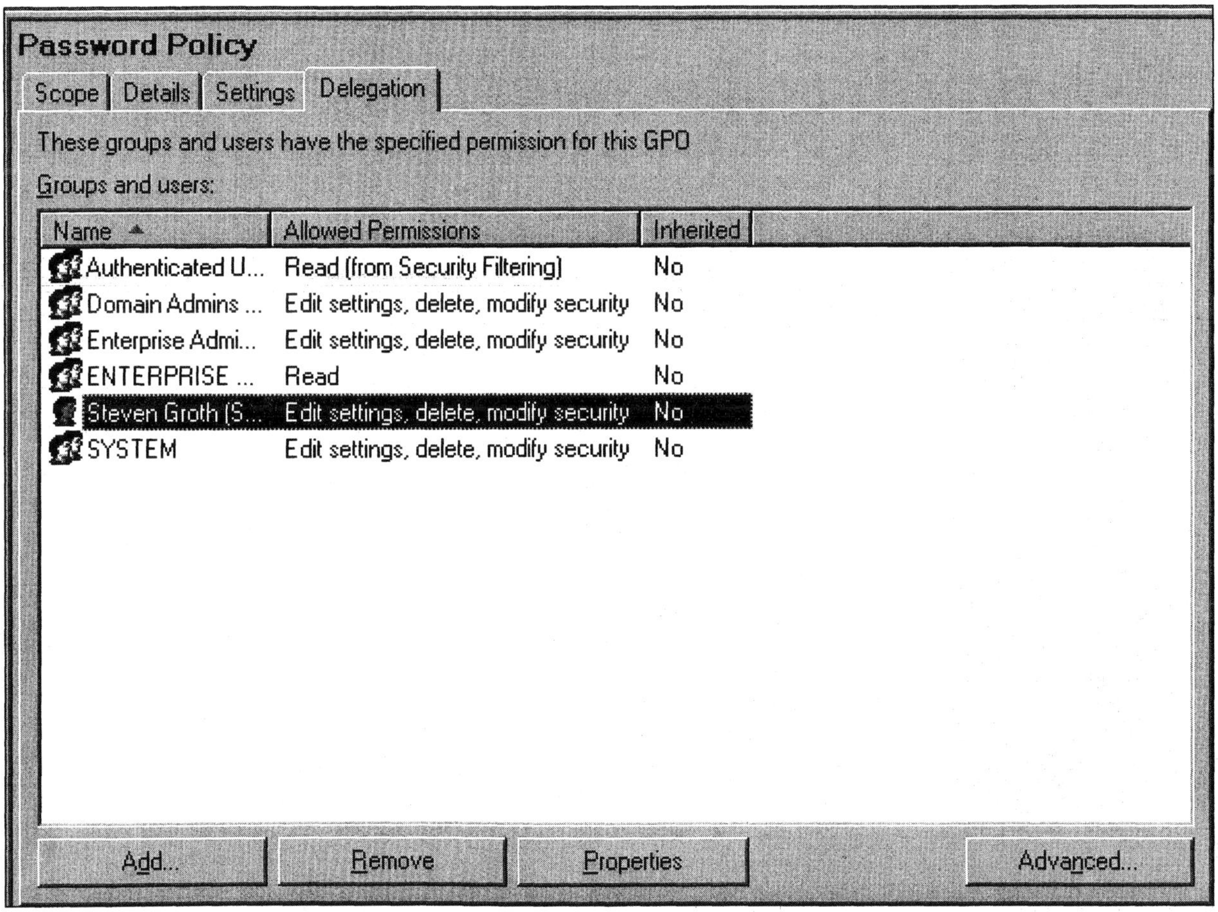

project 9.4

Configuring Policy Settings for a GPO

exam objective

Basic knowledge

overview

After you have created a GPO, you must configure the policy settings to which it will apply. Computer Configuration settings apply to computers, no matter what user logs on, and they are applied to the computer at startup. User Configuration settings apply to users, no matter what computer the user logs on to, and they are applied when the user logs on. In the System node in the User Configuration\Administrative Template node, you can configure a Group Policy to lock client computers when they resume from hibernation or suspension.

learning objective

After completing this project, you will know how to configure the policy settings for a GPO so that users are prompted for a password when the computer resumes from hibernate or suspend.

specific requirements

Administrative rights on SERVERA, the Windows Server 2003 that is acting as a domain controller for apbindustries.com.

estimated completion time

5 minutes

project steps

1. Open the **Group Policy Management** console.
2. Right-click the **Group Policy Objects** node and select **New** to open the **New GPO** dialog box.
3. Type **Power Management** in the **Name** text box and click **OK**.
4. Expand the **Group Policy Objects** node.
5. Right-click **Power Management** and click **Edit** to open the **Group Policy Object Editor** for the GPO.
6. Expand the **User Configuration** node, if necessary. Expand **Administrative Templates**. Expand **System**.
7. Select **Power Management**. In the details pane, double-click **Prompt for a password on resume from hibernation/suspend (Figure 9-8)** to open the corresponding **Properties** dialog box.
8. Select the **Enabled** option button. Select the **Explain** tab to read what the policy will do **(Figure 9-9)**.
9. Click **OK** to close the Prompt for a password on resume from hibernation/suspend Properties dialog box.
10. Close the Group Policy Object Editor.
11. In the **Group Policy Management** console, select the **Power Management** GPO, if necessary.
12. Click the **Delegation** tab.
13. Click the **Add** button to open the **Select User, Computer, or Group** dialog box.
14. Click the **Advanced** button to expand the dialog box. Click **Find Now**.
15. Double-click **Peter Murphy** in the **Search results** list to add his name to the **Enter the object name to select** box. Click **OK**. The **Add Group or User** dialog box opens.
16. In the **Permissions** list box, select **Edit settings, delete, modify security**. Click **OK**.
17. Verify that Peter Murphy has been added to the **Groups and users** list. Peter Murphy has been delegated control over the Power Management GPO.
18. Close the GPMC.

Figure 9-8 Opening the Group Policy Management console

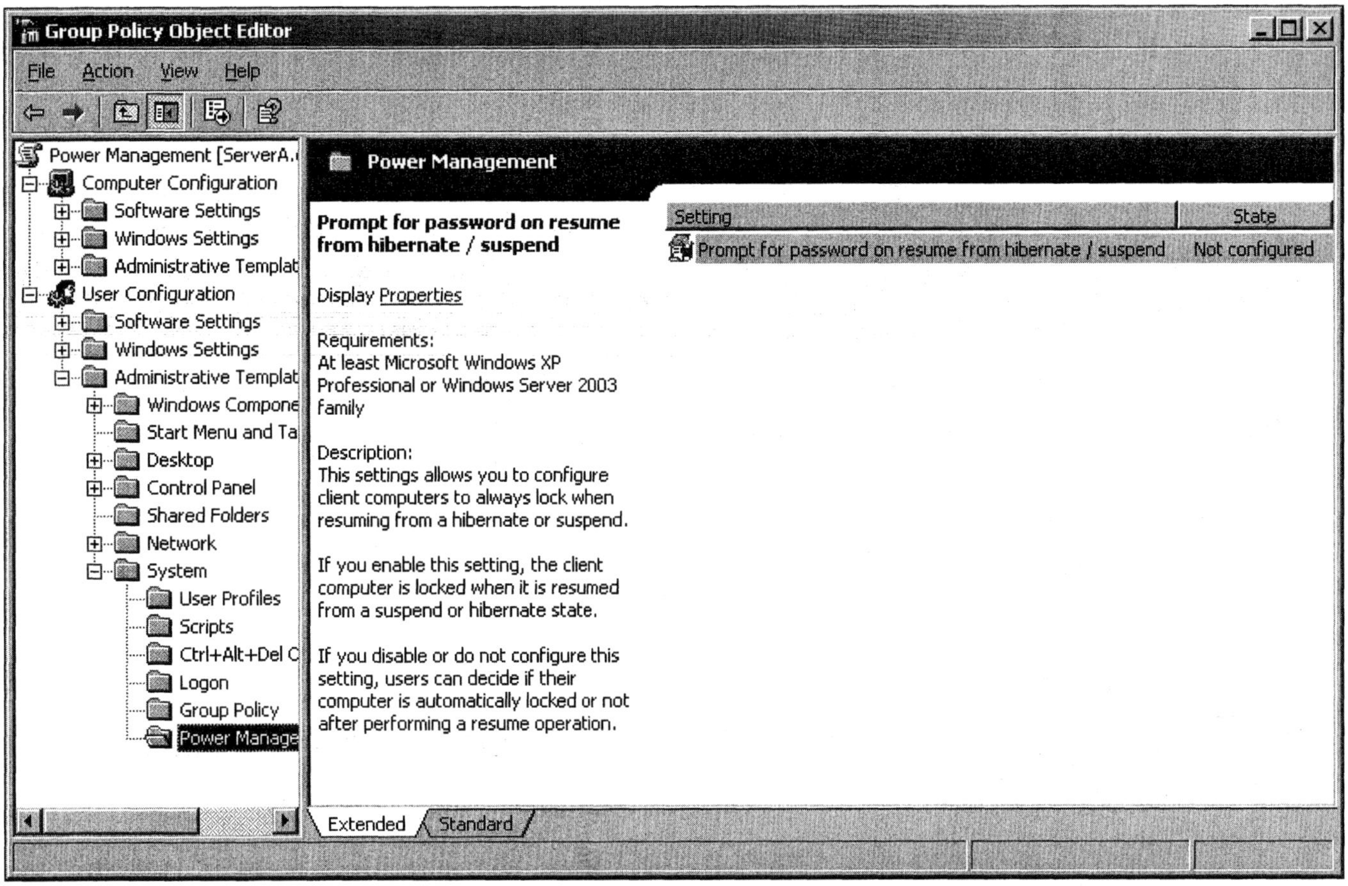

Figure 9-9 Creating a new GPO

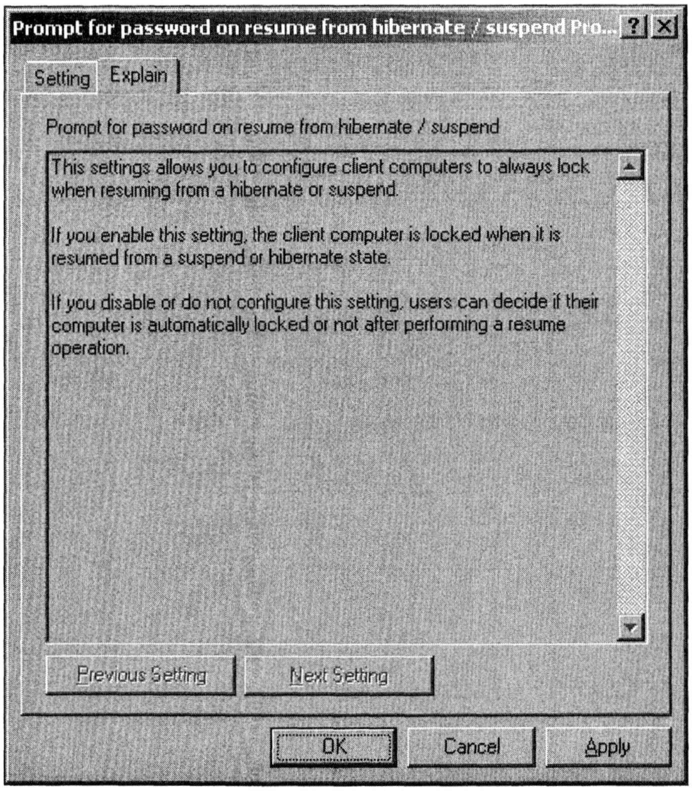

LESSON 10 Configuring Group Policy Settings

Administrators frequently use Group Policy settings to configure the desktop environment for domain users. Policies are configured for GPOs, which are checked by the operating system at startup and logon. If several GPOs are linked to a site, domain, or OU, The GPO list is processed from the bottom up. If there is a conflict between the policies, the last policy applied takes precedence. However, if the Enforced or Block Inheritance options arc applied, or if filtering has been configured, this default behavior is altered. When you set a GPO link to Enforced, you are designating that the policy settings in that GPO link will take precedence over the settings in any child objects. When you set the Block Inheritance option, you are specifying that all policies at higher levels will be blocked. In other words, the children will be prevented from inheriting their parents' Group Policy settings. Filtering is only used to apply a specific GPO to one or more groups of users. Additionally, you can disable a GPO link. Disabling is applied for a specific container object and it is used to block a GPO from being applied for a specific site, domain, or OU.

GPOs can become an encumbrance if they have been applied but are no longer needed, or are no longer serving a purpose. If this occurs, administrators have two options. They can simply remove the link to the GPO (leaving the GPO intact) or remove it altogether. Removing the link allows the GPO to be re-applied later without having to rebuild it. This should be done if there is a good chance that the GPO may be needed in the future. If the GPO is completely removed, it is permanently removed from Active Directory.

Scenario

As the administrator for the apbindustries.com domain, you have been assigned the task of managing the desktop wallpaper for all users in the apbindustries.com domain. In an effort to create a uniform appearance throughout the offices, you must assign a specific background for certain users and groups. You will then be charged with modifying your implementation of the new company policy.

Lesson 10 Configuring Group Policy Settings

Project	Exam 70-294 Objective
10.1 Configuring the User and Computer Environment	Configure the user environment by using Group Policy. Configure user security settings by using Group Policy. Deploy a computer environment by using Group Policy. Configure computer security settings by using Group Policy.
10.2 Modifying the Order of Group Policy Objects	Plan Group Policy strategy.
10.3 Filtering the Scope of a Group Policy Object	Plan Group Policy strategy.
10.4 Linking Group Policy Objects	Plan Group Policy strategy.

General Requirements

To complete the projects in this lesson, you will need administrative rights on SERVERA, the Windows Server 2003 computer that is acting as a domain controller for the apbindustries.com domain. You may also find it helpful to refer to Lesson 10 in your Prentice Hall Certification Series Exam 70-294 textbook for further information about the topics covered by the projects in this lesson.

project 10.1 Configuring Group Policy Settings for a GPO

exam objective

Configure the user environment by using Group Policy. Configure user security settings by using Group Policy. Deploy a computer environment by using Group Policy. Configure computer security settings by using Group Policy.

overview

The CEO of APB Industries has informed you that she no longer wants company employees to be able to personalize their desktop wallpaper because she believes it looks unprofessional and she does not want employees spending company time downloading and changing wallpaper. You have been asked to establish a uniform desktop for the company. The Follow background will be assigned to all employees except for those in the Information Technology department. IT users will be assigned the Crystal background. You will use GPOs to implement this new company policy.

learning objective

After completing this project, you will know how to create and modify GPOs to manage desktop settings.

specific requirements

Administrative rights on SERVERA, the Windows Server 2003 computer that is acting as a domain controller for apbindustries.com.

estimated completion time

15 minutes

project steps

1. Log on to **SERVERA** with an account that has administrative rights.
2. Open the **Group Policy Management** console.
3. Expand the **Forest** and **Domains** nodes, if necessary. Expand **apbindustries.com**, if necessary.
4. Right-click **apbindustries.com** and select **Create and Link a GPO Here** to open the **New GPO** dialog box.
5. Type: **Employees Desktop** in the **Name** text box and click **OK**.
6. Right-click the **Employees Desktop** GPO and select **Edit** to open the **Group Policy Object Editor** for the policy.
7. Expand the **User Configuration** node, if necessary.
8. Expand the **Administrative Templates** and **Desktop** nodes and select **Active Desktop**.
9. Double-click **Enable Active Desktop** to open the **Enable Active Desktop Properties** dialog box.
10. Select the **Enabled** option button and click **OK (Figure 10-1)**.
11. Double-click **Active Desktop Wallpaper** to open the **Active Desktop Wallpaper Properties** dialog box.
12. Select the **Enabled** option button.
13. In the **Wallpaper Name** text box, type ***%Systemroot%*\web\wallpaper\follow.jpg** **(Figure 10-2)**. Click **OK**.
14. Close the Group Policy Object Editor.
15. In the Group Policy Management console, right-click the **IT** OU and select **Create and Link a GPO Here**.
16. Type **IT Desktop** in the **Name** text box and click **OK**.
17. Select the **Group Policy Objects** node, if necessary. On the **Contents** tab, right-click **IT Desktop** and select **Edit** to open the **Group Policy Object Editor** for the policy.
18. Expand the **User Configuration** node, if necessary.
19. Expand the **Administrative Templates** and **Desktop** nodes and select **Active Desktop**.
20. Double-click **Enable Active Desktop**. Select **Enabled**. Click **OK**.
21. Double-click **Active Desktop Wallpaper** and select **Enabled**.

tip

All members of the domain will have the Follow wallpaper, unless they log on as members of the IT OU, which will have the Crystal wallpaper.

caution

By default, Group Policies are refreshed on domain controllers every five minutes. Therefore, the policy may not take effect for up to five minutes.

Figure 10-1 The Enable Active Desktop Properties dialog box

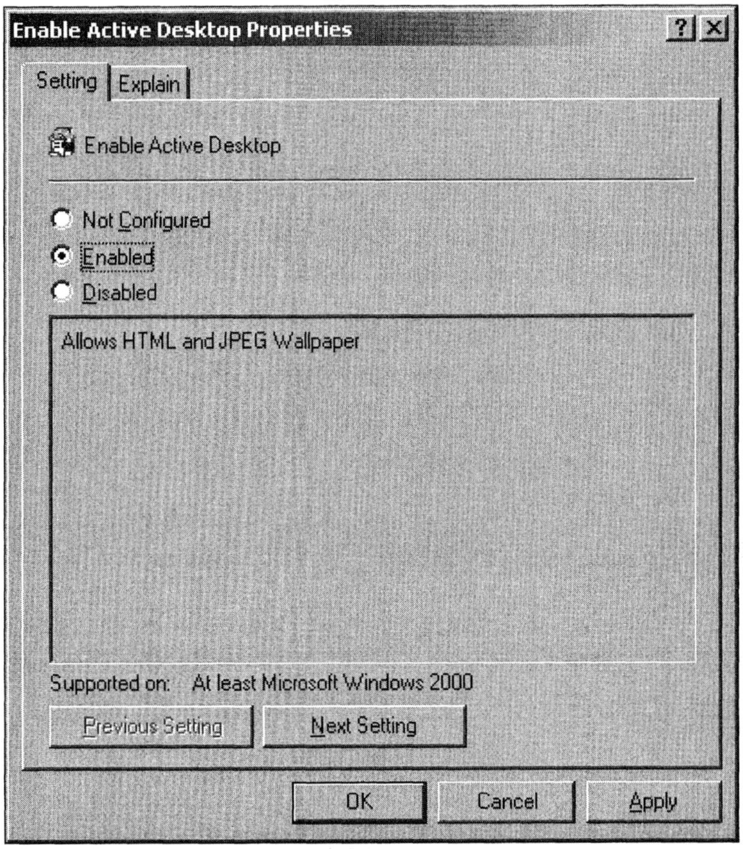

Figure 10-2 The Active Desktop Wallpaper Properties dialog box

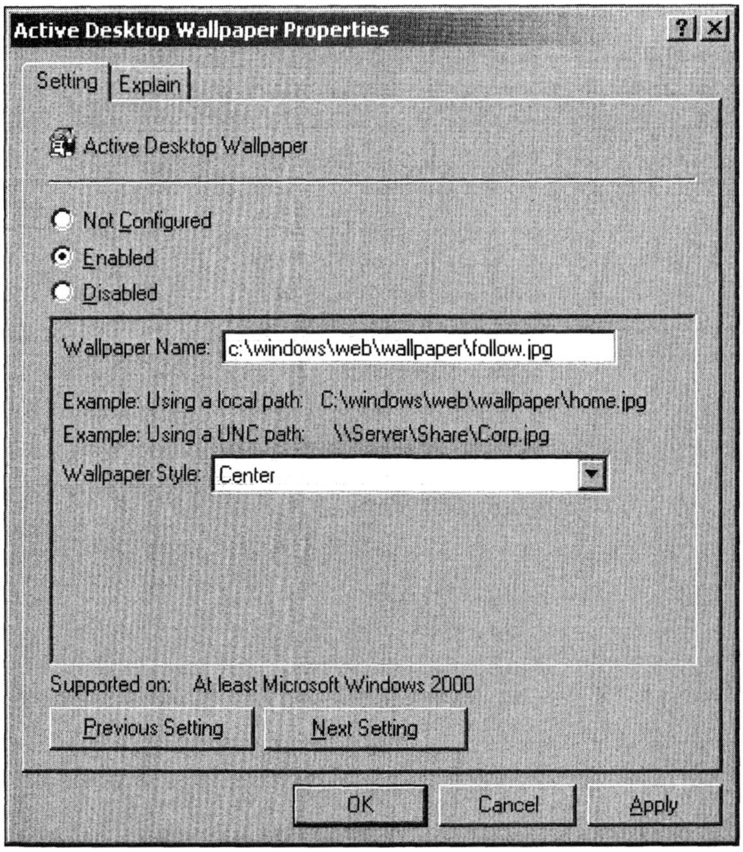

project 10.1

Configuring Group Policy Settings for a GPO (cont'd)

exam objective

Configure the user environment by using Group Policy. Configure user security settings by using Group Policy. Deploy a computer environment by using Group Policy. Configure computer security settings by using Group Policy.

project steps

22. In the **Wallpaper Name** text box, type ***%Systemroot%*** **\web\wallpaper\crystal.jpg** (**Figure 10-3**). Click **OK**.
23. Close the Group Policy Object Editor and the GPMC.
24. Open the **command prompt**.
25. Type **gpupdate** and press **[Enter]** to refresh both User and Computer policy.
26. Close the command prompt and log off.
27. Log on as **Peter Murphy** (**PMurphy**). The desktop should now have the **Follow** background (**Figure 10-4**).
28. Log off.
29. Log on as **Mark Jackson** (**MJackson**). The desktop should now have the **Crystal** background (**Figure 10-5**).
30. Log off.

Figure 10-3 Entering the path to the wallpaper for the IT OU

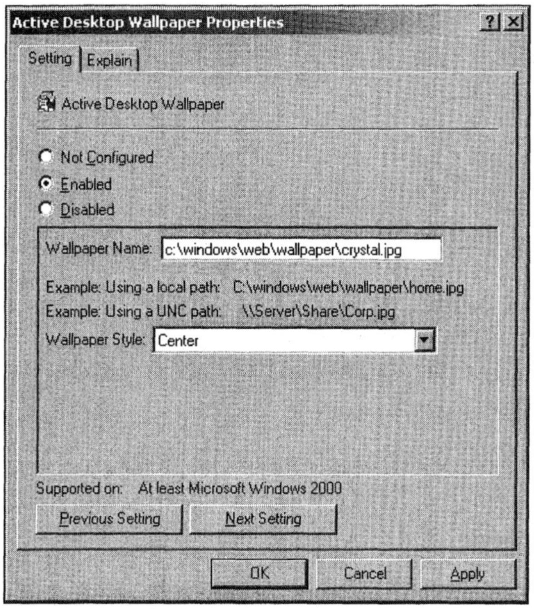

Figure 10-4 The Follow background

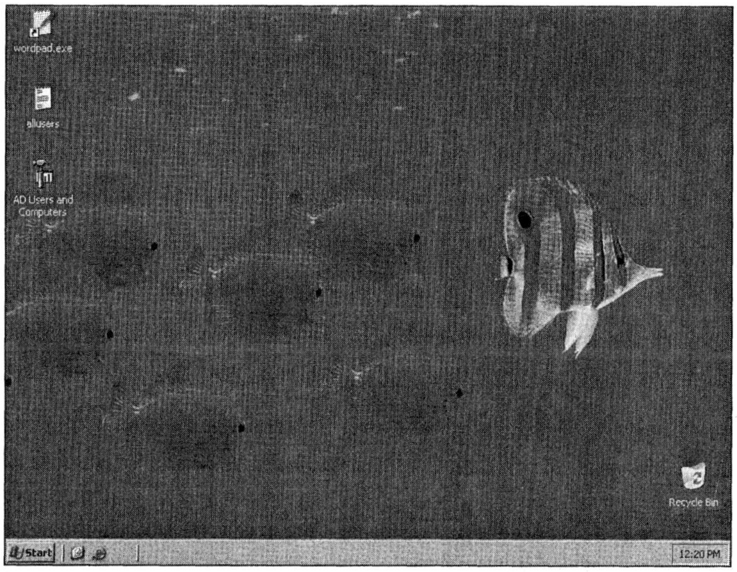

Figure 10-5 The Crystal background

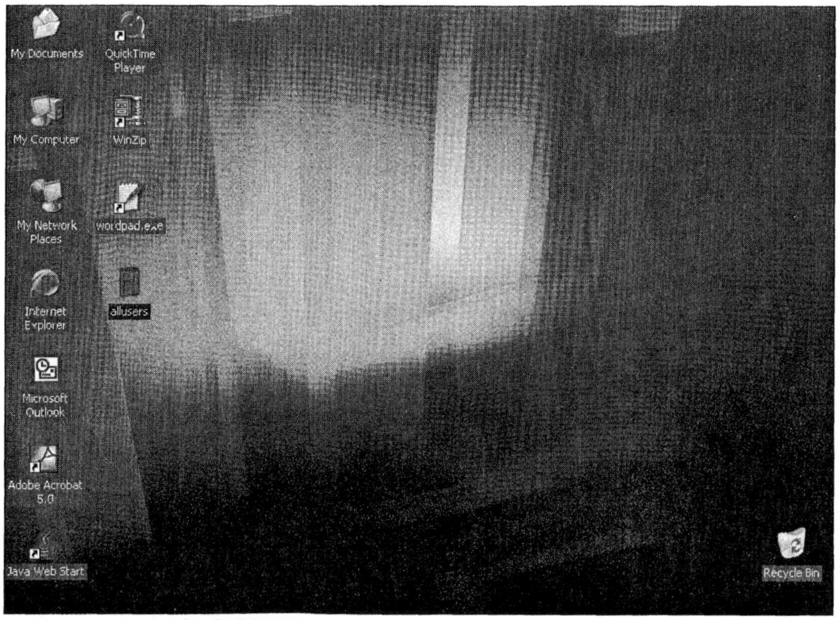

project 10.2

Modifying the Order of Group Policy Objects

exam objective

Plan Group Policy strategy.

overview

After careful thought, you, as the administrator for apbindustries.com, have decided to temporarily rescind the GPO that assigns the Crystal wallpaper to the Information Technology OU. You have decided to have them use the Follow wallpaper along with the rest of the employees of APB Industries. You have decided not to delete the GPO for the Information Technology OU because you may reinstitute the policy later. Instead, you are going to Enforce the Employees Desktop GPO so that it will not be overridden by the IT Desktop GPO. The result will be that all computers in apbindustries.com will use the Follow wallpaper.

learning objective

After completing this project, you will know how to override the default GPO processing order and how to view policy settings in the GPMC.

specific requirements

Administrative rights on SERVERA, the Windows Server 2003 computer that is acting as a domain controller for apbindustries.com, and successful completion of Project 10.1.

estimated completion time

5 minutes

project steps

1. Log on to **SERVERA** with an account that has administrative rights.
2. Open the **Group Policy Management** console.
3. Expand the **Forest** and **Domains** nodes, if necessary. Expand **apbindustries.com**, if necessary.
4. Right-click the **Employees Desktop** GPO and select **Enforced**. This specifies that policy settings in this GPO link will take precedence over the settings for any child object. (The Enforced setting was formerly referred to as the **No Override** option.) GPOs that are Enforced are always applied, even if the Block Inheritance setting has been applied to the container object.
5. With the **Employees Desktop** GPO selected, click the **Settings** tab.
6. Click the **show** link to the right of **Desktop/Active Desktop**.
7. The policy settings display including the path to the wallpaper **(Figure 10-6)**.
8. Click the **hide** link to hide the policy settings.
9. In the GPMC console tree, expand the **IT** OU.
10. Select the **IT Desktop** GPO.
11. Click the **Settings** tab, if necessary.
12. Click the **show** link to the right of **Desktop/Active Desktop**.
13. The policy settings display including the path to the wallpaper **(Figure 10-7)**.
14. Close the GPMC.
15. Open the **command prompt**.
16. Type **gpupdate** and press **[Enter]** to refresh both User and Computer policy.
17. Close the command prompt and log off.
18. Log back on as **Mark Jackson (MJackson)**. The desktop has been changed to the Follow background. Even though the policy settings are still intact, the settings in the Employees Desktop GPO are applied because, with the Enforced setting enabled (refer to Step 4), they have priority and are always applied.
19. Log off.

caution

The Enforced and Block Inheritance options should be used sparingly because when they are used, it can be harder to troubleshoot policy problems.

Figure 10-6 The Employees Desktop GPO policy settings

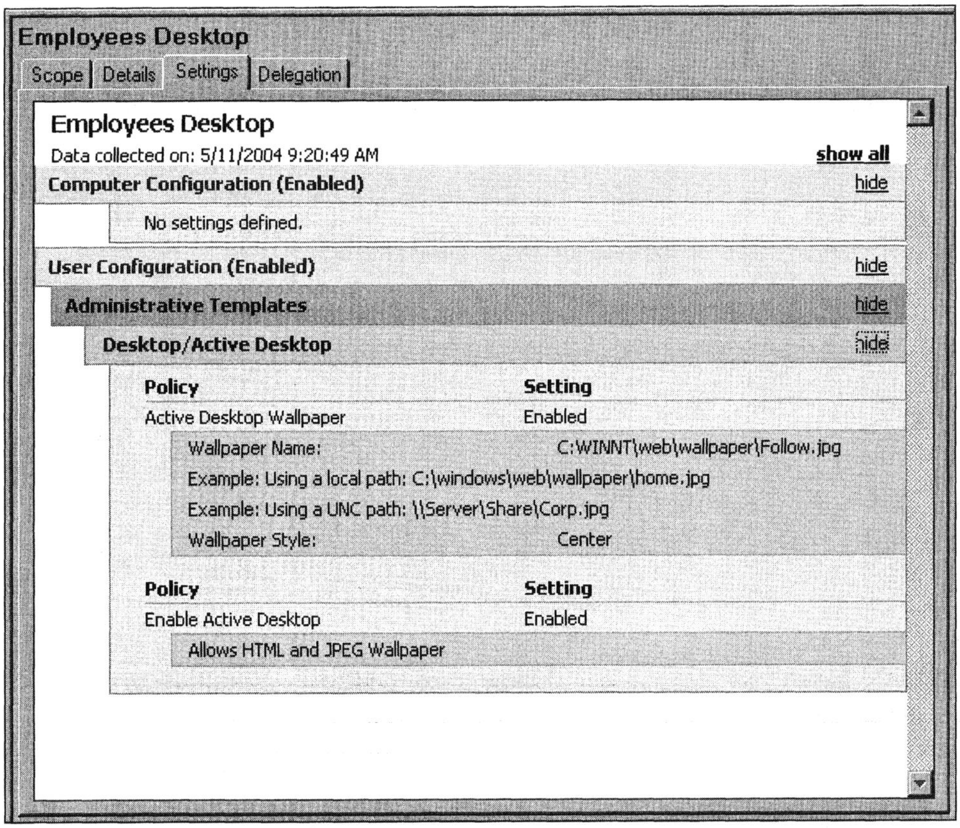

Figure 10-7 The IT Desktop GPO policy settings

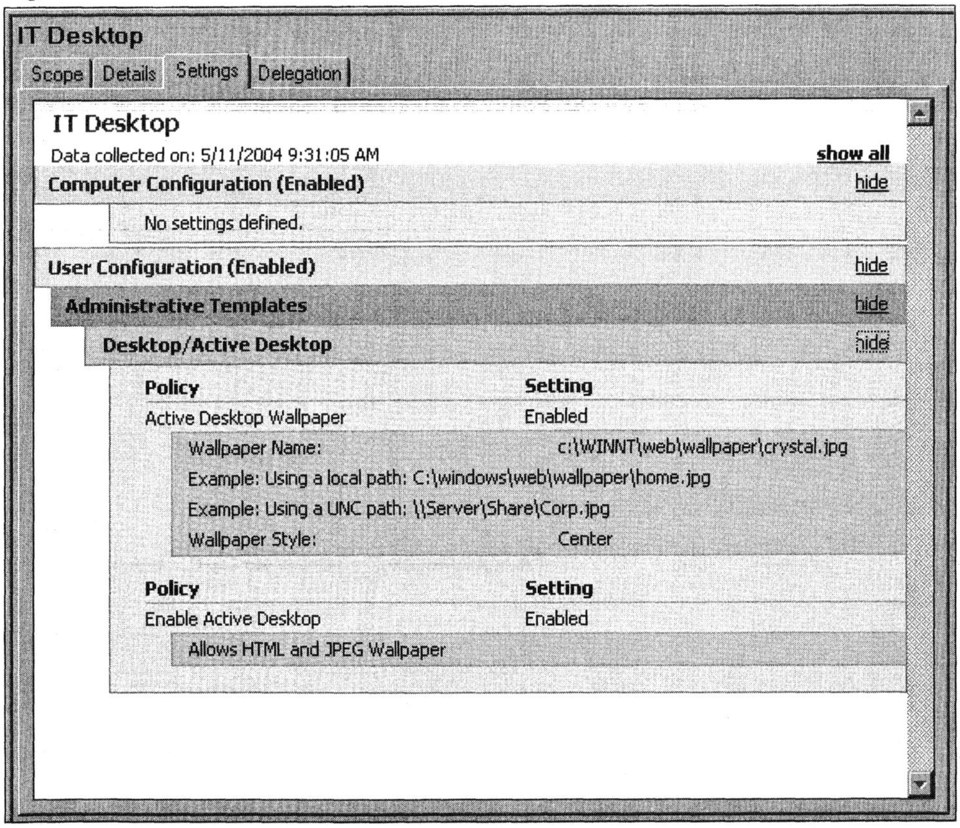

project 10.3

Filtering the Scope of the GPO

exam objective

Plan Group Policy strategy.

overview

In accordance with a new directive from the CEO of APB Industries, you must now make changes to the existing GPO implementation. The CEO has informed you that she has received complaints about the wallpaper limitations from key management personnel. She has decided to offer company employees an incentive (a different wallpaper) if their departments meet certain goals each month. The goals were not met last month by only two departments: Sales and Human Resources. Employees in the Sales and Human Resources groups will still be allowed access to only the Follow wallpaper. After careful thought, you decide to filter the scope of the Employees Desktop GPO so that it will apply to only the Sales and Human Resources groups.

learning objective

After completing this project, you will know how to modify the permissions for existing Group Policy Objects so that you can filter the GPO scope.

specific requirements

Administrative rights on SERVERA, the Windows Server 2003 computer that is acting as a domain controller for apbindustries.com.

estimated completion time

10 minutes

project steps

First, you will filter the scope of the Employees Desktop GPO so that it will apply to only the Sales-G and HR-G groups.

1. Log on to **SERVERA** with an account that has administrative rights.
2. Open the **Group Policy Management** console.
3. Expand the **Forest** and **Domains** nodes, if necessary. Expand **apbindustries.com**, if necessary.
4. Select the **Employees Desktop** GPO.
5. On the **Scope** tab in the **Security Filtering** section, select **Authenticated Users** and click **Remove (Figure 10-8)**.
6. A **Group Policy Management** warning dialog box prompts you to confirm that you want to remove this delegation privilege. Click **OK (Figure 10-9)**.
7. Click **Add** to open the **Select User**, **Computer**, **or Group** dialog box.
8. Type **Sales-G** in the **Enter the object name to select** box.
9. Click **OK** to add the Sales-G group to the **Name** list in the **Security Filtering** section.
10. Click **Add** to reopen the **Select User**, **Computer**, **or Group** dialog box.
11. Type **HR-G** in the **Enter the object name to select** box.
12. Click **OK** to add the HR-G group to the **Name** list in the **Security Filtering** section **(Figure 10-10)**. The Employees Desktop GPO will now apply to only the Sales-G and HR-G groups.

Next, you will examine the permissions that have been granted to the Sales-G and HR-G groups so that the policy is applied.

1. Click the **Delegation** tab **(Figure 10-11)**.
2. Click the **Advanced** button to open the **Employees Desktop Security Settings** dialog box.
3. Select the **HR-G** group in the **Group or user names** box.

tip

You assign the Read and Apply Group Policy permissions for a particular GPO to the users and computers to which you want the Group Policy applied. By default, the Authenticated Users group is granted both of these permissions for all GPOs.

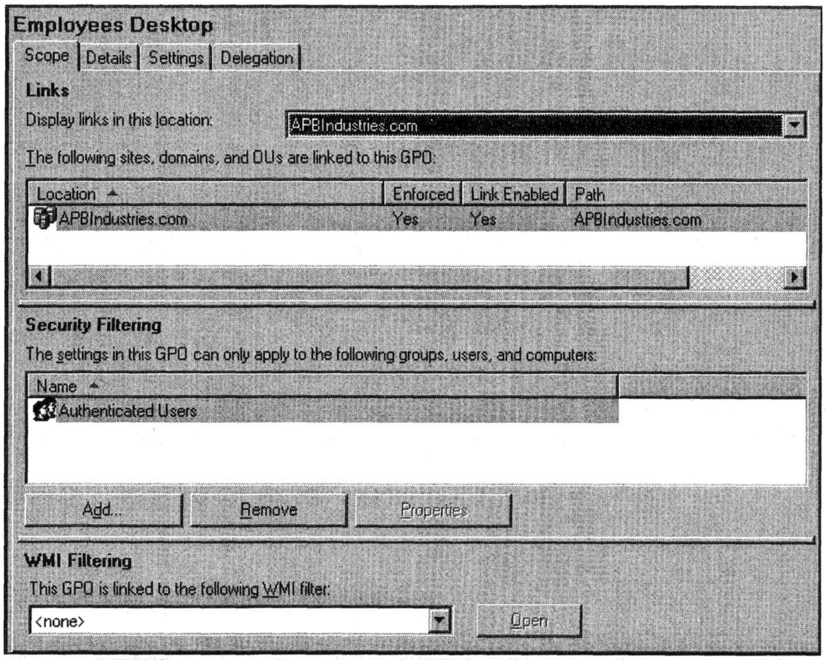

Figure 10-8 Removing the Authenticated Users group

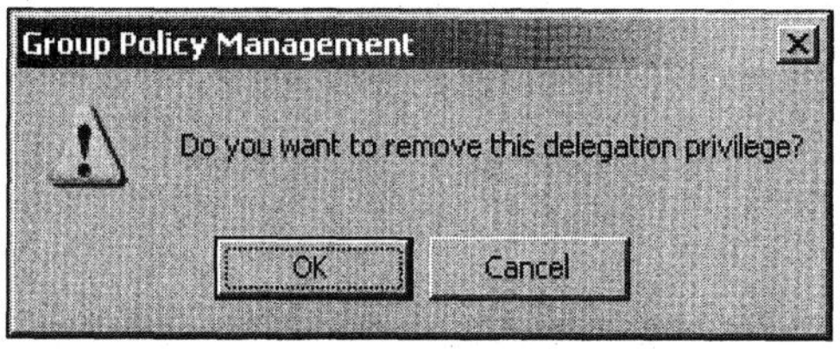

Figure 10-9 Confirming the removal of delegation privileges

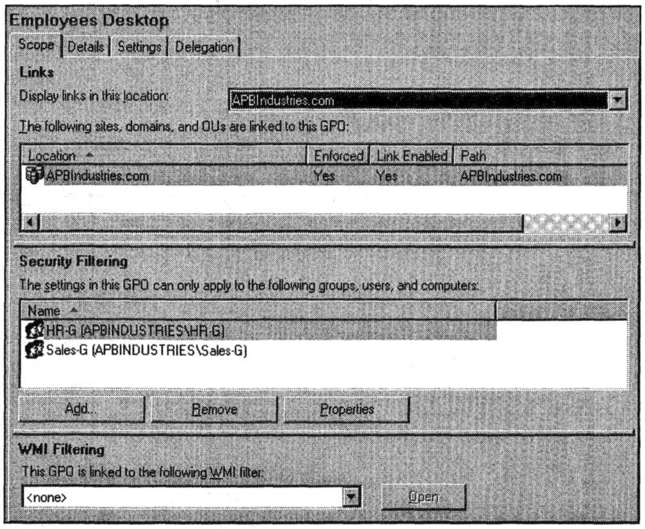

Figure 10-10 Applying Security Filtering to a GPO

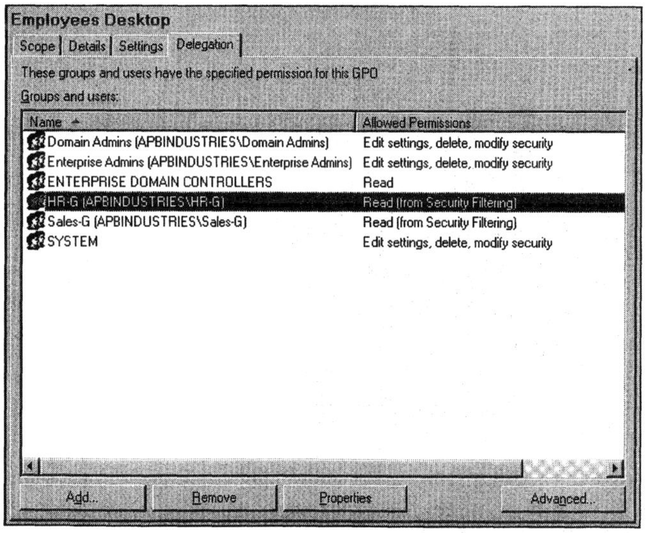

Figure 10-11 The Delegation tab

project 10.3

Filtering the Scope of the GPO (cont'd)

exam objective

Plan Group Policy strategy.

project steps

4. Confirm that the **Read** and **Apply Group Policy** permissions have been assigned to the group **(Figure 10-12)**.
5. Select the **Sales-G** group and confirm that the **Read** and **Apply Group Policy** permissions have been assigned to the group.
6. Click **OK** to close the Employees Desktop Security Settings dialog box.
7. Close the GPMC.

Now, you will add Peter Murphy to the HR-G group so that the Employees Desktop GPO will apply to him.

1. Open the **Active Directory Users and Computers** console.
2. Select the **HR** OU in the console tree.
3. Right-click **HR-G** in the details pane and select **Properties** to open the **HR-G** Properties dialog box.
4. Open the **Members** tab and click **Add** to open the **Select Users**, **Contacts**, **Computers**, **or Groups** dialog box.
5. Click **Advanced** to expand the dialog box.
6. Click **Find Now**. In the **Search results** list, double-click **Peter Murphy** to add him to the **Enter the object names to select** box **(Figure 10-13)**.
7. Click **OK** to add Peter Murphy to the HR group **(Figure 10-14)**.
8. Click **OK** to close the HR-G Properties dialog box.
9. Close the Active Directory Users and Computers console.
10. Run the **gpupdate** command at the command prompt to apply the policy changes.
11. Log off and log back on as **Mark Jackson**. His wallpaper is now Crystal because he is not a member of either the Sales-G or HR-G groups.
12. Log off and log back on as **Peter Murphy**. His wallpaper is Follow because he is a member of the HR-G group.
13. Log off.

tip

Mark Jackson receives the Crystal wallpaper because he does not have the Read and Apply Group Policy permissions for the Employees Desktop GPO assigned at the domain level.

Figure 10-12 Confirming that the Read and Apply Group Policy permissions have been assigned

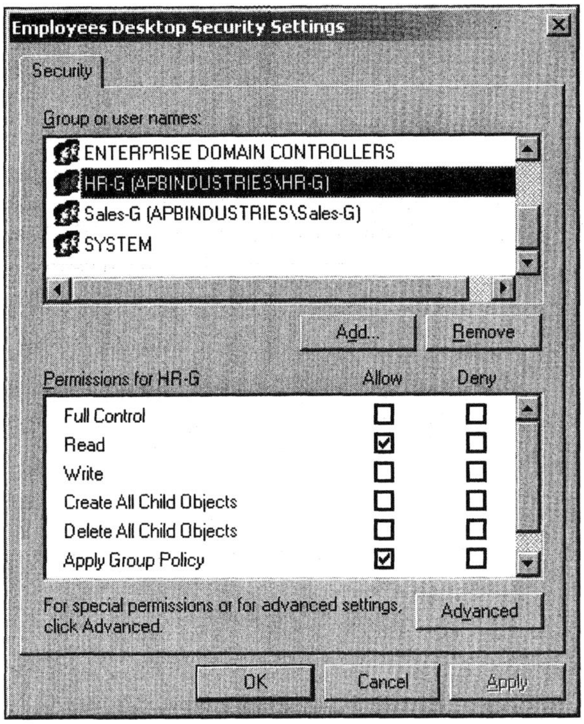

Figure 10-13 Adding Peter Murphy to the HR-G group

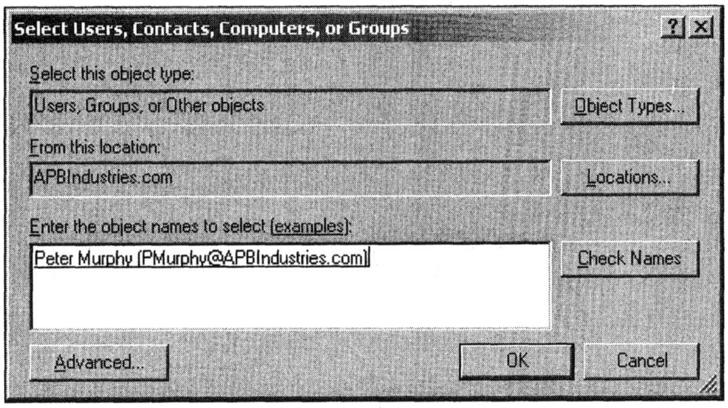

Figure 10-14 Members of the HR-G Group

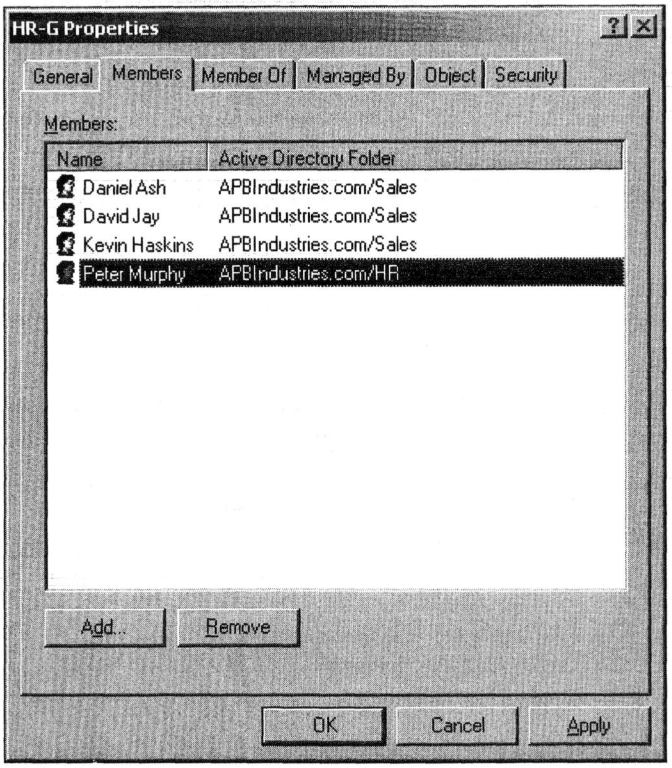

project 10.4 Linking Group Policy Objects

exam objective

Plan Group Policy strategy.

overview

Finally, you have convinced the CEO of APB Industries that it is not a good idea to change GPO configurations on a monthly basis, especially linked to a company incentive plan. She has agreed to have only one background on the desktop of all computers throughout the company. She has allowed you to decide which wallpaper is most appropriate and to complete the task immediately. You have decided that Chateau is the most professional and aesthetic. You will use GPOs to add the Chateau wallpaper to the desktop of all users in the apbindustries.com domain.

learning objective

After completing this project, you will know how to link a single GPO to multiple objects, (sites, domains, or OUs) and how to delete a GPO link and a Group Policy Object.

specific requirements

Administrative rights on SERVERA, the Windows Server 2003 computer that is acting as a domain controller for apbindustries.com, and the successful completion of Project 10.3.

estimated completion time

5 minutes

project steps

1. Log on to **SERVERA** with an account that has administrative rights.
2. Open the **Group Policy Management** console.
3. Right-click **apbindustries.com** and select **Link an Existing GPO** to open the **Select GPO** dialog box.
4. Select **IT Desktop (Figure 10-15)**.
5. Click **OK** to close the Select GPO dialog box. The IT Desktop GPO is now linked to the domain.
6. In the GPMC console tree, right-click the **Employees Desktop** GPO and select **Delete**.
7. A **Group Policy Management** information dialog box prompts you to confirm that you want to delete the link and reminds you that this will not delete the GPO itself (**Figure 10-16**).
8. Click **OK** to delete the GPO link. The GPO is no longer linked to the domain, but it still exists in the domain and in Active Directory.
9. Expand the **Group Policy Objects** node, if necessary.
10. Right-click the **Employees Desktop** GPO and select **Delete**.
11. A **Group Policy Management** dialog box prompts you to confirm that you want to delete this GPO and all links to it in this domain, and reminds you that this will not delete links to this GPO in other domains (**Figure 10-17**).
12. Click **OK** to delete the GPO and all links to it in the domain.
13. The **Delete** dialog box may open to chart the progress of the deletion progress (**Figure 10-18**).
14. Click **OK** to close the Delete dialog box.
15. Right-click the **IT Desktop** GPO and select **Edit** to open the **Group Policy Object Editor** for the policy.
16. Expand the **User Configuration** node, if necessary.
17. Expand the **Administrative Templates** and **Desktop** nodes and select **Active Desktop**.
18. Double-click **Active Desktop Wallpaper** to open the **Active Desktop Wallpaper Properties** dialog box.
19. In the **Wallpaper Name** text box, change the path to ***%Systemroot%*\web\wallpaper\chateau.jpg**.

Figure 10-15 The Select GPO dialog box

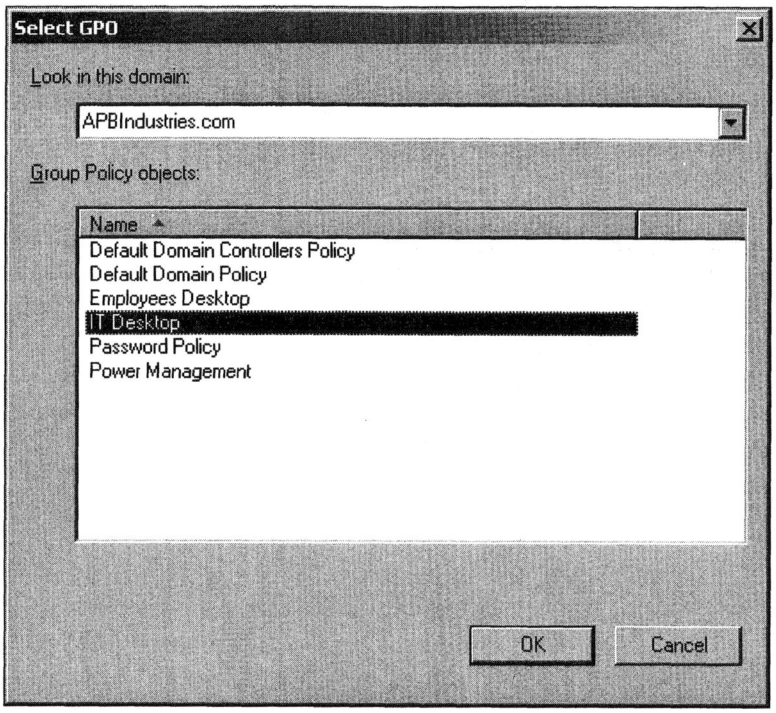

Figure 10-16 Confirming a GPO link deletion

Figure 10-17 Confirming a GPO deletion

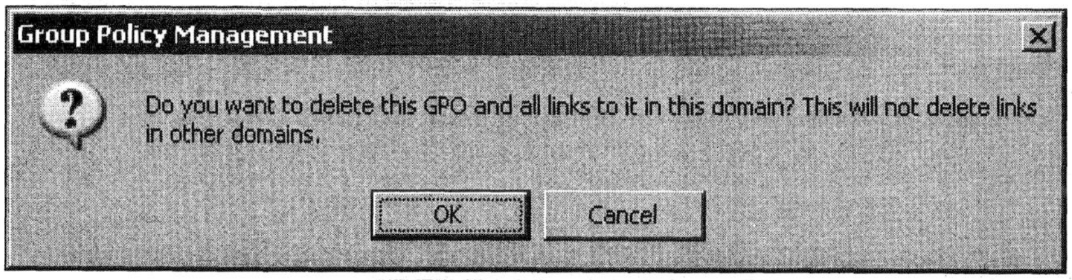

Figure 10-18 The Delete dialog box

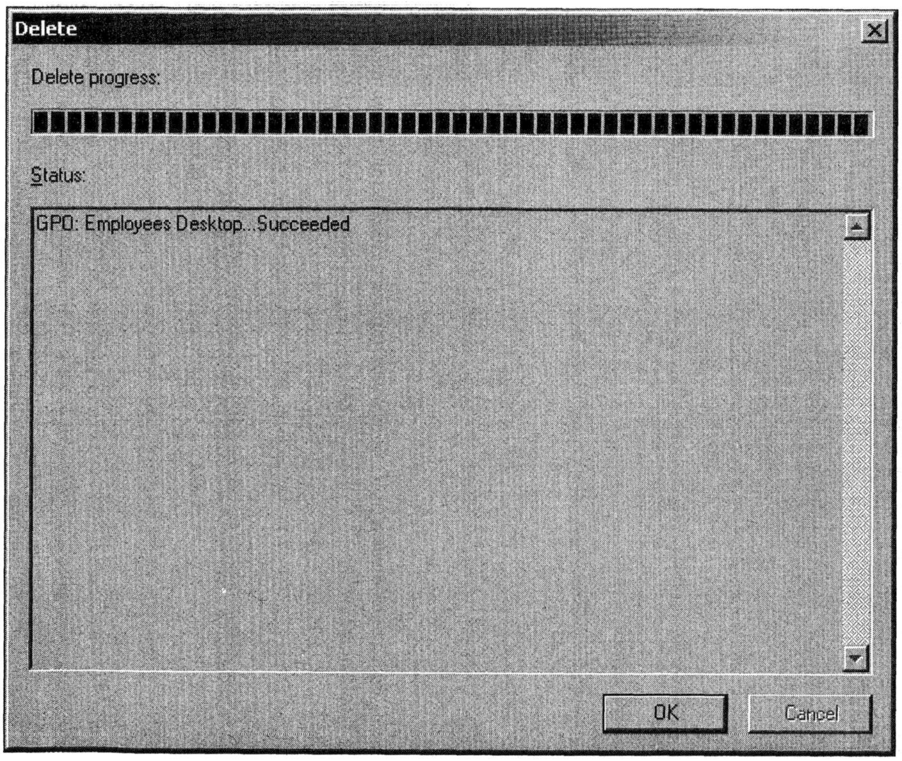

project 10.4

Linking Group Policy Objects (cont'd)

exam objective

Plan Group Policy strategy.

project steps

20. Click **OK** to close the dialog box and apply the change.
21. Close the Group Policy Object Editor and the GPMC.
22. Run the **gpupdate** command from the command prompt.
23. Log off and log back on as Peter Murphy. The wallpaper is now **Chateau** (**Figure 10-19**).
24. Log off.

Figure 10-19 The Chateau desktop

LESSON

11 Using Group Policy to Manage Software

Windows Server 2003 and Windows 2000 provide an environment much more conducive to the mass distribution of software than their predecessors. Through the use of Group Policy Objects, network administrators now have the ability to distribute and manage software remotely and automatically from any administrative workstation.

To do so, you must first create a central software distribution point, then set software installation defaults, and finally use Group Policy to deploy the applications. After an application is deployed, you can also modify its installation properties using a GPO. You can also use Group Policy to implement folder redirection, which allows an administrator to redirect common folders to a network server, saving considerable network bandwidth and considerably reducing the logon time for users with large profiles.

This lesson contains projects that will enable you to practice setting up a software distribution point, deploying software applications, modifying installation properties, and implementing folder redirection.

Scenario

As the administrator for the apbindustries.com domain, you have been assigned the task of software deployment, specifically a package named adminpak.msi (the Windows Server 2003 Administration Tools Pack). You are required to use GPOs to successfully deliver the software package. Later, you will be asked to change the deployment type and implement folder redirection.

Lesson 11 Using Group Policy to Manage Software

Project	Exam 70-294 Objective
11.1 Setting Up a Software Distribution Point	Deploy a computer environment by using Group Policy. Distribute software by using Group Policy.
11.2 Distributing Software Applications	Configure the user environment by using Group Policy. Distribute software by using Group Policy.
11.3 Modifying Installation Properties	Deploy a computer environment by using Group Policy. Distribute software by using Group Policy. Configure the user environment by using Group Policy. Distribute software by using Group Policy.
11.4 Using Group Policy to Manage Folder Redirection	Redirect folders by using Group Policy.

General Requirements

To complete the projects in this lesson, you will need administrative rights on SERVERA, the Windows Server 2003 computer that is acting as a domain controller for the apbindustries.com domain. You also may find it helpful to refer to Lesson 11 of the Prentice Hall Certification Series Exam 70-294 textbook for further information about the topics covered by the projects in this lesson.

project 11.1

Setting up a Distribution Point

exam objective

Deploy a computer environment by using Group Policy. Distribute software by using Group Policy.

overview

As the administrator for the apbindustries.com domain, you have been assigned the task of setting up the preliminary steps to distribute a new software package called Adminpak.msi throughout the network. Although your boss is not quite ready to actually distribute the software, she wants you to have it ready to deliver for early tomorrow morning.

learning objective

After completing this project, you will know how to create a distribution point for software distribution throughout the enterprise.

specific requirements

Administrative rights on SERVERA, the Windows Server 2003 computer that is acting as a domain controller for apbindustries.com.

estimated completion time

5 minutes

project steps

1. Log on to **SERVERA** with an account that has administrative rights.
2. Open **Windows Explorer**. Select **Local Disk (C:)**.
3. Open the **File** menu, point to **New**, and click **Folder** to create a folder on the **C:** drive named **Adminpak_Distrib**. Press **[Enter]**.
4. Expand the ***%System root%*** folder. Select **system 32**. In the contents window, right-click **adminpak.msi** and click **Copy (Figure 11-1)**.
5. In the tree, right-click **Adminpak_Distrib** and click **Paste**.
6. In the tree, right-click **Adminpak_Distrib** and click **Sharing and Security** to open the **Adminpak_Distrib Properties** dialog box on the **Sharing** tab.
7. Click the **Share this folder** option button. In the **Share name** text box, type **Adminpak_Distrib_Share (Figure 11-2)**.
8. Click **Permissions** to open the **Permissions for Adminpak_Distrib_Share** dialog box.
9. Click **Add** to open the **Select Users, Computers, or Groups** dialog box.
10. Type **Administrators** in the **Enter the object names to select** box and click **OK**.
11. Click the **Allow** check box for the **Full Control** permission to grant full control over the share to the Administrators group in apbindustries.com. Only administrators should be granted the Full Control permission for the Software Distribution Point folder. Users should be assigned only the Read permission.
12. Click **OK** to close the Permissions for Adminpak_Distrib_Share dialog box.
13. Click **OK** to close the Adminpak_Distrib Properties dialog box.
14. Close Windows Explorer.

tip

Using a different name, such as **_share**, allows the administrator to easily distinguish between local and network resources.

Figure 11-1 Copying Adminpak.msi from the system32 directory

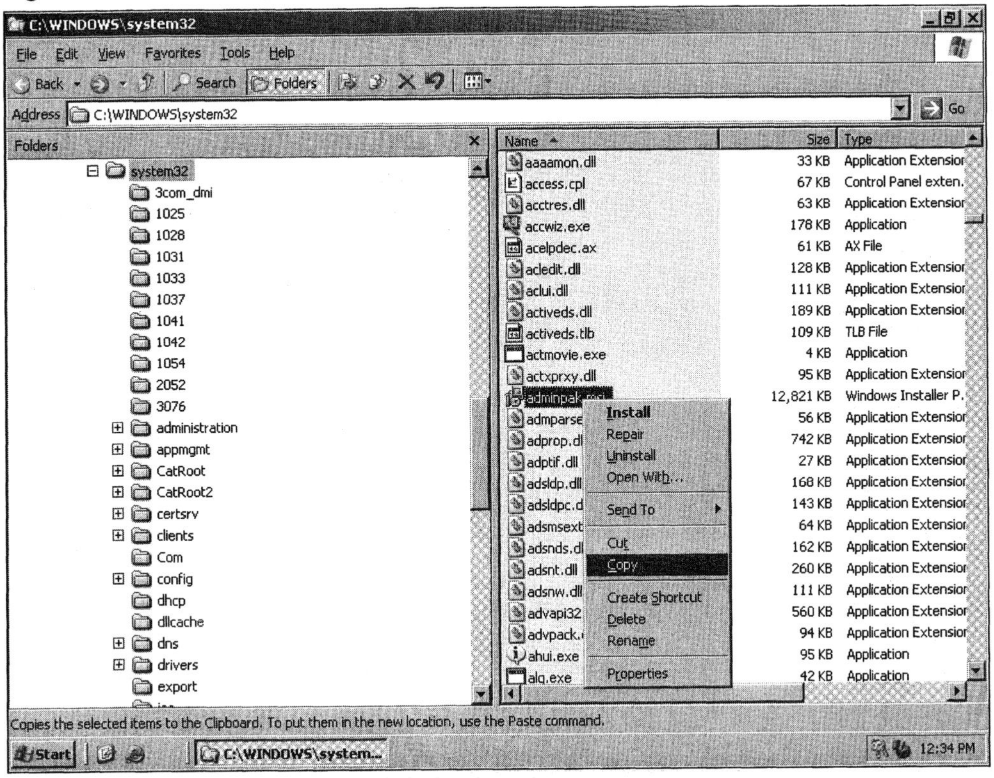

Figure 11-2 Viewing the properties of the newly created Adminpak_Distrib_Share

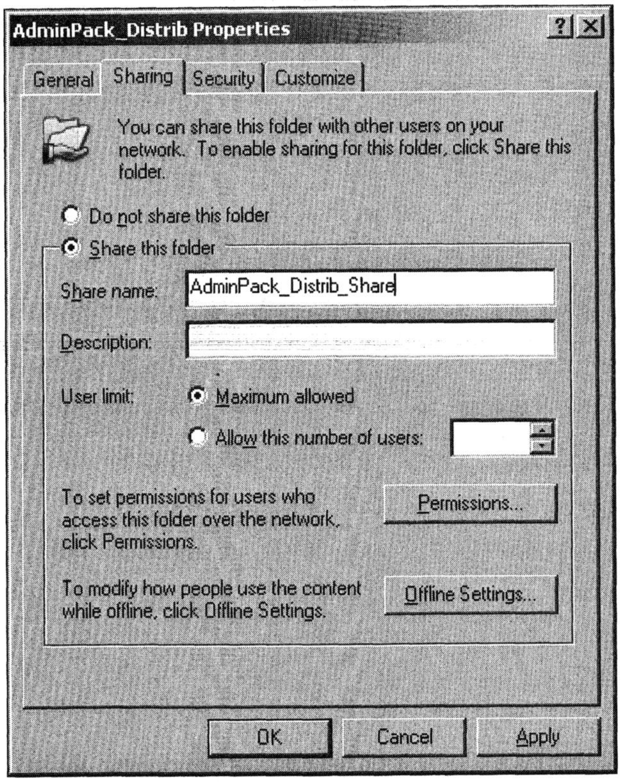

project 11.2 Distributing Software Applications

exam objective

Configure the user environment by using Group Policy. Distribute software by using Group Policy.

overview

After the successful completion of your assigned tasks in Project 11.1, you are now ready to distribute the software package called Adminpak.msi. This project requires you to do so through the use of a GPO.

learning objective

After completing this project, you will know how to modify Group Policies to facilitate the successful distribution of software packages.

specific requirements

Administrative rights on SERVERA, the Windows Server 2003 computer that is acting as a domain controller for apbindustries.com.

estimated completion time

5 minutes

project steps

1. Log on to **SERVERA** with an account that has administrative rights.
2. Open the **Group Policy Management Console (GPMC)**.
3. Expand the **Forest** and **Domains** nodes, if necessary. Expand **apbindustries.com**, if necessary.
4. Right-click **apbindustries.com** and click **Create and Link a GPO Here** to open the **New GPO** dialog box.
5. Type **Adminpak_Distrib** in the **Name** text box and click **OK**.
6. Right-click **Adminpak_Distrib** and click **Edit** to open the **Group Policy Object Editor** for the GPO.
7. Expand the **User Configuration** node, if necessary. Expand the **Software Settings** node.
8. Right-click **Software installation,** point to **New**, and select **Package** to open the **Open** dialog box.
9. In the **Look in** list box, select **My Network Places** (see Caution). Double-click **Entire Network**.
10. Double-click **Microsoft Windows Network**.
11. Double-click **Apbindustries**.
12. Double-click **SERVERA**.
13. Double-click **Adminpak_Distrib_Share (Figure 11-3)**.
14. Select **adminpak.msi** and click **Open** to open the **Deploy Software** dialog box.
15. Click the **Assigned** option button **(Figure 11-4)**. Click **OK**.
16. Close the Group Policy Object Editor and the GPMC.

caution

Be sure to use network locations, not local locations, when browsing to the .msi file.

Figure 11-3 Adminpak_Distrib_Share containing the adminpak.msi file

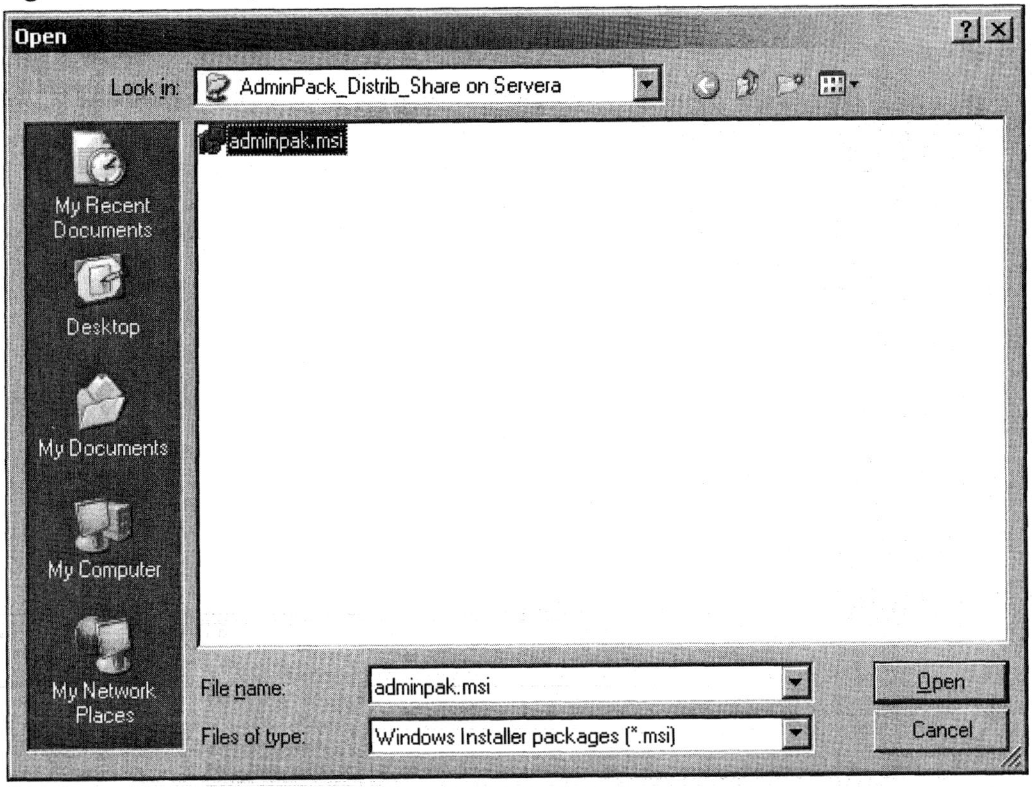

Figure 11-4 Assigned deployment method for software Adminpak.msi

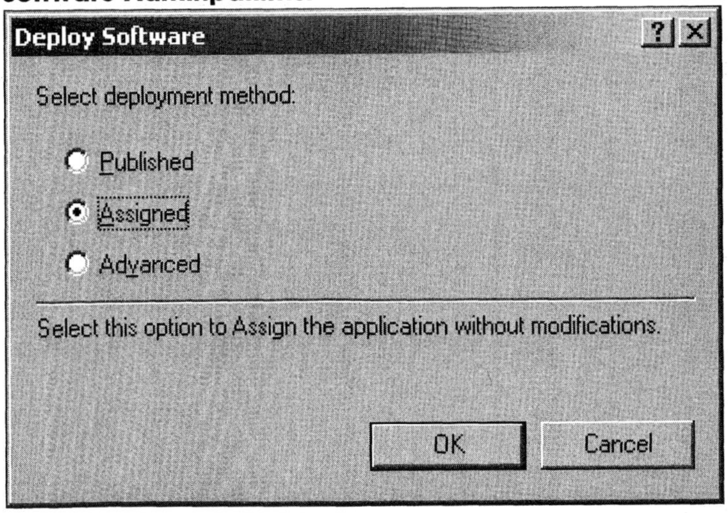

project 11.3

Modifying Installation Properties

exam objective

Deploy a computer environment by using Group Policy. Distribute software by using Group Policy. Configure the user environment by using Group Policy. Distribute software by using Group Policy.

overview

In the previous project, you were required to distribute a software package to a specific group of computers. Due to unforeseen circumstances, you have now decided to amend the existing software package by changing the deployment type to "Published."

learning objective

After completing this project, you will know how to modify an existing software distribution package.

specific requirements

Administrative rights on SERVERA, the Windows Server 2003 computer that is acting as a domain controller for apbindustries.com, and successful completion of Project 11.2.

estimated completion time

5 minutes

project steps

1. Log on to **SERVERA** with an account that has administrative rights.
2. Open the **GPMC**.
3. Expand the **Forest** and **Domains** nodes, if necessary. Expand **apbindustries.com** if necessary.
4. Right-click **Adminpak_Distrib** and click **Edit** to open the **Group Policy Object Editor** for the GPO.
5. Expand the **User Configuration** node, if necessary. Expand the **Software Settings** node.
6. Select **Software installation**.
7. Double-click **Windows Server 2003 Administration Tools Pack (Figure 11-5)** to open the corresponding **Properties** dialog box.
8. Open the **Deployment** tab. In the **Deployment type** section, select the **Published** option button to change the deployment type to Published **(Figure 11-6)**.
9. Click **OK** to close the Windows Server 2003 Administration Tools Pack Properties dialog box.
10. Close the Group Policy Object Editor and the GPMC.

Figure 11-5 Specifying Windows Server 2003 Administration Tools

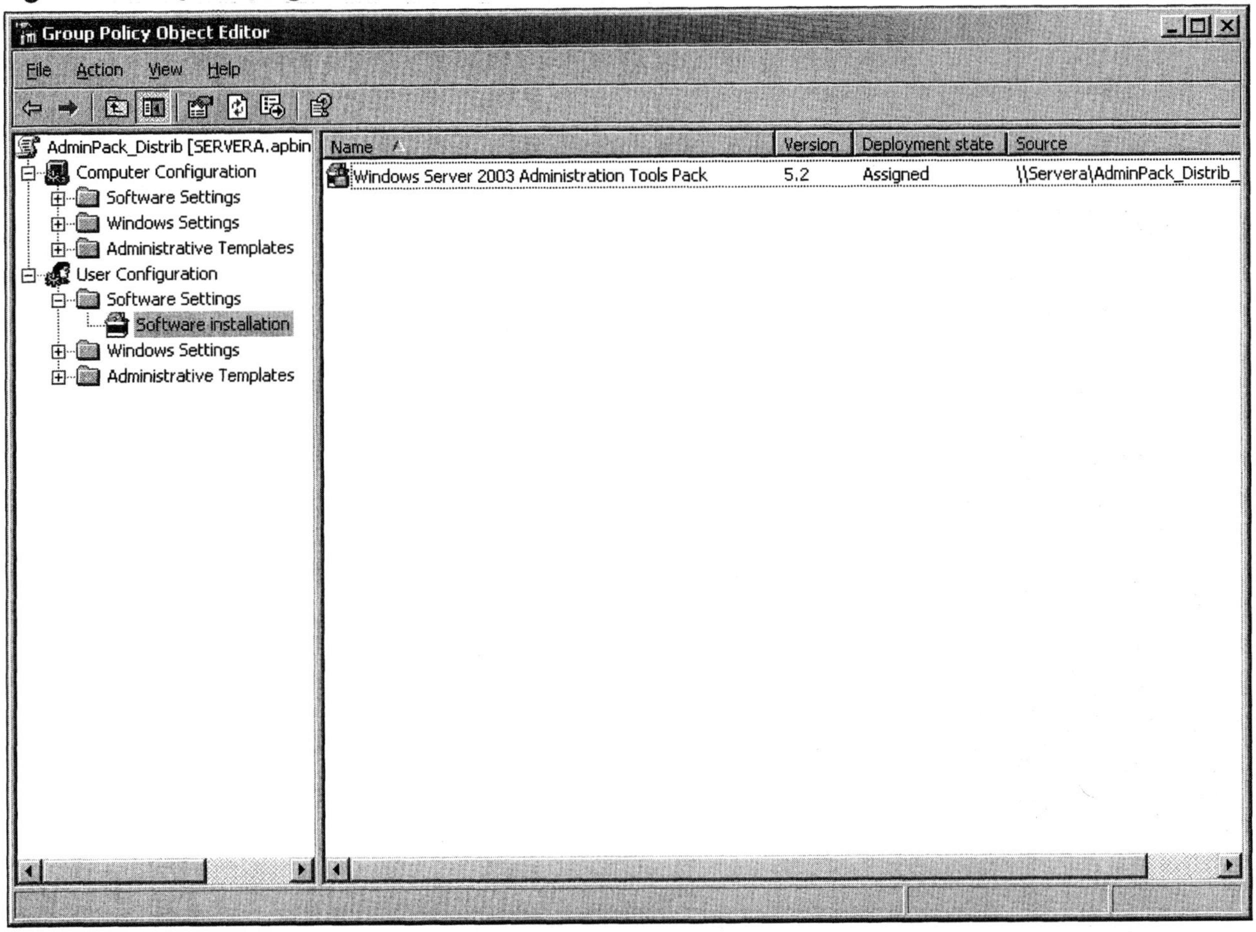

Figure 11-6 Changing Deployment Type to Published

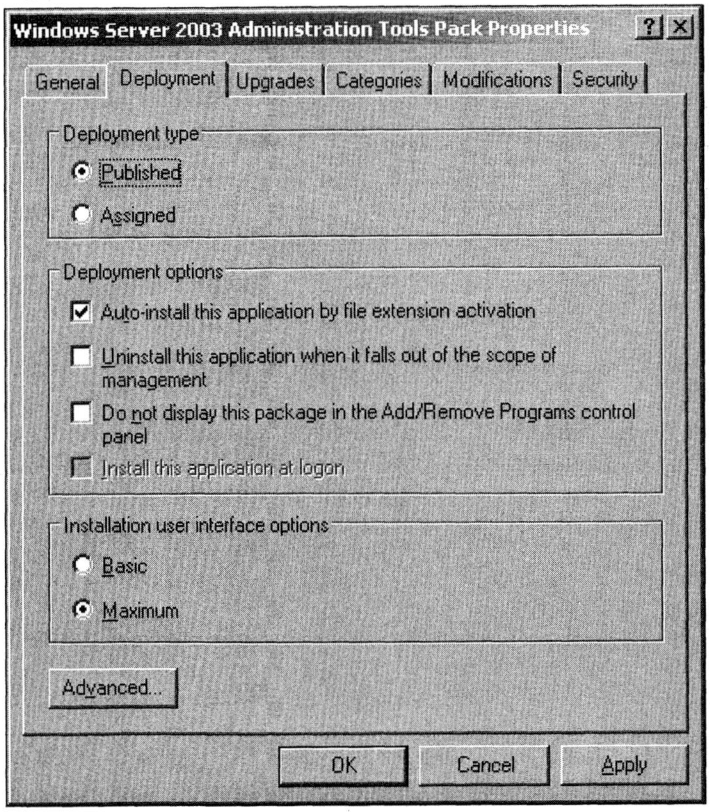

project 11.4

Using Group Policy to Manage Folder Redirection

exam objective

Redirect folders by using Group Policy.

overview

Several weeks ago, the IT Department issued a memo requiring all work to be saved to a network folder rather than locally because the department plans to replace all client computers soon. Images have already been created to distribute to the newly installed machines. It is important that no new software or documents be added to the legacy computers.

During your regular network reviews, you realize that some users are continuing to save work to their My Documents folder. Rather than issuing another memorandum, you decide to redirect the My Documents folders to a network folder on SERVERA named Redirect_My_Documents.

learning objective

After completing this project, you will know how to prevent users from saving locally. They will be forced to save to a network drive, even when they think they are saving locally.

specific requirements

Administrative rights on SERVERA, the Windows Server 2003 computer that is acting as a domain controller for apbindustries.com.

estimated completion time

5 minutes

project steps

1. Log on to **SERVERA** with an account that has administrative rights. Open **Windows Explorer**. Select **Local Disk (C:)**.
2. Open the **File** menu, point to **New**, and click **Folder** to create a folder on the **C:** drive named **Redirected_Folder**. Press **[Enter]**.
3. In the tree, right-click **Redirected_Folder** and click **Sharing and Security** to open the **Redirected_Folder Properties** dialog box.
4. Click the **Share this folder** option button. Name the share **Redirected_Folder_Share (Figure 11-7)**.
5. Click **Permissions** to open the **Permissions for Redirected_Folder_Share** dialog box. Click the **Allow** check box for the **Full Control** permission to grant full control to the **Everyone** group.
6. Click **OK** to close the Permissions for Redirected_Folder_Share dialog box. Click **OK** to close the Redirected_Folder Properties dialog box. Close Windows Explorer.
7. Open the **GPMC**. Expand the **Forest** and **Domains** nodes, if necessary. Expand **apbindustries.com**, if necessary.
8. Right-click **apbindustries.com** and click **Create and Link a GPO Here** to open the **New GPO** dialog box. Type **Redirect_My_Documents** in the **Name** text box and click **OK (Figure 11-8)**.
9. Right-click the **Redirect_My_Documents** GPO and click **Edit** to open the **Group Policy Management Editor** for the GPO. Expand the **User Configuration** node, if necessary. Expand the **Windows Settings** and the **Folder Redirection** nodes.
10. Right-click **My Documents** and click **Properties** to open the **My Documents Properties** dialog box. In the **Setting** list box, select **Basic – Redirect everyone's folder to the same location**. In the **Target folder location** section, click **Browse** to open the **Browse for Folder** dialog box.
11. Expand the following in order: **My Network Places**, **Entire Network**, **Microsoft Windows Network**, **Apbindustries**, and **Servera**.
12. Select **Redirected_Folder_Share (Figure 11-9)** and click **OK** to close the Browse for Folder dialog box.
13. In the **Target folder location** list box, select **Create a folder for each user under the root path**, if necessary **(Figure 11-10)**.
14. Click OK to close the My Documents Properties dialog box. Close the GPMC.

Figure 11-7 Redirected_Folder Properties dialog box

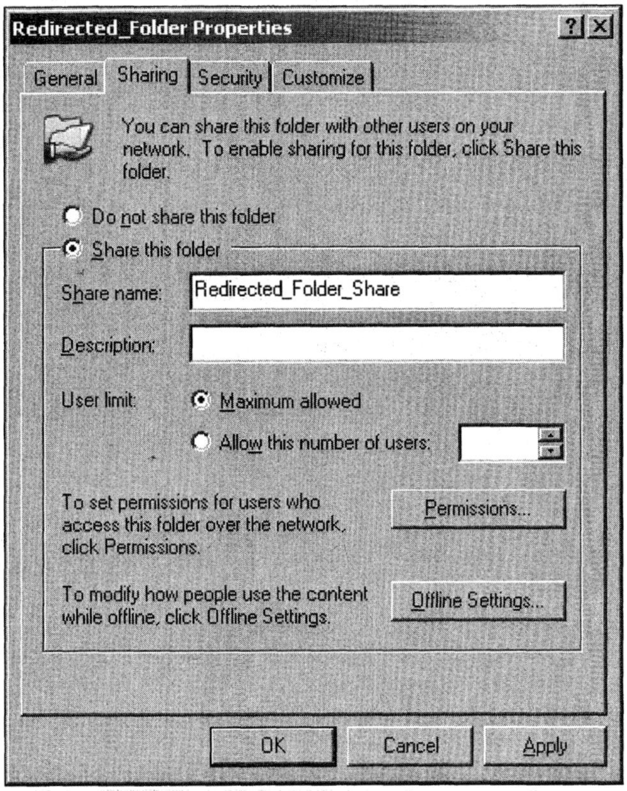

Figure 11-8 New GPO dialog box

Figure 11-9 The Browse for Folder dialog box

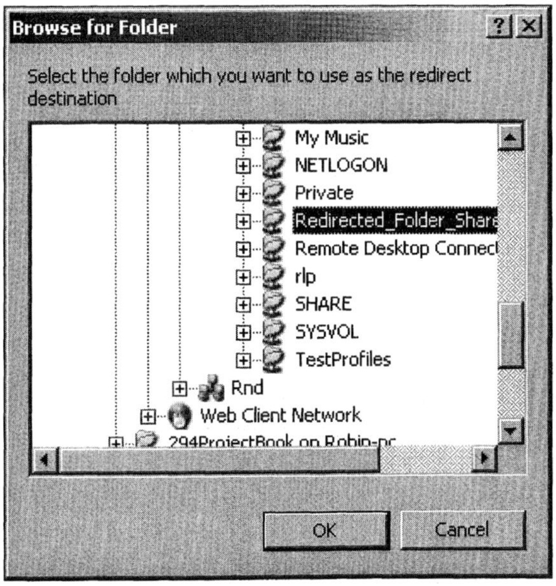

Figure 11-10 Creating a new folder in the target location

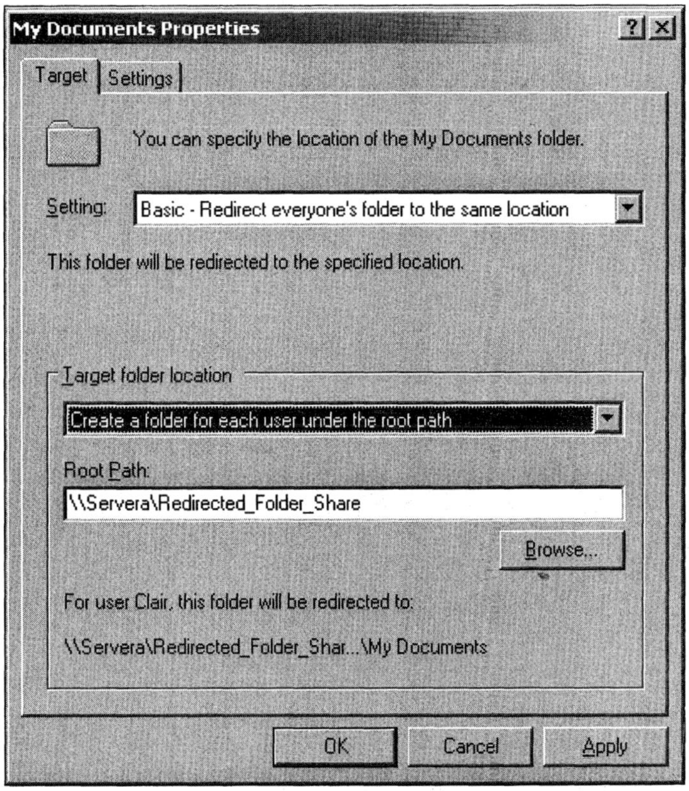

LESSON 12

Configuring Active Directory Security

Networks exist to share resources among users. However, for various reasons, all users will rarely have access to all resources. It is the responsibility of the network administrator to grant access to specific network resources only to authorized users. Administrators must also audit access to vital resources to ensure that unauthorized users are not gaining access.

Information such as directory and file access can be recorded by Windows Server 2003 as part of the auditing process. This information can be reviewed to determine the normal processes and procedures of everyday network operations. If these parameters are exceeded, it can be a red flag for network administrators.

Organizations must have security measures in place in order to prevent unauthorized users from accessing resources, while still maintaining uninterrupted communications. Auditing must be balanced against available system resources, because auditing can consume a large amount of disk space, as well as a great deal of administrative time to monitor and analyze events.

Network administrators must have a solid understanding of the security tools provided by Windows 2003, including the Group Policy security settings, the Security Templates and Analysis tools, and audit policy, in order to create a secure and efficient network.

Scenario

As the network administrator for APB industries, one of your chief concerns is security. In order to achieve a satisfactory security level, you must create and properly configure audit policies on the domain controllers. You must also use various tools and templates to set up and manage network security for existing files and folders.

Lesson 12 Configuring Active Directory Security

Project	Exam 70-294 Objective
12.1 Configuring Security	Basic knowledge
12.2 Setting Audit Policy on Domain Controllers	Basic knowledge
12.3 Auditing Files and Folders	Basic knowledge
12.4 Using Security Logs to Handle Events	Basic knowledge
12.5 Exporting Security Settings to a Security Template	Plan a user authentication strategy. Create a password policy for domain users.

General Requirements

To complete the projects in this lesson, you must have administrative rights on SERVERA, the Windows Server 2003 computer that is acting as a domain controller for the apbindustries.com domain. You must also have successfully completed the projects in Lesson 7. You may also find it helpful to refer to Lesson 12 in your Prentice Hall Certification Series Exam 70-294 textbook for further information about the topics covered by the projects in this lesson.

project 12.1

Configuring Security

exam objective

Basic knowledge

overview

Active Directory networks use time stamps throughout the replication process. It is important that all computers on the network agree on the correct time. You have decided to use a GPO to grant authority to change the time to one of your managers by assigning him the Change the system time user right.

learning objective

After completing this project, you will know how to use the Security Settings extension in the Group Policy Object Editor.

specific requirements

Administrative rights on SERVERA, the Windows Server 2003 computer that is acting as a domain controller for apbindustries.com.

estimated completion time

10 minutes

project steps

1. Log on to **SERVERA** with an account that has administrative rights.
2. Open the **Group Policy Management** console.
3. Expand the **Forest** and **Domains** nodes, if necessary. Expand **apbindustries.com**, if necessary.
4. Expand the **Domain Controllers** OU.
5. Right-click the **Default Domain Controllers Policy** GPO and click **Edit** to open the **Group Policy Object Editor** for the GPO.
6. Expand the **Computer Configuration** node, if necessary.
7. Expand the **Windows Settings**, **Security Settings**, and **Local Policies** nodes.
8. Select **Users Rights Assignment (Figure 12-1)**.
9. Double-click **Change the system time** to open the **Change the system time Properties** dialog box **(Figure 12-2)**.
10. Click **Add User or Group** to open the **Add User or Group** dialog box.
11. Click **Browse** to open the **Select Users, Computers, or Groups** dialog box.
12. Click **Advanced** to expand the dialog box.
13. Click **Find Now**. In the **Search results** list, double-click **Mark Jackson** to add the user account to the **Enter the object names** to select box.
14. Click **OK** to close the Select Users, Computers, or Groups dialog box and add **APBINDUSTRIES\MJackson** to the **User and group names** text box.
15. Click **OK** to close the Add User or Group dialog box.
16. APBINDUSTRIES\MJackson is added to the list of users and groups in the Change the system time Properties dialog box.
17. Click **OK** to close the Change the system time Properties dialog box.
18. Close the Group Policy Object Editor and the GPMC.
19. Open the command prompt and run the **gpupdate** command.
20. Logoff and log back on as **MJackson**.
21. Double-click the **system clock** to open the **Date and Time Properties** dialog box and verify that Mark Jackson can access the clock.
22. Click **Cancel**.
23. Logoff and log back on as **PMurphy**.
24. Double-click the **system clock**. The **Date and Time Properties** information dialog box opens to inform you that you do not have the proper privilege to change the System Time **(Figure 12-3)**.
25. Log off.

tip

By default, Group Policies are refreshed on domain controllers every five minutes. Therefore, the policy may not take effect for up to five minutes. However, you can run the gpupdate command at the command prompt to force an immediate policy refresh.

Figure 12-1 User Rights Assignments

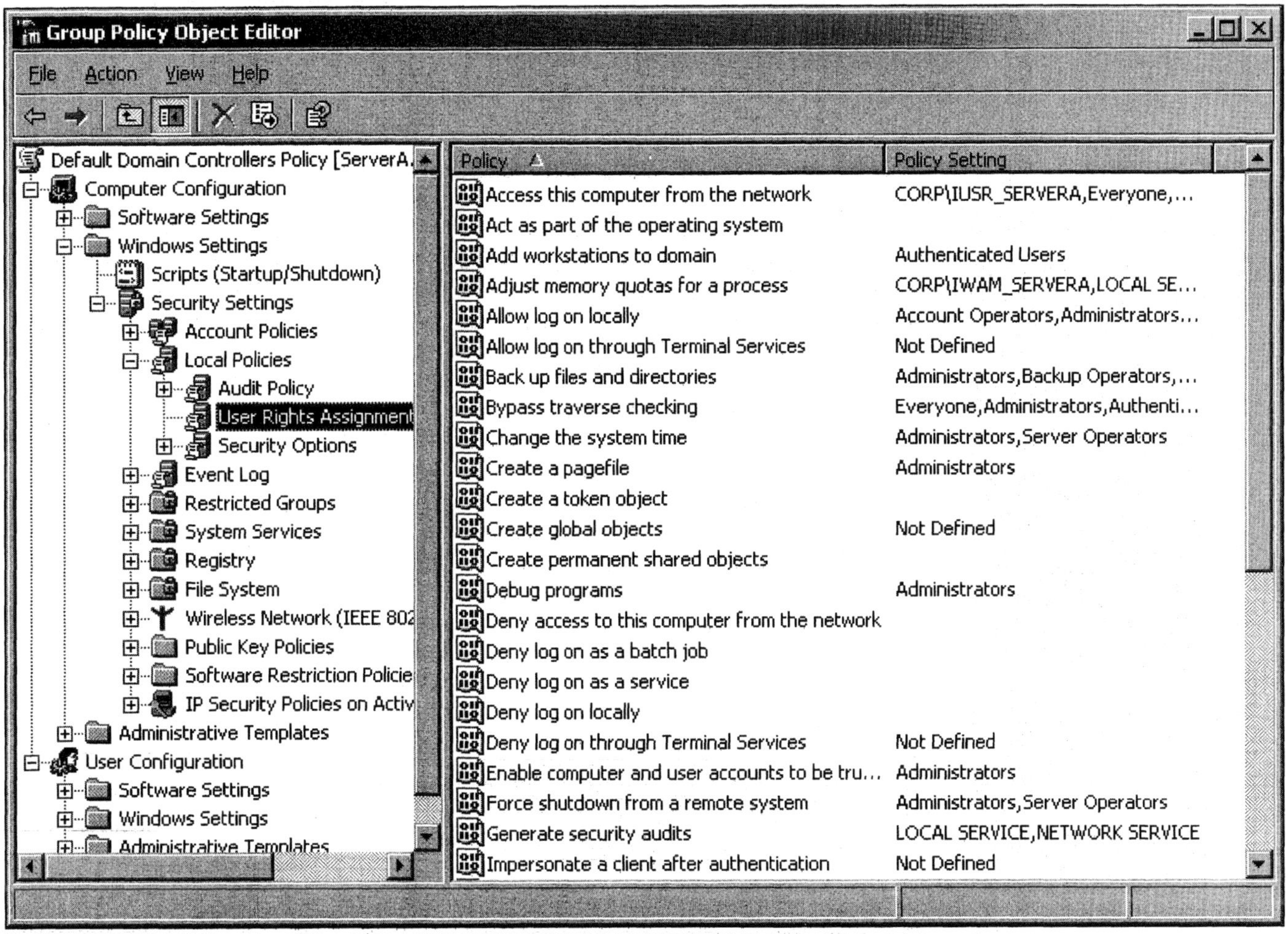

Figure 12-2 The Change the system time Properties dialog box

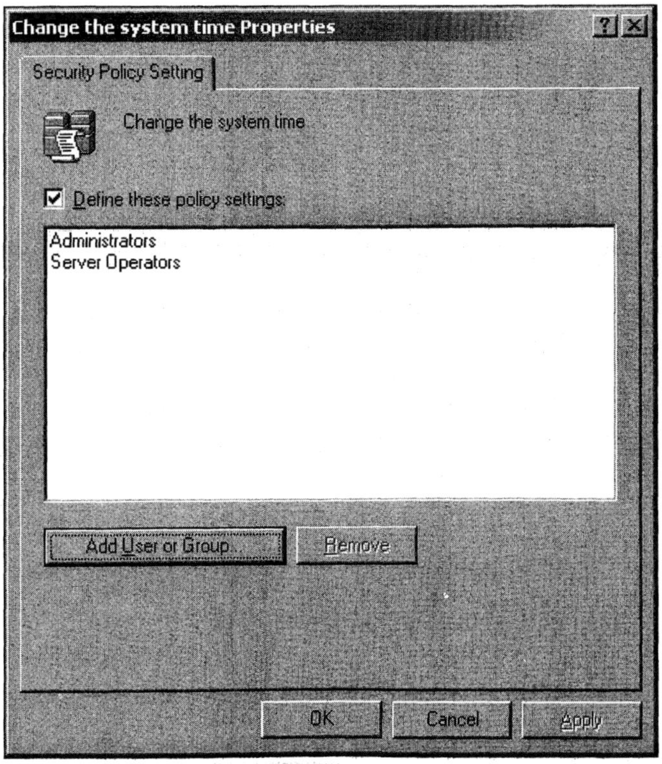

Figure 12-3 The Date and Time Properties information dialog box

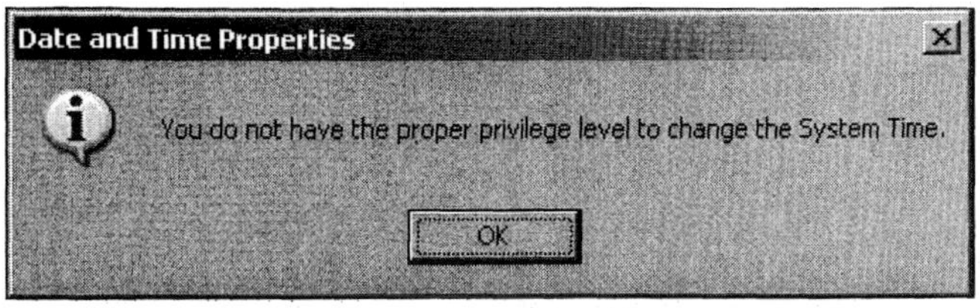

project 12.2

Setting Audit Policy on Domain Controllers

exam objective

Basic knowledge

overview

Audit policy is configured on a domain controller to monitor attempts to gain access to the domain through the domain controller. It is your responsibility as the network administrator for apbindustries.com to create audit policies to monitor all logons to the domain, as well as all local logons to the domain controller. You must also enable auditing for object access so that you can audit access to a sensitive folder.

learning objective

After completing this project, you will know how to implement audit policies on a domain controller.

specific requirements

Administrative rights on SERVERA, the Windows Server 2003 computer that is acting as a domain controller for apbindustries.com.

estimated completion time

10 minutes

project steps

tip

If events are non-existent in the Security Log, remember that group policies are refreshed every five minutes and auditing will not begin until before then.

1. Log on to **SERVERA** with an account that has administrative rights.
2. Open the **Group Policy Management** console.
3. Expand the **Forest** and **Domains** nodes, if necessary. Expand **apbindustries.com**, if necessary.
4. Expand the **Domain Controllers** OU.
5. Right-click the **Default Domain Controllers Policy** GPO and click **Edit** to open the **Group Policy Object Editor** for the GPO.
6. Expand the **Computer Configuration** node, if necessary.
7. Expand the **Windows Settings** node.
8. Expand the **Security Settings** and **Local Policies** nodes.
9. Select **Audit Policy**.
10. Double-click **Audit account logon events** to open the **Audit account logon events Properties** dialog box.
11. Select the **Define these policy settings** check box, if necessary, to activate the audit policy setting.
12. Select the **Success** and **Failure** check boxes **(Figure 12-4)**.
13. Click **OK** to close the dialog box. This setting audits all logon attempts sent to the domain controller.
14. Double-click **Audit logon events** to open the **Audit logon events Properties** dialog box.
15. Select the **Define these policy settings** check box, if necessary.
16. Select the **Success** and **Failure** check boxes **(Figure 12-5)**.
17. Click **OK** to close the dialog box. This setting audits all local logon attempts.
18. Double-click **Audit object access** to open the **Audit object access Properties** dialog box.
19. Select the **Define these policy settings** check box, if necessary.
20. Select the **Success** and **Failure** check boxes **(Figure 12-6)**.
21. Click **OK** to close the dialog box. The details pane now shows **Success**, **Failure** for each of these policies **(Figure 12-7)**.
22. Close the Group Policy Object Editor and the GPMC.
23. Logoff and log back on as **PMurphy**.
24. Log off. Attempt to log back on with an account that has administrative rights, but use an incorrect password. Log on correctly.

Figure 12-4 The Audit account logon events Properties dialog box

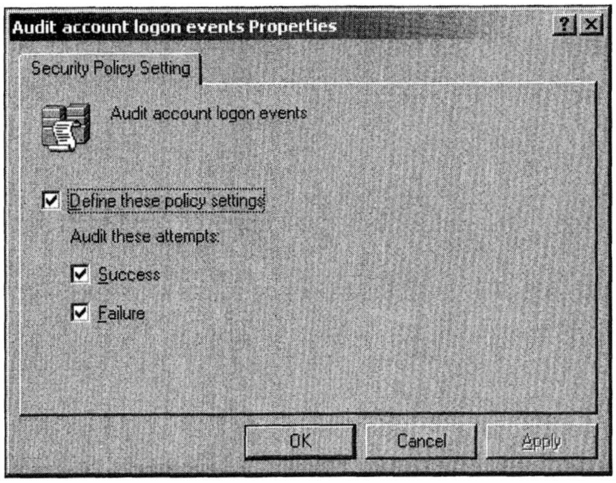

Figure 12-5 The Audit logon events Properties dialog box

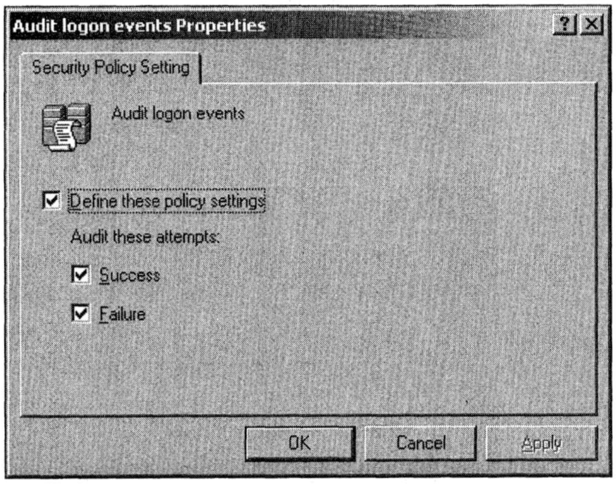

Figure 12-6 The Audit object access Properties dialog box

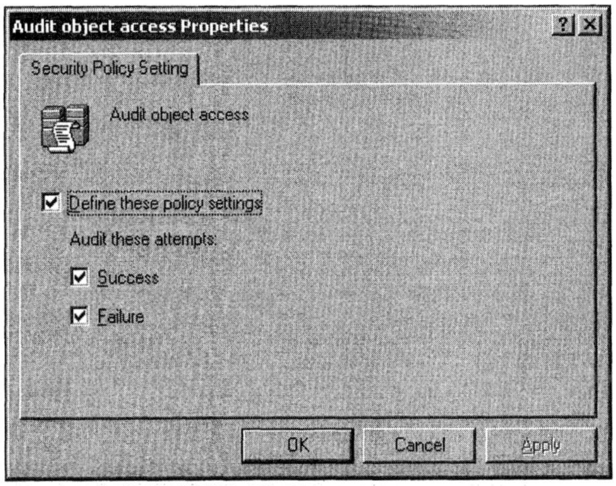

Figure 12-7 The configured audit policies

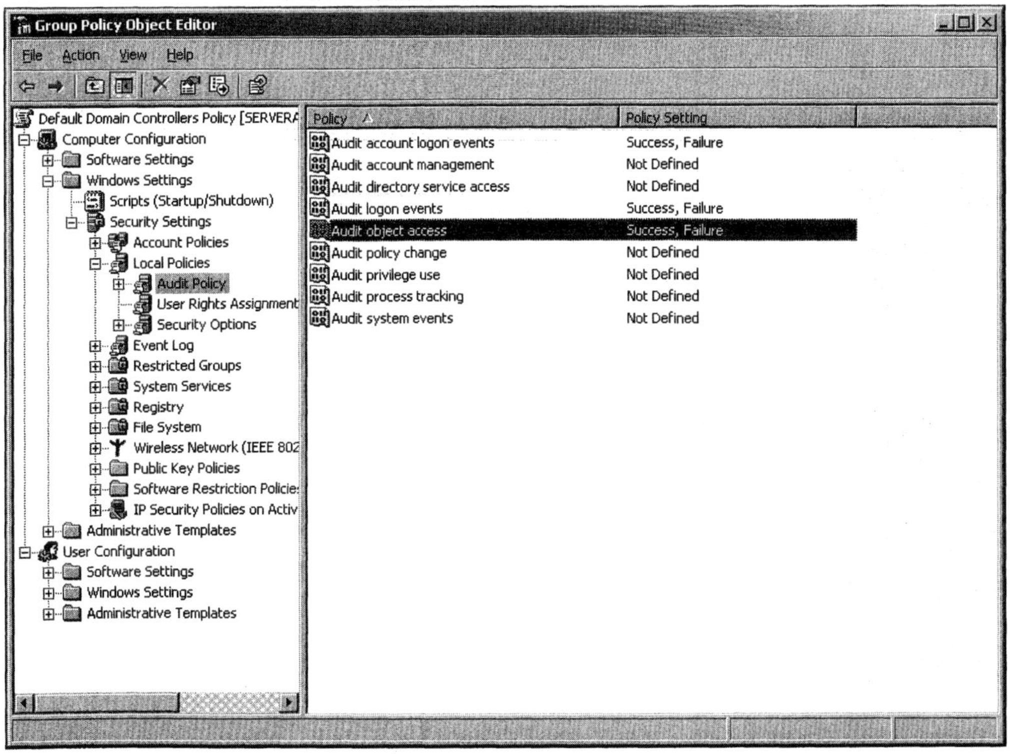

project 12.2

Setting Audit Policy on Domain Controllers (cont'd)

exam objective

Basic knowledge

project steps

25. Click **Start**, point to **Administrative Tools**, and click **Event Viewer** to open the **Event Viewer** console.

26. Select **Security** to view the Security log and verify the existence of the Account Logon and Logon/Logoff events **(Figure 12-8)**.

27. Close the Event Viewer.

Figure 12-8 The Security log in the Event Viewer

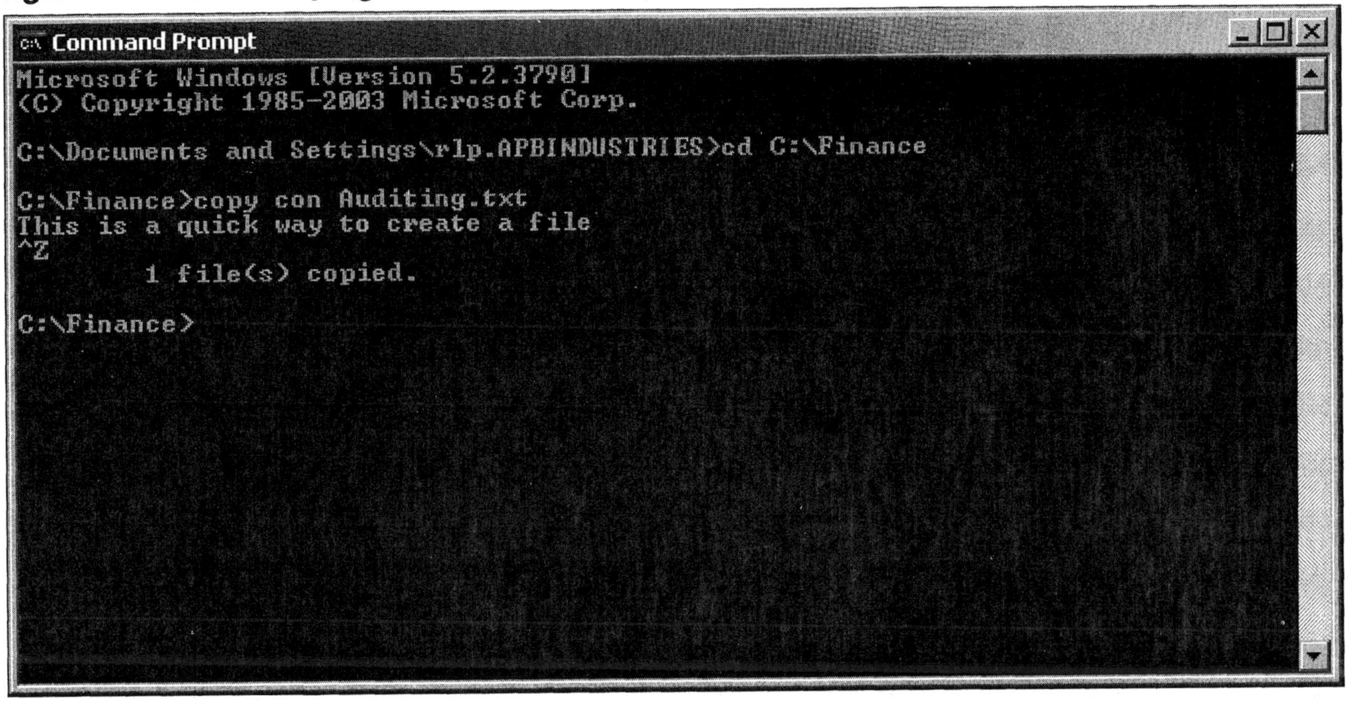

project 12.3

Establishing Auditing for Files and Folders

exam objective

Basic knowledge

overview

Windows Server 2003 allows you to monitor access and attempts to access files and folders. You have decided to create an audit policy for apbindustries.com to monitor successful and failed attempts to access a sensitive file, Auditing.txt, which is stored in the Finance folder.

learning objective

After completing this project, you will know how to audit object access.

specific requirements

Administrative rights on SERVERA, the Windows Server 2003 computer that is acting as a domain controller for apbindustries.com.

estimated completion time

10 minutes

project steps

tip

Auditing is one of the few times the use of the Everyone group is a best practice.

1. Open **Windows Explorer** and select **Local Disk (C:)**.
2. Open the **File** menu, point to **New**, and click **Folder** to create a new folder.
3. Name the new folder **Finance**. Press **[Enter]**.
4. Click **Start** and then **Run** to open the **Run** dialog box.
5. Type **cmd** in the **Open** text box and press **[Enter]** to open the command prompt.
6. Type cd **C:\Finance** and press **[Enter]** to change the directory to the Finance folder.
7. Type **copy con Auditing.txt** and press **[Enter]**. This is a quick way to create a text file named Auditing in the Finance folder.
8. Type **This is a quick way to create a file** and press **[Enter]**. This is the text that will be entered in the Auditng.txt file.
9. Hold down the **[Control]** key and simultaneously press **Z**.
10. Press **[Enter]** to copy the Auditing.txt file to the Finance folder **(Figure 12-9)**.
11. Type **exit** and press **[Enter]** to close the command prompt.
12. In Windows Explorer, double-click the **Finance** folder in the details pane to confirm that the **Auditing.txt** file has been created.
13. Right-click the **Finance** folder in the tree and select **Properties** to open the **Finance Properties** dialog box **(Figure 12-10)**.
14. Open the **Security** tab and click **Advanced** to open the **Advanced Security Settings for Finance** dialog box.
15. Open the **Auditing** tab **(Figure 12-11)**.
16. Click **Add** to open the **Select User, Computer, or Group** dialog box.
17. Click **Advanced** to expand the dialog box.
18. Click **Find Now**. In the **Search results** list, double-click the **Everyone** group to enter it in the **Enter the object name** to select box.
19. Click **OK** to close the Select User, Computer, or Group dialog box.
20. The **Auditing Entry for Finance** dialog box opens.
21. Select the **Successful** and **Failed** check boxes for the **List Folder/Read Data** and **Create Files/Write Data** access levels **(Figure 12-12)**.
22. Click **OK** to close the Auditing Entry for Finance dialog box.
23. Click **OK** to close the Advanced Security Settings for Finance dialog box.
24. Click **OK** to close the Finance Properties dialog box. Close Windows Explorer.

Figure 12-9 Creating a text file at the command prompt

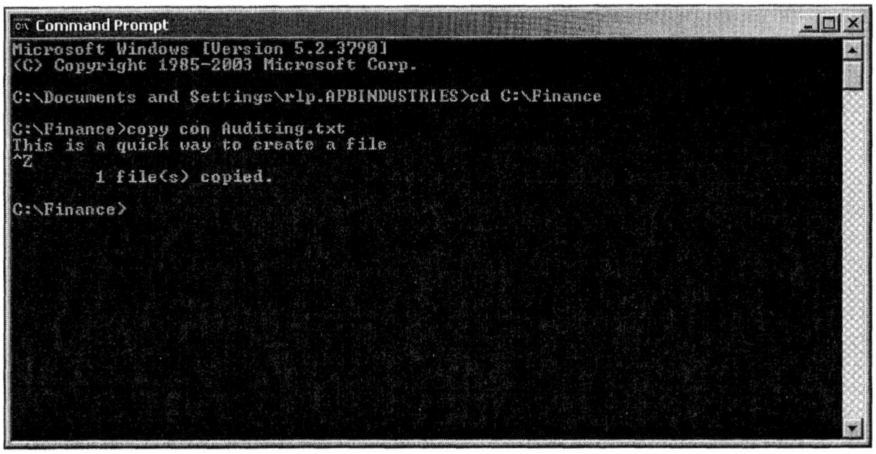

Figure 12-10 The Finance Properties dialog box

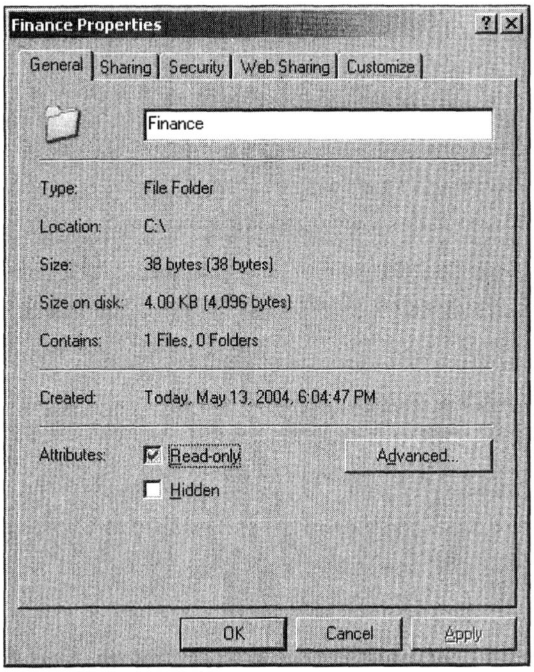

Figure 12-11 The Auditing tab on the Advanced Security Settings dialog box

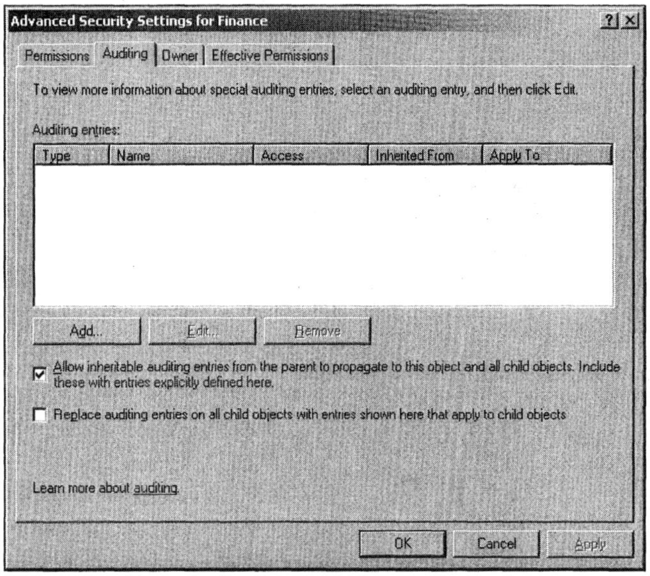

Figure 12-12 Selecting auditing entries

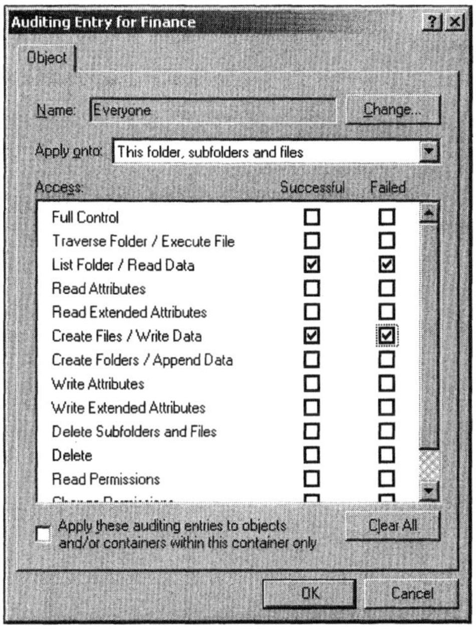

project 12.4

Using Security Logs to Handle Events

exam objective

Basic knowledge

overview

Now that you have created a folder that is monitored with specific audit policies, you must establish permissions for the Finance folder to enable auditing of the Auditing.txt file.

learning objective

After completing this project, you will know how to create, monitor, analyze, and troubleshoot audit policies using security logs.

specific requirements

Administrative rights on SERVERA, the Windows Server 2003 computer that is acting as a domain controller for apbindustries.com.

estimated completion time

15 minutes

project steps

First, you will assign the Full Control permission to the IT-U group for the Finance folder.

1. Open **Windows Explorer** and select **Local Disk (C:)**.
2. In the folder tree, right-click **Finance** and select **Properties** to open the **Finance Properties** dialog box.
3. Open the **Security** tab.
4. Click **Add** to open the **Select Users, Computers, or Groups** dialog box.
5. Click **Advanced** to expand the dialog box.
6. Click **Find Now**.
7. In the **Search results** list, select the **IT-U** group.
8. Click **OK** to enter the IT-U group in the **Enter the object names to select** box.
9. Click **OK** to close the Select Users, Computers, or Groups dialog box.
10. Click the **Allow** check box for the **Full Control** permission for the IT-U group **(Figure 12-13)**.

Next, you will remove all inherited permissions so that only the IT-U group will have access to the Finance folder.

1. Click **Advanced** to open the **Advanced Security Settings for Finance** dialog box.
2. Clear the **Allow inheritable permissions from parent to propagate to this object** checkbox **(Figure 12-14)**.
3. A **Security** dialog box opens to inform you that the parent permissions entries that apply to child objects will no longer be applied **(Figure 12-15)**.
4. Click **Remove**. Only the IT-U group now has permission to access the Finance folder **(Figure 12-16)**.
5. Click **OK** to close the Advanced Security Settings for Finance dialog box.
6. Click **OK** to close the Finance Properties dialog box. Close Windows Explorer.

Now, you will attempt to access the Finance folder with a user account that is not a member of the IT-U group as well as with a user account that is a member of the IT-U group.

1. Logoff and log back on as **PMurphy**.
2. Open Windows Explorer, select **Local Disk (C:)**, and attempt to access **C:\Finance**. Access should be denied **(Figure 12-17)**.
3. Click **OK** to close the **Local Disk (C:)** Access is denied dialog box and close Windows Explorer.

Figure 12-13 Assigning Full Control to the IT-U group

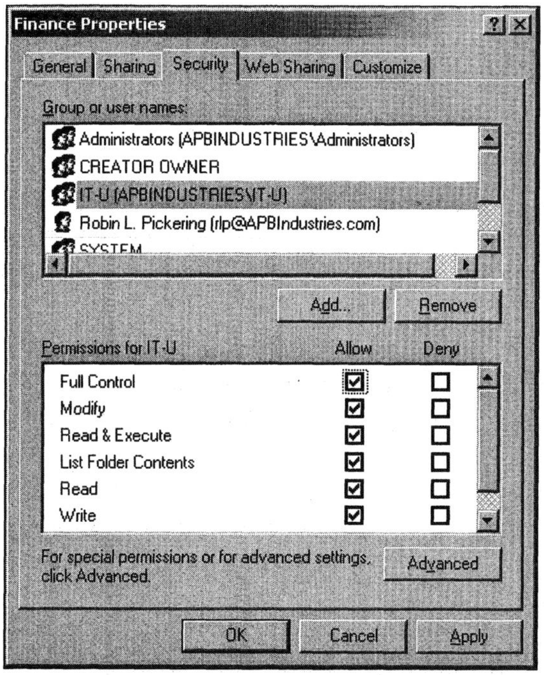

Figure 12-14 The Advanced Security Settings dialog box

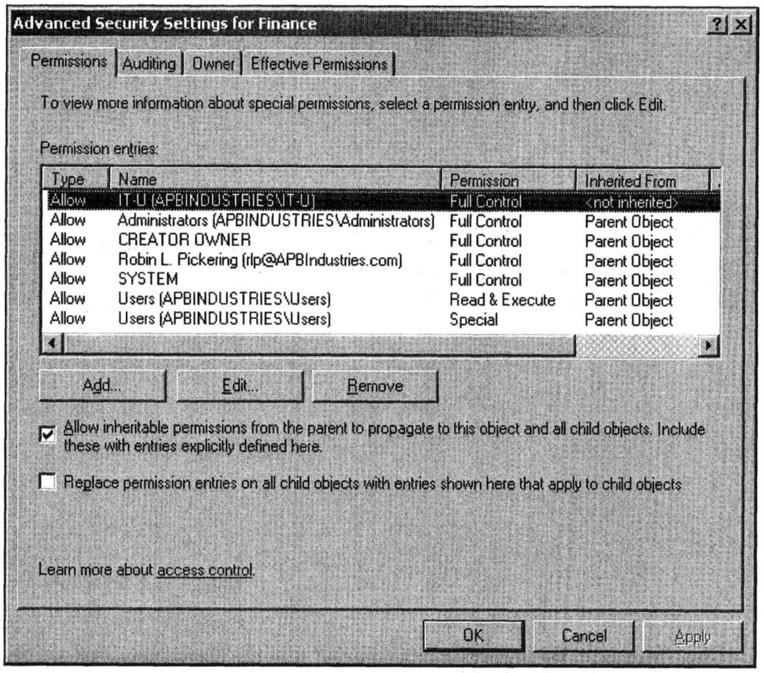

Figure 12-15 A Security information dialog box

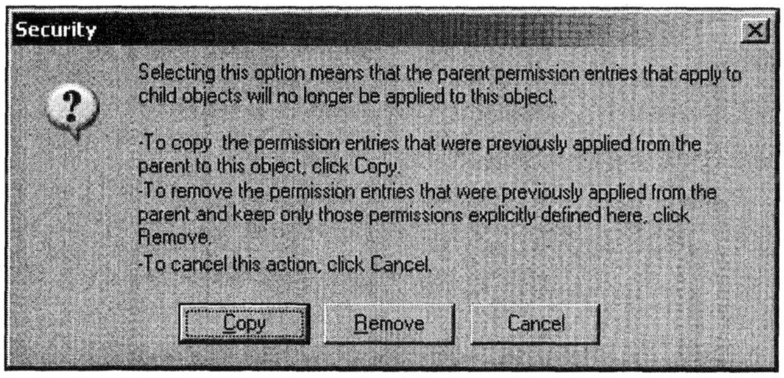

Figure 12-16 The parent permissions have been removed

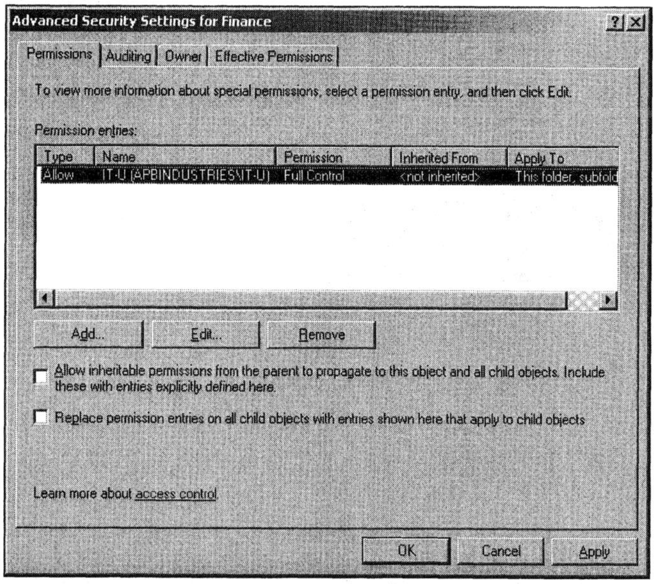

Figure 12-17 An Access is denied message box

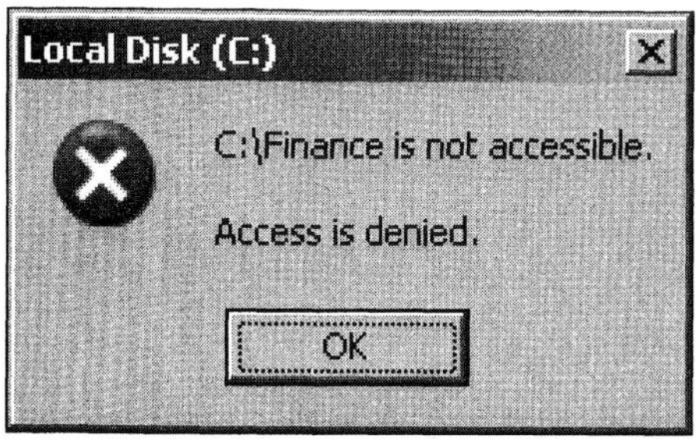

project 12.4

Using Security Logs to Handle Events *(cont'd)*

exam objective

Basic knowledge

project steps

4. Logoff and log back on as **MJackson**.
5. Open Windows Explorer and open **C:\Finance**.
6. Double-click **Auditing.txt** in the details pane. The file will open in Notepad (**Figure 12-18**).
7. Close Notepad and Windows Explorer.

Finally, you will filter the entries in the Security log to view only Object Access events and view the auditing entry that was created when access was denied to PMurphy for the Finance folder.

1. Logoff and log back on with an account that has administrative rights.
2. Click **Start**, point to **Administrative Tools**, and click **Event Viewer** to open the **Event Viewer** console.
3. Click **Security** to view the Security log.
4. Open the **View** menu and click **Filter** to open the **Security Properties** dialog box on the **Filter** tab.
5. In the **Event source** list box, select **Security**.
6. In the **Category** list box, select **Object Access (Figure 12-19)**.
7. Click **OK** to close the Security Properties dialog box.
8. Double-click the first audit entry (on the top) to open the **Event Properties** dialog box.
9. Click the **down arrow** button until you locate the failure audit entry for PMurphy with **C: Finance** as the **Object Name (Figure 12-20)**.
10. Click **OK** to close the Event Properties dialog box.
11. Close the Event Viewer.

Figure 12-18 Auditing.txt

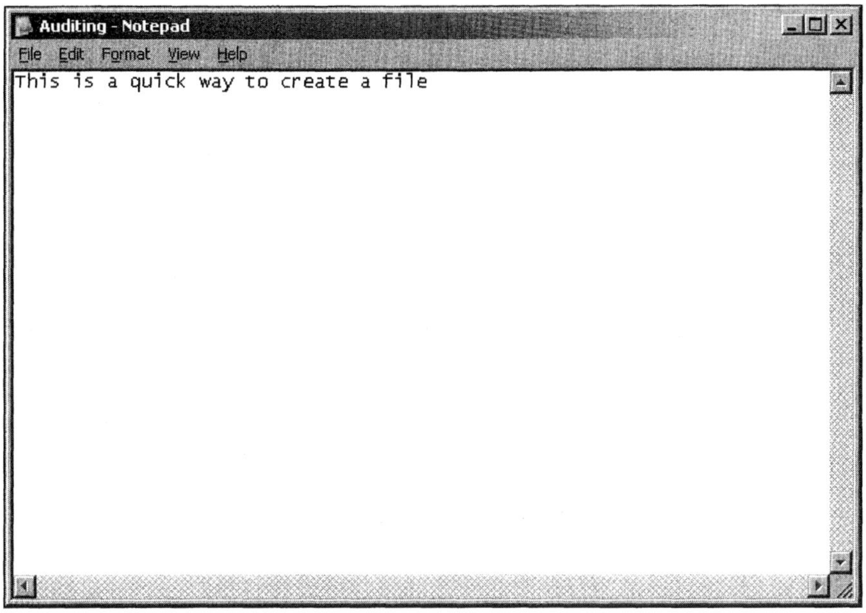

Figure 12-19 Filtering Security events

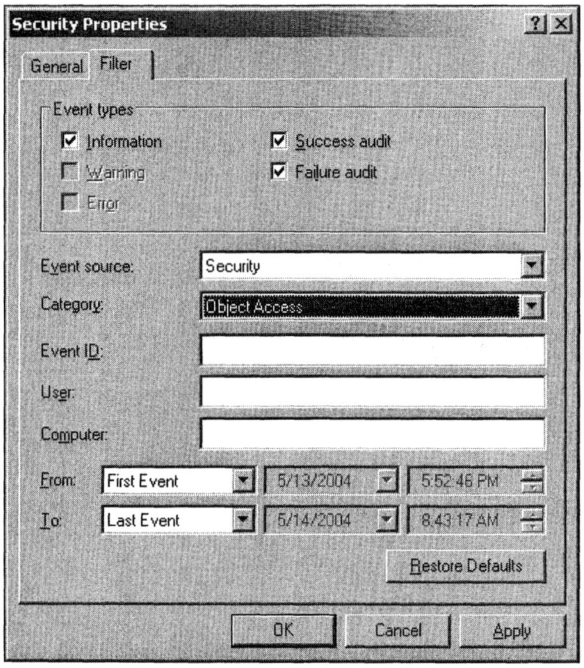

Figure 12-20 The Event Properties dialog box—a failure audit for Object Access

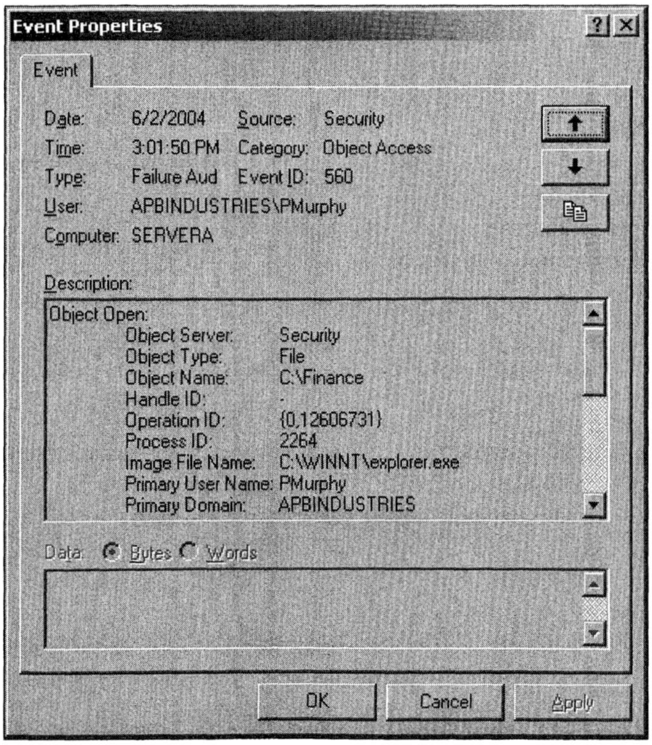

project 12.5

Exporting Security Settings to a Security Template

exam objective

Plan a user authentication strategy. Create a password policy for domain users.

overview

When there are many types of computers on a network, you will usually need more than one security configuration. Security templates allow you to configure security for more computers in less time. Security templates can be imported into GPOs in order to apply a set of common security settings to computers with similar functionality.

You have decided to create a security configuration on a local computer that requires a minimum password length of eight characters and to export the settings to a newly created security template named 8charpwd.inf that you can apply to other computers.

learning objective

After completing this project, you will know how to export the domain controller security settings to a security template.

specific requirements

Administrative rights on SERVERA, the Windows Server 2003 that is acting as a domain controller for apbindustries.com.

estimated completion time

15 minutes

project steps

First, you will import one of the predefined security templates.

1. Log on to **SERVERA** with an account that has administrative rights.
2. Click **Start** and then **Run** to open the **Run** dialog box.
3. Type **mmc** in the **Open** text box and click **OK**.
4. Open the **File** menu and click **Add/Remove Snap-in** to open the **Add/Remove Snap-in** dialog box.
5. Click **Add** to open the **Add Standalone Snap-in** dialog box.
6. Double-click **Security Configuration and Analysis** and **Security Templates (Figure 12-21)**.
7. Click **Close** to exit the Add Standalone Snap-in dialog box.
8. Click **OK** to close the Add/Remove Snap-in dialog box.
9. Right-click **Security Configuration Analysis** and select **Open Database** to open the **Open database** dialog box.
10. Type **8charpwd** in the **File name** list box.
11. Click **Open** to open the **Import Template** dialog box.
12. Select **DC security.inf (Figure 12-22)**. Click **Open**.

Next, you will analyze the security configuration of the computer compared to the database settings in the imported security template and modify the database settings to create a custom security template.

1. Right-click **Security Configuration and Analysis** and select **Analyze Computer Now** to open the **Perform Analysis** dialog box.
2. Click **Browse** to open the **Locate error log file** dialog box.
3. Select **Desktop** in the **Look in** list box and click **Open** to enter the path to the error log file in the **Error log file path** text box.
4. Click **OK** to close the **Perform Analysis** dialog box.
5. The **Analyzing System Security** dialog box opens and the system is analyzed (**Figure 12-23**).
6. Expand the **Security Configuration and Analysis** node, if necessary.

Figure 12-21 The Add Standalone Snap-in dialog box

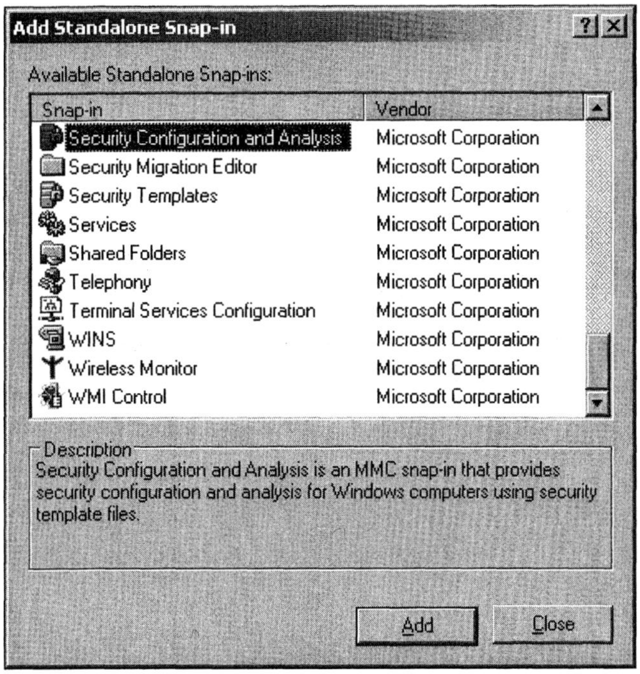

Figure 12-22 The Import Template dialog box

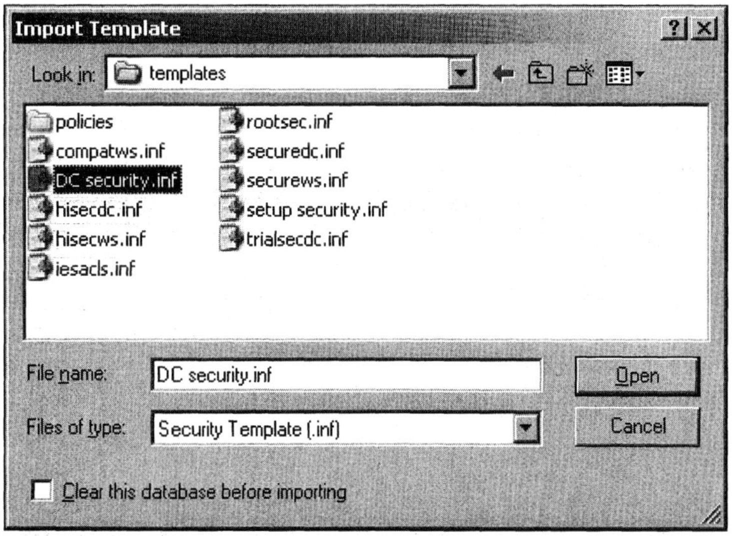

Figure 12-23 Analyzing System Security

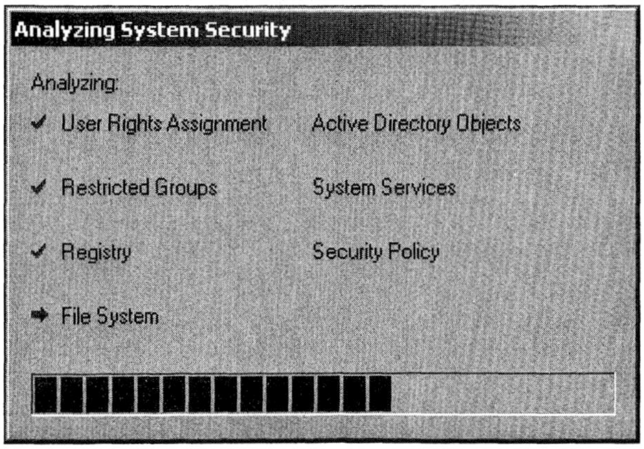

project 12.5

Exporting Security Settings to a Security Template *(cont'd)*

exam objective

Plan a user authentication strategy. Create a password policy for domain users.

project steps

7. Expand **Account Policies**.
8. Select **Password Policy**.
9. Double-click **Minimum password length** to open the **Minimum password length Properties** dialog box.
10. Select the **Define this policy in the database** check box. Type **8** in the **Password must be at least ____ characters** spin box **(Figure 12-24)**.
11. Click **OK** to close the dialog box.
12. Unless password policy has already been configured for the domain or for the domain controllers in the domain, there will be a red "X" over the **Minimum password length** because the database setting and the computer setting do not match.

Next, you will configure the computer with the database settings in the custom 8charpwd security template.

1. Right-click **Security Configuration Analysis** and select **Configure Computer Now** to open the **Configure System** dialog box.
2. Click **Browse** to open the **Locate error log file** dialog box.
3. Select **Desktop** in the **Look in** list box and click **Open** to enter the path to the error log file in the **Error log file** path text box.
4. Click **OK** to close the Configure System dialog box.
5. The **Configuring Computer Security** dialog box opens and the security configuration is applied **(Figure 12-25)**.

Finally, you will analyze the security settings on the computer compared to the database settings in the custom 8charpwd security template to confirm that the settings have been applied and export the 8charpwd security template to the templates folder.

1. Right-click **Security Configuration Analysis** and select **Analyze Computer Now** to open the **Perform Analysis** dialog box.
2. Click **OK** to accept the default path to the error log file (the desktop).
3. The **Analyzing System Security** dialog box opens and the system is analyzed.
4. Double-click **Account Policies**.
5. Double-click **Password Policy**.
6. The **Minimum password length**, **Database Setting and Computer Setting** are now in compliance **(Figure 12-26)**.
7. Right-click **Security Configuration and Analysis** and select **Export Template** to open the **Export Template To** dialog box.
8. Type **8charpwd.inf** in the **File name** list box **(Figure 12-27)**.
9. Click **Save** to close the dialog box and export the template.
10. Close the mmc console. Do not save the console settings when prompted.

Figure 12-24 The Minimum password length Properties dialog box

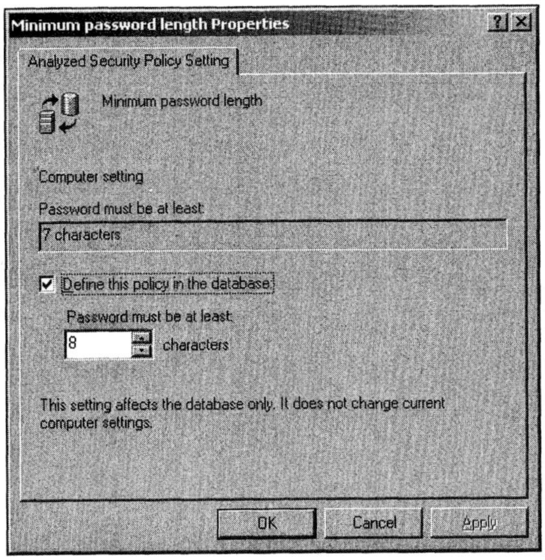

Figure 12-25 Configuring Computer Security

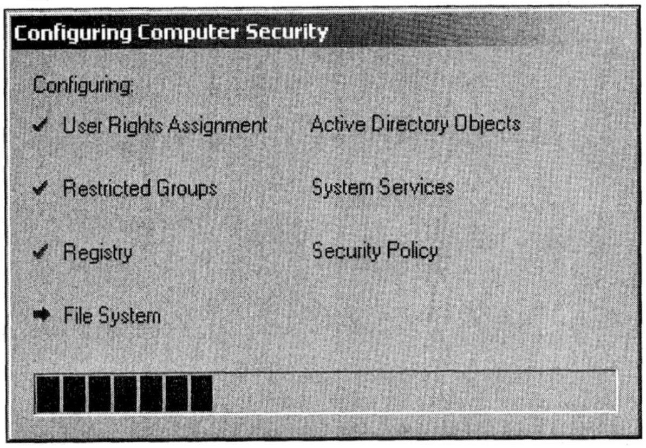

Figure 12-26 The configured password policy

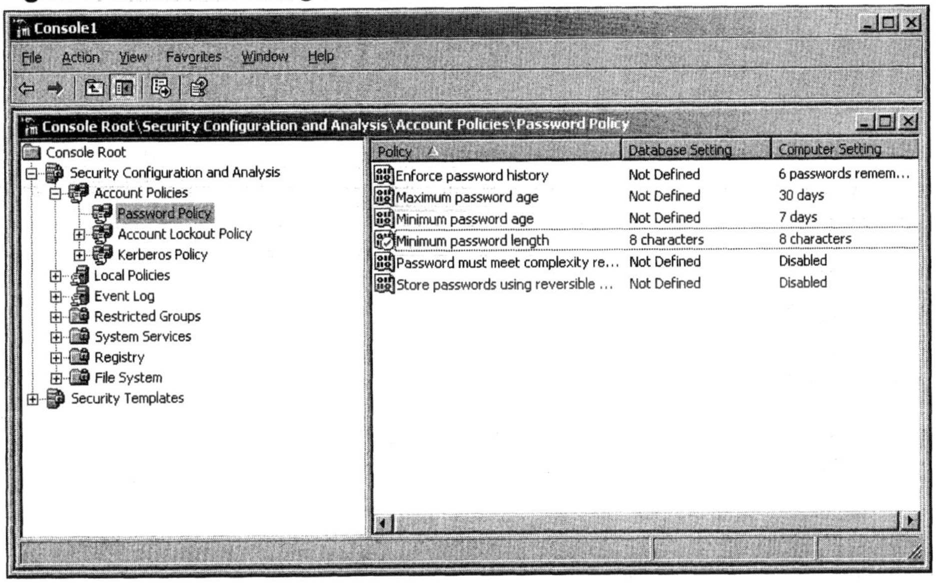

Figure 12-27 The Export Template To dialog box

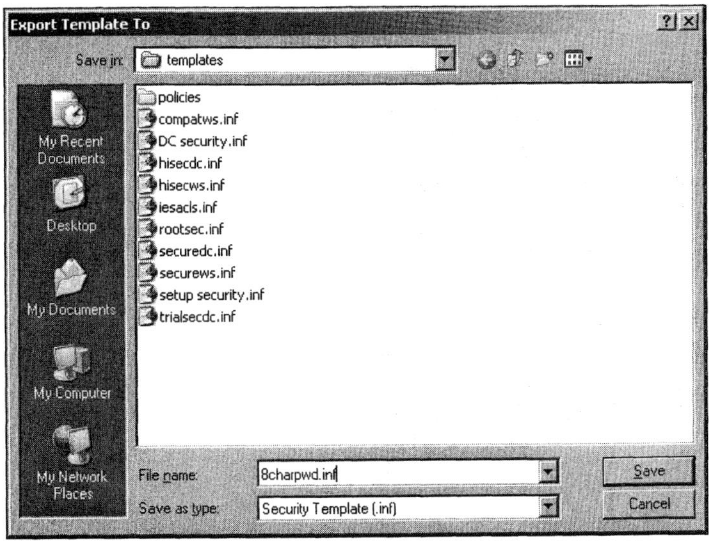

LESSON 13

Monitoring Active Directory Performance

The measure of the success of a network implementation is the secure and efficient sharing of resources. This level of efficiency is only achieved through constant monitoring and tweaking of network configurations. It is important to monitor your key servers and your network so that you can catch problems early before they cause a major disruption. You can use tools such as the Performance console and the Event Viewer to diagnose and troubleshoot Active Directory issues.

The Performance console consists of the System Monitor and Performance Logs and Alerts snap-ins. The System Monitor functions as a library for system services throughout the network, as well as for information about hardware performance. The Performance Logs and Alerts snap-in is used by administrators to create counter logs, trace logs, and system alerts pertaining to specific events. You use the information obtained from the logs to identify system bottlenecks and to diagnose and troubleshoot Active Directory problems. After you have identified a potential problem, you can reconfigure your network infrastructure, upgrade or add servers, or take whatever measures are called for to improve optimal performance.

Scenario

Network users at APB Industries are complaining of slow network response times at different periods throughout the day. The slow response times seem random, but the calls are consistently coming into your office. Some users have gone so far as to complain to your boss. She informs you that she wants an explanation and a solution by the end of the week. You have decided to use the tools in the Performance console to identify the source of the problem.

Lesson 13 Monitoring Active Directory Performance

Project	Exam 70-294 Objective
13.1 Monitoring Active Directory Performance Counters	Monitor Active Directory replication failures. Tools might include Replication Monitor, Event Viewer, and support tools. Monitor Active Directory replication.
13.2 Creating Performance Logs and Alerts	Monitor Active Directory replication failures. Tools might include Replication Monitor, Event Viewer, and support tools. Monitor Active Directory replication.

General Requirements

To complete the projects in this lesson, you must have administrative rights on SERVERA, the Windows Server 2003 computer that is acting as a domain controller for the apbindustries.com domain. You must also have successfully completed Lesson 12. You may also find it helpful to refer to Lesson 13 in your Prentice Hall Certification Series Exam 70-294 textbook for further information about the topics covered by projects in this lesson.

project 13.1

Monitoring Active Directory Performance Counters

exam objective

Monitor Active Directory replication failures. Tools might include Replication Monitor, Event Viewer, and support tools. Monitor Active Directory replication.

overview

The Performance console is arguably the most widely used tool for monitoring Active Directory performance and replication. It allows administrators to monitor computers throughout the network. You have decided to record data in the System Monitor for SERVERA so that you can discover if there is a problem with the domain controller for apbindustries.com. You are going to include counters for the processor, memory, disk, and network to see if you can discover the source of the problem.

learning objective

After completing this project, you will know how the Performance console tracks and organizes system and network processes.

specific requirements

Administrative rights to SERVERA, the Windows Server 2003 that is acting as a domain controller for apbindustries.com.

estimated completion time

10 minutes

project steps

1. Click **Start**, point to **Administrative Tools**, and click **Performance** to open the **Performance** console.
2. Notice that the **Pages/sec**, **Avg. Disk Queue Length**, and **%Processor Time** counters are already in operation. This is a new default in Windows Server 2003.
3. Click the **Plus** sign button on the Performance Monitor toolbar **(Figure 13-1)** to open the **Add Counters** dialog box.
4. Make sure that **Processor** is selected in the **Performance object** list box. The processor is the default performance object.
5. In the **Select counters from list** scrolling list box, **select Interrupts/sec**.
6. Click **Add** to add the counter to the System Monitor.
7. In the **Performance object** list box select **Memory**.
8. In the **Select counters from list** scrolling list box, select **Pool Nonpaged Bytes** **(Figure 13-2)**.
9. Click **Add** to add the counter to the System Monitor.
10. In the **Performance object** list box select **PhysicalDisk**.
11. In the **Select counters from list** scrolling list box, verify that the selected counter is **% Disk Time**.
12. Click **Add** to add the counter to the System Monitor.
13. In the **Performance object** list box select **Network Interface**.
14. In the **Select counters from list** scrolling list box, verify that the selected counter is **Bytes Total/sec**.
15. Select the **All instances** option button.
16. Click **Add** to add the counters to the System Monitor.
17. Click **Close** to exit the **Add Counters** dialog box.
18. The counters are added to the System Monitor and the statistics are continually recorded **(Figure 13-3)**.
19. Click the **Highlight** button (the light bulb) on the toolbar.
20. Open a folder and several files. Open the GPMC.
21. Return to the **Performance** console and observe the effect on the performance counters.

tip

In order to most effectively use the Performance console, the first thing you must do is establish a performance baseline. Collect baseline data during normal network operation so that you will be able to recognize potential problems later.

Figure 13-1 The Performance Monitor tool bar

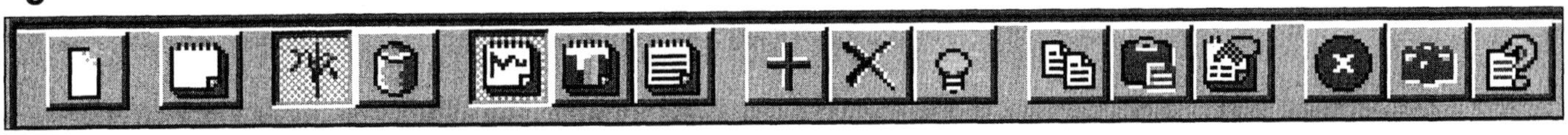

Figure 13-2 Adding the Pool Nonpaged Bytes/Memory counter

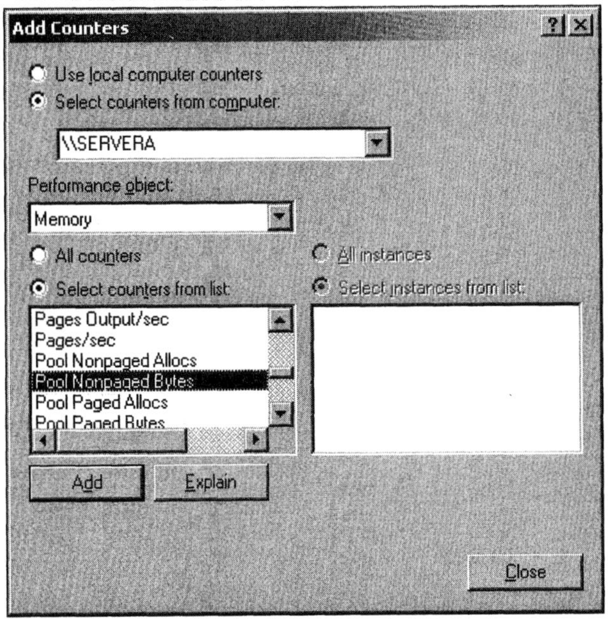

Figure 13-3 Counter tracking activity

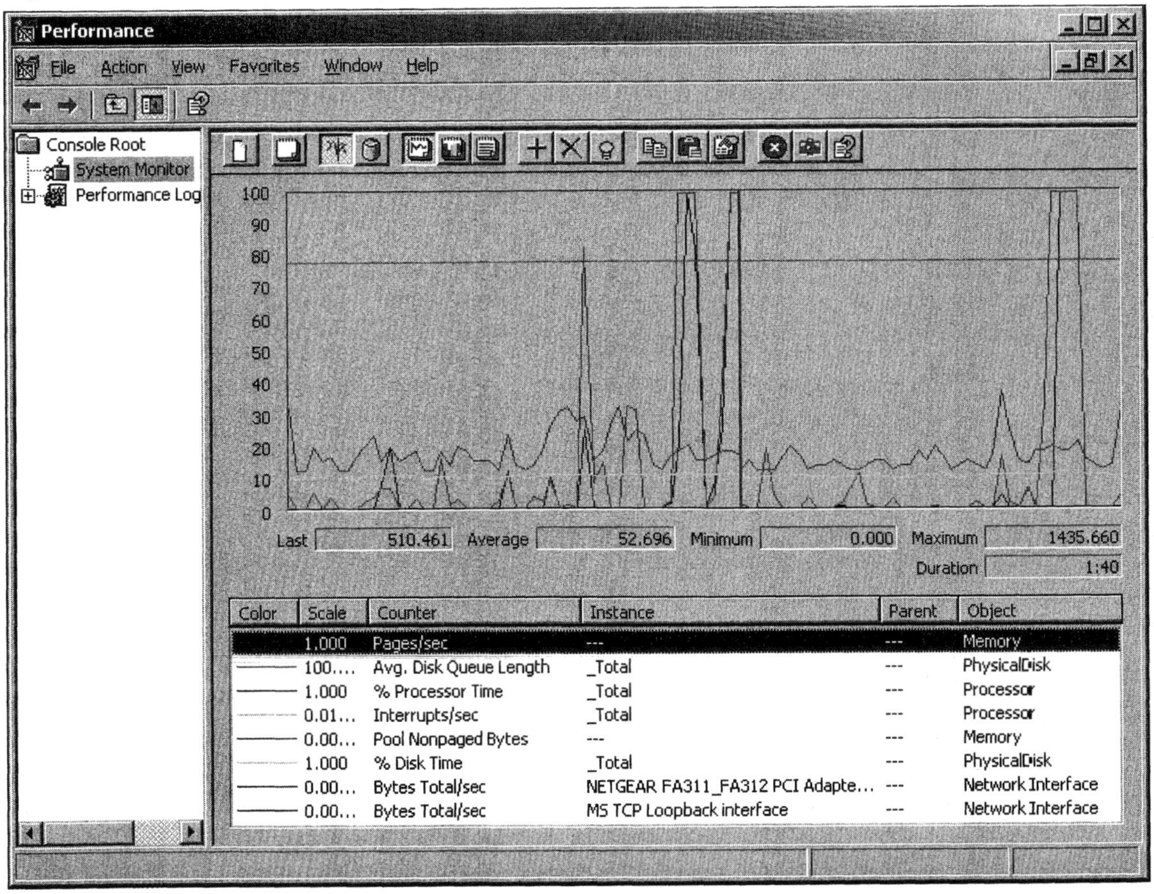

project 13.1

Monitoring Active Directory Performance Counters *(cont'd)*

exam objective

Monitor Active Directory replication failures. Tools might include Replication Monitor, Event Viewer, and support tools. Monitor Active Directory replication.

project steps

22. Move the **Up** and **Down** arrow keys on the keyboard to highlight the graph line that corresponds to the selected counter in the pane at the bottom of the Performance console (**Figure 13-4**).

23. Close the GPMC and the folder and files you opened.

24. Close the Performance console.

Figure 13-4 A highlighted graph line

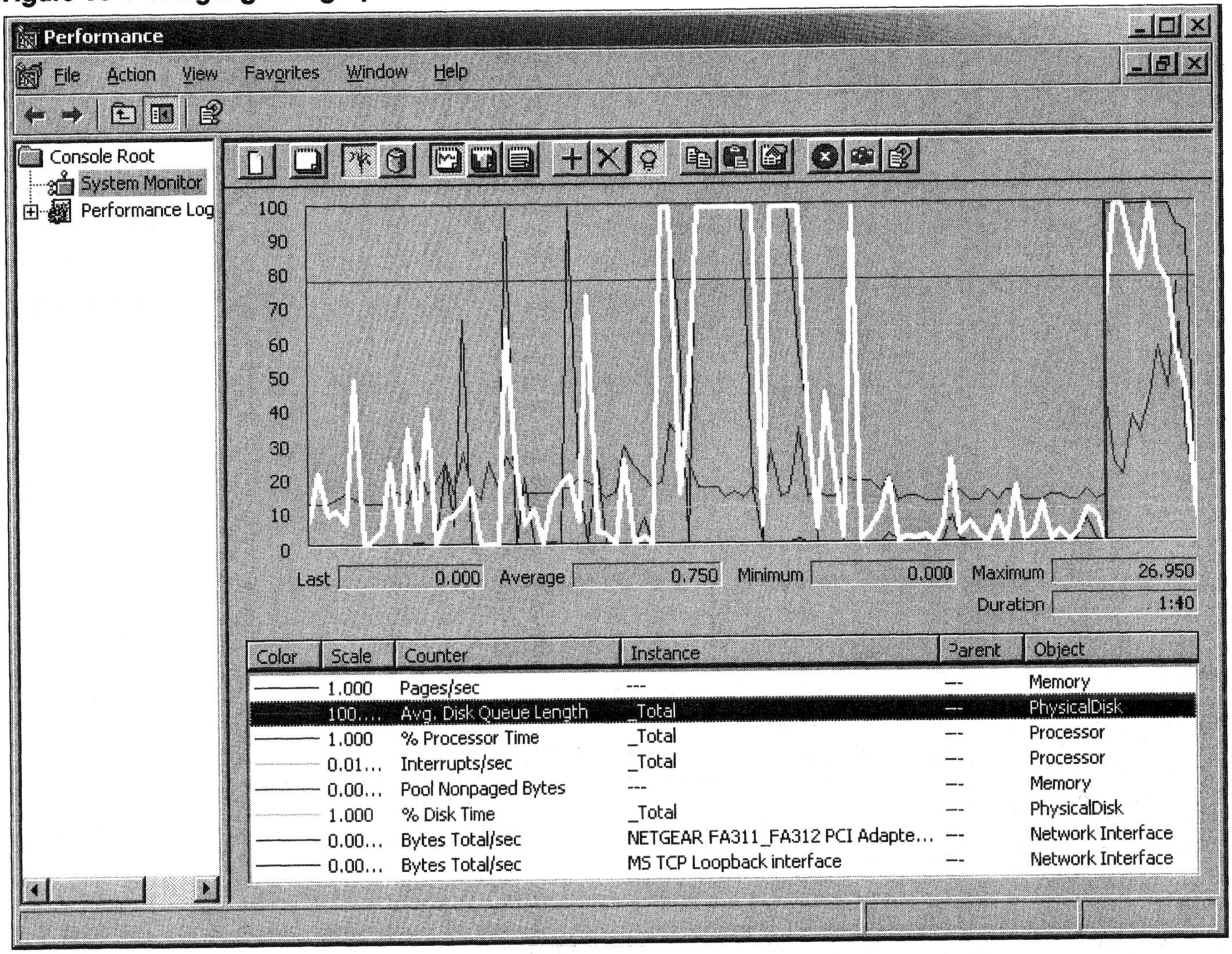

project 13.2

Creating Performance Logs and Alerts

exam objective

Monitor Active Directory replication failures. Tools might include Replication Monitor, Event Viewer, and support tools. Monitor Active Directory replication.

overview

You use the Performance Logs and Alerts snap-in to create counter logs, trace logs, and performance alerts. You have decided to create an alert that will be triggered when the processor utilization on the domain controller exceeds 10%.

learning objective

After completing this project, you will know how to use the Performance Logs and Alerts snap-in to create an alert.

specific requirements

Administrative rights to SERVERA, the Windows Server 2003 that is acting as a domain controller for apbindustries.com.

estimated completion time

10 minutes

project steps

First, you will start the Messenger service.

1. Click **Start**, point to **Administrative Tools**, and click **Services** to open the **Services** console.
2. Double-click **Messenger (Figure 13-5)** to open the **Messenger Properties** dialog box.
3. In the **Startup type** list box, select **Manual (Figure 13-6)**.
4. Click **Apply** to change the startup type.
5. Click **Start** to start the Messenger service.
6. Click **OK** to close the **Messenger Properties** dialog box.
7. Close the **Services** console.

Next, you will create an alert to send a message to the Administrator account when the %Processor Time exceeds 10%.

1. Click **Start**, point to **Administrative Tools**, and click **Performance** to open the **Performance** console.
2. Select **Performance Logs and Alerts**.
3. In the details pane, double-click **Alerts**.
4. Right-click an empty space in the details pane and select **New Alert Settings** to open the **New Alert Settings** dialog box.
5. In the **Name** text box, type **Processor-10**.
6. Click **OK** to name the alert and open the **Processor-10** dialog box.
7. Click **Add** to open the **Add Counters** dialog box.
8. Click **Add** to add the **%Processor Time** counter to the alert **(Figure 13-7)**.
9. Click **Close** to exit the Add Counters dialog box.
10. In the **Alert when the value is** list box, select **Over**, if necessary.
11. In the **Limit** text box, type **10**.
12. Open the **Action** tab.
13. Select the **Send a network message to** check box and type **Administrator** in the text box.
14. Click **OK** to close the Processor-10 dialog box.
15. If processor utilization exceeds 10%, a **Messenger Service** dialog box will inform you that the counter has tripped its alert threshold **(Figure 13-8)**.
16. To stop the popup messages, right-click **Processor-10** and select **Stop** to stop the alert. It may take a few minutes for the alert to stop.
17. Close the Performance console.

tip

Always try to avoid running **Performance** on the machine you are monitoring as it generates a substantial load on its own that will affect your results.

Figure 13-5 The Messenger Service

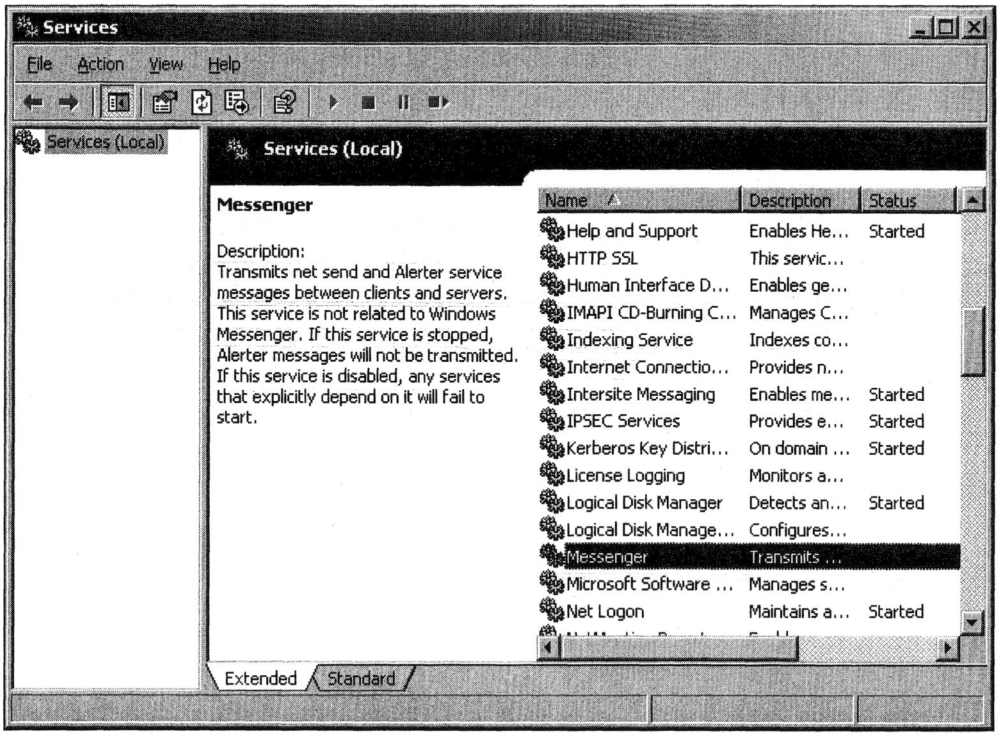

Figure 13-6 Setting a service startup type

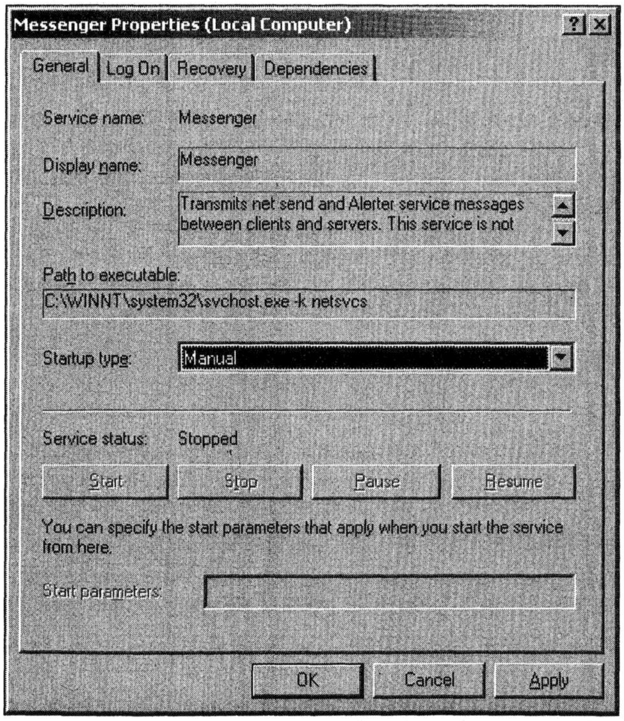

Figure 13-7 Adding the %Processor Time counter

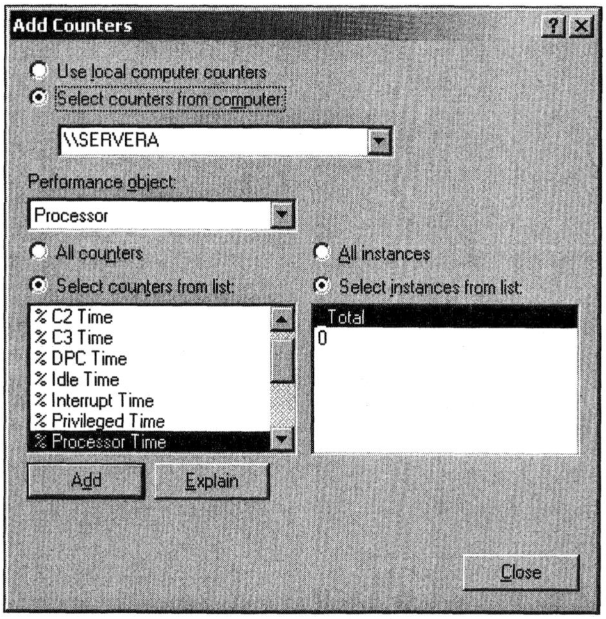

Figure 13-8 The Messenger Service message box when a counter surpasses its alert threshold

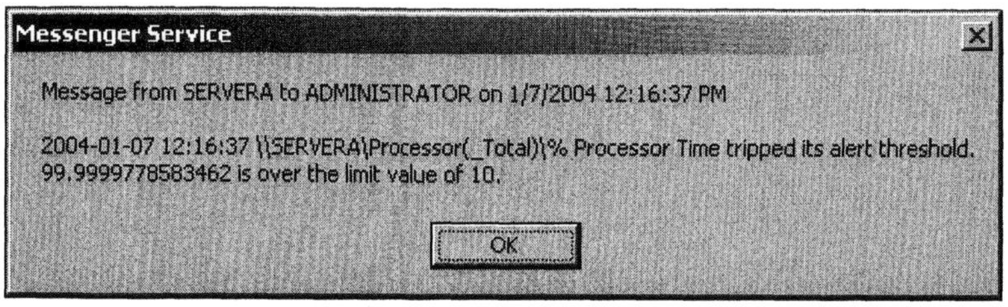

LESSON 14

Implementing Remote Installation Services (RIS)

Time is very important to most network administrators. However, there is seldom enough of it. Problems arise constantly and without warning. These issues, as well as scheduled maintenance, must be addressed immediately in order to ensure optimal network performance. In an effort to free up network administrators for troubleshooting, Windows Server 2003 includes Remote Installation Services (RIS) to speed up the process of installing operating systems on multiple machines. In conjunction with Dynamic Host Configuration Protocol (DHCP), Domain Name Service (DNS), and Active Directory, RIS enables administrators to install operating systems remotely with minimal user intervention. You can also use RIPrep imaging to install applications and customize desktop settings on a number of RIS client computers simultaneously. After RIS is installed and configured, you can use the Check Server Wizard to verify that there are no configuration errors.

Before you can use RIS, the RIS component must be added to the computer destined to become the RIS server. Next, you run the Remote Installation Services Setup Wizard to install and configure RIS. Configuring RIS entails making sure that the appropriate installation and image options are made available to users.

The RIS server must meet certain hardware and software requirements. It must have at least a Pentium or Pentium II 166 MHz processor (200 MHz or faster is recommended), 64 MB RAM (128 MB if Active Directory, DHCP, and DNS are to be installed), a 2 GB hard disk or partition dedicated to the RIS directory tree, and a network card. The DNS and DHCP services and Active Directory must be available on the network. They can either be running on different network servers or on the RIS server. The RIS clients must have at least a Pentium 166 MHz processor, 32 MB RAM (64MB recommended), an 800 MB hard disk, and a supported PCI Plug and Play network adapter card. RIS clients can either be computers that support PXE DHCP-based remote boot ROMS or computers with network cards that the RIS boot disk supports. PXE DHCP-based computers can start an operating system installation from a remote source. If a computer does not support PXE DHCP-based remote boot technology, you can use Rbfg.exe to create a RIS boot disk. Rbfg.exe emulates PXE remote boot technology, enabling computers to boot directly from a network image. The RIS boot disk includes drivers that are compatible with approximately 30 different models of network cards. NICs are defined by their chipset, and most network cards use similar chipsets, so even if your network card is not listed, it may still be compatible.

In order to perform an installation using RIS, you need a DHCP server, a Windows 2000 or Windows Server 2003-compliant DNS server, and the Active Directory service. The DHCP server provides the Internet Protocol (IP) address to the client computers. DNS is needed to enable the RIS server to find and use Active Directory. Active Directory enables the RIS server to determine user rights and permissions.

Scenario

APB Industries has called a special meeting of its managerial staff. Due to recent and steady growth in the company, it has been decided that 100 new computers will be added to the existing network. As the growth was somewhat unexpected, a great deal of pressure is being put on the Information Technology Department to get these new machines set up as quickly as possible.

As the network administrator for the apbindustries.com domain, you are in close contact with the Chief Information Officer (CIO). You both decide Remote Installation Services is the best plan for such an implementation.

Lesson 14 Implementing Remote Installation Services (RIS)

Project	Exam 70-294 Objective
14.1 Configuring a RIS Server	Basic knowledge
14.2 Verifying RIS Server Installation	Basic knowledge
14.3 Customizing RIS Client Installation Options	Basic knowledge

General Requirements

To complete the projects in this lesson, you will need administrative rights on ServerA, a domain controller in the apbindustries.com domain. ServerA must be running the DHCP and DNS services along with Active Directory. It must also have a second NTFS partition or volume with at least 2 GB of free space. You will also need the Windows Server 2003 installation CD-ROM. You may also find it helpful to refer to Lesson 14 of the Prentice Hall Certification Series Exam 70-294 textbook for further information about the topics covered by the projects in this lesson.

project 14.1 Configuring a RIS Server

exam objective

Basic knowledge

overview

The CEO of APB Industries has asked you to set up nearly 100 new computers in the apbindustries.com domain. Among these, 10 will be servers. Time is important and staffing in the Information Technology Department is limited. You decide to deploy the servers yourself using RIS to create an image and to delegate the client deployment to the IT department.

learning objective

After completing this project, you will know how to install RIS and create an image.

specific requirements

Enterprise Administrative rights on ServerA, the Windows Server 2003 computer that is acting as the domain controller for apbindustries.com.

estimated completion time

20 minutes

project steps

1. Log on to **SERVERA** with an account that has administrative rights.
2. Click **Start**, point to **Control Panel**, and click **Add or Remove Programs** to open the **Add or Remove Programs** window.
3. Click **Add/Remove Windows Components** to start the **Windows Components Wizard**.
4. Double-click **Networking Services** to open the **Networking Services** dialog box.
5. Select the **Dynamic Host Configuration Protocol (DHCP)** check box **(Figure 14-1)**, if necessary. If there is already a DHCP server on your network, you will not have to perform this step.
6. Click **OK** to close the Networking Services dialog box.
7. In the **Components** box, select the **Remote Installation Services** check box **(Figure 14-2)**.
8. Click **Next** to start copying the installation files.
9. The **Configuring Components** screen opens and the **Insert Disk** dialog box prompts you to insert the Windows Server 2003 installation CD-ROM. Insert the CD-ROM and click **OK** (or **Exit** to close the **Autorun** screen, if your server is configured to autorun CDs).
10. After the components are installed, the **Completing the Windows Components Wizard** screen opens. Click **Finish**.
11. The **System Settings Change** dialog box prompts you to restart the system. Click **Yes**.
12. After the system restarts and you have logged back on, click **Start**, point to **Administrative Tools**, and click **Remote Installation Services Setup** to start the **Remote Installation Services Setup Wizard**.
13. Click **Next** to open the **Remote Installation Folder Location** screen.
14. Type **F:\RemoteInstall** in the **Path** text box, where **F** is the second NTFS partition or volume on the server, to specify the location to store the RIS files. You cannot install the remote installation folder on the same drive as the server's operating system **(Figure 14-3)**.
15. Click **Next** to open the **Initial Settings** screen.
16. Select the **Respond to client computers requesting service** check box **(Figure 14-4)**.
17. Click **Next** to open the **Installation Source Files Location** screen.
18. Click **Browse** to open the **Browse for Folder** dialog box.
19. Navigate to the **i386** folder on the Windows Server 2003 installation CD-ROM. After you have located and selected the i386 folder, click **OK** to close the dialog box and enter the path to the source files in the Path text box **(Figure 14-5)**.

tip

If a RIS client does not have a PXE DHCP-based boot ROM, you must create a RIS boot disk before you can use RIS. If the network card or the chipset of the RIS client is supported by the RIS boot disk, a RIS-based installation can be performed on it. You use the Remote Boot File Generator (Rbfg.exe) utility to create the RIS boot disk. Refer to Lesson 14, Skill 7 in your Prentice Hall Certification Series Exam 70-294 textbook for information on how to create a RIS boot disk.

Figure 14-1 Installing DHCP

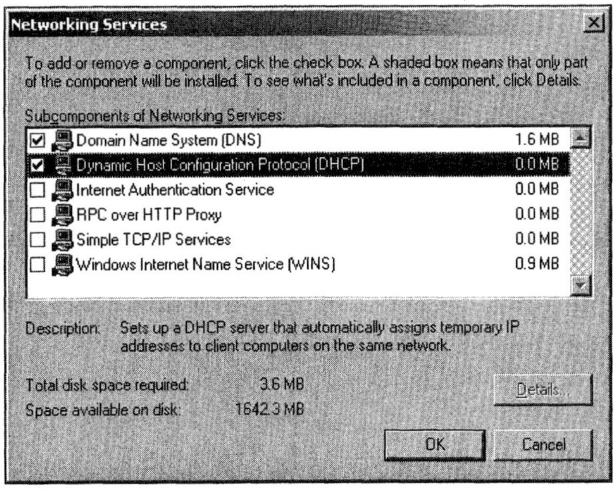

Figure 14-2 Installing RIS

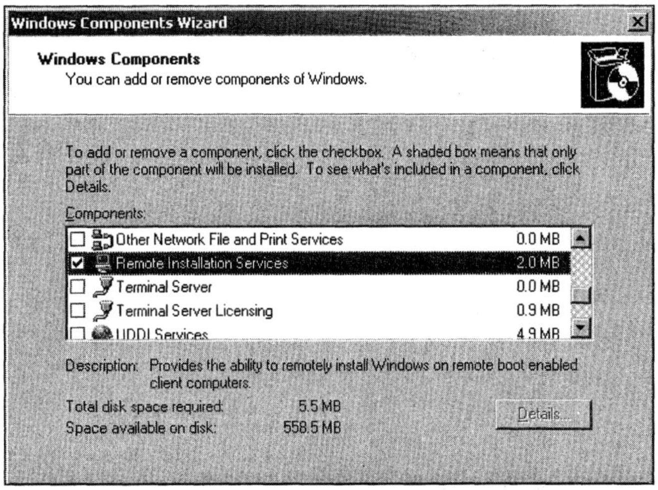

Figure 14-3 The Remote Installation Folder Location screen

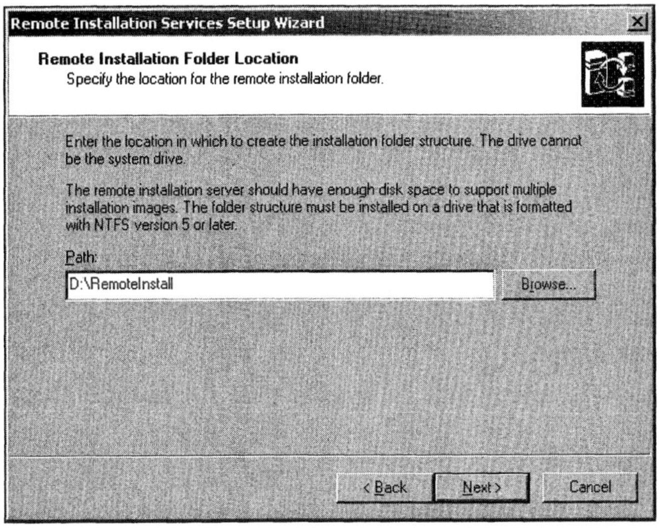

Figure 14-4 The Initial Settings screen

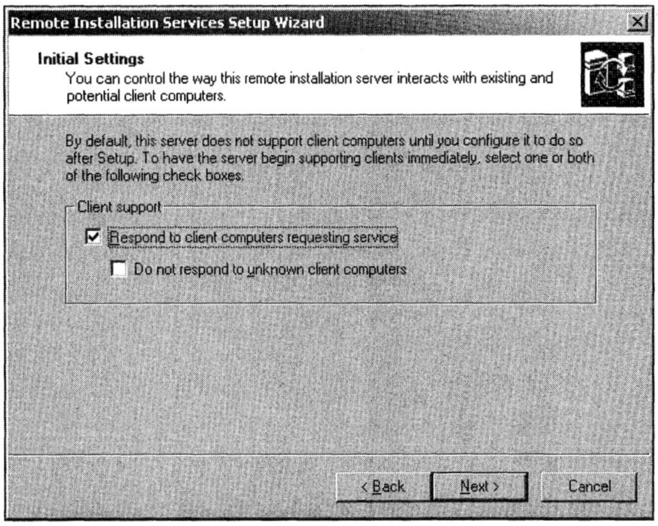

Figure 14-5 The Installation Sources Files Location screen

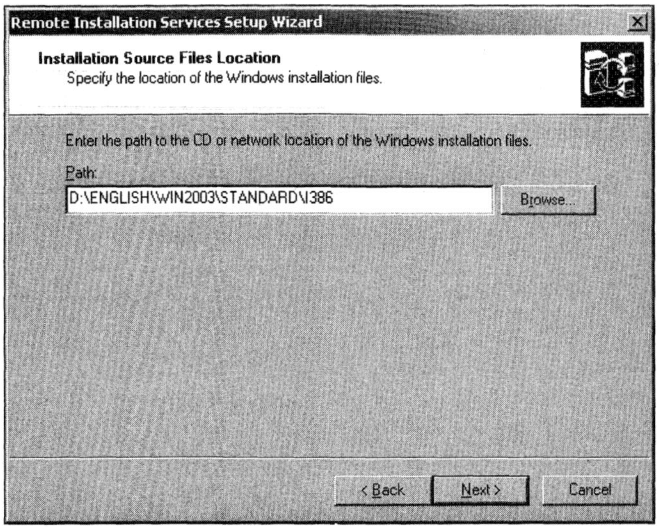

project 14.1

Configuring a RIS Server *(cont'd)*

exam objective

Basic knowledge

project steps

20. Click **Next** to open to the **Windows Installation Image Folder Name** screen (**Figure 14-6**).

21. Click **Next** to accept the default name (**WINDOWS**) in the **Folder name** text box and open the **Friendly Description and Help Text** screen (**Figure 14-7**).

22. Click **Next** to accept the default description and help text and open the **Review Settings** screen (**Figure 14-8**).

23. Click **Finish**.

24. The **Remote Installation Services Setup Wizard** dialog box opens (**Figure 14-9**).

25. When the configuration is complete, click **Done**.

26. Click **Start**, and then **Run** to open the **Run** dialog box.

27. In the **Open** text box, type **C:\Windows\system32\adminpak.msi** to install the supplemental administrative tools. Press **[Enter]**. If the **Administrative Tools Pack** is already installed on the server, you will not have to perform Steps 26 through 28.

28. The **Welcome to the Windows Server 2003 Administrative Tools Pack Setup Wizard** opens (**Figure 14-10**). Click **Next**.

29. When the installation is complete, click **Finish**.

30. Close any open dialog boxes and windows.

Figure 14-6 The Windows Installation Image Folder Name screen

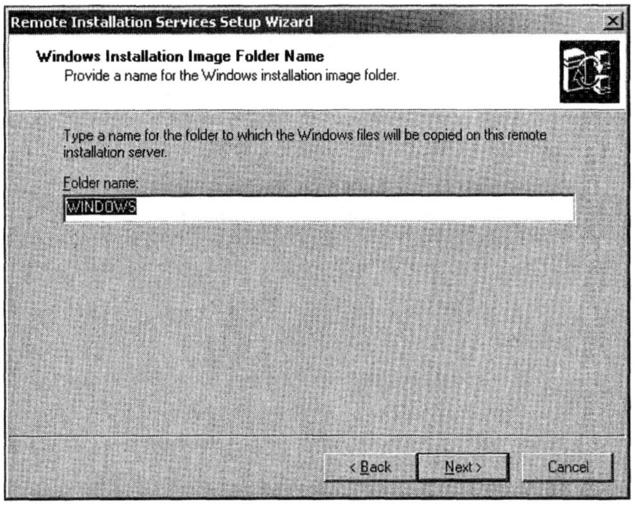

Figure 14-7 The Friendly Description and Help Text screen

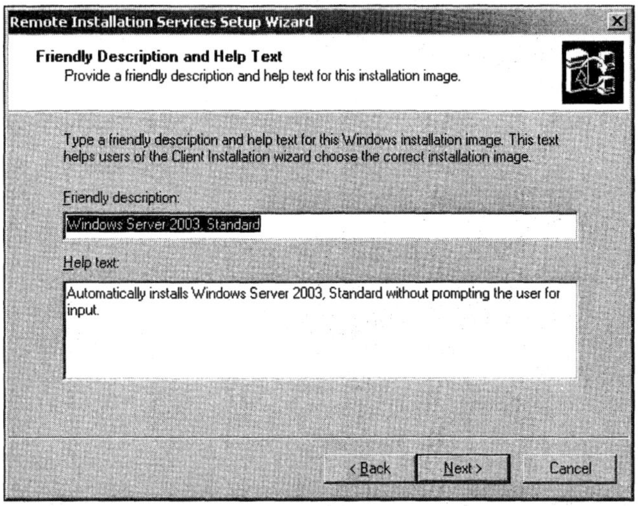

Figure 14-8 The Review Settings screen

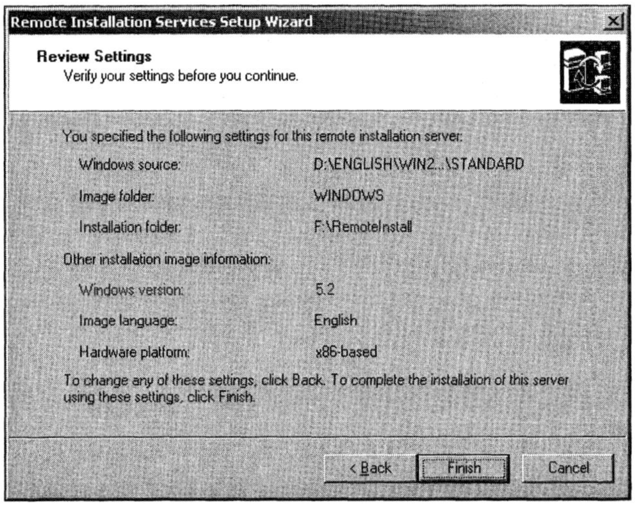

Figure 14-9 The Remote Installation Services Setup Wizard dialog box

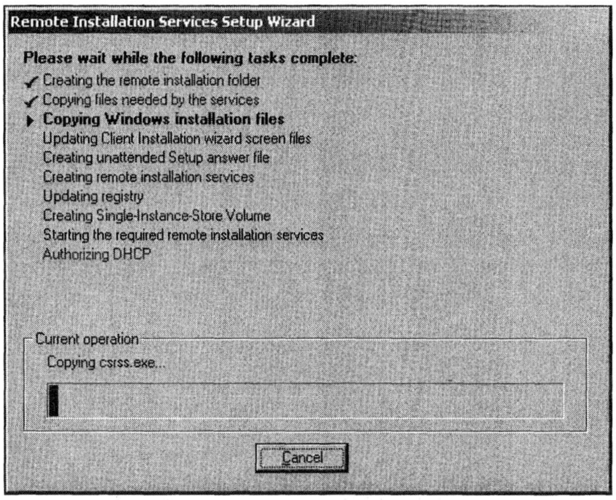

Figure 14-10 The Windows Server 2003 Administrative Tools Pack Setup Wizard

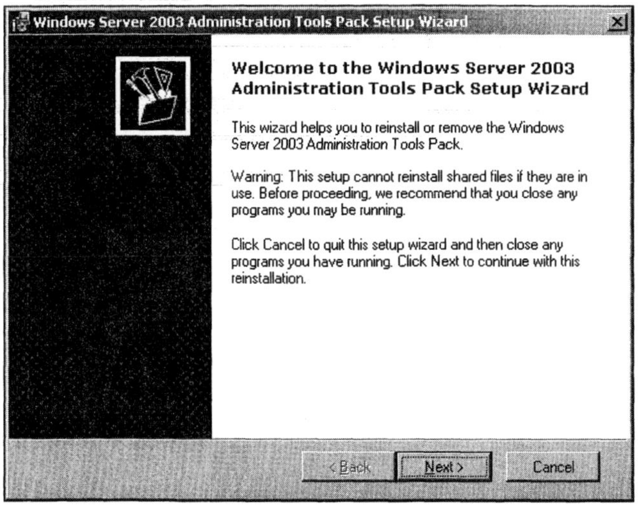

project 14.2 Verifying RIS Server Installation

exam objective

Basic knowledge

overview

In this project, you will confirm that RIS is properly installed and is functioning correctly.

learning objective

After completing this project, you will know how to verify Remote Installation Services.

specific requirements

Enterprise administrative rights on SERVERA, the Windows Server 2003 computer that is acting as the domain controller for apbindustries.com.

estimated completion time

5 minutes

project steps

1. Open the **Active Directory Users and Computers** console.
2. Expand **apbindustries.com**.
3. Select the **Domain Controllers** OU.
4. Right-click **SERVERA** and click **Properties** to open the **SERVERA Properties** dialog box.
5. Click the **Remote Install tab (Figure 14-11)**.
6. Verify that **Respond to client computers requesting service** check box is selected.
7. Click **Verify Server** to open the **Check Server Wizard**.
8. Click **Next** to start the verification process.
9. When the verification is complete, the **Remote Installation Services Verification Complete** screen opens **(Figure 14-12)**.
10. Review the RIS configuration information and click **Finish** to restart or unpause RIS.
11. A **Remote Installation Services Setup Wizard** dialog box opens while the required remote installation services are started and DHCP is authorized **(Figure 14-13)**.
12. Click **Done**.
13. Close the SERVERA Properties dialog box and the Active Directory Users and Computers console.
14. Click **Start**, point to **Administrative Tools**, and click **DHCP** to open the **DHCP console**.
15. Expand the **servera.apbindustries.com** node.
16. Right-click **servera.apbindustries.com** and verify that the RIS server is an authorized DHCP server by making sure that the **Unauthorize** command is available. Do *not* click **Unauthorize**.
17. Close the DHCP console.

Figure 14-11 The Remote Install tab in the SERVERA Properties dialog box

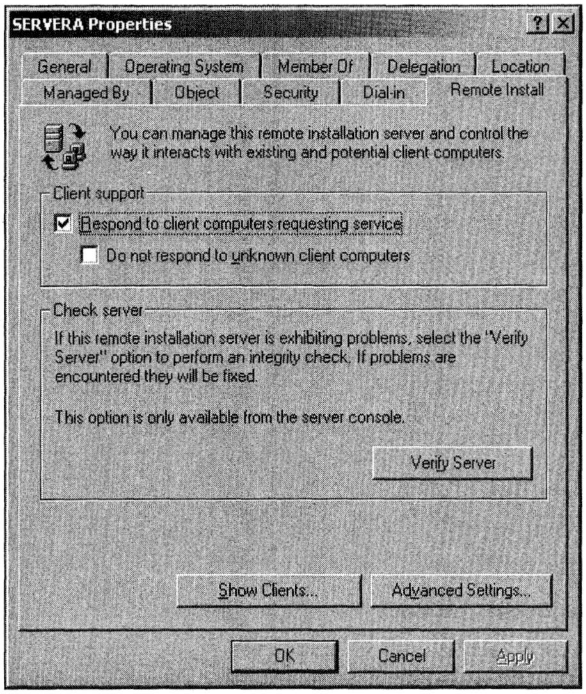

Figure 14-12 The Remote Installation Services Verification Complete screen

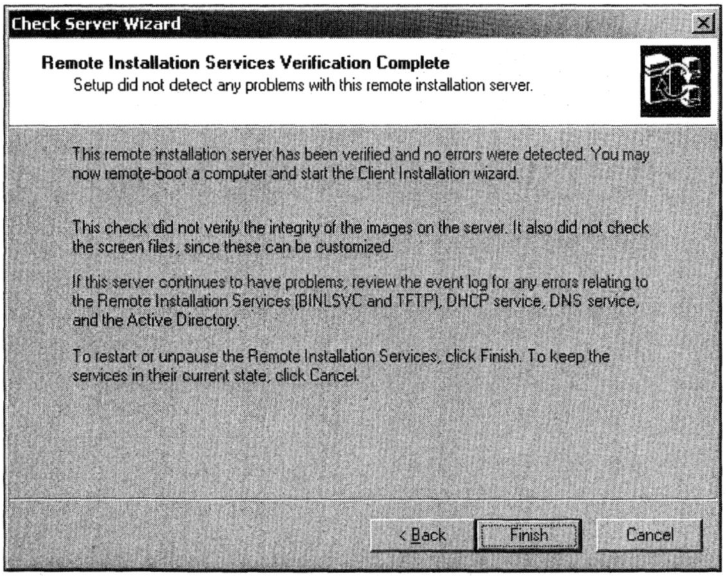

Figure 14-13 Starting RIS and authorizing DHCP

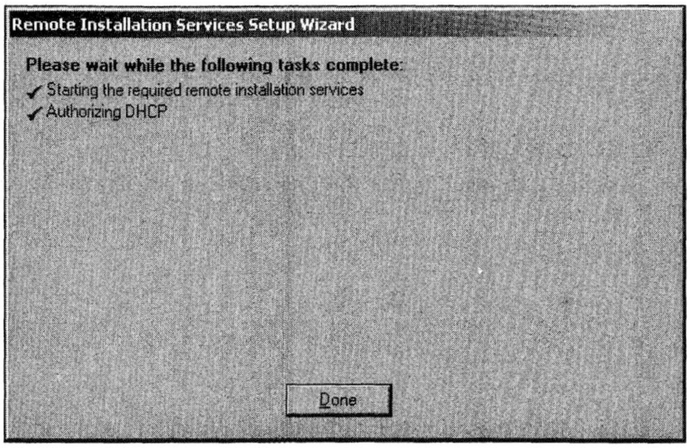

project 14.3

Creating Options for RIS Client Installation

exam objective

Basic knowledge

overview

You have decided to construct an answer file to be used for the deployment of the ten new servers in the domain. You will use the Setup Manager and RIS to create an unattended answer file so that you can quickly configure the new servers. The CIO has instructed you to accept all default network settings, time zone, and display settings during the installation process.

learning objective

After completing this project, you will know how to install Setup Manager on the desktop and how to create a custom answer file for RIS deployment.

specific requirements

Administrative rights on SERVERA, the Windows Server 2003 that is acting as a domain controller for apbindustries.com.

estimated completion time

15 minutes

project steps

tip

The answer file is text file that can be directly modified using Notepad.

1. Log on to **SERVERA** with an account that has administrative rights.
2. Insert the Windows Server 2003 installation CD-ROM.
3. When the **Introduction** screen opens, click **Exit**.
4. First, you will install Setup Manager on the desktop. Open **Windows Explorer**.
5. Browse to the **CD**.
6. Locate and double-click the **Support** folder. Double-click the **Tools** folder. Double-click **Deploy.cab**.
7. Press **[Ctrl]** + **[A]** to select everything in the window.
8. Right-click the selected files and click **Extract (Figure 14-14)**.
9. The **Select a Destination** dialog box opens.
10. Select **Desktop** and click **Extract (Figure 14-15)**.
11. Close Windows Explorer.
12. On the desktop, double-click the **Setup Manager** icon.
13. Click **Next** to open the **New or Existing Answer File** screen. The **Create new** option button is selected by default.
14. Click **Next** to open the **Type of Setup** screen. Select the **Remote Installation Services (RIS)** option button **(Figure 14-16)**.
15. Click **Next** to open the **Product** screen. Select the appropriate edition of **Windows Server 2003 (Figure 14-17)**.
16. Click **Next** to open the **User Interaction** screen. Select **Fully automated (Figure 14-18)**.
17. Click **Next** to open the **License Agreement** screen. Select the **I accept the terms of the License agreement** check box.
18. Click **Next** to open the **Name and Organization** screen.
19. In the **Name** text box, type **Apbindustries**; in the **Organization** text box, type **Apbindustries**.
20. Click **Next** to open the **Display Settings** screen.

Figure 14-14 Extracting the Deploy.cab directory

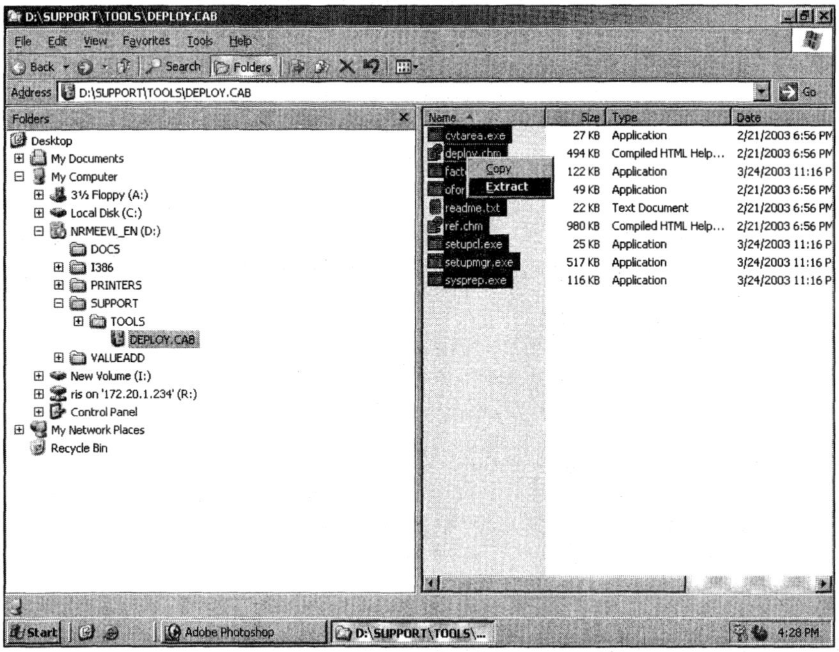

Figure 14-15 The Select a Destination dialog box

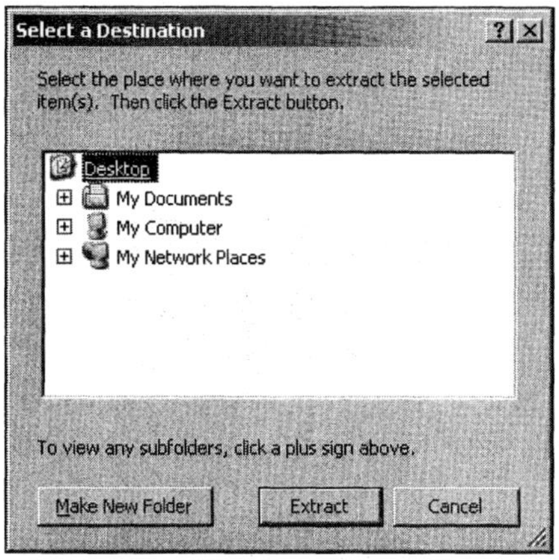

Figure 14-16 The Type of Setup screen

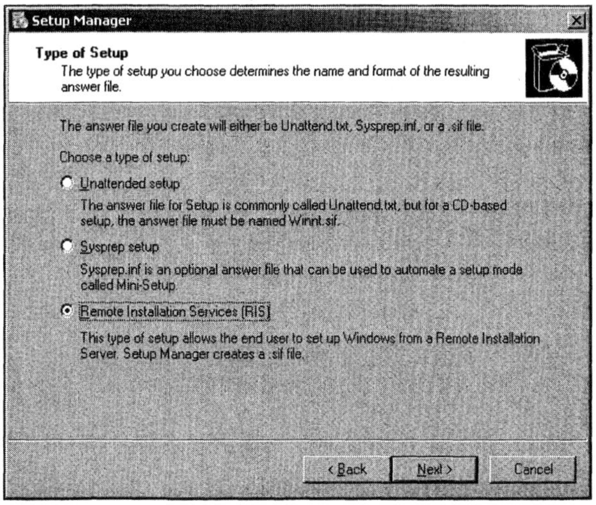

Figure 14-17 The Product screen

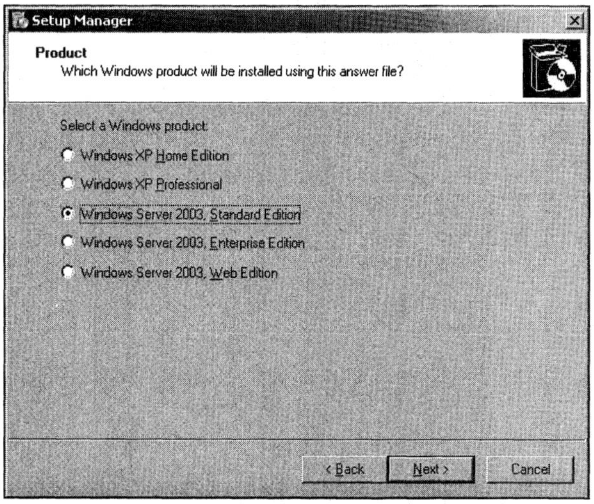

Figure 14-18 The User Interaction screen

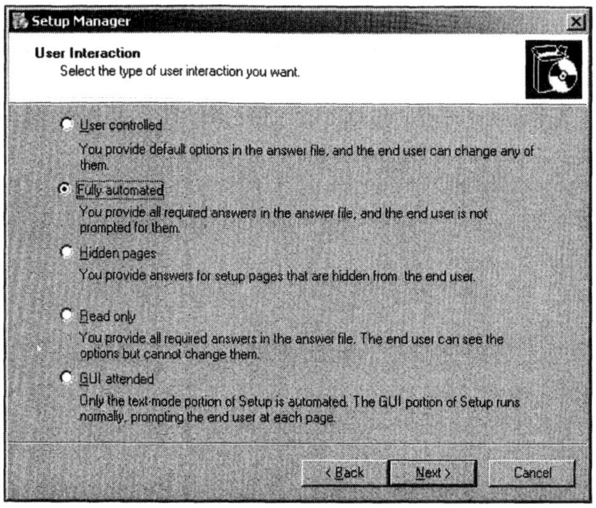

project 14.3

Creating Options for RIS Client Installation (cont'd)

exam objective

Basic knowledge

project steps

21. Click **Next** to accept the default settings and open the **Time Zone** screen (**Figure 14-19**).
22. Click **Next** to set the time zone the same as the server and open the **Product Key** screen
23. Enter the **product key** for your CD.
24. Click **Next** to open the **Licensing Mode** screen.
25. Click **Next** to accept the default licensing mode and open the **Administrator Password** screen. You can specify an administrator password on all destination computers, if desired.
26. Click **Next** to open the **Networking Components** screen.
27. Continue to click **Next** to accept the defaults while noting the options that can be configured. The default settings are the normal way that many networks are configured. It is important to understand that these can be changed to conform to specific network configurations.
28. When you reach the **Setup Information File Text** screen, click **Finish**.
29. The **Setup Manager** dialog box opens (**Figure 14-20**).
30. Click **OK** to accept the default path and filename for the answer file.
31. Close the Setup Manager.
32. Open **Windows Explorer**.
33. Select **Local Drive C:**. Select **windist**.
34. Right-click **remboot.sif** and click **Open**.
35. Select the **Select the program from a list** option button (**Figure 14-21**).
36. Click **OK** to open the **Open With** dialog box.
37. Select **Notepad** and click **OK**.
38. Examine the contents of **remboot.sif** (**Figure 14-22**).
39. Close the answer file and Windows Explorer.

Figure 14-19 The Time Zone screen

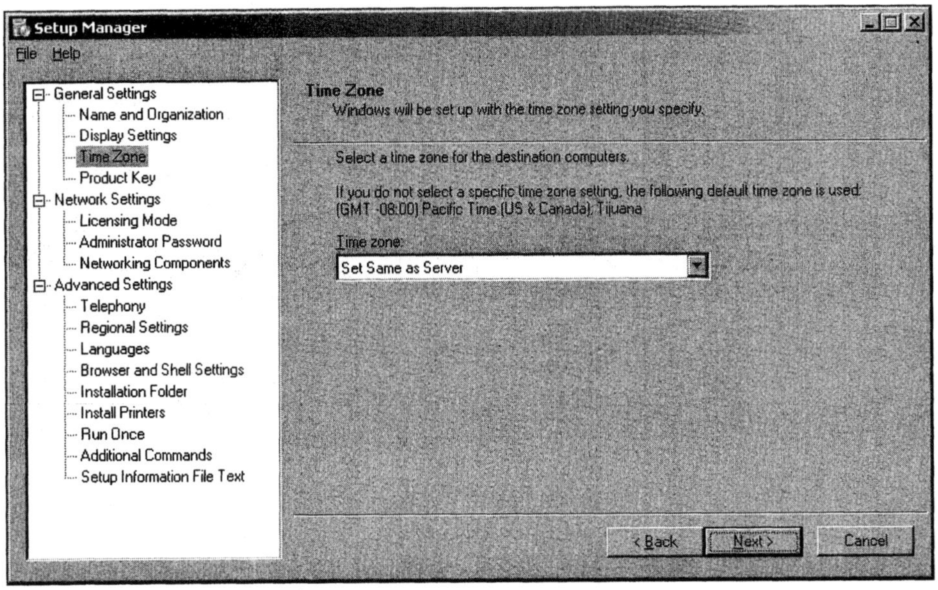

Figure 14-20 Saving the answer file

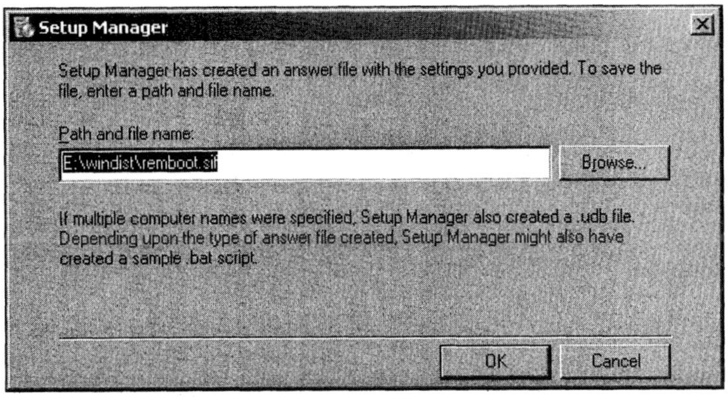

Figure 14-21 The Select the program from a list option button

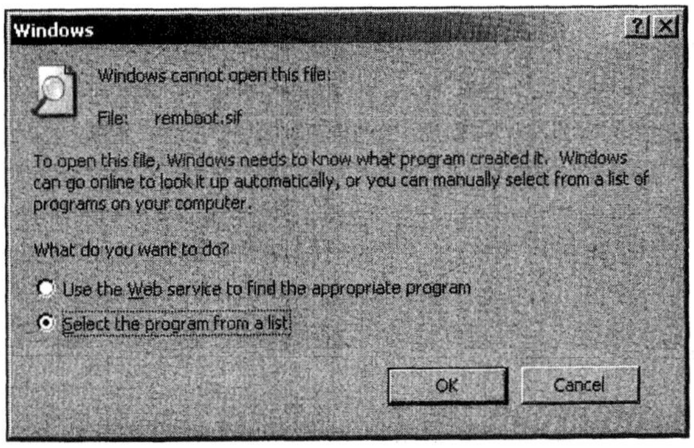

Figure 14-22 The remboot.sif answer file

LESSON 15

Managing a Remote Installation Services (RIS) Implementation

In order to make sure that remote installations are performed correctly, you will have to manage the client installation images, the RIS clients, and user permissions and rights. CD-based images are the default image type. When you install RIS, the files that are used for CD-based images are typically installed. As you have learned, answer files are used to set values for a number of settings including network settings, time zone settings, and display settings. These values are used by the system when an unattended installation is performed. If you want to specify different settings for different images, you will need separate answer files. Each answer file uses the same CD-based image. Another option is to use RIPrep images, which use the CD-based image as a base image and have their own answer files.

You can also set a particular naming convention to be used for the RIS clients. Naming conventions can follow a number of pre-set patterns using the user's last and first name, or they can use the username. You can also create a custom naming convention. For example, you can use the formula %[0][n]# to create computer names that include an incremental number containing n digits. If you use %03#, for instance, a three-digit number in the range 001 to 999 will be created.

RIS clients can be pre-staged, which allows you to create the computer account in the domain prior to using RIS. If you do not pre-stage the RIS clients, you must grant the users of those clients the right to join computers to the domain. However, granting users this right presents a security hazard, because users can connect any computer to the network, perform a RIS-based installation, join a domain, and access network resources. When you pre-stage a RIS client, you use the globally unique identifier (GUID) or Universally Unique ID (UUID) to create the computer account in the domain before you deploy the operating system. Pre-staging also enables you to designate the computers that the RIS server will service.

Scenario

You are using GPOs and RIS throughout the processes and procedures in the apbindustries.com domain. The number of employees has been steadily increasing and you have no reason to believe the numbers will not continue to increase. Employee retention has also become a noticeable issue. You want to keep the network infrastructure as neat as possible, while continuing to provide an efficient level of security.

Lesson 15 Managing a Remote Installation Services (RIS) Implementation

Project	Exam 70-294 Objective
15.1 Managing CD-based Images	Basic knowledge
15.2 Pre-Staging a RIS Client	Basic knowledge

General Requirements

To complete the projects in this lesson, you will need administrative rights on SERVERA, the Windows Server 2003 computer that is acting as a domain controller for the apbindustries.com domain. You may also find it helpful to refer to Lesson 15 of the Prentice Hall Certification Series Exam 70-294 textbook for further information about the topics covered by the projects in this lesson.

project 15.1 Managing CD-based Images

exam objective

Basic knowledge

overview

There are many reasons why an administrator may want to change the RIS default naming convention. Turnover is ordinarily the main reason to modify the naming convention so that new employees will not have computer names that are associated with employees who have long since left the company. You have decided to modify the default computer naming convention to use an incremental number to avoid this problem.

learning objective

After completing this project, you will know how to modify the RIS naming convention to use an incremental number.

specific requirements

Administrative rights on SERVERA, the Windows Server 2003 computer that is acting as a domain controller for apbindustries.com.

estimated completion time

5 minutes

project steps

1. Log on to **SERVERA** with an account that has administrative rights.
2. Open the **Active Directory Users and Computers** console.
3. Double-click the **Domain Controllers** OU.
4. Right-click **SERVERA** and click **Properties** to open the **ServerA Properties** dialog box.
5. Click the **Remote Install** tab (**Figure 15-1**).
6. Click **Advanced Settings** to open the **ServerA Remote Installation Services Properties** dialog box (**Figure 15-2**).
7. Click **Customize** to open the **Computer Account Generation** dialog box.
8. In the **Format** text box, type **%#machine (Figure 15-3)**.
9. Click **OK** to close the Computer Account Generation dialog box. Every RIS client will now get a unique, incremental number during the installation process.
10. Click **OK** to close the ServerA Remote Installation Services Properties dialog box.
11. Click **OK** to close the ServerA Properties dialog box.
12. Close the Active Directory Users and Computers console.

Figure 15-1 The Remote Install tab

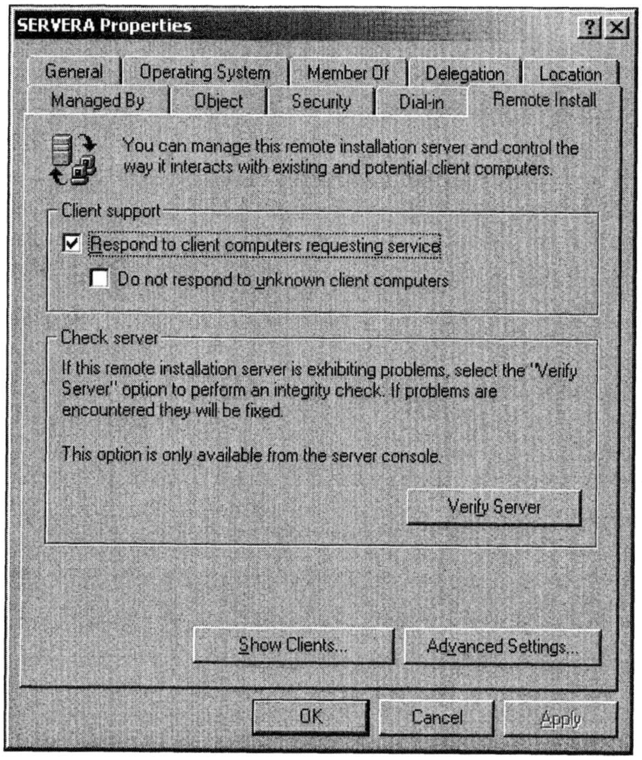

Figure 15-2 The Remote-Installation-Services Properties dialog box

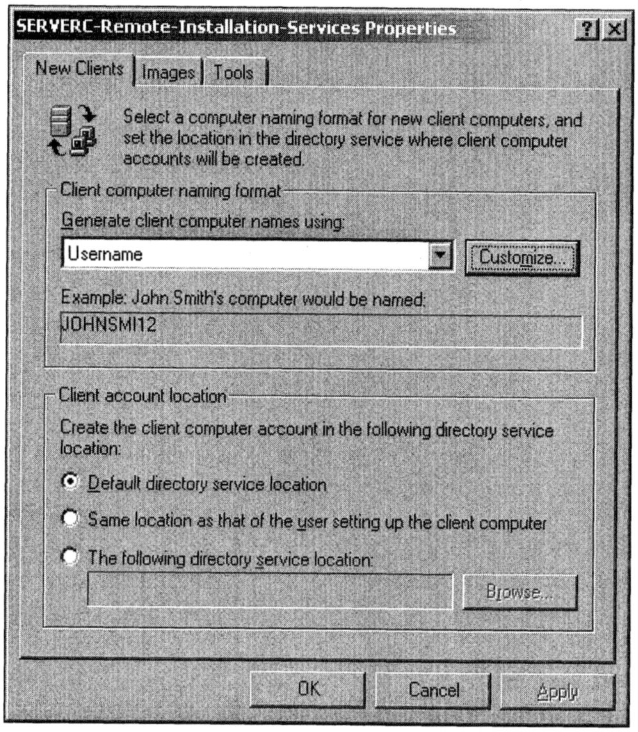

Figure 15-3 The Computer Account Generation dialog box

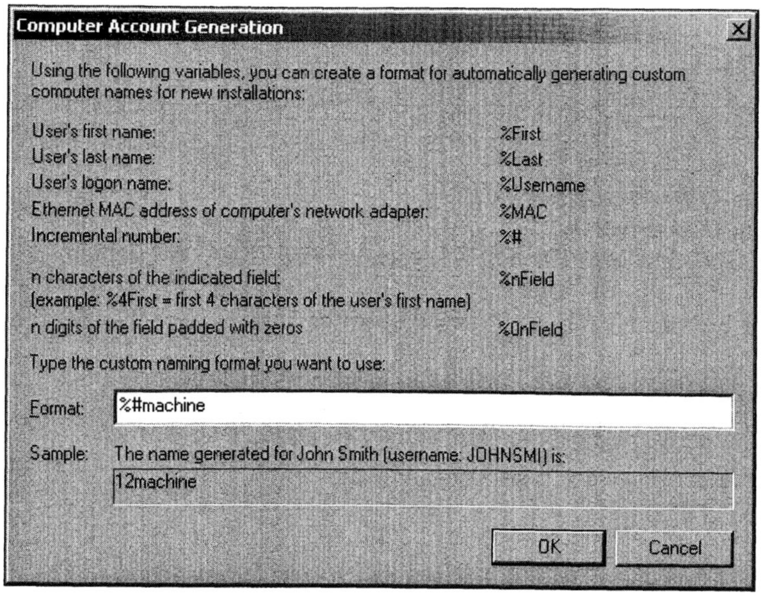

project 15.2 Pre-Staging a RIS Client

exam objective

Basic knowledge

overview

For security purposes, you have decided to pre-stage the ten servers that you are going to deploy using RIS. This way, you will not have to grant any users the right to join the servers to the domain. When you pre-stage a RIS client, the computer account is created in the domain prior to the RIS installation. Then, you will configure the RIS server to respond only to the pre-staged computers. In this project, you will create the computer account for one of the servers using a fictitious globally unique identifier (GUID) and configure the RIS server to respond only to known client computers.

learning objective

After completing this project, you will know how to pre-stage RIS clients and how to configure a RIS server to respond only to specific computers.

specific requirements

Administrative rights on SERVERA, the Windows Server 2003 computer that is acting as a domain controller for apbindustries.com and the successful completion of the projects in Lesson 14.

estimated completion time

10 minutes

project steps

1. Log on to **SERVERA** with an account that has administrative rights.
2. Open the **Active Directory Users and Computers** console.
3. Right-click the **Computers** container, point to **New**, and click **Computer** to open the **New Object – Computer** dialog box.
4. Type **13machine** in the **Computer name** text box to specify a name for the RIS client **(Figure 15-4)**.
5. Click **Next** to open the **Managed** dialog box. If you do not select the **This is a managed computer** check box, the computer name will be assigned to any RIS client randomly.
6. To specify the GUID, select the **This is a managed computer** check box and type the GUID, for example, **{921AC974-ED22-22DE-ABCD-00BB0063B998}** in the **Computer's unique ID (GUID/UUID)** text box **(Figure 15-5)**. Note that if you specify a GUID that is associated with an existing computer account, an error message will open when you click **Next**.
7. Click **Next** to open the **Host server** dialog box.
8. Select the **The following remote installation server** option button.
9. Type **ServerA** in the corresponding text box **(Figure 15-6)**.
10. Click **Next** to open the **New Object – Computer** dialog box, which shows a summary of the settings you specified **(Figure 15-7)**.
11. Click **Finish** to create the computer account.
12. Select the **Domain Controllers** OU.
13. Right-click **SERVERA** and click **Properties** to open the **SERVERA Properties** dialog box.
14. Open the **Remote Install** tab. Select the **Do not respond to unknown client computers** check box.
15. Click **OK** to close the SERVERA Properties dialog box.
16. Close the Active Directory Users and Computers console.

tip

GUIDs consist of hexadecimal digits. There are 8 digits before the first hyphen, 4 digits in the next three hyphenated sections, and 12 digits in the last section. The hexadecimal digits must be enclosed in curly brackets: {dddddddd-dddd-dddd-dddd-dddddddddddd}.

tip

If the RIS installation fails on clients that are not pre-staged, the RIS server probably is configured to respond to only known computers. To resolve the problem, clear the Do not respond to unknown client computers check box on the Remote Install tab in the Properties dialog box for the RIS server.

Figure 15-4 Setting the computer name for the RIS client

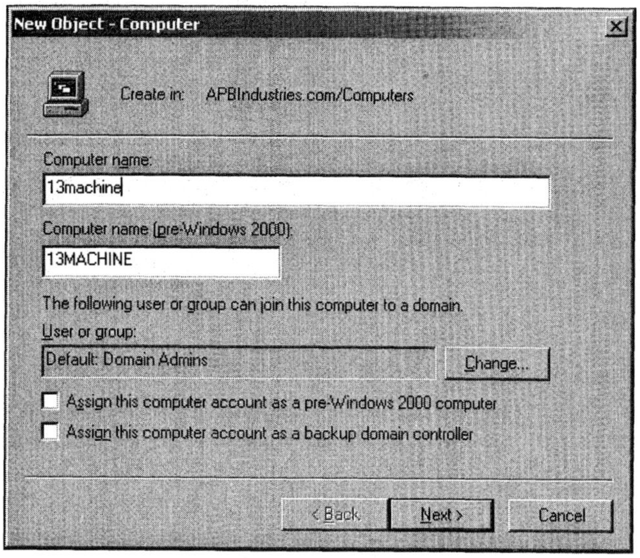

Figure 15-5 Specifying the GUID for the RIS client

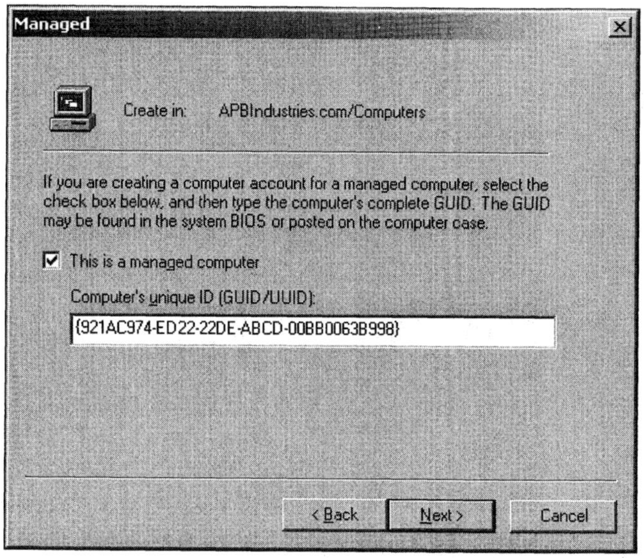

Figure 15-6 Specifying the host RIS server

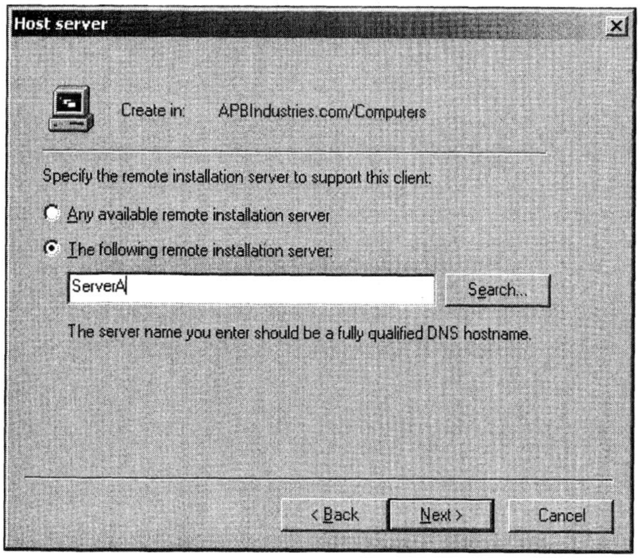

Figure 15-7 Reviewing the pre-stage settings

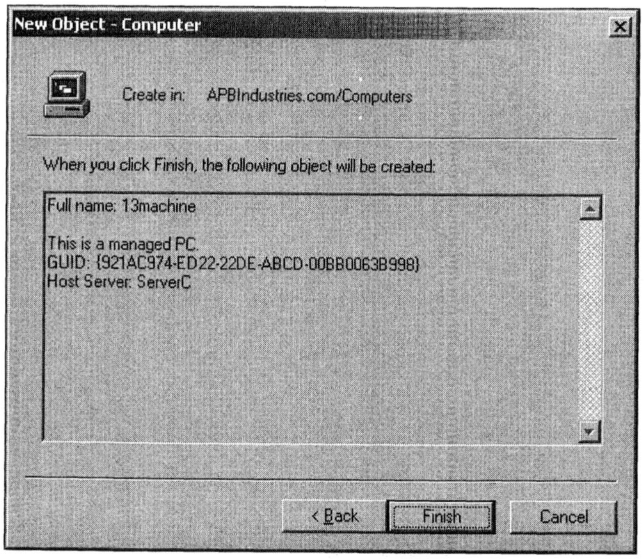

LESSON 16

Applying Certificate Services in Active Directory Infrastructure

The Public Key Infrastructure (PKI) consists of protocols, standards, and technologies that provide both authentication and encryption services. A PKI implementation uses Certificate Authorities (CAs) to authenticate the parties involved in electronic communications. The purpose of a CA is to act as a trusted third-party in a communication exchange or other digital transactions. Certificates contain a unique public key, as well as identifying data about the entity to which it is being issued. Certificates can be issued to user accounts, computers, and services. The CA signs each certificate that it issues to guarantee its authenticity and to pledge that the public key belongs to the certificate owner.

An internal CA can be configured so that all of the computers on the local network trust it. Network users, computers, and services can then make requests to the CA to issue them a certificate. The CA must confirm the information sent by the requester. Each CA has a policy module that dictates how the process of verification takes place. It also has a private key that it uses to digitally sign the certificate prior to issuance. The policy module may require a company letterhead, or corporate seal, or any type of identifying information from the user to verify who they are such as a driver's license or other ID card, a credit card number, or simply a list of physical attributes for the user.

CAs generally belong to a hierarchical system in which one CA certifies another CA to manage certificates over a part of a network. Trust relationships are at the core of this hierarchy, which is also referred to as CA chaining. The trust relationships begin with the root Certificate Authority, which is the most highly trusted CA in the CA organizational structure. The root CA must be kept secure, because if a security breach occurs at the root CA level, all certificate-based security on the network is jeopardized. The root CA has the authority to issue certificates to other CAs. There are two classes of CAs: either enterprise or stand-alone. Within each class there are root CAs and subordinate CAs. An Enterprise root CA is the root CA for an Active Directory integrated hierarchy. Enterprise subordinate CAs request certificates from the Enterprise root CA. A Stand-alone root CA is the root CA for a hierarchy of CAs that does not require Active Directory. Stand-alone CAs cannot issue certificates for Active Directory related functions. Stand-alone subordinate CAs request certificates from a Stand-alone Root CA.

Scenario

As the network administrator for APB Industries, you must configure a safe, cost-effective security strategy. You have decided to implement Certificate Services as one facet of your security implementation.

Lesson 16 Applying Certificate Services in Active Directory Infrastructure	
Project	**Exam 70-294 Objective**
16.1 Using Certificate Services in the Active Directory Infrastructure	Basic knowledge
16.2 Using Automatic Enrollment to Enroll User Certificates	Configure the user environment by using Group Policy. Automatically enroll user certificates by using Group Policy.
16.3 Using Automatic Enrollment to Enroll Computer Certificates	Deploy a computer environment by using Group Policy. Automatically enroll computer certificates by using Group Policy.
16.4 Using Web Enrollment Services	Basic knowledge

General Requirements

To complete the projects in this lesson, you must have administrative rights on SERVERA, the Windows Server 2003 computer that is acting as a domain controller for the apbindustries.com domain and on SERVERB, the Windows Server 2003 computer that is acting as a domain controller for the rnd.apbindustries.com domain. You also may find it helpful to refer to Lesson 16 in your Prentice Hall Certification Series Exam 70-294 textbook for further information about the topics covered projects in this lesson.

project 16.1

Using Certificate Services in the Active Directory Infrastructure

exam objective

Basic knowledge

overview

As the network administrator for APB Industries, you have decided to use Certificate Services to issue certificates. You have decided to use a Certificate Services hierarchy that is integrated with Active Directory. First, you must install the Enterprise root CA.

learning objective

After completing this project, you will know how to install and configure an Enterprise root CA.

specific requirements

Administrative rights on SERVERA, the Windows Server 2003 computer that is acting as a domain controller for apbindustries.com. In order to support certificate enrollment using the Web enrollment pages, you must have the Internet Information Services World Wide Web service installed before you install Certificate Services.

estimated completion time

20 minutes

project steps

1. Log on to **SERVERA** with an account that has administrative rights.
2. Click **Start**, point to **Administrative Tools**, and click **Internet Information Services (IIS) Manager** to open the **Internet Information Services (IIS) Manager** console.
3. Expand the **SERVERA** node.
4. Select the **Web Server Extensions** folder.
5. In the details pane, select **Active Server Pages** and click the **Allow** button **(Figure 16-1)**.
6. Close the Internet Information Services (IIS) Manager console.
7. Click **Start**, point to **Control Panel**, and click **Add or Remove Programs** to open the **Add or Remove Programs** window.
8. Click **Add/Remove Windows Components** to start the **Windows Components Wizard**.
9. In the **Components** list box, select **Certificate Services**. A warning dialog box informs you that after you install Certificate Services, you will be unable to change the computer name or the domain membership for the computer. After reading the warning, click **Yes** to continue **(Figure 16-2)**.
10. Click **Next** in the **Windows Components** dialog box to open the **CA Type** screen.
11. Verify that the **Enterprise root CA** option button is selected.
12. Click **Next** to open the **CA Identifying Information** screen.
13. Type **Enterprise Root CA** in the **Common name for this CA** text box. The distinguished name is entered in the **Preview of distinguished name** label. Note that the default validity period for the CA is five years **(Figure 16-3)**.
14. Click **Next**. The **Cryptographic Key** screen opens briefly as the key is generated and then the **Certificate Database Settings** screen opens.
15. Click **Next** to keep the default settings for the **Certificate database and Certificate database log**.

tip

The Certificate Authority Web enrollment pages require Active Server Pages (ASP) in order to function.

Figure 16-1 Enabling Active Server Pages on IIS

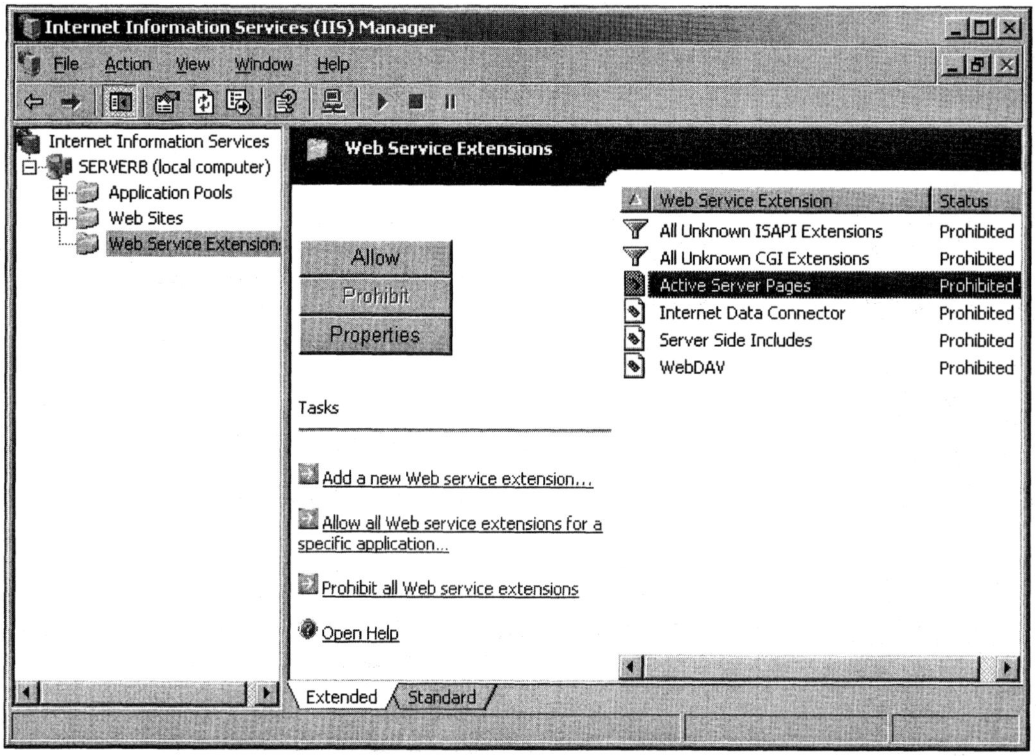

Figure 16-2 A Microsoft Certificate Services warning dialog box

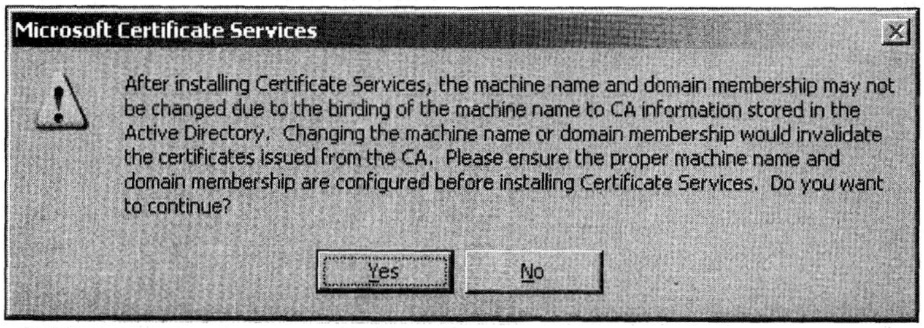

Figure 16-3 The CA Identifying Information screen

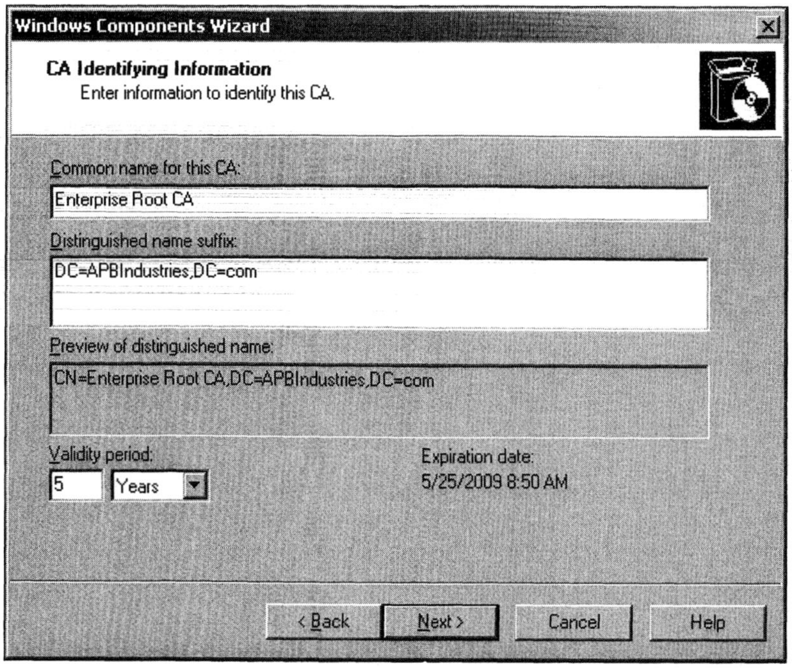

project 16.1

Using Certificate Services in the Active Directory Infrastructure (cont'd)

exam objective

Basic Knowledge

project steps

16. A **Microsoft Certificate Services** warning dialog box opens if Internet Information Services is running to warn you that Certificate Services must temporarily stop IIS. Click **Yes (Figure 16-4)**.
17. The **Configuring Components** screen opens while the component configuration process begins.
18. The **Insert Disk** dialog box may open to prompt you to insert the Windows Server 2003 CD-ROM (If so, and your computer is configured to auto-run CD-ROMs, click **Exit** to close the Autorun window that opens when you insert the CD-ROM).
19. When the components are installed the **Completing the Windows Components Wizard** screen opens. Click **Finish**.
20. Close the Add or Remove Programs window.
21. Click **Start**, point to **Administrative Tools**, and click **Certification Authority** to open the **Certification Authority** console and confirm the installation **(Figure 16-5)**.
22. Close the Certification Authority console.

Figure 16-4 A Microsoft Certificate Services warning dialog box

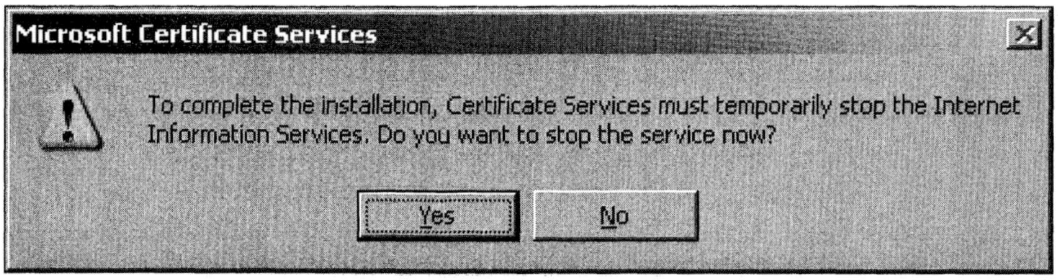

Figure 16-5 Verifying the CA Installation

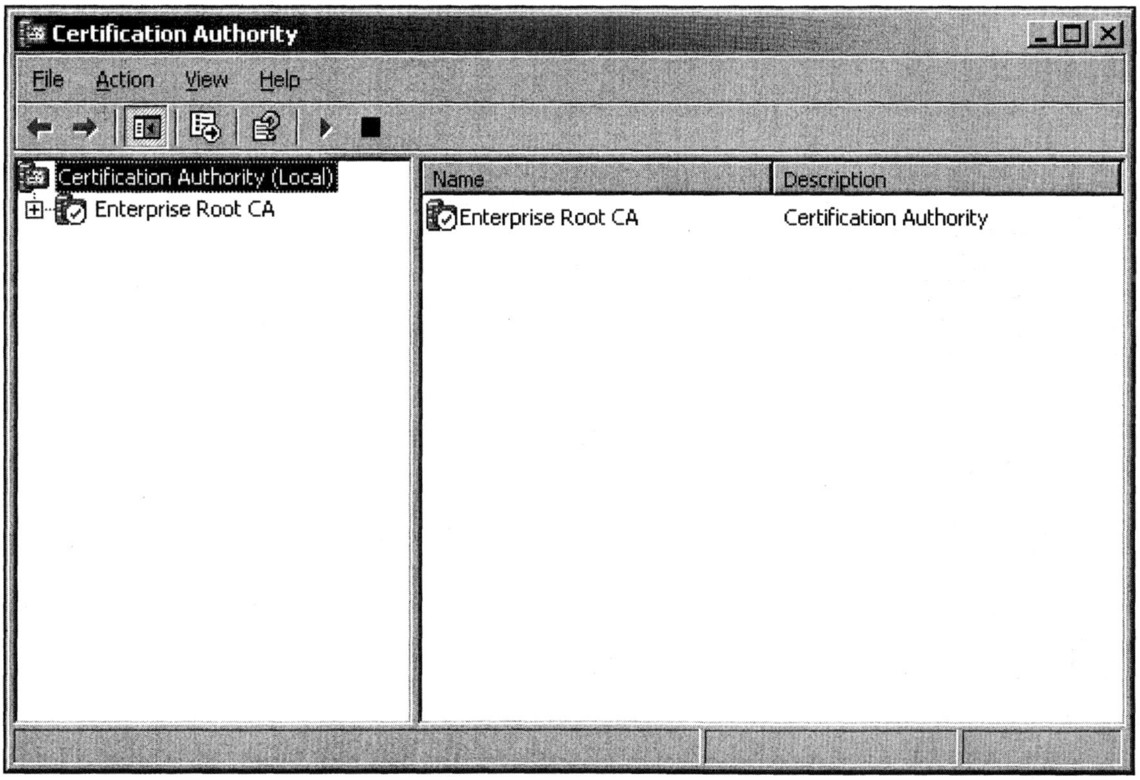

project 16.2

Using Automatic Enrollment to Enroll User Certificates

exam objective

Configure the user environment by using Group Policy. Automatically enroll user certificates by using Group Policy.

overview

You have been asked to configure automatic enrollment for user certificates in the apbindustries.com domain. In order to do so, you must create a certificate template for your user accounts and apply the appropriate access permissions. You will also need to configure the Enterprise CA to issue the appropriate certificates based on the template. Finally, you must configure Group Policy to enable Automatic Enrollment.

learning objective

After completing this project, you will know how to enable automatic enrollment for user certificates.

specific requirements

Administrative rights on SERVERA, the Windows Server 2003 computer that is acting as a domain controller for apbindustries.com.

estimated completion time

15 minutes

project steps

First, you will create a certificate template for your user accounts and grant all Authenticated Users permission to request a certificate that is based on the template.

1. Log on to **SERVERA** with an account that has administrative permissions.
2. Click **Start**, point to **Administrative Tools**, and select **Certification Authority** to open the **CA console**.
3. Expand the **Enterprise Root CA** node.
4. Right-click **Certificate Templates** and select **Manage** to open the Certificate Templates console.
5. Select the User template **(Figure 16-6)**.
6. Right-click the User template and select **Duplicate Template** to open the **Properties of New Template** dialog box.
7. Type **Auto-enrolled User** in the **Template display name** text box and verify that the **Publish certificate in Active Directory** check box is checked **(Figure 16-7)**.
8. Open the **Request Handling** tab and select the **Enroll subject without requiring any user input** option button, if necessary.
9. Open the **Subject Name** tab and remove the check from the **Include e-mail name in subject name** check box.
10. Clear the **E-mail name** check box.
11. Open the **Security** tab and select **Authenticated Users**, if necessary.
12. Select the **Allow** check boxes next to the **Enroll** and **Autoenroll** permissions **(Figure 16-8)**.
13. Click **OK** to close the Properties of New Template dialog box.
14. Close the Certificate Templates console.

Next, you will add the Auto-enrolled User certificate template to the Enterprise CA so that it can issue the appropriate certificate based on the template.

1. In the **Certification Authority** console, right-click the **Certificate Templates** folder, point to **New**, and select **Certificate Template to Issue** to open the **Enable Certificate Templates** dialog box.
2. Select **Auto-enrolled User (Figure 16-9)**.
3. Click **OK** to close the dialog box.
4. Close the Certification Authority console.

Figure 16-6 The User template in the Certificate Templates console

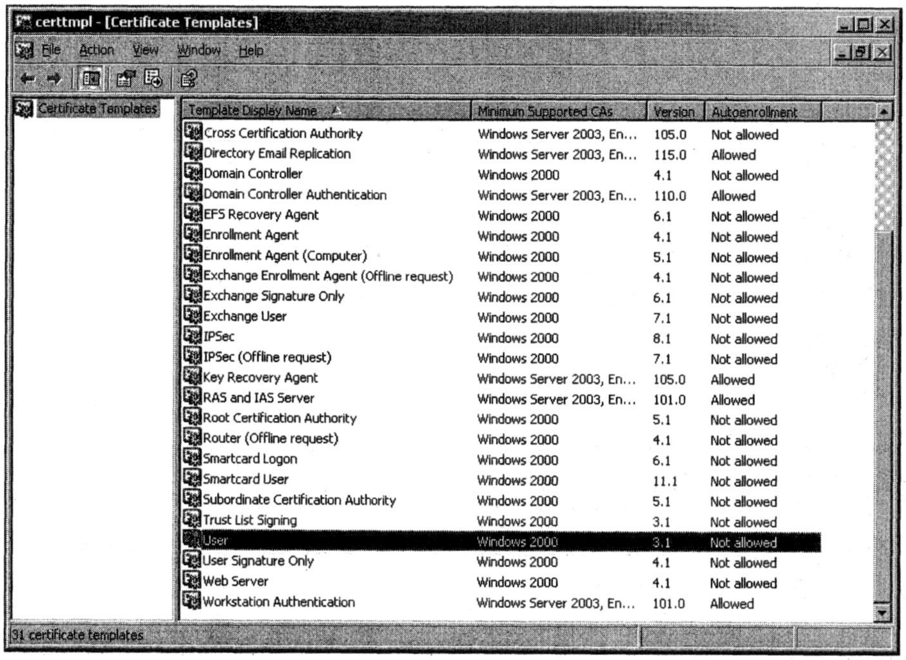

Figure 16-7 Creating a new Certificate template

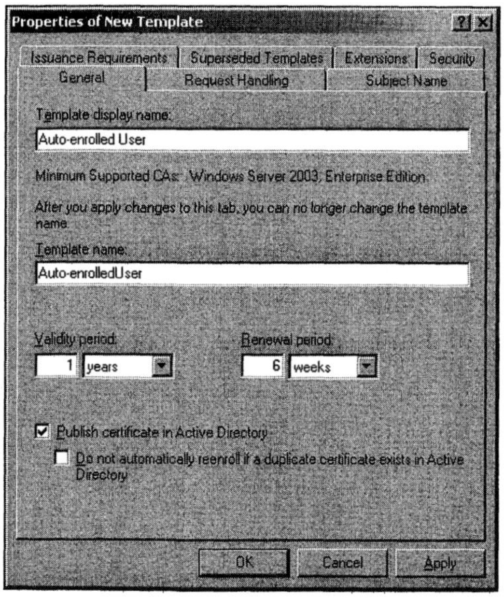

Figure 16-8 Assigning Auto-enrollment permissions

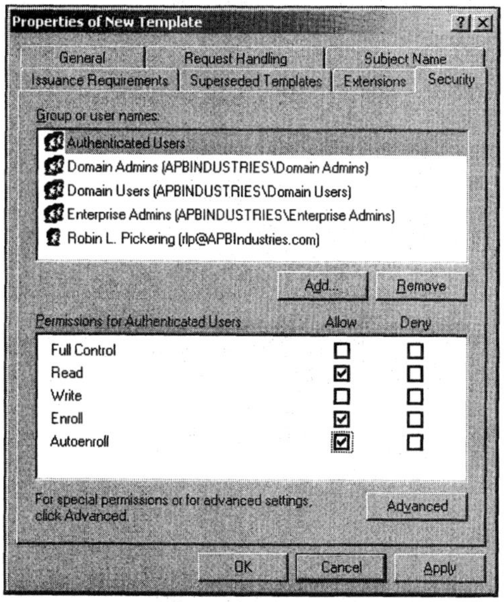

Figure 16-9 The Enable Certificate Templates dialog box

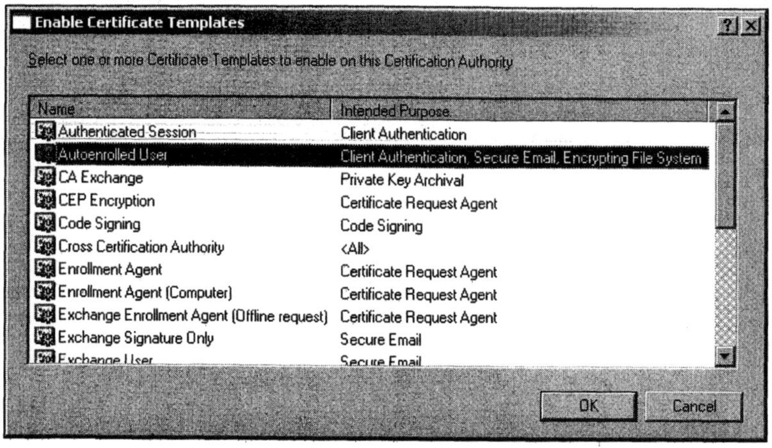

project 16.2

Using Automatic Enrollment to Enroll User Certificates (cont'd)

exam objective

Configure the user environment by using Group Policy. Automatically enroll user certificates by using Group Policy.

project steps

Finally, you will configure Group Policy to enable Automatic Enrollment.

1. Open the **Group Policy Management** console.
2. Expand the **Forest** and **Domains** nodes, if necessary.
3. Expand **apbindustries.com**.
4. Right-click **Default Domain Policy** and click **Edit** to open the **Group Policy Object Editor**.
5. Expand the **User Configuration** node, if necessary.
6. Expand the **Windows Settings** and **Security Settings** nodes.
7. Select **Public Key Policies (Figure 16-10)**.
8. Double-click **Autoenrollment Settings** to open the **Autoenrollment Settings Properties** dialog box.
9. Select **Enroll certificates automatically**, if necessary.
10. Select the **Renew expired certificates**, **update pending certificates, and remove revoked certificates** and **Update certificates that use certificates templates check boxes** check boxes **(Figure 16-11)**.
11. Click **OK** to close the Autoenrollment Settings Properties dialog box.
12. Close Group Policy Object Editor and the GPMC. Users logging on to Windows Server 2003 or Windows XP computers will now be automatically enrolled for certificates.

Figure 16-10 User Configuration Public Key Policies

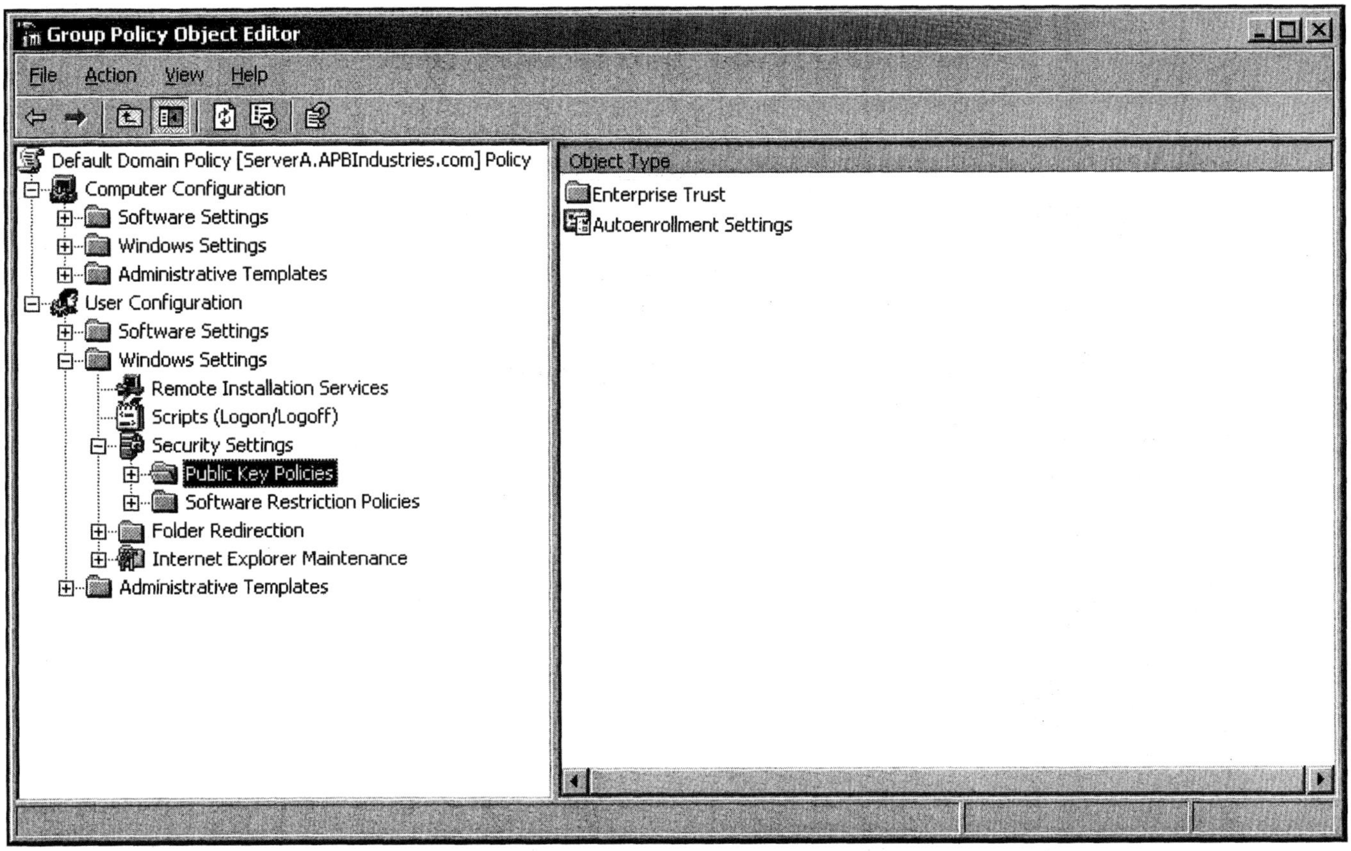

Figure 16-11 The Autoenrollment Settings Properties dialog box

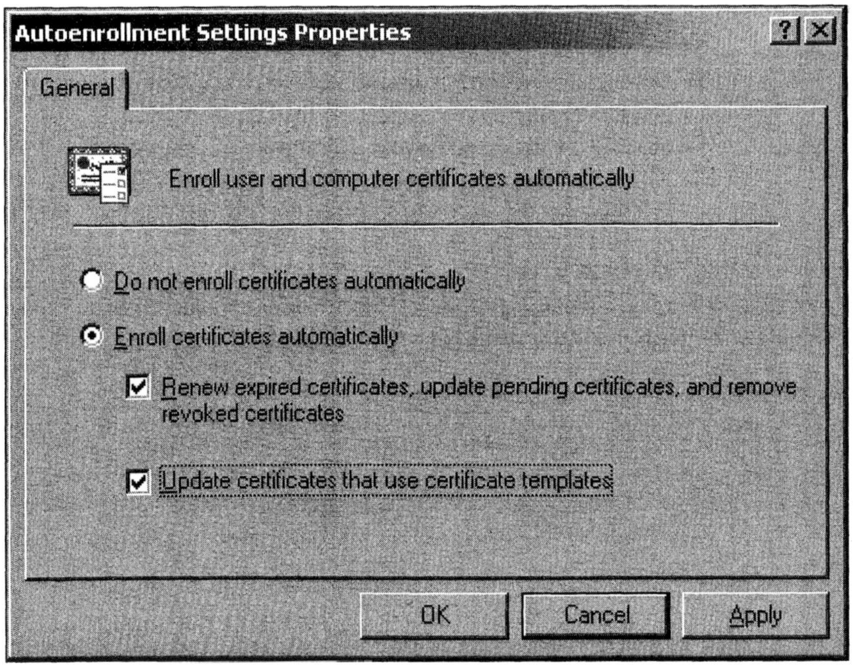

project 16.3

Using Automatic Enrollment to Enroll Computer Certificates

exam objective

Deploy a computer environment by using Group Policy. Automatically enroll computer certificates by using Group Policy.

overview

To finalize the certification strategy, you must create an environment for automatic computer enrollment. You will use Certificate Services to allow automatic enrollment for computers with no manual interaction from the user.

learning objective

After completing this project, you will know how to enable automatic enrollment for computer accounts.

specific requirements

Administrative rights on SERVERA, the Windows Server 2003 computer that is acting as a domain controller for apbindustries.com.

estimated completion time

15 minutes

project steps

1. Log on to **SERVERA** with an account that has administrative permissions.
2. Click **Start**, point to **Administrative Tools**, and click **Group Policy Management** to open the **GPMC**.
3. Expand the **Forest** and **Domains** nodes, if necessary.
4. Expand **apbindustries.com**.
5. Right-click **Default Domain Policy** and click **Edit** to open the **Group Policy Object Editor**.
6. Expand the **Computer Configuration** node, if necessary.
7. Expand the **Windows Settings** and **Security Settings** nodes.
8. Select **Public Key Policies (Figure 16-12)**.
9. Double-click **Autoenrollment Settings** to open the **Autoenrollment Settings Properties** dialog box.
10. Select the **Enroll certificates automatically**, if necessary.
11. Select the **Renew expired certificates, update pending certificates, and remove revoked certificates** and **Update certificates that use certificates templates** check boxes **(Figure 16-13)**.
12. Click **OK** to close the Autoenrollment Settings Properties dialog box.
13. Close the Group Policy Object Editor and the GPMC. Computer accounts will now automatically enroll for certificates.

Figure 16-12 Computer Configuration Public Key Policies

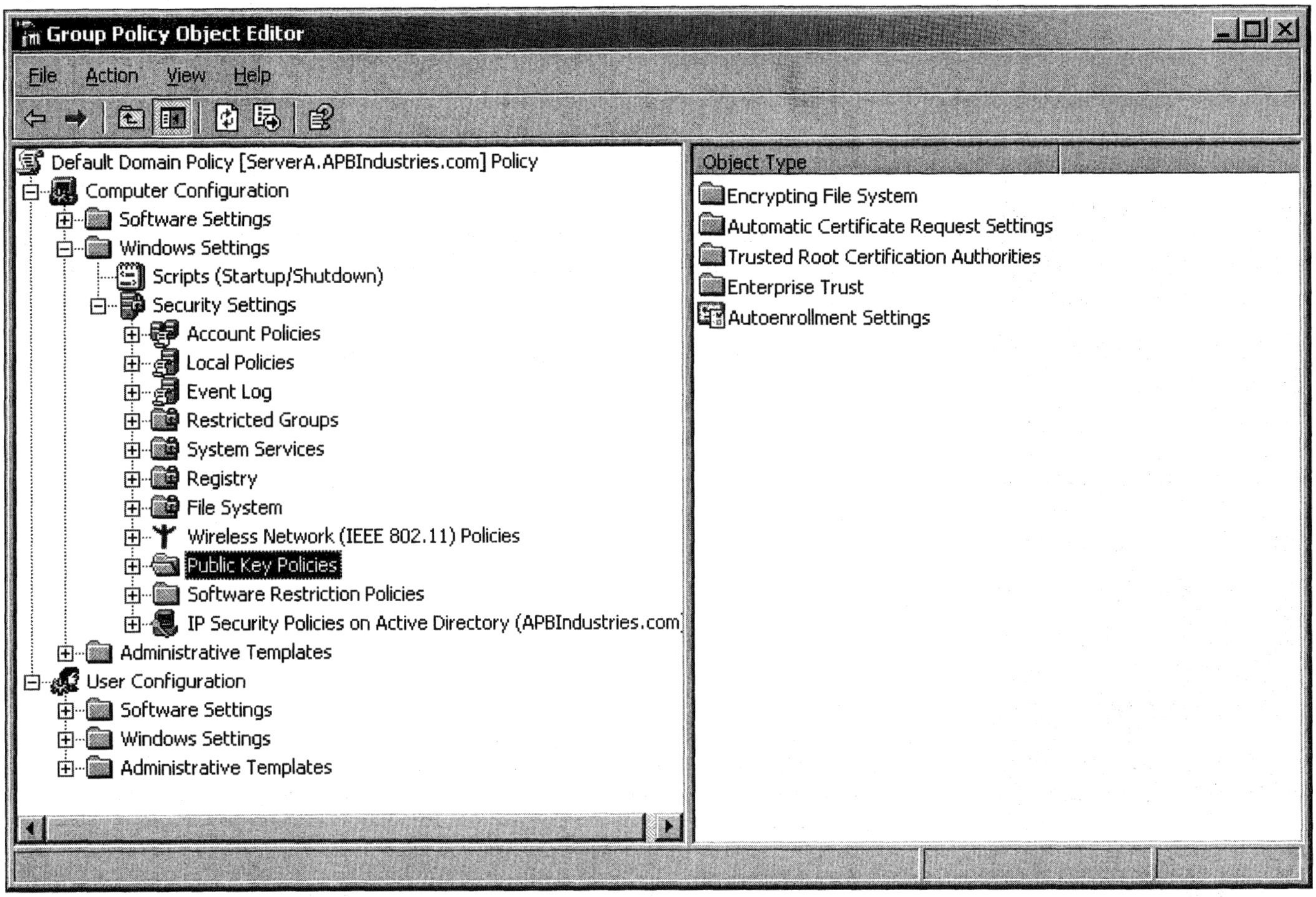

Figure 16-13 Automatically enrolling computer certificates

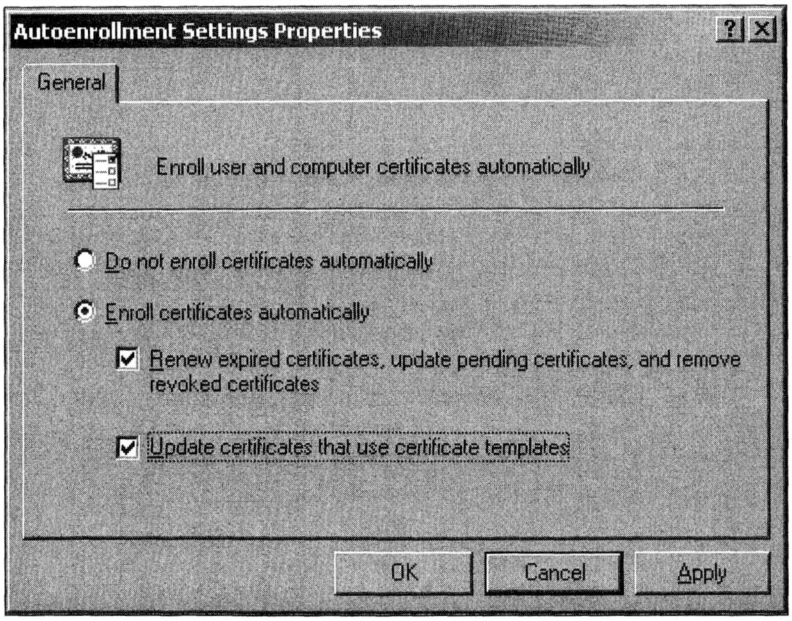

project 16.4 Using Web Enrollment Services

exam objective

Basic knowledge

overview

Now that you have the Public Key Infrastructure in place for apbindustries.com, you can start to issue certificates. You are going to use the Web enrollment pages to request and install a user certificate.

learning objective

After completing this project, you will know how to use Web Enrollment Services to enroll a user certificate.

specific requirements

Administrative rights on SERVERA, the Windows Server 2003 computer that is acting as a domain controller for apbindustries.com and on SERVERB, the Windows Server 2003 computer that is acting as a domain controller for rnd.apbindustries.com.

estimated completion time

15 minutes

project steps

1. Log on to **SERVERB** with an account that has administrative permissions.
2. Click **Start**, point to **All Programs**, and click **Internet Explorer**.
3. In the **Address** bar, enter **http://servera/certsrv**, and press **[Enter]** to open the Microsoft Certificate Services Web enrollment page.
4. Under the **Select a task** heading, click the **Request a certificate** link.
5. On the **Request a Certificate** page, select **User Certificate (Figure 16-14)**.
6. On the **User Certificate—Identifying Information** page, click **Submit**.
7. The **Potential Scripting Violation** warning dialog box opens to warn you that you should only allow trusted Web sites to request a certificate for you. Click **Yes** to request a certificate (**Figure 16-15**).
8. Depending on your Internet Explorer security settings, you may receive a second prompt warning you that sending information to a trusted site may be viewed by others. Click **OK** to continue.
9. When you submit your request, you will see a Generating Request message. Next, the **Certificate Issued** screen will open.
10. Click **Install this certificate**.
11. The **Potential Scripting Violation** warning dialog box opens to warn you that the Web site is adding one or more certificates to the computer and that allowing an untrusted Web site to update your certificates is a security risk. Click Yes to install the certificate (**Figure 16-16**).
12. The **Certificate Installed** screen informs you that the certificate has been successfully installed (**Figure 16-17**).
13. Close Internet Explorer.
14. On **SERVERA**, click **Start**, point to **Administrative Tools**, and click **Certification Authority** to open the **Certification Authority** console.
15. Expand the **Enterprise Root CA** node.
16. Select the **Issued Certificates** folder. In the details pane, you should see the issued user certificate (**Figure 16-18**).
17. Close the Certification Authority console.

Figure 16-14 Certificate Services Web enrollment pages

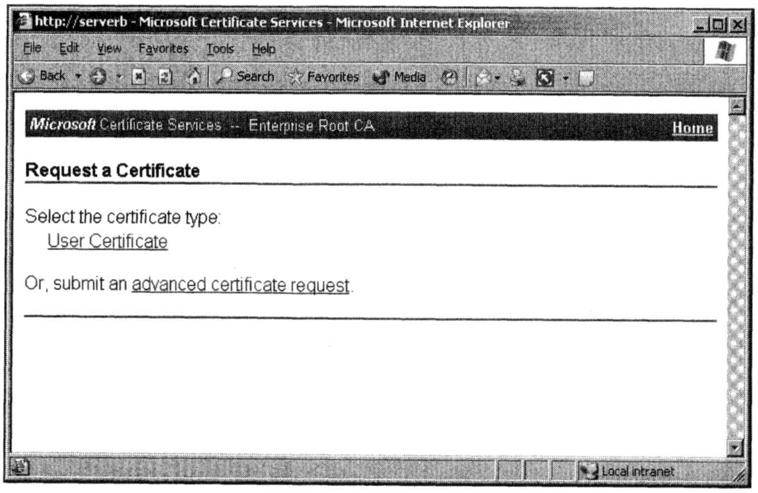

Figure 16-15 A Potential Scripting Violation warning dialog box (Step 7)

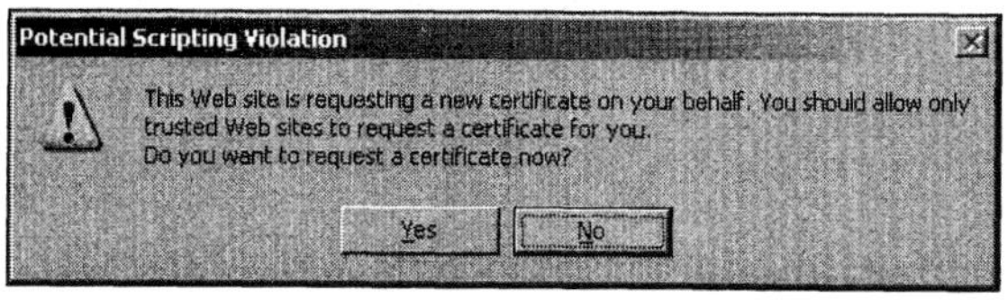

Figure 16-16 A Potential Scripting Violation warning dialog box (Step 11)

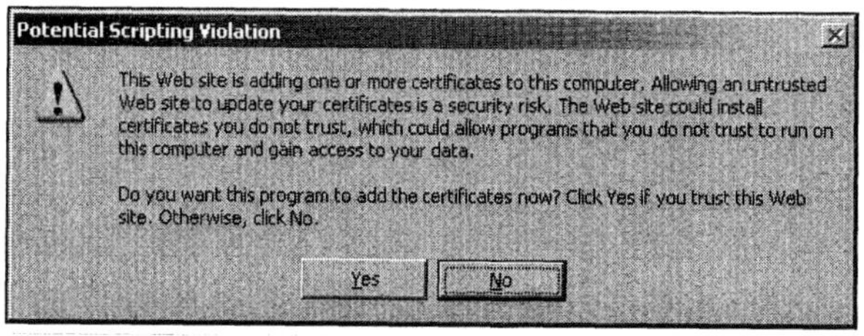

Figure 16-17 The Certificate Installed screen

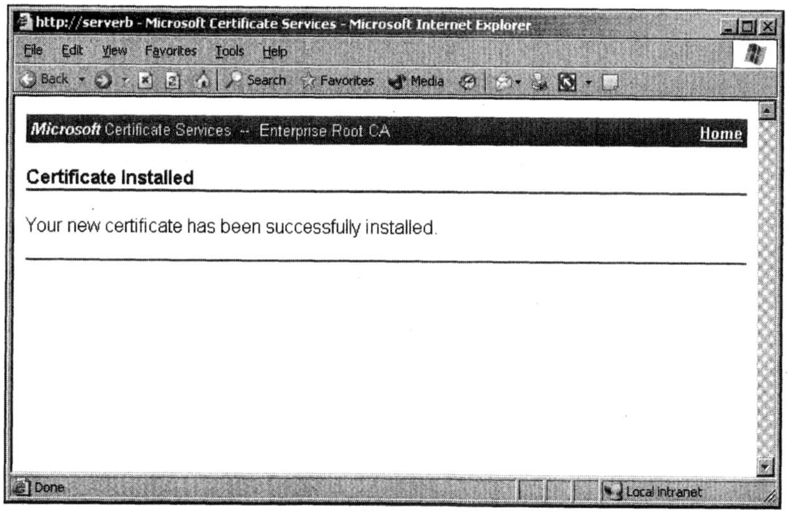

Figure 16-18 The new user certificate in the Certification Authority console

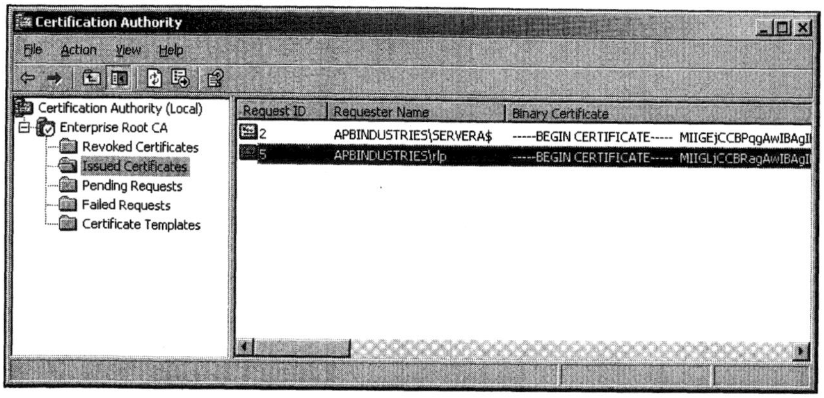

16.16 Notes

Glossary

Access Control Entry (ACE) An entry in the Discretionary Access Control List that notes the type of access required in order for a user to gain access to the resource. A user cannot gain access to a resource unless there is an ACE for the user, or for the groups to which the user belongs, in the DACL. An ACE contains the SID of the user or group allowed or denied, as well as the permissions associated with that user or group.

Access Control List (ACL) A set of security descriptors that defines how an object can be accessed. An extra security feature of Active Directory-integrated zones is that you can use the Access Control List (ACL) to restrict access to specific zones or resource records in the zone.

Acldiag.exe A command-line tool used to diagnose and troubleshoot problems related to permissions that are set for Active Directory objects.

Active Directory Directory service for Windows 2000 Server and Windows Server 2003 used for storing information in a logical and hierarchical manner.

Active Directory Domains and Trusts console Administrative tool used to manage the trust relationships between two or more domains in the same forest or different forests. It is also where you add alternative UPN suffixes.

Active Directory Schema snap-in MMC snap-in extension used to view and modify the Active Directory schema.

Active Directory Services Interfaces (ADSI) Used to create scripts that interact with Active Directory.

Active Directory Sites and Services console Administrative tool used to create sites, subnets, site links, and connection objects, as well as to add or remove global catalog servers.

Active Directory Users and Computers console Administrative tool used to create and delete most objects, to modify their properties, and to set their permissions.

Active Directory zone replication Zone replication technique that is only used for ADI zones. With ADI zones, each domain controller can act as a primary DNS server, and replication between these servers is automatically performed by Active Directory.

Active Directory-integrated zone Type of DNS zone in which the zone data is stored and replicated as a part of the Active Directory database.

Add Installation Image Wizard Wizard used with RIS to add CD-based images, specify the installation source files location, set the Windows installation image folder name, and all other tasks associated with adding an additional CD-based image.

Alert Utility used to send a message, run a program, or start a log in System Monitor, when the value of a specific counter passes the threshold value.

All Users folder Folder used to add settings to all profiles used on a specific machine.

Application Advertising Displaying the Start menu shortcut and/or desktop icons for an application, making it appear as if the application is already installed. When an application is advertised by a GPO, however, it is not installed until the first time the user attempts to run it.

Application Data Partition Special database structure in Active Directory that holds information specific to a particular application.

Application log Event log in which warnings, alerts, and messages that are generated by applications are recorded.

Archive attribute A property for files and folders that is used to identify them when they have changed. When a file has changed, the archive attribute, which is actually an attribute of the file header, is automatically selected. Some backup types remove the archive attribute to mark files as having been backed up, while others do not. Some backup types use the archive attribute to determine which files to back up, and others ignore it.

Attributes Distinct characteristics that represent an object.

Authoritative restore Active Directory restore that allows you to recover deleted objects. When an object is deleted, the deletion is replicated to other domain controllers and the USN for the object is updated. If you restore the object non-authoritatively, it will subsequently be removed because it has a lower USN than the deletion. In order to force the object back into Active Directory, an authoritative restore increases the USN by 100,000, so that it is higher than the deleted USN.

Automatic RIS Setup The default RIS installation option. The installation starts as soon as the user logs on and users will not be prompted for any of the settings that are normally requested during an installation including computer names, network settings, and time zone settings. However, you can still present users with the list of available operating system images. In an automatic setup installation, the RIS server generates the machine name, and the client account is created in the location specified in the RIS server settings.

Binding information Service information that when published allows clients to connect to services that do not have well-known bindings, so that connections can be automatically established with these services.

Boot Information Negotiation Layer Service (BINLSVC) One of the services added when RIS is installed on a server. The BINL service listens for client network service requests and manages the RIS environment. It controls the response to network service requests from RIS clients. When it receives these requests, BINLSVC ensures that the correct files, configuration, and policy settings are sent to the client.

Bridgehead server Contact point for sending and receiving replication information between sites. The bridgehead server is the only server in a site allowed to replicate to other sites. This functionality reduces the amount of replication traffic between sites, because all servers are not attempting to replicate with all other servers; however, it also increases the load on the bridgehead server.

Built-in domain local groups Domain local groups that are automatically created only on domain controllers and which cannot be deleted, They are stored in the Users container in the Active Directory Users and Computers console. The number of domain local groups will be different on each domain controller, depending on the type of services the domain controller is running. The names generally identify the function of the group. For example, the DnsAdmins group is for users who can manage DNS servers in the domain.

Built-in global groups Global groups that are automatically created on domain controllers. They are stored in the Users container in the Active Directory Users and Computers console. These groups have predefined group memberships. Domain-wide rights and privileges must be assigned to members of these groups. Rights can be assigned to built-in global groups either directly or by adding them to domain local groups.

Built-in local groups Local groups that are created on all Windows Server 2003 computers. They can be viewed in the Groups folder in the Computer Management snap-in on all non-domain controllers and in the Builtin container in the Active Directory Users and Computers console on domain controllers.

Built-in system groups Also referred to as special identities, these groups are populated with users based upon how they access a computer or a resource. Network administrators cannot add, modify, or delete user accounts from a built in system group. The operating system does this automatically. For example, a user who connects to the network via a dial-up connection is automatically added to the Dial-up built-in system group.

Built-in user accounts Accounts created automatically during the installation of Windows Server 2003. Examples include the Administrator and Guest accounts. Built-in accounts cannot be deleted, but they can be disabled and renamed. Renaming the Administrator account is a common security practice.

Caching-only name server DNS servers that do not have their own local zone database file.

Centralized GPO design GPO implementation strategy in which an organization's network is maintained by a small number of large GPOs. For example, if one GPO handles an entire domain, the logon process for this GPO would be faster, but it would be difficult to delegate administrative control over this GPO because of its large number of settings.

Check Server Wizard Wizard used to check the settings of an RIS server and to record any problems with the BINL, SIS, or TFTPD services in the event log. The Check Server Wizard also fixes the problems, if possible, and displays a summary of the RIS configuration.

Child domain Domains under a parent domain.

Closed Set The object and all references to the object.

COM+ Class Registration database Database that stores entries for dynamic link library (.dll) and executable (.exe) files on a computer.

Computer Configuration settings Group Policy settings that apply to computers when the operating system starts up, regardless of which user logs on.

Configuration information Service information that when published allows you to distribute current configuration information for a particular application to all clients in a domain.

Connection objects The one-way, individual communications channels that the Knowledge Consistency Checker (KCC) typically creates between individual servers for replication. Whereas site links correspond to connections between sites, connection objects correspond to connections inside sites.

Contacts Objects that are used only for distribution list and e-mail purposes. Unlike user accounts they are not security principals and cannot log on and access shared resources.

Contiguous namespace An Active Directory tree—sometimes called a domain tree—forming a contiguous namespace. A domain tree is formed as soon as a child domain is created and associated with a given root domain. For a technical definition, a tree is a contiguous DNS naming hierarchy.

Counter log Logs used to record the state of object counters at specific intervals of time that you set.

Custom RIS Setup RIS installation option that allows users to override the computer name generated by the RIS server. Users also can specify an alternate location for the client account rather than the one specified in the RIS server settings.

Data Store (ntds.dit file) File where the records that make up Active Directory's database are stored. The Ntds.dit file contains the schema information, global catalog, and all of the objects stored on the domain controller. It is stored in the *%systemroot%*\Ntds folder, by default.

Database Layer Active Directory service layer that provides an object view of database information, thereby isolating the upper layers of the directory service from the underlying database system. All database access is routed through the Database layer.

Decentralized GPO design GPO implementation strategy that uses separate GPOs for specific policy settings. This approach increases the number of GPOs and thus lengthens logon time. On the other hand, its flexibility simplifies administration.

Default trust A trust that is automatically established between the forest root domain and the root of each tree in the forest, as well as between each child domain and each parent domain. Default trusts are always two-way and transitive.

Default User profile The profile that all profiles are copied from the first time a user logs on. The Default User profile is stored in the Documents and Settings folder as are all other profiles, but the folder it is contained in is marked as a hidden folder by default. You must change your display settings in order to view the folder.

Delegation of control The process of giving other users or administrators rights to Active Directory objects so that the administration of the network is evenly distributed.

Delegation with Central Control Design or **Distributed Control Design** GPO design approach is based on delegating administrative control over OUs to various administrators in an organization. When you implement this strategy, you maintain centralized control while distributing managerial control to a number of OU administrators.

DHCP Server Server that runs the DHCP service. This service automatically provides clients with IP addresses, subnet masks, and can provide additional IP configuration (such as DNS server addresses), thus saving the administrator from having to manually configure static IP addresses for each machine.

Direct replication partner A domain controller for which the originating domain controller has a connection object.

Directory database Repository of information about network objects.

Directory service Database that stores information about network objects, such as files, applications, users, or printers, in the network.

Directory Service log Event log in which alerts, messages, and informational messages relating to Active Directory are recorded.

Directory Services Restore Mode Special safe mode that enables you to restore the System State data on a domain controller.

Directory System Agent (DSA) Active Directory service layer that represents the process that provides access to the Data store, which contains the physical store of directory information located on a hard disk. The DSA is the server-side process that creates an instance of a directory service. Clients use one of the supported interfaces to connect (bind) to the DSA and then search for, read, and write Active Directory objects and their attributes. Applications need to connect to the DSA layer to access objects in Active Directory through one of the supported interfaces such as LDAP or ADSI.

Discretionary Access Control List (DACL) A list of all user accounts and groups granted access permissions to Active Directory objects, and the type of access granted. For every user who attempts to gain access to a resource, the DACL must contain an Access Control Entry (ACE) in order to access to the resource.

Disjointed namespace A DNS infrastructure that includes two or more top-level domain names. The domains in the Active Directory tree are interrelated but do not always share a common root domain name. A forest is a disjointed namespace.

Distinguished Name (DN) Distinct name that provides a unique identity to an object. All objects can be referenced using a Distinguished Name. Example: CN=Gregory Johnson, OU=Accounting, DC=ABC Corp, DC=com.

Distribution group Groups that are used only for the distribution of messages by applications such as Microsoft Exchange Server. They cannot be used to assign permissions to users.

DNS name server A server that runs the DNS server service and is used to resolve host names to IP addresses or vice versa.

DNS notification A feature of the DNS service that uses a push mechanism for notifying a selected set of secondary servers for a zone whenever the zone is updated.

DNS Server log Log file that contains basic events logged by the DNS Server service, including when the DNS Server service starts and stops on the DNS server.

DNS zone An area of authority over a namespace or collection of contiguous namespaces.

Domain A collection of network resources grouped together under a single domain name and security boundary.

Domain controller A computer that stores a replica of the directory database. A domain controller also stores the security policies and security accounts for a domain and authenticates users to log on to the domain and access the shared resources.

Domain local group Groups created in Active Directory on a domain controller. The scope of a domain local group is the domain in which the group was created. You can add members to a domain local group from any domain, but members can only be assigned permissions for resources in the domain in which the domain local group is created.

Domain Name System (DNS) The main name resolution service for Windows Server 2003. It is used to access computers on a TCP/IP network using the host name instead of an IP address. The DNS service enables clients on a network to register and resolve fully qualified domain names.

Domain namespace Naming scheme used by DNS to organize domains in a hierarchical structure

Domain Naming Master role The domain controller holding the domain naming master role can add or remove domains in a forest. Only one domain naming master role can exist in the entire forest.

Domain user accounts Account used to access resources on a computer in a domain

Domain-wide operations master roles Tasks that are controlled by a single server for each domain.

Dsacls.exe A command-line tool used to manage ACLs. Using this tool, you can query and modify security attributes of Active Directory objects to troubleshoot problems relating to permissions.

Dsastat.exe A command line tool used to diagnose replication problems. You use Dsastat to compare two directory trees across replicas within the same domain, or for a global catalog server, across different domains. You can obtain capacity statistics including megabytes per server, objects per server, and megabytes per object class, and you can use this tool to compare the attributes of replicated objects.

Dynamic Domain Name System (DDNS) The capability to dynamically create and modify records in a DNS zone. This feature is included in Windows Server 2003 and BIND (8.1.1 or higher) DNS servers.

Environment subsystems Component of the user mode layer that allows operating systems to run applications not otherwise compatible with the operating system.

Event log A log that is used to record an entry when certain events occur. Warnings, alerts and informational messages specific to a service, an application, or the operating system are recorded in a number of service-specific logs including the Application log, Security log, System log, Directory Service log, File Replication Service log, and DNS log.

Event Viewer Snap-in used to monitor information about server events. Events are documented in event logs as errors, warnings, or information. The default event logs are the Application, Security, and System logs. A DNS server has the DNS Server log which you can use as a troubleshooting aid. A domain controller will also include the Directory Service log and the File Replication Service log. A DNS server will have the DNS Server log.

Extensible Storage Engine (ESE) layer This Active Directory service layer has direct contact with the records in the Data Store. It is based on an object's relative distinguished name attribute. This layer can support a database up to a maximum of 16 terabytes (TB) in size.

External trust Also called an explicit trust, a trust established between different Windows 2000 forests, between Windows Server 2003 and Windows 2000 forests, and between Windows NT and Windows 2000 or Server 2003 domains. External trusts are always NT trusts; that is, an external trust is always one-way and non-transitive. However, a two-way external trust can be mimicked by creating two one-way, external trusts.

File Replication service (FRS) Service that is responsible for ensuring that the Sysvol folder is replicated between domain controllers. The FRS is also responsible for all automatic replication of Dfs replicas.

Firewall A combination of hardware and software security systems that secures a network from unauthorized access from outside the network, usually using stateful packet filtering techniques.

Floating/Flexible Single Master of Operations (FMSO) A server that performs one of the specific Active Directory roles that require single-master replication.

Folder Redirection Process of redirecting common folders to a network server. Rather than downloading the full folder at logon, your users will instead browse the remote folder, just as if they were browsing a network share. When a user opens an item in a redirected folder, the individual item is downloaded. This functionality saves considerable network bandwidth and can considerably reduce the logon time for users with large profiles.

Forest Discrete administrative Active Directory unit that consists of one or more trees joined together through a common forest root domain. This set of domain trees share a common schema and configuration, common global catalog, are secured by Kerberos trust, and share a disjointed namespace

Forest-wide operations master roles Tasks that are controlled by a single server for the entire forest.

Forward lookup zones DNS zone type that is used to resolve host names to IP addresses using forward lookup queries.

Forwarders Servers that your DNS server should query to resolve addresses that are not locally resolvable. Forwarders are used in situations where root hints are unusable or deemed inefficient for resolving other domains.

Fully Qualified Domain Name (FQDN) The full DNS path name, containing all domains and subdomains along the path to the host. For example, www.sales.corp.com. is an example of a FQDN. www is the hostname (the name of the computer), sales is a sub-domain, corp is the second level domain, com is the top-level domain, and the "." at the end signifies the root of DNS.

Functional role (or Team design) GPO design GPO implementation strategy that is based on the structure of the organization. The functional roles of users are used to apply Group Policies. To implement this strategy, first create an OU structure that corresponds to the functional structure of your organization. Then create a customized GPO for each OU that is tailored to the needs of the OU.

General Protection Fault (GPF) GPFs cause Windows applications to crash. They most commonly occur when one application attempts to use a block of memory that has been assigned to another application. GPFs can also be caused by running applications with insufficient resources, using incorrect hardware device drivers, corrupt or missing Windows files, and data exchanges between applications that fail because they cannot be read.

Global catalog Domain controller that stores the information about all of the objects on the domain where it resides and partial information about the objects in other domains.

Global Catalog server Domain controller that stores a full copy of its own domain database, and a partial copy of all other domain databases in the forest. The partial databases include all objects, but do not include all attributes of each object. Global catalog servers are required in Active Directory to facilitate enterprise searching, User Principal Name (UPN) lookups, and Universal group storage.

Global group Groups whose members can be drawn from only the domain in which the group was created, but which can assign permissions to members for resources in any domain.

Globally Unique Identifier (GUID) A 128-bit number that defines the identity of an object in Active Directory. When you create an object in Active Directory, the Directory Service Agent (DSA) automatically assigns a GUID to the object. Even if you move an object from one domain to another, the GUID remains the same.

Gpresult.exe A tool for troubleshooting Group Policy application in Windows Server 2003. Stored in *%systemroot%*\System32, it performs nearly the same functions as RSop; however, Gpresult is a command line tool.

Group A collection of users, computers, contacts, and other group objects within a forest.

Group Policy Set of rules that apply to a part of the directory structure, such as an OU, domain, or site. A set of configuration settings applied by administrators to objects in Active Directory, which are used to centrally manage users and groups.

Group Policy Container An Active Directory component that contains GPO attributes, extensions, and version information.

Group Policy Modeling Wizard A simulation tool implemented or a “what if” scenario in order to see what the results of a particular GPO implementation is or would be.

Group Policy Object A storage place for a collection of Group Policy settings that enable an administrator to control various aspects of the computing environment. Consists of a Group Policy container (GPC) and a Group Policy template (GPT).

Group Policy Results Wizard A tool that queries the target computer for the RSoP data applied to that computer and that displays the policies applied to that computer or a particular user thereon.

Group Policy Template A collection of folders stored in *%Systemroot%*\SYSVOL\sysvol \<*domain_name*>\Policies on each Windows 2000 and Windows Server 2003 domain controller. The GPT contains all of the Registry entries and associated files and folders required to implement the various GPO functions.

Home folder Private network location in addition to the My Documents folder where users can store personal files.

in-addr.arpa Second-level, which contains name-to-IP address mappings indexed by IP address. It was to simplify the process of reverse lookup queries, which are requests to resolve a known IP address to a host name.

Infrastructure master role The domain controller holding this role is responsible for updating all cross-domain object references (such as a group from Domain A being added as a member of another group in Domain B).

Integral subsystems Component of the user mode layer that performs important operating system functions such as security and session management.

IntelliMirror A set of powerful features native to Microsoft Windows 2000 and later for desktop change and configuration management.

Inter-forest trust Also known as a forest trust, a trust established between two Windows Server 2003 forest root domains. Forest trusts can be either one-way or two-way, and are always transitive.

Inter-site replication Active Directory replication that occurs between sites.

Inter-site Topology Generator (ISTG) A special service in Active Directory that is used to check for the availability of domain controllers in remote sites and calculate the best replication paths between sites using the cost fields of the site links.

Intra-site replication Active Directory replication that occurs between servers in a single site.

IP replication Replication using the Remote Procedure Call protocol; also known as RPC over IP.

Iterative query A query performed on behalf of a DNS client to assist in answering a recursive query. It allows DNS servers to send back pointers or referrals if it does not have the answer.

Kernel mode Windows Server 2003 architectural layer that has direct access to system data and hardware.

Knowledge Consistency Checker (KCC) Active Directory process responsible for creating connection objects to ensure that each computer has at least two replication partners, and that all intra-site replication conforms to the three-hop rule.

Ldp.exe A graphical tool that provides you with information about objects. This tool also enables you to connect to domains and to search, modify, add, delete, and bind to LDAP-compatible directories. If you are experiencing a problem with Active Directory, you can use this tool to troubleshoot the problem.

Lightweight Directory Access Protocol (LDAP) LDAP is both a protocol and an API. The LDAP protocol is the Active Directory core protocol and is the preferred method of interacting with Active Directory; the LDAP API provides access to the LDAP protocol. LDAP is used by clients to query, create, update, and delete information stored in Active Directory and domain controllers to communicate with each other.

Local group Groups that are used to manage local user accounts on a single server or a stand-alone computer. The access level for these groups is limited to resources located on the computer on which the group is created. Local groups are mainly used in peer-to-peer or workgroup networks or on stand-alone computers that are not part of a domain. You populate local groups with user accounts that are stored in the local security database of a single computer.

Local user accounts Allow users to log on only to the computer where the local user account was created.

Local user profile User profile created the first time a user logs on to a computer and stored on a system's local hard disk. Any changes made to local user profile remain specific to the computer on which the changes were made.

Logical AD structure AD arrangement that reflects the logical setup of an organization and is made up of domains, OUs, trees, and forests.

Mandatory software removal Software removal configuration that automatically removes an application from a computer the next time the user logs on or the computer restarts.

Mandatory software upgrade Software upgrade configuration used when the latest versions of an application must be installed on network computers.

Mandatory user profile A read-only roaming profile that can be used to specify particular settings for specific users or groups of users. Changes made to the desktop settings by a user are not permanently saved.

Many-to-one mapping Mapping multiple certificates to one user account.

Master name server The DNS server from which the secondary name server gets the copy of the zone database.

Member server A Windows NT4.0, 2000 or Server 2003 computer that is part of a domain but does not store a replica of the directory database. A member server can perform all Windows Server 2003 services except Active Directory services.

Mixed mode Domain mode that allows the coexistence of Windows NT domains, Windows 2000, and Windows Server 2003 domains.

Modifications .mst files that allow you to customize the installation of Windows Installer packages at the time of deployment.

Movetree.exe A utility that is used to move objects such as users, computers, and OUs between domains.

Multi-master replication Method of creating multiple copies, known as read/write replicas, of the directory database and making them available throughout the network.

Multiple domain model A type of domain model in which the network objects are placed in more than one domain.

Name resolution Process by which the names that people use to identify objects can be converted into the numbers that computers use to identify objects.

Name server A server with the DNS Server service installed and running. While a name server usually also includes one or more zone files (DNS databases) used for authoritatively resolving queries to one or more zones, it is not required.

Namespace Bounded area where the names that people use to identify objects can be converted into the numbers that computers use to identify objects. All directory services provide a namespace. A telephone directory is a namespace where the names of the subscribers are resolved or translated into telephone numbers

Native mode If your domain consists of only Windows 2000 domain controllers, you can switch to Windows 2000 Native mode. This mode supports Windows 2000 and Windows Server 2003 domains

Nesting The process of adding a group to other groups or consolidating the groups within a network.

Netdom.exe A utility that is used to move workstations and member servers between domains.

Nltest.exe A command-line tool used to perform network administrative tasks. You can use this tool to check the status of trust relationships between domains and the connectivity and flow of traffic between domain controllers and computers in a network. You can also use Nltest to obtain a list of the primary domain controllers on your network, to check domain controller replication, to force a remote shutdown, and to obtain data about Active Directory objects.

Nonauthoritative restore Active Directory restore that allows you to recover Active Directory, while keeping any changes that have occurred since the last backup. The information in the directory will be only as recent as the last backup set and will be brought up-to-date through the normal replication process.

No-Refresh interval (Zone Aging/Scavenging) The period of time during which a record can be updated, but not refreshed. By default, this is seven days.

Non-transitive trust A trust that does not follow through; that is, it does not pass from domain to domain, so each domain must explicitly trust the other domains. See also transitive trust.

NSLookup A command-line utility that can be used to test the DNS domain namespace.

Ntdsutil Active Directory support tool used to manage the directory database files with authoritative restorations, database copying, database moving, offline defragmentations, and metadata cleanups. It is also used to list sites, domains, and server information, to manage operations masters, to perform authoritative restores, and to create domains.

Object Any "thing," either tangible or intangible (non-physical), about which data is stored such as files, applications, users, or printers.

One-to-one mapping Mapping a single certificate to a single user account.

One-way trust A trust that allows a domain to access another domain's resources, but not vice-versa. See also two-way trust.

Optional software removal Software removal configuration in which existing applications are left as is, but no new users can install the software.

Optional software upgrade Software upgrade configuration that provides flexibility to users because it allows them to install the upgrade when they need it.

Organizational Unit (OU) A container object that is an Active Directory administrative partition. OUs can contain users, groups, resources, and other OUs. Organizational Units enable the delegation of administration to distinct sub-trees of the directory.

Parent domain Any domain immediately above another domain.

Performance console MMC console that is used to collect and monitor information about system resources.

Performance counter Performance measures for an object that can be quantified, such as the percentage of time the processor is busy (%Processor Time).

Performance Logs and Alerts Snap-in in the Performance console that is used to store performance data in log files and to create alerts.

Performance object A system resource such as a processor, disk, network interface card (NIC), or memory whose performance can be monitored.

Physical AD structure AD arrangement that reflects the physical locations of components in an organization and is made up of sites and domain controllers.

Pre-staging The process of preparing the computers on which you want a RIS-based installation to be performed and configuring the RIS server to respond only to these computers. Pre-staging involves identifying RIS clients using their globally unique identifiers (GUIDs) or Universally Unique IDs (UUIDs) and creating computer accounts for them.

Primary DNS server Another name for a Primary name server.

Primary domain controller (PDC) emulator role The domain controller holding this role acts as a Windows NT primary domain controller to any Windows NT 4.0 backup domain controllers. It processes password change requests from Windows NT clients and replicates updates to the Windows NT backup domain controllers. In native mode, it receives preferential replication of security. Finally, and perhaps most importantly, the PDC emulator is responsible for clock synchronization between domain controllers in a domain, which is an extremely important function in Active Directory because the primary method Active Directory uses to resolve conflicts is to accept the last modification.

Primary name server The name server with the primary copy of the zone. Modifications are made on this server, and the changes are forwarded to secondary name servers. Also called a primary DNS server.

Proxy A device that, in its most basic form, performs Network Address Translation. Typically, a proxy will also provide some firewall functions, and may also cache copies of remote data for faster access.

Published folders Shared folders that have been listed in Active Directory.

Realm trust A trust between a Windows Server 2003 domain and a Unix Kerberos realm. A Kerberos realm resembles a domain in Active Directory. A realm trust can be either one-way or two-way, and can be transitive or non-transitive.

Recovery Console A command-line interface that is used to resolve complex system problems when a full system boot is not available.

Recursive query A type of forward lookup query that is used to request that a DNS server provides the full and complete answer to the query. The receiver, not the sender, will perform recursion as necessary to retrieve the requested record. The DNS name server will not return a referral or pointer to another DNS server to the sender, but rather will follow the query to its completion.

Refresh interval (SOA Properties) How often a secondary server will query a primary server for changes to the zone. This process is accomplished by a transfer and comparison of the serial number field in the SOA record.

Refresh interval (Zone Aging/Scavenging) The period of time during which a record can be updated or refreshed. By default, this is seven days.

Registry Database that stores the configuration data for a computer.

Relative Distinguished Name (RDN) Naming convention for an object that consists of one of the attributes for an object that is a part of the DN name. It is the portion of the Distinguished Name that uniquely identifies an object within the object's parent container. For example, the RDN for the user object Gregory Johnson is CN = Gregory Johnson.

Relative identifier (RID) master role The domain controller responsible for this role issues unique blocks of RIDs to each domain controller in the domain. RIDs are a part of each object's SID (Security ID), and are required to ensure the domain-wide uniqueness of SIDs.

Remote Installation Services (RIS) Services that enables you to automate the installation of the Windows 2000, Windows Server 2003, and Windows XP Professional operating systems. You can create installation images of these operating systems that can include applications and desktop configurations, which can then be made available to users at client computers. The client computers must support PXE ROM or must be started with a RIS boot floppy.

Repadmin.exe A command-line tool used to diagnose replication problems. You use this tool to modify and view your replication topologies, view replication information, and force replication between domain controllers. You will need to force replication if you want to propagate important Active Directory updates to other domain controllers immediately

Replication The act of exchanging directory information. For example, a domain controller is a Windows Server 2003 computer that authenticates user logon attempts and exchanges the directory information with other domain controllers.

Replication topology Arrangement that defines the path for replication of Active Directory from one domain controller to another until all the domain controllers have the same directory information.

Replmon.exe Tool that graphically represents the replication status, replication topology, and performance of domain controllers. Replmon can also report on changes that have not replicated from a specified domain controller. Using this tool, you can troubleshoot replication-related problems, and force synchronization between domain controllers.

Requests for Comments (RFCs) A regularly growing series of technical reports, proposals for protocols, and protocol standards used by the Internet community.

Resolver The service responsible for formulating the initial DNS query. A resolver queries other DNS name servers, including the root servers on behalf of the client. If the local DNS name server cannot resolve the host name to it IP address, it sends an iterative query on behalf of the client to assist in answering a recursive query.

Resource record Entries in a DNS database that contain information about the resources in a DNS domain.

Restart RIS Setup RIS installation option that is useful if there is an incomplete setup attempt. If a user cancels an installation after specifying a few options or if the setup fails, the user can select this option to restart the setup. The complete installation begins again, but the user will not be prompted for any values.

Resultant Set of Policy (RSoP) A useful tool for troubleshooting Group Policies. This tool shows the effective Group Policy settings applied to a user, and which GPOs those settings are inherited from. RSoP is a new feature in Windows Server 2003.

Reverse lookup query Request to resolve a known IP address to a host name, A second-level domain called in-addr.arpa, which contains name to IP address mappings indexed by IP addresses, was created to simplify this task.

Reverse lookup zones DNS zones that are used to resolve IP addresses to host names using reverse lookup queries.

RIPrep (Remote Installation Preparation) image A copy of the CD-based image along with applications and desktop settings. After this image has been created, it can be used to install the operating system, applications, and desktop settings simultaneously on multiple clients using RIS.

RIS boot disk Boot disk that simulates the PXE architecture in order to allow computers that are not PXE remote boot-enabled to use RIS for remote installation.

Roaming user profile User profile used primarily when users are required to work on multiple computers. The network administrator sets up a roaming user profile on a network server so that the profile is available to the user on all of the computers in the domain.

Root domain Domain at the top of the DNS hierarchy.

Run as command Command that runs as part of the Secondary Logon service to allow administrators to access administrative tools and perform administrative tasks while logged on using a normal Users or Power Users account

Schema Active Directory database design It provides a set of definitions to describe the type of objects that can be created in Active Directory, formal definitions of every object class that can be created in an Active Directory forest, and formal definitions of every attribute that can exist in an Active Directory object. The schema can be extended by adding new object classes or new attributes.

Schema master role The domain controller performing this role controls all updates and modifications to the schema.

Sdcheck.exe A command-line tool that lists the security descriptors for Active Directory objects.

Secondary DNS server Another name for a secondary name server.

Secondary name server The name server that maintains a copy of the zone database file from the primary DNS server of the zone. Also called Secondary DNS server.

Security descriptor Every Active Directory object is associated with a security descriptor, which contains the two access control lists (ACLs): the Discretionary Access Control List (DACL) and the System Access Control List (SACL).

Security groups Groups that are used to define the rights and permissions users will have to access resources on a computer or a network. When a user requests access to a network resource, the credentials for the user are validated against the group permissions to verify whether or not the user is allowed access. Security groups have all of the same capabilities as distribution groups, so they can also be used to distribute e-mail to multiple users.

Security ID (SID) A unique number (usually 80 bits in size) used to represent the identity of a user account or group.

Shared system volume (SYSVOL) The folder structure, present on all Windows Server 2003 domain controllers, that is created during Active Directory installation. This directory stores a copy of the public files for domains such as scripts and group policy objects. The contents of this folder are automatically replicated by the File Replication Service (FRS) to all the domain controllers in a domain.

Shared system volume (SYSVOL) A shared folder that is created when Active Directory is installed. It contains all publicly available files for domains, such as scripts and group policy objects, that users and other domain controllers will need for domain access.

Shortcut trust A trust established to reduce the normal Kerberos trust resolution path between domains.

SID Unique number used by Active Directory that identifies each object in Active Directory.

SIDHistory A security field that stores the old SID information including the security settings.

Single domain model A type of domain model in which only one domain stores the network objects.

Single Instance Store (SIS) One of the services that is added when RIS is installed on a server. The SIS service minimizes the disk space required to store the RIS installation images on the RIS server. SIS searches for duplicate files in the RIS volume, tries to identify all files related to the installation, and links them all together. It removes redundant copies, thereby saving space on the server.

Site A logical representation of your physical structure from within Active Directory.

Site license server In Windows Server 2003 Server, the License Logging service in a site replicates the licensing information to a centralized database on a server called the site license server for the site.

Site link The logical representation of the physical connections between locations (sites).

Site link attributes The site link cost, replication frequency, and replication schedule.

Site link bridges A means of linking two or more site links to allow replication when a direct site link does not exist between two sites.

SMTP replication Replication method that uses e-mail messages to transmit replication data. SMTP can only be used to replicate between different domains.

Software Distribution Point (SDP) A shared network folder in which you store software. After you have published or assigned applications to users, or assigned applications to computers, users can access them from this location.

Special permissions A set of very specific permissions that are used to achieve a finer grained control over objects than can be achieved used standard permissions.

Standard permissions The most commonly assigned access permissions, such as Read and Write.

Standard primary zone When a DNS server is the primary server for a zone, the zone type is configured as standard primary. All updates are made on the primary zone.

Standard secondary zone When a DNS server is the secondary server for a zone, the zone type is standard secondary. The changes in standard primary zone are replicated through a one-way zone transfer on the secondary zone.

Standard zone replication The process of copying the text-based DNS zone database using a process known as zone transfers. It is used by standard primary and standard secondary zones.

Stub Zone Stub zones are similar to delegated zones, but they cache the SOA, NS, and core A records for the zone to reduce query time slightly. Stub zones do not participate in zone transfers.

Subnet A collection of host computers on a TCP/IP network that are not separated by routers. Also known as a segment. In Active Directory, a subnet is simply a range of IP addresses, and may or may not match your physical subnets.

System Access Control List (SACL). List that identifies the users and groups that are being audited and records the actions being audited such as when they successfully access or fail to access an object.

System boot files Files that are used to load and configure the Windows Server 2003 operating system.

System Monitor MMC console that is used to collect and view real-time or previously collected performance data.

System State data Critical data that consists of several key components related to the operating system or applications. It includes the Registry, the boot and system files, the COM+ Class Registration database, all files under Windows File Protection, and various other components depending on the role of the server. On a domain controller, it includes the Active Directory database and SYSVOL.

Task Scheduler Service that enables you to program tasks to run at a specified date and time.

Tombstoning Process that essentially marks objects "dead," which makes them unusable, and updates the update sequence number (or the version number) for the object. This is done so that a "deletion" is properly replicated. On a domain controller, once every night, a process known as Garbage Collection is run. Any Active Directory object that has been tombstoned for more than 60 days (by default) is now actually deleted.

Tools RIS Setup RIS installation option that enables users to use troubleshooting tools before the operating system has been installed. These tools can include system BIOS flash updates and memory virus scanners.

Trace log Logs used to monitor a particular value continuously. Events are logged by a system provider or by a non-system provider that you specify.

Transitive trust A trust that follows through, meaning they pass from domain to domain. See also non-transitive trust.

Transitive site links Site links that are combined to create a site link bridge.

Tree Discrete administrative Active Directory unit that consists of a set of one or more domains in a hierarchical structure. Domains under the root domain possess contiguous names in which the child domain always contains the name of the parent domain.

Trivial File Transfer Protocol Daemon (TFTPD) One of the services that is added when RIS is installed on a server. In RIS, the TFTPD service manages file transfer requests from RIS clients during a remote installation. It is used to download initial files such as the bootstrap files that are required in order for the installation to start. TFTPD is also used to download the Client Installation Wizard (CIW).

Trust relationship A logical relationship between domains to facilitate the exchange of authentication information.

Two-way trust One that allows both domains to access each other's resources. See also one-way trust.

Unicode characters A standard for encoding text that is compatible with multiple character sets, unlike ASCII, which is only useful for Latin-based character sets (most notably, American English).

Universal group Groups used when there are multiple domains in a forest. Members can be drawn from many different domains and permissions can be assigned for resources in any domain. Universal groups are available only when Active Directory is running in Windows 2000 native mode or Windows Server 2003 mode.

Universal group caching Active Directory feature which allows a standard Windows Server 2003 domain controller to store universal group memberships so that a global catalog server is not required for logons.

Universal groups Groups that can contain members from any domain and are visible in all domains. Universal groups are unique in that they are stored entirely on global catalog servers. Thus, a change to the membership of a universal group will cause global catalog replication throughout the entire forest. Universal groups are used when there are multiple domains in a forest. Members can be drawn from many different domains and permissions can be assigned for resources in any domain. Universal groups are available only when Active Directory is running in Windows 2000 native mode or Windows Server 2003 mode.

Update Sequence Number (USN) Unique number assigned by Active Directory to a new or modified object. The update sequence number is used to keep track of the number of updates made to an object. It is USNs that make multi-master replication possible.

User account Account that contains information about a user such as user logon name, first name, last name, and password.

User Configuration settings Group Policy settings that apply to users after the user profile is loaded, regardless of what computer the user logs on to.

User Principal Name (UPN) The name of a system user in an e-mail address format. The user name is followed by the "at sign" followed by the name of the DNS domain with which the user is associated. An example might look like: GJohnson@ABCCorp.com. The UPN is used to identify an Active Directory object and is an acceptable format for user authentication.

User profile A collection of folders that stores a user's customized desktop environment.

Windows 2000 mixed mode Domain mode that allows for the coexistence of Windows NT and Windows 2000 domain controllers in the same domain. You can switch from mixed mode to native mode, but this process is irreversible.

Windows 2000 native mode Domain mode available only when all domain controllers in the domain are running either Windows 2000 Server or Windows Server 2003. You cannot switch from native mode to mixed mode.

Windows 2003 mode Windows Server 2003 domain mode supports only Windows Server 2003 domain controllers, and gives you the additional ability to rename domain controllers at any time.

Windows Installer A Windows Server 2000, 2003, and XP component that defines and manages a standard format for application setup and installation, as well as tracks components such as registry entries and shortcuts.

Windows Management Instrumentation (WMI) An entity built from query strings that can filter the application of Group Policy based on customizable metrics.

Windows Server 2003 interim mode Domain mode used when you upgrade an NT 4.0 PDC (primary domain controller) to Windows Server 2003 and there are only NT 4.0 and Windows Server 2003 domain controllers in the domain. There cannot be any Windows 2000 domain controllers. Interim mode must be used if you have NT 4.0 groups with more than 5000 members because Windows 2000 does not allow groups with over 5000 members.

Windows Server 2003 Interim mode Domain mode that permits the Windows Server 2003 Active Directory to operate with a domain composed only of Windows NT 4.0 domain controllers It is used in environments that are upgrading directly from NT4 to Windows Server 2003 and can support groups with more than 5000 members, which the Windows 2000 modes cannot.

Windows Server 2003 mode Domain mode that can only include Windows Server 2003 domain controllers. You can switch to Windows Server 2003 mode only when all of your domain controllers have been upgraded to Windows Server 2003 server and you will not be adding any new Windows 2000 domain controllers.

Zone An area of authority consisting of one or more contiguous domains.

Zone database file Contains all of the DNS records associated with a given zone.

Zone delegation The process of assigning responsibility for a section of the DNS namespace to a separate zone.

Zone file The file on the DNS server that contains information about a zone.

Zone replication The process of replicating zone data to all secondary zones at each server.

Zone transfer The process of synchronizing standard secondary zones with the primary zone.